Enjoying Global History

Henry Abraham
Irwin Pfeffer

AMSCO SCHOOL PUBLICATIONS, INC.
315 Hudson Street   New York, N.Y. 10013

Henry Abraham is former Chairman of the Social Studies Department at William Cullen Bryant High School in Long Island City, N.Y. **Irwin Pfeffer** is former Chairman of the Social Studies Department at Thomas Jefferson High School in Brooklyn, N.Y. The two men are the co-authors of *Enjoying American History.*

When ordering this book, please specify
either **R 625 S** *or* ENJOYING GLOBAL HISTORY

ISBN: 0-87720-890-5

8 9   04 03

PREFACE

Over the years, some of our students have complained that their history courses were dull and lifeless. "Why can't history be interesting?" they asked. *Enjoying Global History* was written to show students that the study of the past is not just memorizing names, dates, battles, and treaties. History is about all of these things, of course, but it is also about people. Real people made history—our past was their present.

Enjoying Global History surveys the history of the world from prehistoric times to the present day. The twelve units are chronological as well as topical. Each unit presents stories and narratives that highlight the world's major civilizations in their place and time. In addition, each unit has one or more major themes that tie the stories together.

We have taken a multicultural approach to global history. Civilizations of the Middle East, Africa, Asia, Europe, the Indian subcontinent, and the Americas are well represented in this book. Over 100 stories tell about people and events spanning a period from 9500 years ago to the present day. Many of the characters in our stories were or are real people. The stories tell about men and women whose ideas and deeds shaped their worlds. The stories also tell about people who grew the food, made the goods, kept the records, and fought the wars. While some of the incidents in these stories are fictional, all are based on fact.

Each unit is preceded by an overall introduction that contains motivating material about the events in the stories. These introductions raise questions that will help students anticipate outcomes and focus on the material at hand. Each story in turn is introduced by a historical narrative that sets the time and place and explains in easy-to-understand terms the political, social, and economic setting. When a name or term that may cause difficulty is used for the first time, its definition is given. The story is concluded by a summary that highlights the effects of the story's events and points to future developments.

We have used a variety of literary forms—short stories, plays, newspaper reports, interior monologues, and letters—to present our historical narratives. The illustrations—line drawings, photographs, and maps—are visual records of the past. They will help students understand the people and events in the story. We have included a full world map at the beginning of each unit to show the areas of the globe where the stories take place. The maps in the stories focus on the areas where the stories occur. Many of these maps are the basis for comprehension questions in the end-of-story exercises. The maps thus not only offer pictures of where events took place, they also help develop skills in geography.

Following each story are five questions for review. These may either be integrated into the lesson as do-now exercises or used as homework questions. A section of short-answer questions follows in the Understanding the Story section. In the Activities and Inquiries section, students have the opportunity to do research and develop portfolios as well as sharpen other social studies skills.

It is our hope that the stories in *Enjoying Global History* will interest students and give them insight about how people lived and the forces that shaped their lives. This knowledge and insight may, in turn, help students reflect on their own world and gain an understanding of the forces that have shaped their own lives.

Henry Abraham
Irwin Pfeffer

CONTENTS

Unit IV Meetings of Cultures   *139*

Unit V New Empires, New Ideas   *187*

Unit VI Absolutism Versus Freedom   *231*

Unit VII   Nationalism and the Industrial Revolution   293

Unit VIII   Imperialism   *333*

Unit IX   World War I   *393*

Unit X   Twentieth-Century Dictatorships   *421*

Unit XI   World War II and Its Aftermath   *469*

Unit XII   The Present Day   *537*

MAPS

Enjoying
Global History

UNIT I

The Cradles of Civilization

The stories in this first unit introduce the achievements of the earliest known civilizations. These civilizations arose in the Middle East, Africa, and Asia.

Africa. Before we look at these civilizations, however, we will take a step further back in history and, in our first story, visit a typical human settlement in East Africa, about 9,500 years ago. Human beings there were in the process of making a major change in their life-style. People were learning how to settle down, cultivate (grow) their own food, and live and work together. This was the beginning of life based on agriculture.

Middle East. By the time of our second story, set some 5,000 years later in Mesopotamia, in the Middle East, people had adapted so well to

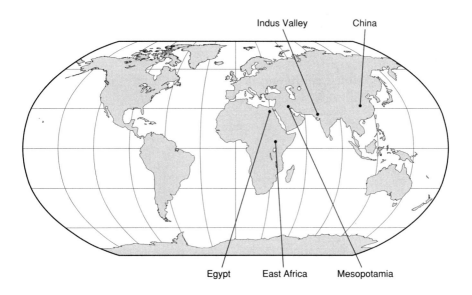

settled living that they were able to engage in many other activities besides farming. They built great cities in a land known as Sumer, and they invented history's first system of writing. A civilization arose.

Our third story takes place over 700 years later. The land of Sumer had become part of the Babylonian Empire. The center of this empire was the city of Babylon, where great buildings were decorated with hanging gardens. The ruler of Babylon had ordered that, for the first time, all the traditions (customs) and laws of the land were to be written down and followed by everyone. From that time on, all the people would know what was expected of them and what to expect from their rulers.

Asia. Our fourth story is set in India, early in this century. Archeologists (people who study the remains of past civilizations) are impressed by their discovery of a society that existed in India some 4,000 years ago. But there are many mysteries about this Indus Valley civilization, some of which have not been solved to this day.

Africa. The fifth story is set in North Africa during one of the greatest periods of Egyptian civilization, some 3,500 years ago. A rich and secure civilization had existed in Egypt for 1,500 years before our story takes place. The storyteller is one of Egypt's most unusual rulers—the only pharaoh (supreme ruler) who was a woman. She tells what she had to do to acquire power, and what she did after she had it.

Asia. Our sixth story is set in Asia, almost 3,300 years ago. The Shang, the first dynasty to rule China, had been in power for several hundred years. They had accomplished many things. The narrator of our story built a great new capital. In ruling his empire, he used a mixture of hard-headed common sense and a belief in the power of written signs to communicate with past rulers and to foretell the future.

1. Hunter or Farmer?

Humanlike creatures have existed on the earth for millions of years. Fossils of the oldest human ancestors have recently been discovered in Africa. These apelike creatures lived over 4.4 million years ago. Earlier, also in Africa, scientists found the footprints and physical remains of beings that walked upright over 3.5 million years ago. Some 2.5 million years ago, humanlike creatures made the first known stone tools. These people had larger brains than any previously known human ancestors.

No one knows exactly when modern humans first appeared on the earth. Intelligent beings known as Neanderthals (named for the place in Germany where their remains were first found) appeared about 200,000 years ago. The Neanderthals were short, heavyset, had short arms and legs, and walked with a forward-leaning gait. They made tools of stone and blades of flint. The Neanderthals probably believed in an afterlife, since they buried food and tools with their dead.

Some scientists believe that our first truly human ancestors originated in Africa between 250,000 and 165,000 years ago. (Others dispute the date but not the place.) Some of these human ancestors probably left Africa about 115,000 years ago and began a slow migration across the earth. The best-known of these prehistoric people were the Cro-Magnons, who were named for the place in France where their remains were first found. The Cro-Magnons flourished between 40,000 and 10,000 years ago. They were taller and more slender than the Neanderthals, stood upright, and, most important, had brains better able to make decisions and adapt to change. They made tools from animal horns and bones. They made fishhooks and harpoons for fishing; needles for sewing clothing of leather and animal skins; and knives and bows and arrows for hunting. They left striking examples of their art in caves in France and Spain. Some believe that the more intelligent Cro-Magnons were better able to survive the great Ice Ages than the Neanderthals, who disappeared about 35,000 years ago. During the Ice Ages, the climate was much colder and drier than it is today. Much of northern Europe and North America was buried under great sheets of ice.

About 12,000 years ago, the last of the Ice Ages ended. The world's climate slowly grew warmer, the ice retreated, and the landscape and animals changed. Up to this time, humans had been *nomads*—they had no settled homelands. Instead, people lived in small groups that followed and hunted the huge animals, such as mammoths and bison, living at the time, and they gathered wild grains, fruits, and nuts.

By about 10,000 years ago, many human groups had settled down and were growing their own food. Some of these farmers had also begun to *domesticate* (care for and raise) once-wild animals such as cattle and sheep. These early agricultural groups settled in fertile lands that had good supplies of water. Later in this unit we will tell about the lives of some of the people who settled in the river valleys of the Middle East, Africa, and Asia.

The hunters did not all turn immediately to farming or raising animals. Wild animals were still available, and hunting appealed to many people. The man in our story seems determined to remain a hunter. But his friends have found new ways of caring for themselves and their families. As you read the story, ask yourself what you would do if you were faced with the same circumstances as Ogg the hunter.

Prehistoric hunters in France, c. 5000 B.C., painted scenes of their adventures on the walls of caves.

East Africa   7500 B.C.

My name is Ogg, and I am a hunter. I usually walk a great distance each day to find my food. The animals often fight back, and I have been attacked and bitten many times by deer and goats. Twice I have come close to losing my life to lions.

I continue to hunt for a living, even though many of my friends have given up. They have learned to plant crops and keep animals. They live in houses made of brick, stone, and grass.

One day, while returning from the hunt, I happened to pass the field of my friends Ulana and Lute. Ulana was working in the hot sun. She called out, "Ogg, how tired you look! Your life is so hard and dangerous!"

"I would rather hunt than work in a hot, dusty field," I answered.

"Look how well we live," Ulana replied. "We have a steady supply of meat, milk, vegetables, and wool. In fact, we have everything we need."

"But you are paying a high price for these goods," I answered.

"What price?"

"You are paying with your freedom. You must spend all of your time tending to your crops and animals. You are not free to come and go as you please."

"Your old friends are happy to live this way," she responded. "We are not afraid, nor are we hungry. We all work together and help one another. Some till the soil. Others care for the animals. Still others make weapons and tools. We trade goods with people in other villages. You should give up the hunt and join us, Ogg. You will have a better life."

I answered, "If I settle down and become a farmer, I will have to live according to the rules of the group. On the hunt, the only rules I have to follow are my own. Besides, the hunt is exciting. I even enjoy the danger. No, I will not join with your group."

I left Ulana and continued to hunt for my food. But last week I returned from the hunt empty-handed every day. I was cold, tired, and hungry. For the first time, I wanted the comfort and security that Ulana and her people had. I decided to go and talk to Lute and Ulana.

Postscript

The people in our first story had bows and arrows for hunting, and knives and tools for farming. They built houses of stone, mud brick, and grasses, and made their clothing from animal skins. But they did not have the two essentials of civilization: a written language and cities. Everything these people knew was told to them by their parents or by other people. All human knowledge was passed along from one generation to the next by this *oral tradition*. It would take thousands of years of living in communities before written languages and cities evolved.

QUESTIONS FOR REVIEW

1. How did the Cro-Magnons differ from the Neanderthals?
2. How did the lives of nomads and farmers differ?
3. Why did Ogg refuse to change his life-style from hunter to farmer?
4. Why did Ulana feel that her way of life was better than Ogg's?
5. Why did Ogg finally decide to talk to Lute and Ulana?

UNDERSTANDING THE STORY

A. Write T for each statement that is true and F for each statement that is false.

1. No one knows exactly when modern humans first appeared on earth.
2. The Neanderthals first appeared in France about one million years ago.
3. The Cro-Magnons left examples of their art in caves in Spain and France.
4. During the Ice Ages, the climate was much colder and drier than it is today.
5. About 10,000 years ago, all hunters became farmers.
6. All of Ogg's friends were hunters.
7. Ulana encouraged Ogg to become a farmer like Lute and herself.
8. Ogg often wrote letters to his friends.

B. Assume that you have the choice of becoming a hunter like Ogg or a farmer like Ulana. Which would you prefer? Explain fully.

ACTIVITIES AND INQUIRIES

1. Imagine that you are a reporter. You interview Ogg. What questions would you ask to find out his true feelings?
2. You interview Ulana. What questions would you ask her?
3. Compare your life in the United States with that of either Ogg or Ulana.
4. Which person in the story would be better able to cope with life in your city or town? Why? What would you do to help either Ogg or Ulana adjust to your way of life?
5. Using your school or local library, prepare a report on the plants and animals that Ulana and Ogg would have known.

2. How to Succeed in Sumer

Over 9,000 years ago, people began to settle in a wide valley between the Tigris and Euphrates rivers, in the southern part of a land called Mesopotamia. (Today, this country is called Iraq.) To the south and west of this land were the Syrian and Arabian deserts. To the east and north were the mountains of Persia (present-day Iran) and Armenia. Mesopotamia was the eastern region of an area of rich lands called the Fertile Crescent. One area of settlement was known as Sumer, and the inhabitants were called Sumerians.

Through the years the Sumerians dug ditches and built up the riverbanks to control the flow of the rivers' waters. They drained the swamps and deepened some of the ditches into canals. Thus, the Sumerians created an irrigation system that made the most of the valley's fertile farmland. The farmers grew large quantities of wheat, barley, and vegetables.

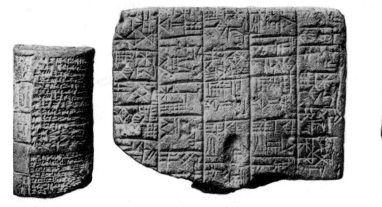

Cuneiform tablets from Sumer and Babylonia, c. 3000 B.C.

As the population of Sumer grew, the people built their houses closer to one another, and villages were formed. Some of these villages continued to grow, and in time they developed into the first cities. It was in a Sumerian city, in about the year 3000 B.C., that the first written records of the daily lives of men and women were kept. Here, recorded history begins. The Sumerians developed the first civilization of the ancient world. They built many cities, with such names as Ur, Lagash, and Uruk.

Sumerian cities were protected by high walls. The basic building material was clay. A mold was invented to make a uniform-size brick. Each house had a courtyard and a doorway that opened into a straight, narrow street. The tallest building was the *ziggurat* (temple), which was covered with millions of pieces of glazed, colored tiles. The people believed that the god who ruled the city lived in a building at the top of the ziggurat.

The Sumerians were a creative people. They were the first people to use the wheel for wagons drawn by animals. They invented the potter's wheel. They imported metals such as bronze and copper, and they used arches and domes in their buildings. In each Sumerian city, many people worked at specialized jobs. One could find carpenters, potters, metalworkers, stone carvers, boat builders, jewelers, weapons makers, merchants, scribes (people who kept written records), and religious leaders.

Perhaps the most important contribution of the Sumerians to history was the first written language. The Sumerians did not create an alphabet. At first, they drew pictures to represent objects. Later, the pictures became symbols that represented syllables (parts of words). The Sumerians used a pointed stick to press wedge-shaped symbols (cuneiform) into soft clay tablets. When these tablets dried and hardened, they became the permanent records of business dealings, court proceedings, school work, grain harvests, and laws.

Many scribes were needed to read and write the Sumerian language. In our story, a scribe wants his son to follow in his footsteps. The father has some definite ideas about the importance of education.

Uruk　2500 B.C.

Our story takes place in a quiet part of the city, away from the clatter of oxcarts, the hammering noises of workers' tools, and the whirring of potter's wheels. Houses here are larger than in the center of the city because of the greater wealth of the residents. There is no glass in the window openings. A man and his son are seated on backless chairs.

"Why weren't you in school today, my son?" asked the father, Eninnu, angrily.

"I *was* in school, Father," replied Eanna. "I'll show you the lessons I wrote on my tablets."

"Never mind," said Eninnu. "I've spoken to your school father (teacher), and he says that you were seen wandering around the public square during school hours."

"I'm tired of spending every minute of the day in school, from sunrise to sunset, in summer and winter," complained Eanna. "I'm always uncomfortable—either roasting or freezing in that windowless room. Everyday, the school father and monitors find something wrong with my work. I work hard, but they are never pleased. Without warning they whack me with a cane. If I complain, they hit even harder. I've got bruises all over."

"I don't feel sorry for you, Eanna. Do your work and the school father will never touch you."

"I wish that were true, Father, but I don't think that the school father likes me. I write on my tablets, study them, and recite as best I can. The other day, I wrote on my clay tablet what the school father told us about the great god Gilgamesh. When I recited my tablet, the school father said I had made two mistakes. I was given two whacks across my back."

"My son, the errors are your fault," said Eninnu. "The school father tells me that you do not pay attention in class. Worst of all, he says that your copying is poor. You must improve or you will never become a scribe."

"That's all I ever hear: Become a scribe! Well, I don't want to be a scribe. I don't like to write, and I don't want to keep records."

"You will never amount to anything unless you become a scribe," Eninnu warned.

"Why not?" asked Eanna.

"Because the best jobs are open only to those people who are educated scribes. Whether you want to be an ambassador, a tax official, an accountant, or a priest, if you first work hard and well as a scribe, you will be promoted to the job that you desire."

"Father, I'm not interested in those professions."

"All right, then," asked Eninnu wearily, "what would you like to do?"

Eanna thought for a moment. "I want to make things with my own hands, not keep records of what other people produce. I think I might like to be a metalworker and make objects of copper or bronze. Or I could become a carpenter. I might consider leatherworking. I think I would enjoy tanning animal hides and making shoes, saddles, and harnesses."

"My son," Eninnu said, "even the metalworker, the carpenter, and the leatherworker must be able to write clearly and correctly. They must order tools and materials, measure and estimate accurately, and keep business records. You are not ashamed to work with your hands. Are you too proud to work with your mind?"

Eanna quickly replied, "Father, I understand what you mean. I'll be in school early tomorrow morning. I'll work hard! Am I going to surprise my school father!"

Eninnu smiled. "The mind and the hands must work together as a team. When this happens, we are on the path to success."

Postscript

For many years the cities of Sumer struggled with one another for control. After a succession of rulers, Sargon of Akkad established the first great military empire in the 2300s B.C. Sargon ruled for 56 years. During

ANCIENT MESOPOTAMIA: SUMER AND BABYLONIA

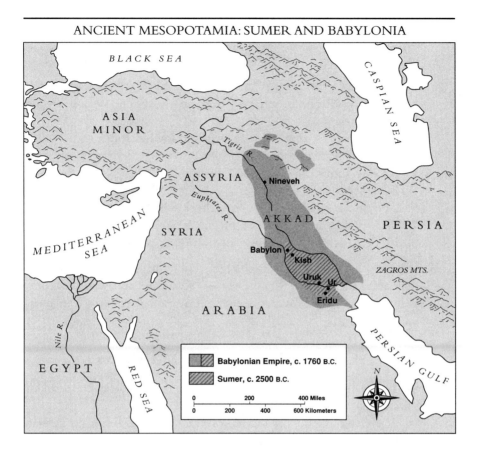

this time, he claimed all of the land from the Mediterranean Sea to the Persian Gulf. The Akkadian Empire lasted for nearly 100 years after Sargon's death. Then the Sumerians regained control until they were defeated by the Amorites. They, in turn, created the Babylonian Empire (see map).

QUESTIONS FOR REVIEW

1. How did the Sumerians turn the marshes and desert into fertile farmland?
2. Why are the Sumerians called a creative people?
3. How did Sumerian writing differ from our own?
4. Why was the work of the scribes so important in Sumer?
5. How did the father, Eninnu, convince his son, Eanna, that he should become a scribe?

UNDERSTANDING THE STORY

A. Write F for each statement that Eninnu made or might have made and S for each statement that Eanna made or might have made.

1. Your school father says you were in the public square during school hours.
2. I'm always uncomfortable in that windowless room.
3. I don't feel sorry for you.
4. I wrote about the great god Gilgamesh.
5. I don't want to be a scribe.
6. The best jobs are open only to those who are educated scribes.
7. Work hard and you will be promoted to the job you desire.
8. I'll be in school early tomorrow and will work hard.

B. Imagine that Eanna is an exchange student at your school. Assume that he can speak and write English. Would he do well in school? Why or why not? Would you do well in Eanna's school? Explain.

ACTIVITIES AND INQUIRIES

1. Study the map of Mesopotamia on page 11. Choose the term or phrase that best completes each statement.
    a. The city of Uruk was located on the (1) Tigris River (2) Persian Gulf (3) Euphrates River.
    b. Akkad was (1) north of Sumer (2) part of the Arabian Desert (3) east of Persia.
    c. The Tigris and Euphrates rivers flow southeast into the (1) Arabian Desert (2) Red Sea (3) Persian Gulf.
    d. The distance from Uruk to Babylon was about (1) 125 miles (2) 200 miles (3) 60 miles.
    e. The city of Nineveh was (1) southeast of Uruk (2) northwest of Uruk (3) west of Uruk.
2. Using your local or school library, prepare a report on farming, architecture, or religion in Sumer.
3. You interview Eninnu. What does he tell you about life in Sumer?
4. You talk to Eanna. What does he tell you about his hopes for a future career? Compare his hopes with yours.
5. Prepare a list of the courses offered in Eanna's school. Compare them with your courses. What similarities and differences do you see?
6. Compare your education with that of Eanna with regard to *(a)* method of writing *(b)* treatment by teachers *(c)* classroom conditions.

3. Crime and Punishment in Babylonia

The city of Babylon was located near the point where the Tigris and Euphrates rivers flow closest to each other. Much of the trade of the civilized world of the period after 1900 B.C. moved through Babylon and the other cities of the Babylonian Empire. The Babylonians created a great center of business and trade. They mined copper, lead, iron, silver, and gold, and they wove textiles of cotton and wool. Babylonian products were shipped throughout the Middle East and as far away as China and India. The caravans that arrived daily filled Babylon's shops with goods from these parts of the world.

The Babylonians continued to use Sumerian cuneiform writing. They studied the stars and planets and developed the science of astronomy. In order to measure time, the Babylonians also invented the water clock and sundial.

The power of Babylonia grew, in part, because it had capable rulers. King Hammurabi was an especially able ruler. During his reign (1792–1750 B.C.), the laws were collected and organized into a written code that covered business contracts, farming methods, debts, wages, marriage, divorce, and the treatment of women. The Code of Hammurabi also specified punishments for a variety of crimes.

Our story takes place during the great king's reign. Two businesspeople, who are husband and wife, express their opinions about the punishments contained in the code.

Ask yourself why this code was so important. What difference do you see between Babylonian law and United States law?

Babylon   1760 B.C.

Our story is set in a two-story mud-brick home. Nabushum and Nasira are seated in the inner courtyard. The doors and windows of their large house are made of woven reeds set into wooden frames.

King Hammurabi receives the code of laws bearing his name from a Babylonian god. Do we believe that our laws come from a human or a divine source?

"Husband, I understand that your friend Zakir is in great trouble," said Nasira. "Last month, he was in charge of the royal estates. Today, he is in prison."

Nabushum replied, "Indeed, he is in great trouble. Zakir is going to be executed."

"That's terrible," Nasira said, shocked. "Why?"

"King Hammurabi ordered Zakir to go to the city of Kish to oversee the harvest on the royal estates," said Nabushum. "Unfortunately, Zakir fell ill and could not travel, so he hired a friend to go in his place. Someone discovered this and told King Hammurabi. The king was furious. Zakir was put on trial, was declared guilty, and was sentenced to die."

"Zakir never hurt anyone!" Nasira exclaimed. "Why must he die simply because he failed to make one trip to Kish? I say he should be fined and even put in jail. But he should not be executed."

Nabushum thought for a moment. "There is a good reason why Zakir is going to be executed. He violated the spirit of King Hammurabi's law. The law says that whatever a person says he or she will do must be done efficiently, correctly, and professionally. An architect must be sure to build a house that will not collapse and hurt the owner. A doctor must not bring harm to a patient. A person who has a duty to perform—such as Zakir—cannot send someone else to do the job that is his or her responsibility alone."

Nasira nodded in agreement.

Nabushum continued. "Zakir's fate disturbs you, Nasira. But you did not object when the thief who broke into our house last year was caught and sentenced to death."

"How can you compare the two crimes?" asked Nasira angrily. "The thief stole our property. Zakir stole nothing."

"All crimes must be punished," said Nabushum. "In the future, people like Zakir will be more reliable and will carry out their superior's orders. Others will be afraid to break into people's houses and steal their possessions."

Nasira shook her head. "I sometimes think that our code of laws is too harsh. You remember what happened when young Ingisil beat his father. They chopped the boy's hand off!"

"That will teach all people to respect their parents," replied Nabushum sternly. "It will be a long time before anyone in this neighborhood hits a parent!"

"Perhaps he should have had a lighter sentence. Is it fair to mutilate a person for life for one wrongdoing?" asked Nasira.

"You are worried that the code is unfair," Nabushum replied. "Under the code, all are responsible for their actions. If I am robbed and the thief is never caught, the city must repay me for my loss because it failed to protect my property. What can be more fair than this?"

Nasira sighed. "I know you believe that the Code of Hammurabi does everything possible to discourage crime and wrongdoing. I fear that the code is itself sometimes unfair and unjust."

Postscript

The Code of Hammurabi was an important milestone. Since the laws were written down, judges could decide someone's guilt or innocence by looking at the written law instead of deciding for themselves what judgment should be passed.

Women held a high position in Babylonian society. They were allowed to go into business, and they had the same rights in business as men did. A wife could return to her family if her husband mistreated her, and a divorced woman was allowed to keep her children.

Hammurabi did more than codify the laws. He increased farm production by enlarging the irrigation system and built granaries to store grain as protection against famine. Hammurabi also set up a system of fair prices and wages. The tax system was made fairer for the poor, and a government housing program was introduced.

QUESTIONS FOR REVIEW

1. How did Babylon become a great commercial center?
2. Why was King Hammurabi considered a great ruler?
3. How were people who broke the law punished, according to the Hammurabi Code?
4. Why was Zakir to be executed?
5. Why is it important to have a written code of laws?

UNDERSTANDING THE STORY

A. Write T for each statement that is true, F for each statement that is false, and O for each statement that is an opinion.

1. Babylonian products were bought and sold throughout the Middle East and Asia.
2. Babylonia would have been more prosperous if the rulers had coined money.
3. The Babylonians used cuneiform writing.
4. Babylon would be the greatest city in western Asia today if it had not been destroyed.
5. Hammurabi was a weak king whose military losses led to Babylon's downfall.
6. Nasira and Nabushum were business people.

7. Nasira and Nabushum agreed about the fairness of the Hammurabi Code.
8. Women in Babylonia probably had as many rights as women in the United States today.

B. Suppose that Nasira and Nabushum were given the opportunity to study United States law. How would each one react to the laws of this country?

ACTIVITIES AND INQUIRIES

1. Prepare a table comparing crime and punishment in ancient Babylonia and the United States. Use the following headings: (*a*) Type of Crime (*b*) Punishment in Babylonia (*c*) Punishment in the United States. Now fill in the chart. What differences do you see between crime and punishment in each country? How do you explain these differences?
2. As a reporter, you interview King Hammurabi. What questions would you ask him about his code? How do you think he would answer your questions?
3. Imagine that you are defending Zakir in a Babylonian court. What arguments would you present to save him from execution?
4. Prepare a report on women's rights in ancient Babylonia.
5. Study the map of Mesopotamia on page 11. Choose the term or phrase that best completes each statement.
    a. In traveling from Babylon to Kish, you would have gone (1) north (2) west (3) south.
    b. In traveling from Babylon to Syria, you would have gone (1) east (2) west (3) north.
    c. Most of the cities on the map were located (1) between the Tigris and Euphrates rivers (2) west of Arabia (3) east of Persia.
    d. A city between the Tigris and Euphrates rivers was (1) Babylon (2) Nineveh (3) Eridu.
    e. In traveling from Babylon to Persia, you would have gone (1) north (2) south (3) east.

4. My Name Is Hatshepsut

At the time that civilization was developing in Mesopotamia, similar forces were at work in North Africa. Nomads in search of water for their herds were moving into the valley of the Nile River. This fertile valley is only 12 miles wide. Each spring, flood waters deposit rich soil along the river-banks. The early settlers in the Nile Valley learned to plant crops of grains and vegetables each year after the floodwaters had receded.

The Nile Valley regularly produced an abundance of food. This enabled the Egyptians to create a secure, rich, and complex civilization. Historical records dating back to 3100 B.C. describe a powerful pharaoh (king) named Menes, who united the lands of upper and lower Egypt under his rule. Egypt would be ruled by dynasties of pharaohs for nearly 3,000 years. (A *dynasty* is a succession of rulers who are all related to a common ancestor.)

Egyptian records were kept by scribes, as in Sumer and Babylonia. The Egyptians had a unique system of picture writing, which we call *hiero-glyphics*. These were picture signs. Some signs stood for the words they represented; others stood for sounds in the Egyptian language.

The Egyptian scribes wrote their history on a paperlike surface made of the papyrus reed that grew in the Nile River. Papyrus writings have been discovered in Egyptian tombs. The Egyptians also carved their history on the great walls of their temples and public buildings. Each pharaoh's life and the accomplishments of the period were recorded, hopefully for eternity. One of these carved records, which was discovered in 1799, gave scholars the keys they needed to decipher (understand) Egyptian hieroglyphics. The carved stone record is called the Rosetta Stone after the place in Egypt where it was found. The stone is a huge tablet with writing in both Greek and Egyptian. Using their knowledge of Greek, scholars were able to understand the Egyptian.

The Egyptians' records tell of their accomplishments in mathematics, astronomy, and medicine. Their engineering feats were superior to any other of the time. A 27-mile-long wall enclosed an irrigation reservoir and resulted in thousands of acres of marshland being turned into farmland. Pillars weighing well over 1,000 tons each were shipped long distances. There is evidence that major centers had sewage systems. The roads were poor, yet the mails were delivered regularly.

The Egyptians worshiped many gods and goddesses, and they believed in an afterlife. The pharaohs were considered divine. The Egyptians built pyramids to serve as monuments and burial places for their pharaohs. Smaller tombs were built for members of the noble families. The bodies of the dead were *mummified* (preserved) and buried with the food, clothing, and objects it was believed they would need in the next life.

The status of women in Egyptian society was the highest in the ancient world. Women worked in many trades and industries. Their legal rights were equal to those of men. Women owned, inherited, and transferred property, and they could file lawsuits. Women also took an active role in religious life. At home, mothers taught religious beliefs to their children.

Our story concerns a highly unusual Egyptian woman, who ruled Egypt for some 20 years. Here is her story.

Thebes   1485 B.C.

My name is Hatshepsut, and I am queen and pharaoh of Egypt. I am the daughter of the great pharaoh Thutmose I and his first wife. When my father died, he was succeeded by his

Queen Hatshepsut ruled Egypt for 22 years. During her reign, Egypt expanded and was prosperous.

son, Thutmose II, my half-brother. His mother was a far less important person than mine. I married Thutmose II and became queen of Egypt. I bore my husband a daughter. Later, my husband had a son, Thutmose III, by another wife, whose social rank was far below mine.

Ten years passed and my husband died. A powerful group of people insisted that Thutmose III had every right to become the next pharaoh and rule all by himself. I thought otherwise. I believed that the boy was too young to rule by himself. He needed someone to advise him, guide him, and share power with him. That someone was me.

My claim was a strong one. I too had powerful people who supported me, and my claim was recognized. The boy Thutmose III would come to the throne as co-pharaoh but as the lesser partner to me.

Now I moved to make myself even more powerful. I claimed that my father, Thutmose I, had really intended for me to rule. I also built a great temple at Thebes, and I created a story that was recorded on the walls. The story tells of Amon-Re, the king of the gods, who promised to give Egypt a future ruler. He then turned himself into Thutmose I and lived with my

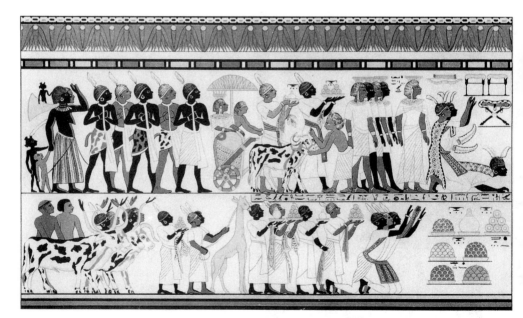

Peoples of the Egyptian Empire bringing gifts to the pharaoh. Note the different groups shown in this wall painting.

mother. Later, the gods helped my mother to deliver me, and then they fed me. Thus people were to believe that I was the daughter of a god.

I was prepared to deal with any who would challenge my right to rule. Many people were confused by a woman who was sitting on what always had been a man's throne. Scribes sometimes referred to me as "he" rather then "she." There are pictures of me in a man's clothing and wearing a beard! Other pictures show me as a woman wearing a dress and a queen's crown. But all that mattered to me was that I was accepted as pharaoh, ruler over all of Egypt.

Now that I had the power, how would I use it? I decided to put my energy into building temples and monuments and in establishing trade with other lands. Under my reign, Egypt prospered. I built new temples and rebuilt others that had been wrecked in wars. By financing trade expeditions, I also brought many new products to Egypt. And best of all, I avoided wars so that the people of Egypt could live full, productive lives.

Perhaps my greatest triumph was my expedition to the land of Punt [believed to be close to modern-day Somalia]. My ships came home bearing gold, ivory, spices, animals, plants, and myrrh trees that would later surround my temple.

And what of the co-pharaoh, young Thutmose III? How he hates me. He thinks that I have stolen his throne and his glory, and perhaps I have. But my royal blood proclaimed my right to rule, and I took that right. The gods have smiled down upon me, and they approve of what I have done. My rule is proof of that.

Postscript

Two years later, Hatshepsut, the only woman ever to sit on the Egyptian throne, was dead. Thutmose III was now allowed to ascend to the throne and rule in his own name. During his reign, Hatshepsut's name and her image were erased from the many temples she had built. Stone tablets recording her achievements were defaced, and statues were smashed and buried. Only in this century have historians been able to reconstruct and understand her achievements. But Hatshepsut's great temple still stands as proof that a woman born of royal blood had once taken power for herself and had used it wisely.

ANCIENT EGYPT

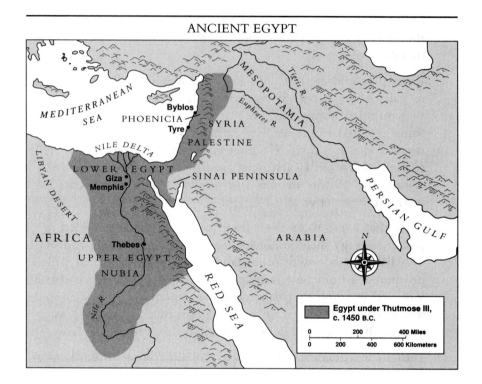

QUESTIONS FOR REVIEW

1. Why was the work of the Egyptian scribes so important?
2. How can we prove that Egyptian engineering was superior to any other of the time?
3. Why did the Egyptians build pyramids?
4. Why did the Egyptians think Hatshepsut was an unusual pharaoh?
5. Why did Hatshepsut think that the expedition to the land of Punt was her greatest triumph?

UNDERSTANDING THE STORY

A. Write F for each statement that is a fact and O for each statement that is an opinion.

1. The Egyptians worshiped many gods and goddesses.
2. The Egyptians would have been better off if the Nile Valley had been 30 miles wide.

3. Scribes kept Egyptian records.
4. Pillars weighing well over 1,000 tons were shipped over long distances.
5. If Hatshepsut were alive today, she would be a successful businessperson or politician.
6. Scribes sometimes referred to Hatshepsut as "he" rather than "she."
7. Hatshepsut built many temples and monuments.
8. Egypt should have had more female pharaohs.

B. Imagine that you are a reporter interviewing Hatshepsut. What questions would you ask her? How do you think she would answer your questions?

ACTIVITIES AND INQUIRIES

1. Study the map of ancient Egypt on page 22. Choose the term or phrase that best completes each statement.
    a. The Nile River flows into the (1) Mediterranean Sea (2) Red Sea (3) Gulf of Suez.
    b. South of the Sinai Peninsula is the (1) Libyan Desert (2) Gulf of Suez (3) Red Sea.
    c. The Nile Delta is in (1) Upper Egypt (2) the Libyan Desert (3) Lower Egypt.
    d. A city in Lower Egypt, near Memphis, was (1) Giza (2) Tyre (3) Thebes.
    e. Hatshepsut's capital city, Thebes, was in (1) Upper Egypt (2) Nubia (3) Lower Egypt.
2. Prepare a report card for Hatshepsut. Grade her from A (highest) to F (lowest) in the following areas and justify each grade: (*a*) claim to the throne (*b*) achievements (*c*) leadership (*d*) solution of problems.
3. Hatshepsut was a very successful pharaoh. Why then was she the only woman ever to succeed to the Egyptian throne? Would Hatshepsut be a successful ruler if she were alive today? Explain.
4. Imagine that you are the editor of an Egyptian newspaper. Write Hatshepsut's obituary (death notice).
5. Prepare a report on life in ancient Egypt.

5. The Ruins Keep Some Secrets

India is named for the Indus River, which flows in the northwest for a thousand miles and empties into the Arabian Sea. The Indian subcontinent covers more than 1.5 million square miles and includes the present-day countries of India, Pakistan, and Bangladesh.

From about 2300 to 1750 B.C., two great cities, Mohenjo-daro and Harappa, as well as many smaller towns and villages, rose and flourished

INDUS VALLEY CIVILIZATION

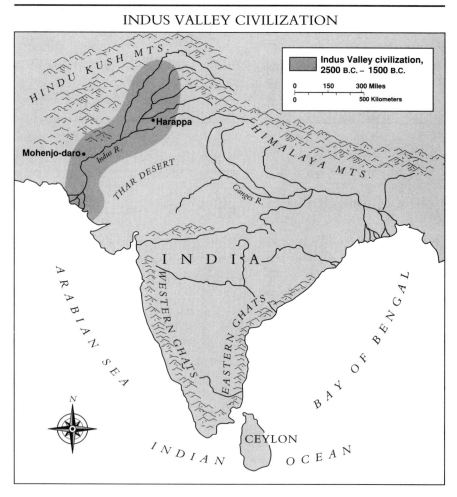

Indus Valley civilization, 2500 B.C. – 1500 B.C.

along the Indus River. The culture of the people is known as the Indus Valley (or Harappan) civilization. Both cities were laid out on a north-south, checkerboard pattern, with wide, straight streets. A large fortress, or citadel, situated in the west, dominated each city. The cities had large buildings that were used both to store grain and house workers. These cities were the equals of or superior to those in Egypt and Babylonia during the same period. Merchant ships carried goods between the Indus Valley, Babylonia, and Egypt.

In our story, twentieth-century archeologists who have been working at the site of Mohenjo-daro are discussing their discoveries.

Mohenjo-daro A.D. 1920

"Just look at all the astonishing things that we have found in these ruins!" exclaimed Karen to the group of archeologists. They were gathered at their camp near the Indus River, at the site of the ancient city of Mohenjo-daro. Many had suggestions and examples to offer of the mysteries they had found.

"These people seem to have been the ancestors of today's Indian civilization," said James excitedly. "Just look at these small statues. They seem to be of a goddess, perhaps an Earth Mother, such as the one that many people in India worship to this day."

Depictions of the bull and the bison were found often at Mohenjo-daro. Scientists think that the people may have worshiped these animals.

"And here are objects made of turquoise and other precious stones," said Mark. "And pictures of bulls, buffaloes, and tigers."

"What is so impressive about the city of Mohenjo-daro is that everything appears so neat and orderly," said James. "The streets were laid out on a grid pattern. The houses were all solidly built of brick. And every house had a bathroom that was connected to a drainage system."

"The Indus Valley people probably traded with Egypt and Babylonia," said Karen. "Certainly, their knowledge of weights and measures would have equipped them to trade with these or any other advanced people of their day."

"Aren't you impressed with the size of the Great Bath here?" asked Mark. "Imagine, finding a pool that measures 39 feet long by 23 feet wide and is eight feet deep! And aren't the granary, marketplace, and palace grounds impressive?"

Karen agreed. "But these buildings pose a great mystery. In all my years of studying ancient civilizations, I have never come across a large city without protective walls. Yet this city had none. These were an intelligent people, superb builders, who had much of value. Why didn't they build walls to protect themselves from outsiders?"

"That is not the only mystery surrounding the Indus Valley people," said James. "We cannot read their writing. It is unlike any other that we know today. And who were the rulers of these people? What were their laws? They buried their dead and believed in an afterlife. Did they have priests and places of worship? We don't even know *why* they disappeared."

"One day we may learn about their religion, rulers, and laws," replied Karen. "But we know that the Indus Valley people had intelligence, energy, and spirit. And they were probably the founders of a civilization that exists to this day."

Postscript

Later scientists found that the Indus Valley civilization declined after 1900 B.C. No one knows why for sure. Some believe that major rivers dried up, leaving the people without water for farming and transporting goods.

Others have guessed that unknown invaders killed many of the people.

About 1500 B.C. people from the north known as the Aryans entered India and settled down. The abandoned cities of Mohenjo-daro and Harappa fell into ruin. A new civilization was formed.

QUESTIONS FOR REVIEW

1. Describe the design of the cities of Harappa and Mohenjo-daro.
2. Why do archeologists think that the people of these cities created the beginning of today's Indian civilization?
3. Why did James say that everything was neat and orderly?
4. Why did Karen think that the buildings posed a great mystery?
5. What are some possible reasons for the collapse of the Indus Valley civilization?

UNDERSTANDING THE STORY

A. Write K for each statement that Karen made or might have made and J for each statement that James made or might have made.

1. Just look at these small statues.
2. Look at the astonishing things we have found.
3. The Indus Valley people probably traded with Egypt and Babylonia.
4. The Indus Valley people seem to have been the ancestors of today's Indian civilization.
5. These buildings pose a great mystery.
6. We cannot read their writing.
7. They buried their dead and believed in an afterlife.
8. One day we may learn about their religion, rulers, and laws.

B. There are many mysteries surrounding the Indus Valley civilization. Visit your school or local library and prepare a report on another ancient civilization that is not fully understood today.

ACTIVITIES AND INQUIRIES

1. Study the Indus Valley map on page 24. Choose the term or phrase that best completes each statement.
    a. The distance from Mohenjo-daro to Harappa was about (1) 100 miles (2) 200 miles (3) 350 miles.
    b. The Indus Valley civilization was found in the (1) northwest (2) southwest (3) southeast.
    c. The Indus River flows into the (1) Bay of Bengal (2) Arabian Sea (3) Indian Ocean.
    d. In traveling from Mohenjo-daro to Harappa, you would have gone (1) northeast (2) south (3) southeast.
    e. Mountains to the northwest of the Indus Valley are the (1) Himalaya (2) Ghats (3) Hindu Kush.

2. Imagine that you are at Mohenjo-daro with Karen, James, and Mark. An Indian reporter interviews you about your discoveries. What would you tell him or her?
3. You have returned to school after your trip to India. You are asked to speak to the school assembly about your adventures. Prepare your speech. How might it differ from your remarks in question 2?
4. Prepare a report on how archeologists carry out their work.
5. Draw a picture or diagram of the city of Mohenjo-daro.

6. The Secrets of a Successful Ruler

Archeologists are uncertain about the origins of Chinese civilization. They know that around 2500 B.C. people lived in the river valley of the Hwang Ho in northern China. These people made excellent ceramics. Later people, known as the Lung-shan, lived in walled villages that were spread along the great rivers of northern China. These people were farmers as well as hunters. They grew crops of millet and rice and kept livestock (cattle and sheep). The Lung-shan people also made fine ceramics.

ANCIENT CHINA: SHANG DYNASTY

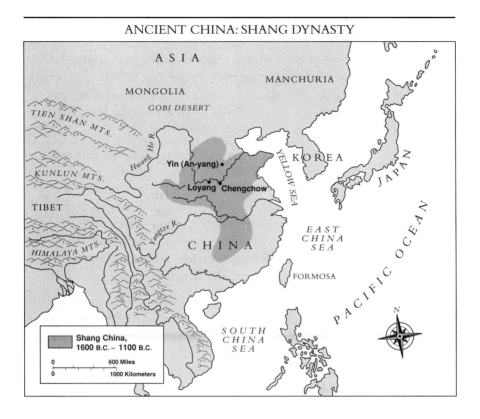

These early Chinese people developed a calendar that helped farmers know when to plant their crops. This calendar had ten-day weeks, and three weeks made one month. The symbol for one month was a moon.

As in Sumer and Egypt, writing in China began with the use of picture signs. Writing developed almost 1,000 years later in China than in these other regions, however. Some people believe that the Chinese borrowed the concept (idea) of writing from Sumer and Egypt.

The first written records in Chinese history were made during the Shang dynasty. This dynasty rose to power in the 1600s B.C. and ruled China until the 1100s B.C. In the 1300s, the emperor Pan-keng moved the Shang capital to the city of Yin, near present-day An-yang. Many Shang treasures were discovered there in this century.

Among the most fascinating examples of early Chinese writing are those that were found on bones and shells discovered at An-yang. In our story, Pan-keng tells about his military triumphs, how he kept his empire running smoothly, and how he used writing on bones and shells to foretell the future.

Yin (An-yang)   1390 B.C.

It was almost easy to conquer those western barbarians!
Backed up by 20,000 foot soldiers, I led my 1,000 noble chari-
oteers into battle. We slaughtered everyone in our way; no
one had a chance to escape. When we arrived at the chiefs'
stronghold, they surrendered at once.

I, Pan-keng, have been criticized for not killing or making
slaves of all the defeated tribal chiefs. But I had a good reason
for sparing their lives. I did not want to be responsible for
running local affairs. I let the chiefs rule their towns and villages, while I make decisions for the whole country. Each
year, the chiefs come to my court bearing costly gifts to prove
their loyalty. They do this because they fear me. They know
the penalty for turning against the Shang ruler!

I have found the secret of how to maintain a successful government. I choose the smartest and most trusted people to run
each division. And then I let each person do his or her job
without interference. For example, a former general knows
more about weapons than I do. Therefore, he supervises the
making and storing of swords and armor.

I follow the same principle when selecting the officials to
oversee the construction of new buildings, maintain irrigation
projects, and collect taxes. My officials have special talents,
and I use them.

Men and women should work at what they do best. I encourage certain farmers to cultivate the silkworm and weave its
threads into fine silk cloth. Other people are skilled at making
clothing. The potters make the fine white ware that we export
to Egypt and Babylon, and the basketweavers and bronze cast-
ers work well at their crafts. Everyone is happy to be employed
and earn good wages.

The Shang people are also skilled builders. We have made the
temples, public buildings, and homes of Yin, our new capital
city, the most splendid in all of China. The noble families have
built great tombs for themselves. There they will be buried in
splendor, with many beautiful objects of jade and bronze that
will be useful to them in the next world.

Oracle bones from Shang China, such as those Pan-keng used to foretell the future and learn the gods' wishes.

Just as the farmers must use the calendar to tell them when to sow their crops, I must have a way of knowing the best time to begin new projects. What is the best month and day to start a war, build a new castle, or begin a long journey? Fortunately, I am a high priest as well as an emperor. I have the power to ask our gods for the answers to these questions.

I have only to take the shoulder bone of an ox or the bottom shell of a tortoise and write my questions on it. Then I drill a small hole and apply a hot point until the bone splits. The gods answer my questions by the way the cracks are formed in the bone. But it is up to me to read their answers accurately. If I read the wrong answers, the army may lose a battle, or a journey may end in disaster. This will mean that I have lost favor with the heavenly spirits of our ancestors. Mighty ruler though I am, even I might lose their trust.

It is good to be able to speak with the spirits and ask them for guidance. But my people must continue to work hard and fight for what is theirs. Then the spirits will be pleased and on our side, and our future will be bright.

Postscript

In the 1100s B.C., people known as the Chou defeated the Shang and established their own dynasty. The great Shang capital was completely destroyed. Not until nearly 3,000 years later did scientists learn of the achievements of the Shang people.

QUESTIONS FOR REVIEW

1. How did the ancient Chinese calendar differ from the Western calendar in use today?
2. Describe the beginnings of Chinese writing.
3. Why did Pan-keng not kill or make slaves of the tribal chiefs he defeated?
4. What were Pan-keng's "secrets" for running a government and choosing officials?
5. How did Pan-keng decide when to go to war or start on a long journey?

UNDERSTANDING THE STORY

A. Write T for each statement that is true and F for each statement that is false.

1. The Chinese developed a calendar that helped farmers know when to plant their crops.
2. Writing in China began with the use of picture signs.
3. Examples of early Chinese writing were found in books.
4. Pan-keng killed all of the defeated tribal chiefs.
5. A former general supervised the making of swords.
6. Nobles were buried in shallow graves.
7. The heavenly spirits would not answer Pan-keng's questions.
8. In the 1100s B.C., the Shang capital was completely destroyed.

B. Pan-keng obviously thought that he was a successful ruler. Prove that he was successful. What less successful events might he have omitted from his story?

ACTIVITIES AND INQUIRIES

1. Study the map of ancient China on page 29. Choose the term or phrase that best completes each statement.
    a. Yin (An-yang) was located (1) in the Hwang Ho River Valley (2) off the South China Sea (3) between the Tien Shan and Kunlun Mountains.
    b. The distance from Yin to Loyang was about (1) 200 miles (2) 600 miles (3) 20 miles.
    c. Northeast of Yin was (1) Formosa (2) Japan (3) Manchuria.
    d. The Hwang Ho River flows into the (1) South China Sea (2) Yellow Sea (3) Bay of Bengal.
    e. The Gobi Desert is located in (1) Korea (2) Mongolia (3) Tibet.

2. Prepare a report card for Pan-keng. Grade him in the following areas, and justify each grade: *(a)* leadership *(b)* accomplishments *(c)* relationships with people *(d)* point of view.

3. Assume that Pan-keng is running for president of the United States. Would you vote for him? Explain.

4. You are a reporter and interview Pan-keng. What questions would you ask him? What answers might he give to each question?

5. You are a modern historian who is studying Pan-keng's life. What would you write about him?

UNIT II

The Ancient World

In this unit, we take a look at some of the highlights of civilization from the years 500 B.C. to A.D. 250. We look at Asia, Europe, Africa, the Middle East, and Mesoamerica.

Asia. In Asia, further changes in government have taken place in India and China. We will focus on how these changes have had a great effect on Indian and Chinese religion and moral values.

Europe. Second, we turn to the European continent, where civilization flowered in Greece and later spread through much of the known world. We will look at several high points of Greek civilization in its

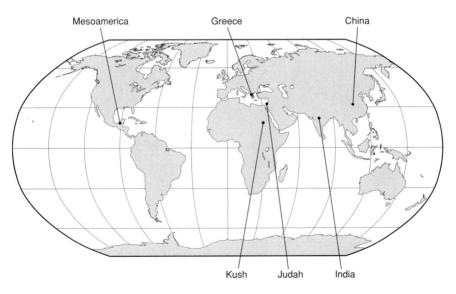

golden age, particularly because Greek thought, government, and culture have influenced civilization directly or indirectly for nearly 2,500 years.

Africa. Next we turn to the African continent, where we study a second important African civilization. Nubia, Egypt's southern neighbor, developed its own way of life and culture, and it both influenced and was influenced by Egypt. It gave birth to the kingdom of Kush (southern Nubia), which flourished from 500 B.C. well into the Christian era. We will see that Kush was a center for one of the most important advances in human technology: the development of iron tools and weapons. Kush was also an important trading link between Africa and the civilizations of the Middle East and Asia.

Middle East. In the Middle East, we will observe the rise and fall of several civilizations. The Babylonians endured for many centuries, then declined. Other civilizations arose, among them the Assyrians and the Persians. The Persians later tried but failed to conquer the Greeks.

The Hebrews, a small group of people originally from Mesopotamia, settled on the eastern shores of the Mediterranean. The major contributions of the Hebrew people were their religious and ethical teachings and the writing of the Bible. We will see how they fought for and gained the freedom to practice their religious beliefs.

Mesoamerica. Our final story takes us to the Americas, where the civilization of the Maya developed in Mesoamerica (middle, or central, America). Gifted mathematicians and astronomers, the Maya built great cities, invented a written language, and left fascinating and puzzling art and monuments.

1. Looking Forward to the Next Life

Around the year 1500 B.C., people known as Aryans invaded India from the north and conquered the Indus Valley. The Aryans had powerful weapons and easily overthrew the peaceful cities of Harappa and Mohenjo-daro. The Aryans also brought with them a system of social class. They established the *caste system*, which grouped people according to their professions. Members of each caste were required to associate only with people of their own caste. They could marry only people in the same caste.

The Brahmans were (and are) the highest social class. Brahmans worshiped Brahman, the supreme, or highest, Hindu god. (Hinduism has many gods.) The high-caste Brahmans included priests, teachers, and thinkers. Next in order of rank came the rulers and military class

Brahman, the highest-ranking god of the Hindu religion.

(*Kshatriyas*), followed by business and professional people (*Vaisyas*). Members of the lowest caste (*Sudras*) were servants and laborers. The caste-less Untouchables performed jobs that members of the castes were forbidden to do. Pariahs were people who had committed serious crimes such as murder, and were expelled from society.

The Aryan invaders of India brought with them their language, which was called Sanskrit. This language was the ancestor of many modern languages, including English. Sanskrit was closely related to the language of the ancient Greeks, whom we shall study later in this unit, and to Latin, the language of the ancient Romans, whom we shall study in Unit III.

The Aryans wrote the earliest known Indian literature, the Vedas, in Sanskrit. The Vedas are mostly hymns to the gods, but they also tell about life in the period from about 1500 B.C. to 450 B.C., especially the book known as the Rig-Veda.

Later Aryan literature includes the Upanishads, which are sacred books somewhat similar to the Bible. They recount the teachings of certain sages (wise persons). The Upanishads contain the doctrine that after a person dies, the human soul is reborn on earth in human or animal form. This is called *reincarnation*. And the soul will have a happy or an unhappy rebirth, depending upon the person's life and works in the previous life.

Other Aryan works of literature include the *Mahabarata* and the *Ramayana*, which are long and detailed narrative-epic poems about gods and human beings. The latter tells of the conquest of a land that may be modern-day Sri Lanka.

The Aryans also continued to settle northern India. By the late fourth century B.C., the first great Indian Empire, that of Chandragupta Maurya, had been founded at Magadha in northern India (322 B.C.).

Hinduism is both the major religion and the way of life of the people of India, and has been so for several thousand years. Unlike Buddhism, Christianity, and Islam (which we shall study in Unit III), Hinduism was not founded on the teachings of one person. Rather, it evolved (grew) from the writings of many spiritual leaders and thinkers over a long period of time. Elements of Hinduism have been found in the civilization of the Indus Valley, which we studied in Unit I.

In the Hindu religion, everything that a person does affects the future of his or her soul. No deed is ever forgotten. A person thus builds a future life through action, or *karma*.

Hindus follow a guide to behavior called *dharma* (the right way). Dharma is many things—divine law, individual duty, the principles of universal and individual existence. Dharma tells the Hindu how to act each day at home and at work. The members of each Hindu caste have different duties and responsibilities.

In our story, a Brahman woman is instructing her daughter in the proper behavior of people of their caste, and in the duties she is expected to perform as a Hindu.

Bombay 500 B.C.

"Mother, I don't understand why I am not permitted to talk to young people from other castes," said Chandra.

"Are you forgetting that you are a Brahman?" replied her mother angrily. "You must stay away from people of the lower castes. And never get close to or speak to an Untouchable! Besides, why would you want to talk to strangers?"

"Mother, I should have the right to talk to anyone I please, Brahman or non-Brahman. If I can't do that, I don't want to be a Brahman!"

Her mother shook her head. "You don't understand how well off you are as a Brahman."

"Why are we favored over all the other castes?" asked Chandra.

Her mother replied, "To begin with, we Brahmans are granted the opportunity to study and learn many things. We are better educated, and we know more about the Hindu religion and customs than the people of other castes do."

"But why can't a non-Brahman be as educated as we are?"

"Chandra, the members of each caste must work at the same jobs or professions as their parents. We Brahmans are well educated because we must teach our Hindu religion and values to the members of the other castes. If a man or woman's parents are lawyers, he or she must be a lawyer. If the parents are farmers, the children must be farmers too. In this way, the social order is preserved. Everyone knows his or her rightful place in society. By associating with our own kind, we pass along our knowledge and experience to those who will make the best use of them."

"Mother, I understand what you mean. Suppose—just suppose—that I meet and wish to marry a man who is not a Brahman. Isn't that my decision to make?" asked Chandra.

"No, it is not, Chandra. If you marry a man from a lower caste, you will become a member of his caste—and so will your parents! Your father and I will never permit this to happen. Besides, you will never choose your own husband. It is our duty to choose him for you."

"But why must everything be this way?" asked Chandra.

"It is the way of the world," replied her mother. "You were not born into the Brahman caste by accident, Chandra. You were born a Brahman because of the way you lived and performed your duties in your past lives. The gods reward those of us who have lived a virtuous life by making sure that our souls are reborn in the bodies of people in a higher caste. But if we have lived a wicked life, the gods see to it that our souls are reborn in the bodies of lower-caste people, or animals!

"You must try to live the best life you can. Listen carefully to the priests' teachings and do exactly as they say. Observe all the rules of our caste," said the mother.

"If you socialize with people of other castes, or marry out of your caste, you tamper with the natural order of things. The people of your caste will turn away from you in this life, and your soul will be punished severely in your next life. Now can you understand why I must forbid such behavior?"

"But, Mother, now that I am a Brahman, a member of the highest caste, what is there for me to look forward to in the next life?"

"Your soul may be released from the wheel of life. Then it will never have to return to the earth. But most souls will continue to be reborn life after life, and our way of life will go on in the same way—forever," her mother said.

Postscript

Great empires arose in India in the centuries that followed. Another great religion, Buddhism (see Unit III) arose in India, but Hinduism remained the dominant spiritual and cultural force. The Indian way of life continued, much as the mother predicted, for many centuries.

In our time, however, much has changed. Contacts among the castes are now encouraged, and there have been intercaste marriages. In education, attempts are being made to offer equal opportunities to men and women. Thanks to the efforts of people like Mohandas Gandhi in our time (see Unit VIII), untouchability is no longer legal, although it still exists in some areas.

Members of the lower castes can improve themselves only by changing their trades. People who deal with animal hides (leather goods), sweep the streets, or care for the dead must change to higher status occupations.

A person's caste is no longer a guarantee of his or her occupation. A Hindu priest is still a Brahman. But many Brahmans have entered other professions. They have become soldiers, police officers, and farmers.

Changes in Indian law have improved women's rights. Wives and husbands now own family possessions jointly. Women have won the right to inherit property, and widows may remarry.

QUESTIONS FOR REVIEW

1. How did the caste system affect the lives of the Indian people?
2. Why were certain castes ranked higher than others?
3. What does Aryan literature tell us about Indian thinking and history?
4. What are the main elements of the Hindu religion?
5. What did the mother tell Chandra about the Brahmans?

UNDERSTANDING THE STORY

A. Write M for each statement that the mother made or might have made and C for each statement that Chandra made or might have made.

1. You must stay away from people of the lower castes.
2. Why are we favored over all the other castes?
3. Never get close to or speak to an Untouchable.
4. I should have the right to talk to anyone I please.
5. Why can't a non-Brahman be as educated as we are?
6. If the parents are farmers, the children must also be farmers.
7. Suppose that I wish to marry a person who is not a member of our caste?

8. If you marry a person from a lower caste, you will become a member of that caste.
9. What is there for me to look forward to in the next life?

B. Draw a ladder of the Hindu caste system. Place the most favored caste on top and the least favored caste on the bottom. Assuming that you are a Hindu, explain why the castes have been ranked in this order. Select two of the castes and tell why you would like to become a member of each.

ACTIVITIES AND INQUIRIES

1. The Hindu guide to behavior is called *dharma*. Outline what you feel would be a proper guide to *your* behavior.
2. The United States is said to be a casteless society. Prove that this is true. Can you think of any examples of caste in this country?
3. Compare your life with that of a Brahman with regard to (*a*) job possibilities (*b*) meeting and associating with people (*c*) opportunities for political and social success.
4. Equal opportunity is one of the features of a democracy such as that of the United States. Is it possible to have a democratic government together with a caste system? Explain.

2. How to Develop a Perfect Society

As we learned in Unit I, the Shang dynasty in China was overthrown by the Chou. The Chou period was a time of change and turmoil in China. Money was introduced. Farming benefited from better plows, fertilizers, and irrigation methods. Iron weapons and tools replaced those made of bronze. Beginning in the eighth century B.C., China expanded south into the Yangtze Valley and east to the coastal regions. Geographically, China was becoming the land it is today.

For the first time in Chinese history, the laws were written down. And China was developing a *bureaucracy*—government workers and employees who saw to it that the laws and regulations were carried out. At the same time, the power of the emperors declined. Princes who controlled vast tracts of land challenged the emperors and fought wars among themselves for more territory.

Many Chinese thinkers wrote about the political and social changes that were taking place. Perhaps the most important was the teacher Confucius (Kung-Fe-tzu), who lived between 561 and 479 B.C..

Confucius opposed the aggressive behavior and constant warfare of the princes. He believed that an all-powerful emperor would bring back the days of China's greatness. The emperor was the "son of Heaven"—his powers originated with the gods, according to Confucius. (This belief is called the *Mandate of Heaven.*)

Confucius felt very strongly about the traditional ways of life that were disappearing. He longed for the polite behavior of the "good old days." He believed in respect for the family and the individual. Confucius spoke of five personal virtues: charity, courtesy, good faith, hard work, and kindness. He was concerned about how people got along with one another. People who lived in a community or group were happier than those who lived alone, he believed. Confucius also understood that no two people are alike. Thus he wondered how a government could pass a law that would perfectly meet the needs of many different citizens.

Confucius believed in education. Through study and hard work, people could improve their lives and advance in society. He disapproved of inherited rank and power. Confucius had many faithful *disciples* (students). In this story, he talks with a former student who disagreed with him and left his school.

Quingdao 501 B.C.

"Welcome, Chen," said Confucius. "I am pleased to see you. You have been away for many months."

Chen hesitated. "I did not think that you would want to speak to me because I disagreed with you."

"You were wrong, Chen," replied Confucius softly. "I am truly happy that you have come back to my school."

"But Master, by disagreeing with you, I have disobeyed you. And you teach that it is important for us to obey our elders. The wife must obey her mother-in-law. Sons and daughters must obey their parents, and the younger brothers and sisters must obey the older ones. The pupil must obey the teacher. I heard you teach this many times, and I still do not know why this must be so."

Confucius answered, "We should follow the advice and counsel of older people because they have lived longer and therefore have acquired more knowledge based on experience. Most important of all, we must obey them because they, in turn, are bound to help us become better people."

"And how can they help us do that?" Chen asked.

"They must provide good examples for everyone to follow," Confucius responded. "They must also teach us wisdom, love, and courage."

"But are older people always wiser?" asked Chen. "Suppose my father sets a poor example for me. Must I accept his bad judgment?"

Confucius shook his head. "No. Chen, if you are *absolutely* sure that your father is wrong, you may gently try to persuade

Confucius taught: "People must never do to others what they would not want others to do to them."

him to change his mind. But even if he refuses, you must still give him the respect that is his due."

"But why must I show respect to someone whose thinking is filled with errors?" asked Chen.

"Because," answered Confucius, "there is a law that all human beings must respect: The family is everything. Within the family, the younger must respect the older. This must always be so, even when the older are in error."

"I have another question, Master. Why should *one* all-powerful man rule our country without limits on what he can do? Are we not better off with many princes controlling their own provinces? In this way, no one will have too much power."

"Chen, power should not be divided or shared. The emperor is like the head of a family. He must be the one responsible for running the entire country. And he, more than any other, must set a good example for all his subjects."

"But where does the emperor's authority to rule come from?"

"Heaven had decreed it so. Our ancient books tell us that the emperor is put here on earth to do the will of the gods. No one else has the power to carry out their wishes."

"How can we know if the emperor rules well?" asked Chen.

Confucius answered, "The person who spends most of his time attending to business, keeps his promises, doesn't spend money foolishly, shows kindness to his subjects, and treats all people fairly is a good ruler."

"What is to be done if the emperor makes serious mistakes and causes the people harm?"

Confucius replied, "Such an emperor must be removed."

"But are you not a peace-loving man?" asked Chen.

"I am speaking of change, not violence," replied Confucius. "We should not use force to remove an emperor. In fact, we should never use force to settle any of our disputes."

"How, then, are we to behave in times of conflict?"

"We should settle disputes by avoiding them."

"And how can we avoid disputes?"

Confucius answered, "We must learn how to develop a perfect society. The ruler must learn to be fair to his subjects. Parents and children must learn to love one another. The young must learn to respect the old."

Chen sighed. "If society is to become perfect, it seems that everyone must play an important role. Yet people seem to offend one another more than they please one another. Is there some way to teach people how not to offend others?"

"That is a wise question," said Confucius. "Yes, there is such a way. People must be taught a simple rule: They must never do to others what they would not want others to do to them. If people would only learn this and practice it, they would never give offense to anyone. This one rule, if practiced, would move us a great deal closer to the perfect society."

Chen thought for a moment and said, "Master, by behaving toward me with patience, kindness, and understanding, you have just taught me the true value of righteous behavior. By not treating me as you would not wish to be treated, you have helped me to understand that which I never understood before. You once said that everyone is born in order to play an important role. For the first time, I am beginning to understand the role that I am expected to fulfill."

Confucius smiled and said, "Chen, with your new wisdom and understanding, you have just brought our society a step closer to perfection."

Postscript

By the second century B.C., Confucianism (the philosophy of Confucius) was firmly established in China. Some people have regarded it almost as a religion, and indeed today throughout China there are hundreds of temples dedicated to Confucius. Confucius set up rules for ideal human behavior and for an ideal society. For over 2,000 years, the Chinese people have lived by these ideals. Confucianism has also been adopted in Japan, Korea, and other countries in Southeast Asia.

Confucian ideas were also a powerful force against change in China. People who wished to pass the difficult civil service examination and obtain jobs in the Chinese government bureaucracy had to memorize long passages of Confucius' writings. Since only well-to-do, upper-class persons could afford to spend the time studying Confucius' writings in order to pass the civil service exam, they dominated the government for many centuries.

The Chinese people were also deeply influenced by another philosophy of life, which arose in India about the time of Confucius. We will learn about Buddhism and its founder in Unit III.

QUESTIONS FOR REVIEW

1. Why was the Chou period a time of change and turmoil in China?
2. Why did Confucius think it was so important that people get along well together?
3. Why should the young obey the old?
4. Why did Confucius believe in a powerful emperor?
5. What did Chen think was righteous behavior?

UNDERSTANDING THE STORY

A. Write T for each statement that is true and F for each statement that is false.

1. During the Chou period, for the first time in Chinese history, the laws were written down.
2. The emperor was regarded as the "son of Heaven."
3. Confucius was happy that the "good old days" were long past.
4. Confucius believed in education.
5. Confucius was unhappy that Chen had returned to school.
6. Young people should not obey older people, according to Confucius.
7. According to Confucius, the family was everything.
8. Every person should have equal power with the emperor.

B. Confucius' school was quite different from yours. What do you think life in Confucius' school was like? What similarities to your school might you have found? What differences?

ACTIVITIES AND INQUIRIES

1. Imagine that you are Chen. You are having a discussion with Confucius. Which of his ideas do you agree with? Which of his points do you disagree with? Explain your answer fully.

2. Chen had been away from Confucius' school for many months. If you were in his place, would you have returned? Why or why not?
3. Confucius believed strongly in the Mandate of Heaven. What do you think of this idea? Could the mandate be applied to the United States government? Explain.
4. Confucius spoke of a perfect society. Describe his perfect society. Now describe your idea of a perfect society. Note the similarities and differences.

3. The Real Source of Athens' Greatness

The first important civilization outside Asia and Africa was centered not on the mainland of Europe but on the island of Crete in the Mediterranean Sea. There, a civilization known as *Minoan* (after a legendary king named Minos) grew and flourished beginning around 2200 B.C. The people of Crete were great seafarers who traded with the people of the eastern Mediterranean, Egypt, and Mesopotamia. They had a written language (Mycenaean Greek). The Cretans left richly decorated palaces, the largest and most important of which was at Knossos.

During the 1450s B.C., Crete came under the influence of the Mycenaean Greeks, who ruled from their capital city of Mycenae on the mainland. The Mycenaeans ruled Crete until the 1300s, when Knossos and other centers were destroyed by invaders.

Around the year 1200 B.C., people from the north called the Dorians invaded Greece. Mycenae collapsed in the 1100s, and Greece was then divided into a land of over a hundred small, independent city-states. A *city-state* was a small territory that was controlled by a king, chieftain, or a small group, which ruled from an urban (city) area. Greece entered a dark age, in which many of the achievements of earlier times—long-distance trade and written language—were lost or forgotten.

Greece is a hilly country, divided by many mountains and the sea. This geographical fact may be one reason why no one city or ruler was able to dominate Greece until the fourth century B.C. and the time of Alexander the Great (see page 60).

By the eighth century B.C., prosperity had returned, and the city-states of Greece had developed a flourishing trade with the people of the Mediterranean and the Black seas. The Greeks traded wine and olive oil for grain, timber, and other goods. Greek colonists settled lands on the eastern coast of the Aegean Sea (present-day Turkey), as far north as the Black Sea, and west in southern Italy and Sicily. Perhaps most important, the Greeks adapted an alphabet from the Phoenician people in the 700s.

Over the centuries, one of the mainland city-states rose to become the most prosperous and powerful in all of Greece. This city-state was Athens. Athens was small by modern standards—it covered just 1,000 square miles. (By comparison, the smallest of the United States, Rhode Island, is slightly over 1,000 square miles in area.)

Athens was a direct democracy. All adult male citizens voted for or against suggested laws in the assembly. This was the first known democratic government in history.

The Athenians had a high regard for learning, the arts, and literature. The Greeks stressed loyalty to their city-state, but the Athenians valued the individual above the group. The Athenians stressed individual thought and action. "Know thyself" was a Greek motto. Students spent much time in the study of music, arithmetic, literature, and writing. The Athenians also stressed physical fitness for men. Their goal was "a sound mind in a healthy body."

Girls did not attend school. Athenian women learned to keep house efficiently, the only training it was believed they required. Some women did learn to read and write at home, but even they were not permitted to hold government office, compete in sports, or take part in public events.

In our story, Cimon, a former slave who recently bought his freedom, tells us about a conversation with Milos, his Athenian employer.

Athens 445 B.C.

Yesterday evening, as I was leaving the olive press where I work, I saw many men walking toward a large open area on the side of a hill. "What is happening?" I asked my employer, Milos.

Milos smiled at me. "Cimon, have you never seen them gather before? You have been in Athens for nearly two years!"

With a proud look he went on. "These men are about to perform the most important duty in Athens. They are gathering in an assembly to decide our laws."

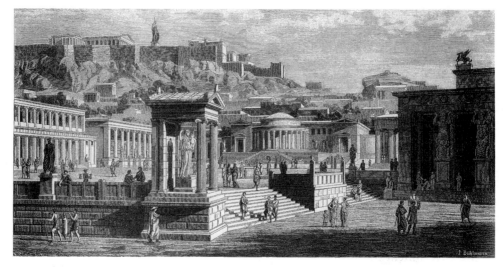

The Athenian marketplace, in the mid-fifth century B.C.

"And who are these men?" I asked.

Milos said, "They are Athenian citizens. In Athens, all male citizens are responsible for governing the city."

I was surprised. In no other city or land that I knew of did ordinary people have anything to say about the way they were governed. Everywhere else, the laws of government were made by a pharaoh or king, as in Egypt and Persia, or by a small group, as in Sparta.

"Were the laws always made this way?" I asked.

"No," Milos replied. "In fact, there was a time when the Athenians who owned land had all the power and took advantage of the rest of the people. For example, if people owed money and could not pay it back, they could be made slaves."

"How did this change?" I asked.

Milos thought for a moment. "We were blessed with wise leaders. They understood that Athens could never become a great city-state unless all of its citizens were treated fairly. This meant that they all had to have a voice in deciding how our city would be governed."

"And, as a result of this, who sees to it that your laws are carried out?" I asked.

Again Milos smiled. "The officials in our council of five hundred, of course. And before you ask your next question, Cimon, let me answer that these council members are chosen by *lot*. Their names are picked from the lists of Athenian citizens."

"What does that mean?"

"It means every citizen has a chance to become a government official?' Milos replied.

"What if a person does not know enough to serve as a government official?" I asked.

"That is the beauty of our system of democracy, Cimon," Milos replied proudly. "Because we Athenians decide our own laws and then enforce them, we make it our business to know as much as possible about the affairs of our city. This knowledge is the real source of Athens' greatness."

"Tell me more about this democracy of yours," I said.

Milos was only too happy to do so. "Thanks to our system of free democracy, we have many schools where teachers with much knowledge instruct our young people. We are taught to think and reason for ourselves. As a result, we Athenians have opened up our minds and accomplished much. Some of us have written fine histories or created great works of art. Others have written wonderful plays or composed fine music. As you can see, we have built many wonderful public buildings, temples, and theaters, which our sculptors have decorated with their finest statues."

"I am fascinated by this," I replied. "How can I, who was born in a faraway land and once was a slave, become a citizen? I too want to feel proud of being an Athenian and help to make and enforce the laws."

Milos shook his head. "Cimon, you can never become a citizen of Athens."

"Why not?"

"Because you were once a slave. Recently, a law was passed that changed the requirements for citizenship. Now, to become a citizen of Athens, a man has to be at least twenty-one years old, and the child of free Athenian parents."

"But how can you hold my origin and former condition against me? Did I not work hard, save my money, and buy my freedom? In fact, how can you Athenians, who prize your freedom and democracy above all things, deny it to others? Why do you continue to own slaves?"

Milos sighed. "There is much freedom here in Athens because Athens is the most powerful city-state in Greece. Many other city-states obey our commands, and they are still free and prosperous. Some people are like those other city-states. They were meant to be ruled. They will never succeed on their own. And others, like yourself, will learn skills and use them to buy their freedom. Slavery exists all over the world, Cimon. I am not ashamed that slavery exists here in Athens, too, because there is a way to rise above it."

But I had been a slave, and I knew that it was wrong for one person to be the property of another.

It appeared that, in spite of their great progress, the people of Athens still had much to learn.

Postscript

Early in the fifth century B.C., the Greeks were at war with the vast Persian Empire. Twice, the Persians attempted to subdue the Greeks. In the years 490 and 480, the Persians launched invasions of Greece, but both times they were defeated by the military skills of combined Greek forces first at Marathon (490) then at Salamis (480) and at Plataea (479). See the map, page 53. The most powerful land army was that of Sparta, while Athens had the strongest navy.

After the defeat of the Persians, Athens and Sparta vied for control of Greece. Each was the leader of an alliance that included many other city-states. Sparta led the Peloponnesian League, and Athens led the Delian League. After the victory over the Persians, the Athenians moved the treasury of the Delian League from Delos to Athens. The Delian League had become the Athenian Empire.

Pericles was the leader of the strongest Athenian political party. He was also the commanding general of all the military forces of Athens. Pericles led Athens for many years—from 460 to 429 B.C. During this time, known as the Age of Pericles, Athens entered a golden age of the arts and philosophy.

THE GREEK WORLD AND THE PERSIAN EMPIRE 500 B.C.

As military commander, Pericles warned that, in case of war between Athens and Sparta, Athens should refuse to fight the Spartan army. Instead, Pericles advocated relying on the powerful Athenian navy. He had an eight-mile-long wall built connecting Athens with its port city, Piraeus. The result was a huge fortress, open only to the sea. Athens was ready for a fight to the finish with Sparta.

QUESTIONS FOR REVIEW

1. Why was Minoan civilization important?
2. Why was Athens a direct democracy? How did it differ from an indirect or representative democracy?
3. How did Athenian education for boys differ from education for girls?

4. Why could Cimon not become an Athenian citizen? What does this tell you about Greek democracy?
5. Why was the Age of Pericles called Athens' golden age?

UNDERSTANDING THE STORY

A. Write F for each statement that is a fact and O for each statement that is an opinion.

1. The people of Crete were the greatest seafarers of their day.
2. A city-state was a small territory controlled by a king or a small group.
3. Greece is a hilly land that is divided by mountains and sea.
4. Athens was the greatest democratic country of all time.
5. The Greeks believed in the motto Know Thyself.
6. In Athens, only male citizens made the laws.
7. Every Athenian citizen might become a great artist.
8. Pericles was the commanding general of Athens' armed forces.

B. Athens was a direct democracy. Could we use this approach in the United States for (*a*) local government (*b*) state government (*c*) national government? Justify each of your answers.

ACTIVITIES AND INQUIRIES

1. Study the map of the Greek world and the Persian Empire on page 53. Choose the term or phrase that best completes each sentence.
   a. In traveling from Athens to Sparta, you would have gone (1) east (2) southwest (3) north.
   b. The island of Crete is in the (1) Mediterranean Sea (2) Aegean Sea (3) Ionian Sea.
   c. Knossos is in (1) Asia Minor (2) Macedonia (3) Crete.
   d. The distance from Athens to Sparta was about (1) 600 miles (2) 100 miles (3) 200 miles.
   e. The city of Mycenae was in (1) Macedonia (2) the Peloponnesus (3) Crete.
   f. The Persian Empire was located (1) west of Greece (2) south of Greece (3) east of Greece.

2. Imagine that you have invited Cimon to speak at an assembly program in your school. What might he tell you about life in ancient Athens?

3. In response to your invitation, Milos also addresses your assembly. How would his remarks differ from those of Cimon?
4. Assume that you are a member of the Athenian Council. Cimon and several other former slaves speak before the council requesting Athenian citizenship. What might they say to convince the council that they deserve to be made citizens? Would you agree? Reply to Cimon with your arguments for or against his proposal.
5. Write a report on Greek civilization during the Age of Pericles. Include information on Athenian art, history, philosophy, and relations with Sparta.

4. A School for Conquest

The city-state of Sparta, although larger than Athens, was also small by modern standards. It covered some 4,000 square miles.

Sparta was ruled by five men who were elected for one year by an assembly of all the male Spartan citizens over the age of 30. (Only 10 percent of the Spartan population were citizens.) These five men, who were called *ephors*, could conduct foreign affairs and control life at home. They could criticize anyone in Sparta, even a king, and they tried to control the minds of the people so that they would always obey their rulers' commands. There was also a council of 28 elders. We call such a government an *oligarchy*—a government in which a few people make all the decisions for the rest.

The Spartans emphasized physical training and military discipline for men, with strict obedience to their superiors' orders. Spartan women also received hard physical training so that they could become healthy mothers of future soldiers.

The Spartans were not allowed to have any kind of luxury or pleasure for fear that it would make them soft. They were also discouraged from having contact with foreigners because foreign ideas might weaken the Spartans' obedience and discipline.

In our story, Penelope, an Athenian woman, describes her visit to Sparta. She has managed to befriend a Spartan woman named Cassandra. Cassandra is trying to answer Penelope's questions about Sparta.

Sparta   435 B.C.

The first thing I noticed about the Spartan people was that they were all strong and healthy-looking. "Where are your sick people?" I asked Cassandra, the Spartan woman I had befriended.

"We have no sick or weak people here in Sparta, Penelope," she replied. "Only the strong and healthy are permitted to live."

"What do you mean?" I asked, a bit bewildered.

Cassandra went on. "If a child is born sickly, it is taken to a mountainside and left to die."

That's cruel, I thought. But I wanted to find out more about the Spartan people from Cassandra, so I kept my thoughts to myself.

"Cassandra, can you tell me more about your people?"

She obliged. "Our male children are sent to live in army schools from the ages of seven to twenty. They serve in the army until they are thirty. Then they may marry and live with their families. But they continue to be soldiers until age sixty, when they are permitted to retire."

"And what happens to your female children?"

Cassandra continued. "They are taught to play games and to build their strength. This makes them fit mothers who bear strong children for our city. They also learn how to manage their households properly. When they are adults, they may engage in business activities, if they wish."

I asked Cassandra if she would take me to see an army school, and she agreed. The first thing we saw was a young boy being whipped by his teacher in front of all his classmates. The boy did not cry out, even though it was clear that he was in great pain.

"Why is he being punished?" I asked.

Vase from the 5th century B.C., *showing two Greek warriors in hand-to-hand combat.*

Cassandra replied, "Perhaps it is because he was caught stealing."

I said, "I know that stealing is wrong, but isn't his punishment too severe?"

Cassandra shook her head at me. "He is not being punished for what he did. He is being punished for getting caught doing it! And as to why, my friend, the answer is simple. We want our children to learn how to take care of themselves. As soldiers they will sometimes have to do risky or dangerous things to stay alive. If they are caught, they will be killed. This boy will become a better soldier because of his whipping today."

"But why must all your men become soldiers?" I asked.

Cassandra answered, "We Spartans have fought many wars. As you well know, Sparta has been the enemy of Athens in the past. Perhaps we may fight each another once again."

"Do you have slaves?" I asked.

"Of course," she replied. "We have taken great numbers of

prisoners in our wars and turned them into slaves. We now have so many slaves that they outnumber us! We Spartans must keep ourselves strong in order to control our slaves. We must also be ready to defend ourselves against any people who try to do us harm."

"But don't the Spartan people complain about always having to live under a state of war?" I asked.

"You don't understand, Penelope," Cassandra answered, a note of anger entering her voice. "We *don't* complain. We Spartans are very proud of our way of life. We are a disciplined people who can make do with very little, and we can take care of ourselves."

"And how do your women feel when they watch their children march off to war? Don't they feel like complaining, even a little bit?" I asked.

Cassandra answered, "The Spartan code of conduct should make us the envy of people everywhere. Do you know what one mother said to her son as he was preparing to go off to war? As she gave him his shield, she told him that she prayed for the day when he would come back alive and victorious, carrying his shield. But if the gods deemed otherwise, and he had to die in battle, she wanted him to be carried back on his shield as proof that he had died defending Sparta."

Soon after, I left Sparta and returned to Athens. The Spartan people continue to trouble me. Can a people who are always prepared to fight a war live in peace with their neighbors? I do not think so.

There are many other Greek cities. Some look to Athens as their leader, while others look to Sparta. There cannot be two leaders. I fear that one day soon, Athens and Sparta will have to fight each other.

Postscript

The Peloponnesian War, pitting Athens and its allies against Sparta and its allies, began in 431 B.C. An epidemic, probably malaria, swept through Athens when all the people from the surrounding countryside were crowded together behind the protective walls. Twenty-five percent of the people died. Pericles was blamed, since the wall was his idea. Two years later, he also perished from the plague. Pericles' successors failed to follow his plan for avoiding land battles with the Spartans. The Athenians paid the price by eventually losing the war in 404 B.C.

Most Greeks assumed that the Spartan victory meant that each city-state would control its own affairs, and they would no longer be under the rule of another government. But they were wrong. The Spartans were now the rulers of Greece. But Sparta's victory was short-lived. In 371 B.C. the city of Thebes defeated the Spartans, ending their rule. Thebes also ruled for a short time, until civil wars resumed. Then the northern kingdom of Macedonia entered the picture. Our next story tells about the two rulers of Macedonia—Philip and his son, Alexander—who would change Greece and much of the civilized world for many years to come.

QUESTIONS FOR REVIEW

1. How was Sparta governed?
2. How did life in Sparta differ from life in Athens?
3. How did the education of Spartan boys differ from that of girls?
4. How were Spartan children taught to take care of themselves?
5. What were the results of the Peloponnesian War?

UNDERSTANDING THE STORY

A. Write T for each statement that is true and F for each statement that is false.

1. Only 10 percent of Sparta's people were citizens.
2. The Spartans were not allowed to have any kind of luxury.
3. There were many weak people in Sparta.
4. All male Spartan children were treated in the same way.
5. Spartan boys were punished for being caught stealing.
6. Sparta and Athens were great friends.
7. The Spartan people lived in a state of war.
8. The Spartan people were trained to live in peace with their neighbors.

B. Name a present-day country where the people are or were trained to live in a state of war. Compare life in that country with ancient Athens and Sparta. Now, compare life in that country with life in the present-day United States.

ACTIVITIES AND INQUIRIES

1. Imagine that you are a reporter. Your assignment is to interview one of the Spartan rulers (ephors) about his goals for his year in office. What questions would you ask him? How might he answer your questions?
2. Prepare a report comparing the Spartan army with the present-day United States army.
3. Make a list of the courses and activities offered in your school. Now do the same for a Spartan school. Discuss the differences and similarities. Which school would you prefer to attend? Why?
4. Compare Spartan attitudes with our own, with regard to: (*a*) crime (*b*) war (*c*) government (*d*) luxuries (*e*) treatment of women.
5. Cassandra emphasized that there were no sick or weak people in Sparta. How was this possible? Do you agree with this idea? Explain.

5. An Idea That Tried to Conquer the World

In the fourth century B.C., military power in the lands around the Aegean Sea shifted to the kingdom of Macedonia, to the north of Greece. When Philip became its king in 359 B.C., he knew that the Greek city-states were still divided, and their continued fighting among themselves had made them weak. Philip's armies easily defeated Athens and Thebes in 338 B.C. Greece was finally united, but under the control of Macedonia.

Philip was an excellent organizer and politician. By the time of his death in 336 B.C., he had made Macedonia into a world power. Philip created the military power and battle tactics with which his son Alexander would conquer much of the known world.

Alexander was born in 356 B.C. From an early age, he aspired to become a great military leader. His goal was to surpass his father's victo-

THE EMPIRE OF ALEXANDER THE GREAT 334–324 B.C.

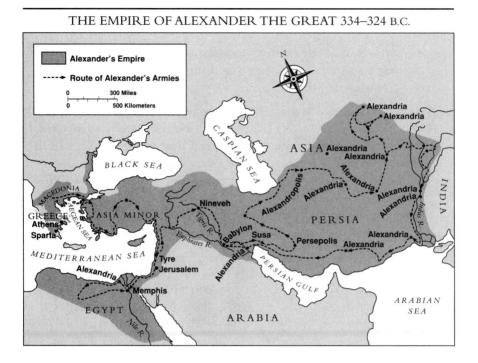

ries—and he succeeded. Alexander had another great teacher—the Greek philosopher Aristotle. Philip engaged Aristotle to teach Alexander about Greek history, literature, and philosophy.

During his years in power, Alexander (who was called "the Great") spent most of his time on the battlefield or in preparation for battle. His armies conquered lands as far east as the Indus River, including the Persian Empire that had threatened the Greeks in the fifth century. Alexander built some 20 cities, all of which he named Alexandria, in the lands he conquered. Each city was a center of Greek culture. Perhaps the most famous Alexandria was in Egypt. This city became a great center of trade and learning.

Alexander's victories opened the door for the spread of *Hellenistic* (Greek) culture and learning throughout the civilized world. (The Greeks called themselves Hellenes, and their land Hellas.) The laws, calendar, and money of the Greeks were introduced wherever they went. Greek became the language of international trade and diplomacy throughout the civilized world. Alexander's soldiers were encouraged to marry women in the lands they conquered and settle in the new cities.

Here is Alexander's story, set in the Babylonian city of Susa.

Susa   323 B.C.

Your name was Alexander, and you wanted to be remembered as the person who conquered and united the entire world as one great civilization.

As a boy, you tamed a wild horse that no one else could manage. You were able to do this because you were more observant and smarter than the others. You realized that the horse was afraid of its own shadow. So you made sure that when you trained it, the horse faced the sun and could not see its shadow. This experience helped to convince you that if you were smarter than your enemies, you would emerge victorious whenever you went to war. You were determined never to be defeated on the field of battle.

You were only 20 years old when you became the king of Macedonia. True to your dream, you united the Greek cities and then went on to win smashing victories against the Persians. Even in victory you were clever. You married a Persian princess and ordered your soldiers to marry Persian women. This made it easier for you to convince the Persian people to accept your rule.

At the same time, you helped to introduce Greek learning and culture to the Persian people. They learned the Greek language. Greek literature, art, culture, laws, and customs were introduced. This was only the beginning. It was your plan to spread the teachings of the Greek people all over the world.

Next, you marched into Egypt, conquered it, and introduced Greek ideas to the Egyptians. But even though you continued to fight and spread Greek culture, the people in the conquered lands kept their own cultures as well. In fact, the conquering Greeks were soon influenced by the cultures of the east. Some Greeks were attracted to eastern religions. Others learned new methods of commerce and trade from the eastern merchants. Greek scientists were inspired to use their knowledge to help solve practical problems. And Greek philosophers began to teach that people should no longer regard only their fellow citizens as their equals. People should, instead, regard men and women all over the world as their fellow citizens.

And even while Greek and eastern ideas were fusing and changing, you continued to conquer. Soon you were leading

Alexander the Great, in a battle near the city of Nineveh (see map, page 61), defeated the Persians under King Darius in 331 B.C.

your troops into India, where you faced an army backed by hundreds of elephants. You won that great battle and urged your army onward to conquer new lands. But your troops had other ideas. They had been away from home for six years, and they were tired and homesick. They begged you to allow them to return home. Reluctantly, you gave your consent.

Your plan was to rest your troops and then gather them together for the final campaign to conquer the rest of the world. But in the Babylonian city of Susa you became ill with fever, and your condition quickly became hopeless. You were 33 years old when you died, and your dream of conquering the entire world died with you.

Your name was Alexander, and you wanted to be remembered as the person who conquered the entire world. You never did conquer the entire world, but 2,300 years after your death you are still remembered.

Postscript

As Alexander lay dying in Susa, he was asked who would rule his vast empire. "The strongest," he is said to have replied. For many years, his followers fought among themselves for control of the empire. But no one person was strong enough to retain control of the empire. Power was divided, and large areas fell under the control of different dynasties.

The Hellenistic Age lasted approximately from the death of Alexander to the Roman conquest of Egypt in 31 B.C. (See Unit III.) Education became more widespread. A great library was founded in Alexandria, Egypt, where the Bible was translated from Hebrew into Greek. Hellenistic philosophers sought truths about the nature of human existence and about the world. Mathematics and the sciences flourished. Euclid formulated his mathematical theorems; Archimedes made discoveries in physics.

The cities that Alexander founded were all constructed on a grid pattern, with long straight streets crossing each other at right angles. International trade flourished from the lands of the Mediterranean to India. In the arts and literature, there was a newfound realism in the depiction of people and emotions. Artists portrayed living, thinking, feeling people.

QUESTIONS FOR REVIEW

1. Why was King Philip of Macedonia so successful?
2. Why was Alexander called "the Great"?
3. How did Alexander encourage the spread of Greek, or Hellenistic, culture?
4. Describe Hellenistic culture.
5. How were the Greeks influenced by the cultures of the east?

UNDERSTANDING THE STORY

A. Write T for each statement that is true, F for each statement that is false, and O for each statement that is an opinion.

1. Alexander was the greatest general the world has ever seen.
2. Alexander refused to permit his soldiers to marry women in the lands he conquered.
3. During his years in power, Alexander spent most of his time on the battlefield.
4. Alexander built many cities that he named Alexandria.
5. If Alexander had lived a few years longer, he would have conquered the entire world.
6. The Greeks were superior to all other people of the time.

7. No one person was strong enough to control all of Alexander's empire after his death.
8. Alexander's soldiers should have continued to fight in India even though they were exhausted.

B. Name a national leader in recent times who set out to conquer other lands. Compare him with Alexander with regard to (*a*) personality (*b*) success or failure to expand his empire (*c*) treatment of conquered people (*d*) effect on the rest of the world.

ACTIVITIES AND INQUIRIES

1. Study the map of the empire of Alexander the Great on page 61. Choose the term or phrase that best completes each statement.
   a. Most of Alexander's conquests were in (1) Egypt and North Africa (2) Asia Minor and Asia (3) Arabia.
   b. Alexander moved from Macedonia to the (1) east (2) west (3) north.
   c. The conquest that was farthest from Macedonia was (1) Egypt (2) Persia (3) India.
   d. A city in Egypt founded by Alexander was (1) Memphis (2) Thebes (3) Alexandria.
   e. A city in Persia was (1) Persepolis (2) Nineveh (3) Tyre.

2. Imagine that you interview Alexander for your school newspaper. Ask him why he feels that he must conquer the world. Then let him explain how he is able to rule his empire when he spends so much time on the battlefield.

3. Imagine that you are writing a book about Alexander. Prepare the table of contents.

4. Prepare a report card for Alexander the Great. Grade him in the following areas and justify each grade: (*a*) leadership (*b*) training (*c*) military ability and battle tactics (*d*) role in spreading Hellenism.

5. Imagine that you are an Egyptian general. You have been told that you will soon be defending your country against Alexander's army. What is your plan for fighting a winning battle against your enemy? What are your thoughts after the battle? Alexander asks your advice about building a city called Alexandria in Egypt. What would you tell him?

6. The Best Swords in the World

In this story, we return to the land of Africa and the Nile River, where the civilization of Egypt flourished for over 3,000 years.

Another civilization also flourished along the banks of the Nile, but upriver from (that is, to the south of) Egypt. Until recently, scholars knew little about the kingdom of Nubia (present-day Sudan). Some of its most important works were flooded when modern Egypt created the Aswan High Dam in the 1960s. But enough was saved and remains in museums

Nubian King Aspelta, 6th century B.C.

and historical records to tell a fascinating story about another great African kingdom.

Nubia was a long, narrow kingdom shaped somewhat like Florida. It covered almost 1,100 miles from Aswan to Khartoum. Scholars date the beginnings of Nubia back almost 6,000 years. The Nubians developed a distinct black African civilization that both influenced and was influenced by Egypt. During its history, Nubia was conquered several times by the Egyptians (the last time just before the reign of Hatshepsut) and regained its freedom. In turn, the Nubians ruled Egypt for almost a century (from 747 to 656 B.C.). The peoples of Egypt and Nubia traded goods such as ivory, gold, animal hides, and ebony. They also exchanged ideas about government, styles of building, and methods of writing. Nubian soldiers served in Egyptian armies and helped drive the invading Asian armies of the Hyksos people out of Egypt.

While the civilizations of Egypt and Nubia intermingled, the Nubians kept their own distinct way of life. They borrowed hieroglyphic writing from Egypt, but invented their own cursive script. Most of their writing has not been deciphered. The Nubians worshiped their own gods and some of Egypt's as well. They buried their kings with great ceremony, but in huge gravel mounds, not in pyramids as in Egypt. The kings of Nubia were buried with many ritual objects, as were the Egyptian pharaohs. The Nubians included magical figurines called *shawabtis* in the kings' tombs. These human figures carry hoes and baskets, and their purpose seems to have been to work in the heavenly grainfields so that the ruler would be assured of a good harvest and plentiful food in the afterlife. The Egyptians may have borrowed the idea of kingship from the Nubians.

The Nubian King Tahargo, who ruled in the 690s, was responsible for a revival of art and architecture in both Egypt and Nubia, and for a revival of Egyptian society, which was in decline. The Nubian rulers of Egypt are seen as black pharaohs in the Egyptian art of the time.

After the Assyrian conquest of Egypt in 656, the Nubians left Egypt and retreated to their own lands. Their capital city was called Meröe, and their land was called the kingdom of Kush. This land is northwest of present-day Ethiopia. Kush survived for many centuries, well into the Christian era. Meröe was a major stopping point on the African trade routes from the Red Sea to Egypt. Goods were transported by caravans from the Red Sea to barges on the Nile River. Large deposits of iron ore were mined near Meröe. The ironworks at Meröe were famous throughout the ancient world, and their products were highly prized.

In our story, two young Kushite men are comparing their work experiences in the economic life of Kush and Meröe.

THE KINGDOM OF KUSH c. 250 B.C.

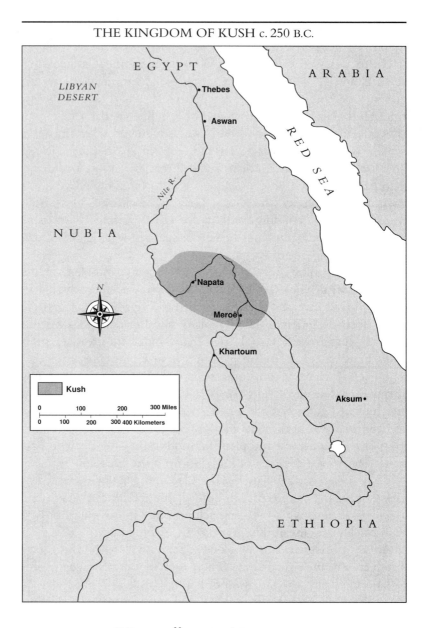

Meroë   250 B.C.

"Shalanka!" cried Tabanka. "I haven't seen you in months. Where have you been?"

"It's a long story," replied Shalanka. "I got a job as a camel driver with a caravan. We carried iron weapons, gold, and

ivory from Meroë to the Red Sea. There we loaded everything onto large merchant ships. We came back with fabrics
and spices from India."

"Weren't you afraid of bandits?" asked Tabanka.

"Not at all," replied Shalanka. "The kingdom of Kush protects
the trade routes between the Nile River and the Red Sea. No
bandits dared attack us."

"You must have seen some really interesting sights."

"I'm afraid not," Shalanka replied sadly. "All I saw was sand:
sand in my mouth, sand in my eyes, and sand in my hair. I
froze all night and roasted all day. No, I saw no interesting
sights!"

"But," protested Tabanka, "you must have visited some towns
you never saw before."

"Towns! What towns?" exclaimed Shalanka. "Every day or
two the experienced camel drivers would tell me that we were
nearing an oasis (watering place). I imagined a paradise with
beautiful gardens and fountains and people my age. Then we'd
come to the oasis. Most of the time it was a half-empty mud-
hole with a few palm trees and scarcely enough water for the
camels to drink."

"But Shalanka, *you* got away from Meroë," replied Tabanka.
"I'm still at the same job, making swords in the iron foundry."

"What you do is very important," said Shalanka. "You've
helped make Kushite swords the best in the world. No army is
a match for the army that fights with our swords. Everyone
wants to buy our iron products."

"Yes, I am proud of what I do. But I wish my working conditions were better," said Tabanka. "The heat in the forge is
often unbearable. And I do the same thing hour after hour,
day after day.

"Still, we ironworkers are better off than those who work in
the mines. Only slaves work down in the mines. I am a free
man. I am skilled, and I get paid well for the work I do."

Shalanka nodded. By the way, how do you feel about our new
ruler, King Ergamenes?"

"I like him very much," replied Tabanka. "The king is

expanding the ironworks. Soon there will be new buildings and equipment to forge more tools and weapons. And the king is opening a new iron mine."

Shalanka smiled and said, "That's wonderful news. Don't you see what this means, Tabanka? With your skill and experience, you will soon be promoted to foreman."

"Shalanka, I can only hope you are right. But what about you? Will you continue to work as a camel driver?"

"When you get your promotion, I'll take your old job in the iron foundry," Shalanka replied.

Postscript

The king of Kush did indeed expand the ironworks at Meroë. As a result, Kushite iron products and iron-smelting methods could be found in many parts of the African continent.

Kush was prosperous for many centuries. During the second century B.C., it was ruled by queens, who were famous as traders of elephants. (They may have supplied the elephants that the Carthaginian general Hannibal used in his invasion of Italy in 218 B.C.) However, Kush was threatened by the rise of Aksum to the south, in what is now Ethiopia. In A.D. 325, Aksum defeated the Kushites, and in 350 destroyed the city of Meroë. For the next 400 years, Aksum controlled the Red Sea trade with the interior of Africa.

Today, many objects from Nubia and Kush—statues, jewelry, weapons, and tools—are displayed in museums throughout the world.

QUESTIONS FOR REVIEW

1. Describe the trade between Nubia and Egypt.
2. Compare the ways of life of Egypt and Nubia.
3. Why was Shalanka unhappy with his job as a camel driver?
4. Why was Tabanka displeased with his working conditions?
5. Why did Tabanka think highly of King Ergamenes?

UNDERSTANDING THE STORY

A. Write S for each statement that Shalanka made or might have made and T for each statement that Tabanka made or might have made.

1. I got a job as a camel driver.
2. The kingdom of Kush protects the trade routes.
3. You must have visited some towns you never saw before.
4. I'm still at the same job, making swords.
5. What you do is very important.
6. Only slaves work down in the mines.
7. The king understands the importance of our ironworks.
8. With your skill and experience, you will soon be promoted to foreman.

B. Compare the working conditions in a modern factory in this country with those in the foundry in Kush where Tabanka worked. Explain the similarities and differences.

ACTIVITIES AND INQUIRIES

1. Study the map on page 68. Choose the term or phrase that best completes each statement.
   a. The city of Meroë was (1) west of the Red Sea (2) south of the Red Sea (3) east of the Red Sea.
   b. Meroë was located on the (1) Zambesi River (2) Senegal River (3) Nile River.
   c. The land of Ethiopia was (1) south of Meroë (2) north of Meroë (3) west of Meroë.
   d. The distance from Meroë to Aksum was about (1) 2,000 miles (2) 1,000 miles (3) 350 miles.
   e. The Egyptian city of Thebes was (1) south of Meroë (2) west of Meroë (3) north of Meroë.
2. Imagine that you meet with Shalanka. What does he tell you about the life of a camel driver? What job in this country might be comparable? Why do you think so? If you cannot think of a comparable job, explain why you found it difficult to make a comparison.
3. According to the story, the manufacture of iron products was very important in Kush. What does this tell you about industry in Africa? Tabanka seems to doubt the importance of his job in the foundry. Convince him that he is doing vital work.
4. Visit your school or public library. Prepare a report comparing Nubia and Egypt, using the following headings: (a) language (b) religion (c) government (d) art and architecture (e) military achievements.
5. Imagine that you are the manager of the foundry in Meroë. Shalanka applies for a job. What questions would you ask him? How might he answer your questions? Would you hire him? Why or why not?

7. Can a Small Group Defeat a Mighty Army?

The eastern coast of the Mediterranean Sea is part of an area that was known in ancient times as the Fertile Crescent. This crescent extended from the Mediterranean north and then east to the lands of Mesopotamia. The land was heavily wooded in some areas; rich soils and sunny conditions led to fine harvests in others. The Fertile Crescent was a land that was much sought after by many different peoples over many thousands of years.

Many groups settled in the Fertile Crescent and made important contributions to civilization. One of these groups, the Hebrews, is highly important to us because their religion influenced the development of two others. That religion is Judaism, and it had profound effects on the development of Christianity and Islam.

The nomadic Hebrew tribes, who migrated from Mesopotamia to the lands of the eastern Mediterranean around the year 1900 B.C., brought with them a belief in one god, Yahweh. Unlike the many gods of the Mesopotamians and the Greeks, Yahweh did not have a human or an animal form. Yahweh was a spiritual force who demanded and received unswerving devotion from his followers. The belief in one god is called *monotheism.*

In the thirteenth century B.C., many of the Hebrews were enslaved in Egypt. After a time, their leader, Moses, persuaded the pharaoh to free them, and he was allowed to lead the people back to their lands. On the long journey, Moses received the Ten Commandments and taught them to his people. After many hardships, they settled in a land they called Palestine.

By the eleventh century B.C., the Hebrew tribes were organized into a loose union. They were too weak to defeat their major enemies, the Philistines, however. In the 1020s, the Hebrews united under a king named Saul. His successor, David, led the people into battle and captured the site of his future capital city of Jerusalem. David's son Solomon built a great temple in Jerusalem to worship Yahweh. Solomon also expanded trade with neighboring countries.

After Solomon died, the tribes split into two kingdoms: the northern

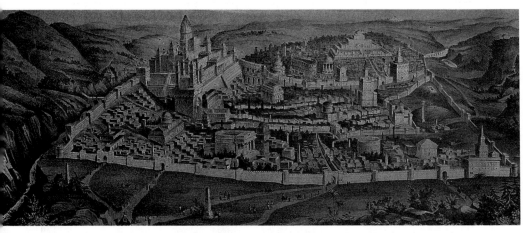

Jerusalem in the middle of the 1st century A.D. *The temple is the tallest building at the highest elevation (left of center).*

one was called Israel, and the southern one was called Judah. Over the centuries, each was weakened by political and social unrest, wars, and bad alliances.

In 722 B.C., the Assyrians defeated the Israelites and took the people into captivity. The northern kingdom of Israel ceased to exist. A similar fate nearly befell the people of Judah. In 586 B.C., the Babylonians invaded, destroyed the temple in Jerusalem, and took many Judeans into captivity.

The people had many spiritual leaders, wise religious persons called prophets. In later centuries, their writings were collected in the holy books that bear their names in the Bible (such as Elijah and Micah).

During their captivity in Babylon, the Judeans, or Jews, turned to the study of the writings of their leaders—the laws of Moses, the psalms (poems) of David, and the books of the prophets—for guidance and consolation. Many of the books of the Bible were collected, organized, and edited at this time. The people came to realize that their god was no longer to be reached just in a single building, but could be found everywhere that worshipers assembled.

King Cyrus of Persia freed the Judeans in 536 B.C. and they returned home. After the death of Alexander the Great in 323 B.C., Egypt governed Judah. In 198, Egypt was defeated by the Seleucid (Syrian Greek) empire. The Jews at first welcomed their new rulers, but they soon changed their minds. Antiochus IV of Syria wanted them to become Hellenized—to follow Greek rather than Jewish customs. To make matters worse, he turned the temple in Jerusalem into a shrine to the Greek god Zeus. Antiochus accused religious Jews of being Egyptian spies. Many who refused to worship the Greek gods were executed.

THE KINGDOMS OF ISRAEL AND JUDAH c. 860 B.C.

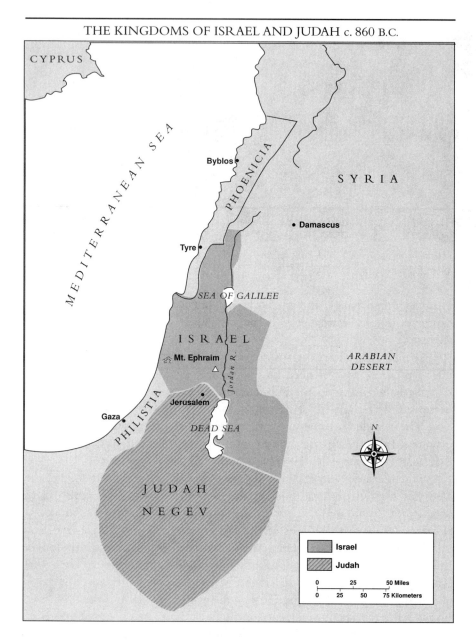

As our story opens, the priest Mattathias Hasmoni, the leader of the religious Jews, and his five sons are in grave danger. They have been forced to flee Jerusalem because they disobeyed the Syrians' orders. They are determined to follow the religion of their choice.

Mountains of Ephraim   166 B.C.

"Are we safe here in the mountains?" asked Mattathias.

"No—we've got to keep moving, Father," replied Judas Maccabeus ("the Hammer"). "You killed Apelles, one of Antiochus' men. Now the Syrians won't stop until they find us."

"I had to kill him. He wanted us to worship their Greek idols," said Mattathias. "I'm too old to keep running. I say stand and fight!"

"Father is right," said Simon. "We *must* fight. We Jews should not be persecuted because of our faith. But how can our small group of believers face the mighty Syrian army?"

"We will never face them in open battle," said Judas. "We will surprise them. We will swoop down on them when they least expect us, kill as many as we can, and dash away."

"Fine," said Eleazer, "but how long can we continue doing this?"

"Until they let us worship in our own way," said Mattathias.

"We'll need more warriors to keep battling the Seleucids," said Jonathan.

"How and where do we find them?" asked John.

"Strong fighting men are hiding all through these lands," said Mattathias. "Jonathan, Eleazer, and John: Slip into the countryside. Speak to the people. Tell them why they must join us. Judas and Simon: Stay with me. We will plan our campaign."

The next day found Mattathias, Judas, and Simon awaiting word from the brothers.

"I hope my brothers return with many volunteers," said Simon.

"They will be very convincing," said Judas. "They will remind the Jews of Antiochus' cruelties."

The three brothers found Jews who were hiding near a farm village. The brothers pleaded with the men to join forces with them. People listened intently to what the brothers said.

"Antiochus has burned Jerusalem to the ground. Thousands

have been killed or sold into slavery. The Syrians have turned the temple, which we dedicated to our god, Yahweh, into a temple honoring Zeus, the chief god of the Greeks. We are forced to eat pork, which is forbidden by our laws, or go to prison. We are not permitted to observe our Sabbath (holy day). The Syrians will kill any Jews who are found with the Torah (Book of the Law).

"Who will join us in the battle for the right to worship our God in our own way?"

Some men stepped forward.

"If we join you, we will surely be killed," said one who did not move.

"I'd rather hide here than in those barren mountains," said another.

"If it will save many lives, why can't we worship a few Greek idols?" asked a third.

"You cannot save your life by worshiping as a Greek. Come with us, or the enemy will kill you!"

Many men now rose and joined the brothers. They swore to defend their faith and liberate their land from the Syrians.

Postscript

Aged and ill, Mattathias died shortly thereafter, and his son Judas Maccabeus became the leader of the rebellion. His band of fighting men lived in the mountains and attacked the enemy whenever they could. Judas's army grew larger and larger as more people rebelled against the rule of the Syrians. (The story of Mattathias and his sons is recorded in the biblical books of the Maccabees.)

In 166 B.C., Judas defeated Antiochus' soldiers. Two years later, the king sent a much larger force to combat the rebels. This time, Judas's army defeated the Syrians even more decisively, and recaptured Jerusalem. The ancient religious ways were observed once again. This victory is celebrated as the Festival of Hanukkah (dedication).

Judas won another major victory in 161, but he was defeated and slain in the following year. In 152, his brother Jonathan was elected high priest of Jerusalem, He was followed by Simon, and Simon's son, John. For the next hundred years, their descendants, the Hasmoneans, were the rulers of Judah.

QUESTIONS FOR REVIEW

1. How did the religious beliefs of the Hebrews differ from those of other peoples in the Middle East?
2. What were the achievements of King Saul and King David?
3. Why did the Hebrews object to the orders of King Antiochus?
4. How did Judas Maccabeus propose to fight the Syrians?
5. What arguments did the three brothers offer to encourage other men to join them?

UNDERSTANDING THE STORY

A. Write M for each statement that Mattathias made or might have made and J for each statement that Judas made or might have made.

1. Now the Syrians won't stop until they find us.
2. I'm too old to keep running.
3. He wanted us to worship their Greek idols.
4. We will never face them in open battle.
5. Strong fighting men are hiding all through these lands.
6. We will fight until they let us worship in our own way.
7. We will swoop down on them when they least expect us.
8. I say stand and fight!

B. The struggle of Judas Maccabeus and his brothers was a fight for religious freedom. Why is this so important? Would you have been willing to join them against the Syrians? Why or why not?

ACTIVITIES AND INQUIRIES

1. Assume that you have joined Judas and his brothers. They now ask your advice in fighting the Syrians. What new tactics would you recommend?
2. Imagine that you are in the Syrian camp. What steps would you recommend taking to defeat the Hebrews?

3. You interview the Syrian king, Antiochus IV. What questions would you ask him? How might he answer your questions?
4. Prepare a report on several groups of people who came to the United States to find religious freedom. Compare their problems with those of the Hebrews.
5. Look at the map on page 74. Locate the area where the Hebrews in the story hid from and struggled against the Syrians.

8. Trying to Understand the Way the World Works

Some 20,000 to 30,000 years ago, the ancestors of the Native American people migrated (traveled) from northern Asia across the Bering Strait land bridge into Alaska and North America. Many of these people remained in the north, but others continued to move farther south and settled in the tropical regions of Mesoamerica (middle, or Central America). Among the most brilliant and creative of these Mesoamerican peoples were the Maya, who settled in parts of present-day Guatemala, Honduras, El Salvador, Mexico, and all of Belize before the year 1000 B.C.

The Maya were an agricultural civilization. They cleared the dense jungle and planted a wide variety of foods, including many items we find in our diets today. Among them were beans, yams, peppers, and above all maize (corn). Maya farmers learned how to make maize, the ancestor of the corn plant, produce abundant crops that fed a large population. They used canals, ditches, and basins to store water from wet to dry seasons.

The Maya were the greatest architects and builders of Mesoamerica. In their cities, they erected great stone temples, terraced pyramids, and monuments. Their towering buildings were covered with stucco and painted in bright colors. The outer walls of the temples and monuments were decorated with elaborately sculpted figures of Maya gods and kings. Maya kings were buried in the great pyramids. The people believed that the kings were related to the gods.

THE MAYA EMPIRE A.D. 250

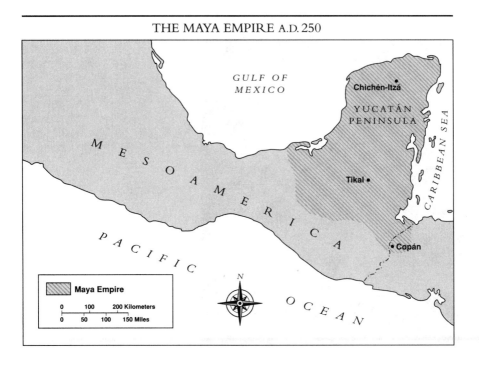

Some Maya cities had populations estimated at 10,000 to 20,000 persons. Long, broad avenues were built of stone covered by cement. The upper classes, or nobility, lived in beautifully decorated buildings apart from the general population of farmers and laborers.

In contrast to the wealth and luxury of the aristocracy, the common people lived simply. Their homes were plain wooden houses with steep thatched roofs. The overhang of roofs provided protection from the hot sun. The common people dressed simply, in cape and loincloth, and painted and tattooed their bodies.

The Maya were gifted astronomers and mathematicians. They made discoveries in these fields that Europeans would not match for centuries. For example, the Maya accurately forecast eclipses of the moon and the positions of stars and the planets. Their calendar was more accurate than the one used in 16th-century Europe.

The Maya were only one of the two pre-Columbian civilizations (prior to A.D. 1492) to develop an original system of writing. (The other was the Olmec people, who lived to the north of the Maya.) The Maya system used hieroglyphics (pictures), which stood for both whole words and phonetic syllables. Recently, scholars have made much progress in decoding the Maya writing, which is found on their great stone columns called *stele*. These columns tell stories about the Maya kings and other rulers.

Pyramids dominated the Maya city of Tikal, in present-day Guatemala.

The Maya built their great cities and maintained their agriculture without many of the things we take for granted. They did not use the wheel (except in children's toys) or have any metal tools. Nor did they use animals to haul heavy loads.

In our story, a woman is teaching her granddaughter important things about the Maya people. The setting is the great city of Tikal.

Tikal A.D. 250

"Why do we always pray for maize (corn), Grandmother?" asked the granddaughter. "I eat it every day, but I wish Mother would give me more beans and sweet potatoes instead."

"Our lives depend on maize," said the grandmother. "That's why, before I plant the corn seeds, I burn incense (scented stick) in front of special ears of corn. It never fails. The corn god hears my prayer, and the crop is always good."

"But we have other food to eat. Why do our lives depend on maize?" asked the granddaughter.

"Let me tell you a little story to help you understand, Granddaughter. Many, many years ago, the gods wanted to create people to live in our world. They realized that maize was the perfect material from which to work. But the gods were *too* successful. The corn people had *perfect* sight and understanding. They were too much like the gods. So the gods weakened the eyes of the people. Now, we see and understand things only when they are close by."

"I think I understand," said the granddaughter. "We must never forget that we *are* maize. The gods made us from maize, and they can just as easily destroy us."

"Or reward us," the grandmother added.

"I have another question to ask you," said the granddaughter. "Sometimes I awaken late at night and I see my father peering at the sky. What is he looking for?"

"Your father is an astronomer," replied the grandmother. "He looks at the heavens (sky) to study the stars, the moon, and the planets.

"As he watches the heavenly bodies, he keeps records of their movements, or paths. The stars, the planets, and the sun and moon have many messages for us."

"But how can he be sure that he is seeing the same stars and planets each time he looks?"

"He uses monuments, buildings, the horizon, crossed sticks—anything that will give him a fixed line of sight, Granddaughter. He's also a mathematician. He is one of the people responsible for keeping an accurate calendar."

"But what's the purpose of keeping our calendar?" asked the granddaughter.

"The record of the reign of each king must be written down accurately for future generations. And how else would we know when to plant and harvest our crops? This is why we made our calendar and learned to tell time," said the grandmother.

The granddaughter said, "Grandmother, even though the gods have weakened us, they seem to have left us with great ability to understand the world they have created for us."

The grandmother nodded and smiled.

Postscript

The civilization of the Maya reached its height between A.D. 100 and 800. Great cities were built, trade with other regions of Mesoamerica flourished, and the population grew. However, the Maya were also constantly at war during this time, as leaders of different city-states battled one another. Some of the most impressive Maya monuments depict scenes of battle and the enslavement and execution of defeated enemies. The Maya also practiced human sacrifice on a large scale. By the year 900, the Maya had abandoned their great cities, the population was declining, and they produced no more art or monuments. Experts now believe that the Maya exhausted their lands and people in constant warfare.

The Spanish conquerors who arrived in Mesoamerica in the 1500s found a society whose achievements were already disappearing under the thick cover of the tropical jungle. The Spaniards deliberately destroyed most of the Maya's written records; only a few books survive in European libraries. Centuries would pass before archeologists began excavating the Maya cities and learned to read their writing.

Some people have called the Maya the Greeks of the Americas. Can you give reasons why?

QUESTIONS FOR REVIEW

1. Why are the Maya considered the most advanced people of Mesoamerica?
2. Compare the lives of the Maya aristocrats and the common people.
3. Describe the Maya system of writing.
4. Why does the grandmother insist that the lives of the people depend on maize?
5. Why was astronomy important to the Maya?

UNDERSTANDING THE STORY

A. Write G for each statement that the grandmother made or might have made and D for each statement that the granddaughter made or might have made.

1. I wish my mother would give me more sweet potatoes.
2. Our lives depend on maize.
3. The gods wanted to create people to live in our world.
4. We must never forget that we are maize.
5. Your father is an astronomer.
6. I see my father peering at the sky at night.
7. He watches the heavenly bodies.
8. But what's the purpose of keeping our calendar?

B. Suppose that the civilization of the Maya had thrived until our day. Compare the accomplishments of the Maya with those of the nations of Europe and the United States.

ACTIVITIES AND INQUIRIES

1. Describe the contributions of the Maya in each of the following areas: (*a*) architecture (*b*) astronomy (*c*) agriculture (*d*) mathematics.
2. The granddaughter says, "We must never forget that we *are* maize." Explain what she means. How might a United States farmer react to the granddaughter's remark? How do you react?
3. Imagine that you interview the grandmother. What questions would you ask her about the Maya? How might she reply?
4. The Maya were astronomers. How did their studies of the heavens differ from ours? What similarities do you see? Suppose that the Maya had been able to use present-day telescopes and modern equipment. What might they have accomplished?
5. Assume that you accompanied the European explorers of Mesoamerica in the 1500s. Describe what you would have seen of Maya culture. Go to your school or local library. Do research on the culture of Spain at the time of the Spanish conquest. Compare Spanish culture and Maya culture.

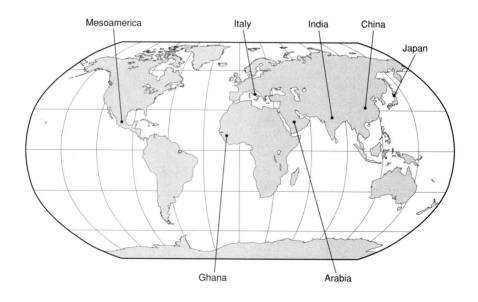

UNIT III

Religions and Empires

This unit spans 1,900 years of recorded history. We begin in India in 500 B.C., journey to Europe, Asia, the Middle East, and Africa, and end in Mesoamerica with the mighty Azetc Empire, in the year A.D. 1410.

India. We begin with the great Indian spiritual teacher Buddha, who sets down guides to personal conduct and the spiritual life.

Europe. On our historical journey, we will witness the growth, flowering, and decline of the Roman Empire in Europe. A second great spiritual leader, Jesus, lived in the early days of the Empire, and his teachings were slowly accepted by the people and their rulers.

Asia. The Han Empire of China flourished at the same time as the Roman Empire. Some of China's riches and achievements traveled to the West along a trading route called the Silk Route. China also influenced its Asian neighbors Korea and Japan. In Japan, an ancient religion taught that the gods existed in nature.

Middle East. On the Arabian peninsula, a third great spiritual leader, Muhammad, arose in the seventh century to lead the people. In just a few hundred years, his teachings had converted and conquered much of the Middle East and North Africa.

Africa. In West Africa, south of the Sahara Desert, a mighty trading empire flourished in the land of Ghana. Our story tells why its rulers were believed to be the richest people in the world.

Mesoamerica. Finally, we see see what the Aztec people of Mesoamerica did to keep their gods happy and their empire strong.

1. Buddhism: The Middle Way

Buddhism is the second of the world's great religions that began in India. Unlike Hinduism, Buddhism traces its origins to a specific time in India and to one person: Siddhartha Gautama (563–483 B.C.). A prince of the powerful and wealthy Shakya clan of warriors, he was born and grew up in the foothills of the Himalayas, in present-day Nepal.

As a young man, Siddhartha lived a happy and privileged life. He married and had a son. But at about the age of 29, he saw that life was filled with sadness and decay. He realized that he understood little about life. He left his home and family and for six years wandered about the land fasting and searching for truth. He studied with wise persons, but even they could not give him the answers he was seeking.

One day, while meditating, Siddhartha suddenly understood why there was so much suffering in the world. (The cause of our suffering is found in humankind's imperfect nature.) From that time on, he was known as the *Buddha*—the *Enlightened One*. For the next 45 years, until his death, the Buddha devoted himself to the service of others. He gathered together a group of disciples and taught them his beliefs. A rich merchant built a monastery for the Buddha and his followers (monks) at Jetavana (Nepal). Buddha allowed all men and women to join the communities, no matter what caste they belonged to. Buddhist monks live in a monastic order or community (called a *sangha*) to this day.

The Buddha taught that people should follow a path of right living and thinking in order to achieve salvation (*nirvana*). Universal laws or truths about human existence may be learned through reason. Buddhism prohibits certain activities, such as lying, killing, and stealing, and it advocates others, such as right speech, proper action, and meditation. The Buddha rejected both the caste system of Hinduism and the idea of a divine creator.

In our story, the Buddha talks with Ananda, a cousin who has become one of his disciples.

Jetavana 495 B.C.

"Master," said Ananda, "you have often spoken about how to live properly. Please explain your rules of how we should live."

The Buddha said: "The right attitude toward life is the basis for sound living." Do you agree?

"Here are my commandments," said the Buddha. "Let us not kill any living thing. Never take what has not been given to you. Do not tell lies. Do not drink anything that will make you drunk. Always live a pure and wholesome life."

"But can we expect ordinary people to live like this?"

"Ananda, all of us can live this way. In fact, I would go much further. If a person hurts me, I will help that person. If I am abused, I will remain silent. The worse a person treats me, the better I will try to be."

"I am truly sorry, Master, but I fear that I cannot be like you."

"Perhaps you don't understand what I am trying to teach you. Let me give you an example of how to behave. Once, a person insulted me, but I said nothing. Finally, I asked the person a question. 'If a person refuses to accept a present that is offered, to whom does it belong?' The person replied, 'It belongs to the person who offered the present, of course.'

'Good,' I said. 'Therefore, I will not accept your nasty remarks. Keep them for yourself!' You see, I did not insult the person, but I showed how foolish the person's remarks and attitude were."

"Master, I have another question for you," said Ananda. "You once were a rich man, with many luxuries and beautiful things. Then you gave up everything and were very poor and had nothing. Which way is better?"

"Neither," replied the Buddha. "On the one hand, if we think only of riches and possessions or live only for pleasure, we will never have the time to search for the true meaning of life. On the other hand, those who have little or nothing are constantly concerned with survival and have neither the time nor energy to seek enlightenment. No, Ananda, we must have the opportunity and the willingness to look inside ourselves. Then we will find the way to truth."

"How can we find this middle way?" asked Ananda.

"The right attitude toward life is the basis for sound living," said the Buddha. "We must constantly seek to teach the true way to all persons. Everyone must learn to respect all living creatures, to do good works, to help the poor and sick, and not to fight or steal."

"Master, do you think I have a chance of achieving nirvana?" asked Ananda. "I want to experience the peace that you have."

"Of course you can reach nirvana. But first, Ananda, you must want absolutely nothing. Devote yourself entirely to helping others. When you have lost interest in yourself and want nothing, you will have found the true meaning of your existence, and you will be at peace."

Postscript

In the third century B.C., during the reign of Asoka (265–238), the last major emperor of the Maurya dynasty, Buddhism spread to other lands. Asoka sent missionaries—among them his son and daughter—to Burma, Ceylon (present-day Sri Lanka), and Egypt. At home, Asoka followed Buddhist teachings and renounced war in favor of good works. Asoka

Chinese bodihsattva, a Buddhist goddess of mercy, from the Tang dynasty period.

granted freedom of religion, built public works, and established communities for Buddhist monks.

Buddhism did not survive in India, however. Hinduism absorbed (took over) parts of Buddhism and became the religion of the majority of the Indian people.

In later years, Buddhism was adopted by people throughout Asia—in Myanmar, Thailand, Cambodia, Laos, Vietnam, and Tibet. In some areas, Buddhism became part of the complex set of beliefs that people held. For example, in China, Buddhism was joined with Confucianism. In Japan, Buddhism and Shinto (see page 118) eventually intermingled ideas and rituals. The Japanese branch called Zen Buddhism has attracted Western followers in the twentieth century.

QUESTIONS FOR REVIEW

1. Why did Siddhartha leave his home and family?
2. How are Buddhists to achieve salvation, or nirvana?
3. How are Buddhists to find the road to truth?

4. How can Buddhists find the middle way?
5. What did the Emperor Asoka do in order to follow Buddhist teachings in his own life?

UNDERSTANDING THE STORY

A. Write B for each statement that the Buddha made or might have made and A for each statement that Ananda made or might have made.

1. Here are my commandments.
2. Can we expect ordinary people to live like this?
3. I am truly sorry, Master, that I cannot be like you.
4. Once, a person insulted me, but I said nothing.
5. We must be willing to look inside ourselves.
6. How can we find the middle way?
7. The right attitude toward life is the basis for sound living.
8. Do you think I have a chance of achieving nirvana?

B. Assume that you are given the opportunity to become one of the Buddha's followers or students. Would you accept? Why or why not? What would you expect to learn from the Buddha?

ACTIVITIES AND INQUIRIES

1. On an outline map of Asia, indicate the countries or areas where Buddhism has been adopted.
2. Buddhism teaches that nirvana can be achieved by following a path of right living. Explain what the Buddha meant by "right living." Outline your own ideas of "right living."
3. Ananda asked the Buddha several questions. What other questions would you have asked him? How might he have answered your questions?
4. Prepare a report on the accomplishments of the Emperor Asoka. Then pretend to interview him and find out why and how he followed Buddhist teachings.

2. The Struggle for Equal Rights

The Italian peninsula juts out into the Mediterranean Sea at its widest point. With its fertile lands, temperate, healthy climate, and central location, Italy attracted many groups of people, including the Greeks, who established Italian colonies in the eighth century B.C. Here, we are concerned with the people who are known to us as the Romans, after the name of their great capital city and empire. The ever-expanding Roman territories later came to include all of Italy and finally the entire Mediterranean region. The Romans built an empire that, at its peak, was larger than that of Alexander the Great. It reached from England in the north to Assyria in the east and included present-day Spain, France, southern Europe, and much of the Middle East.

Rome's origins were humble, however. The hills of Rome were settled around the middle of the seventh century B.C. by tribes of Latin and Sabine shepherds and farmers. The first settlements were a small group of villages located about 15 miles from the mouth of the Tiber River. The villages were well situated and easily protected, and they prospered. Eventually, they united to form the city-state that became Rome. The Romans traded with many other groups, including the Greek colonists in the south.

At about the time that Rome was founded, people from Asia Minor who are known to us as the Etruscans entered the Italian peninsula. First settling in Etruria (present-day Tuscany), they later expanded south to the Bay of Naples and north to the Po River. Etruscan kings ruled Rome in the sixth century until they were overthrown by the Roman people in 509 B.C. The Etruscans left beautiful and imaginative works of art and sculpture. Gifted builders and engineers, they taught their skills to the Romans.

In the century after the overthrow of the Etruscans, Rome began to expand and conquer. Roman customs were written down in a set of laws known as the Twelve Tables (450 B.C.). The city was attacked and nearly destroyed by people known as the Gauls in 390 B.C., but it recovered and grew steadily.

In the years after the overthrow of the Etruscan kings, the Romans developed a republican form of government. A *republic* is a government in which the people's elected representatives run the affairs of state. In some republics, the people have the final say about the laws and their leaders. In others, one person or a small group is actually in control of everything.

By the fourth century, the Roman republic was ruled by a small group of persons, the *patricians*. These were the wealthy landowning families. They controlled the senate (the lawmaking body) and the army. The majority of the people (the *plebeians*) were citizens, but they had few rights. The plebeians included farmers, soldiers, skilled workers, merchants, and traders. The plebeians had a political council, which tried to protect them from the patricians' actions.

Slaves were even worse off. Former prisoners of war or plebeians imprisoned for debt, they farmed the patricians' lands or worked as their house servants. Slaves were not citizens, and they had no legal rights.

In our story, Rome is in turmoil. The plebeians have gone on strike to gain more rights. They refuse to work at their jobs and do not report for military service. Here, two Romans, a patrician and a plebeian, argue about their differences.

Rome   367 b.c.

"Marcus, I have always thought of you as a reasonable person. Don't you agree that, as loyal Roman citizens, you and the other plebeians should resume your duties?" asked Lucius.

Marcus replied, "No, we will not. And we will not be satisfied until we have destroyed your one-sided patrician government!"

"How can you speak to me like that?" said Lucius. "We've been friends since childhood. Haven't I always treated you fairly?"

"Yes, Lucius, we were friends once. But how can I ever forget the enormous differences between us? You are a wealthy land-holding patrician. I am just a poor carpenter. I can barely afford to feed my family."

"But I've never used my wealth to take advantage of you," Lucius protested.

"That's not true! You and the other patricians have always taken advantage of people like me," said Marcus bitterly. "You are one of the three hundred members of the senate. Were any of you elected? Of course not! You are a senator only because your family is a member of the ruling class!"

Lucius replied, "Most of us in the senate have held important government jobs, Marcus. Among the senators are former judges, generals, and consuls. I myself have been head of a province. What experience in government have you plebeians had? Admit it: we patricians know how to run Rome."

"I admit no such thing!" Marcus cried. "We ordinary people don't have your experience because all of the important government jobs are closed to plebeians. Lucius, this is supposed to be a republic, not a government of the rich. We poor people deserve the same rights and privileges as you rich people."

"What do your people really want, Marcus?"

"We want justice," said Marcus. "The laws that were written down years ago are harsh. Many crimes are punished by death, and debtors are treated severely. But the written law was a step forward because people knew what was legal and what was not. The problem, Lucius, is that all the judges are patricians. And they favor their own people."

"You don't need plebeian judges because Roman law protects you. No Roman can be executed without a trial, and a judge's sentence can be appealed to a higher court. A person condemned to die can always go into exile (leave the country) instead."

"Lucius," said Marcus, "as long as there are no plebeian judges, we plebeians will never be judged fairly. And Rome will never have the loyalty of its plebeian citizens so long as its most important jobs are closed to them."

"If you are granted these things, then will you resume your responsibilities?" asked Lucius.

"Not quite," replied Marcus with a slight smile. "We must also have plebeians in the senate, and we want to be able to marry members of patrician families."

"I understand your desire to be in the senate, but marriage between people of different classes—that's not possible."

Marcus replied, "Without the plebeians, Rome is not possible, patrician wealth is not possible, and patrician privilege is not possible. When you and the other patricians finally come to understand that you cannot do without us, you will give us the things we ask for. It may take time, but we plebeians have little to lose and much to gain. We will wait, and we will continue to withhold our services."

Postscript

Marcus was right. The Roman patricians could not do without the plebeian workers and soldiers. By the end of the fourth century, after many years of struggle, the plebeians had achieved most of their goals. Plebeians could hold all public offices, the actions of the plebeians' assembly became law, and some marriages between classes did take place. But the wealthy, especially the plebeians who had recently acquired fortunes, kept actual control of the government.

By 264 B.C., Rome had conquered all of the Italian peninsula. In North Africa, Rome fought with the North African state of Carthage for control of the western Mediterranean. After a long struggle (three wars, fought over more than a century), Carthage was finally defeated, and the city (near present-day Tunis) was totally destroyed in 146 B.C.

At the same time, Rome extended its conquests into the eastern Mediterranean. By 133 B.C., much of what had been the empire of Alexander the Great belonged to Rome.

ROME: REPUBLIC AND EMPIRE

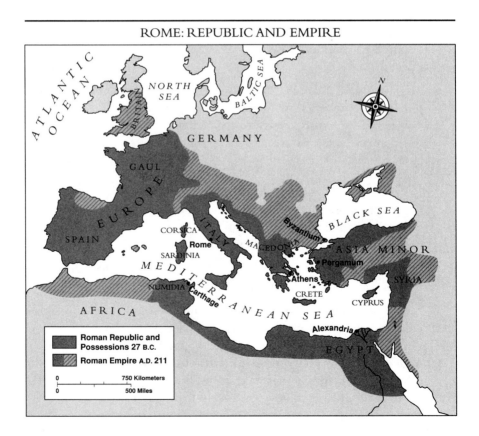

Expansion brought prosperity to businesspeople and to bankers. But the peasants who farmed small plots of land could not compete with the large landowners. Many peasants moved to the cities, particularly to Rome, where they found themselves without jobs. Attempts at moving the people out of the cities and limiting the size of farms failed.

During the first century, the Roman republic could not cope with economic depression, food riots, and attacks from hostile tribes. People lost confidence in the government and, in some cases, actually rebelled. Citizens switched their loyalties from the republic to military leaders. They in turn fought among themselves for political control.

Julius Caesar, a nobleman who was a great military leader, overcame his rivals and became dictator of Rome. (A *dictator* is a person who has the power to make all government decisions by himself or herself.) From 49 to 45 B.C., Caesar fought successful military campaigns in Spain, the Middle East, and North Africa, and he restored Rome's power in its provinces (outlying territories).

Julius Caesar gave land to the poor, reformed the calendar, and resettled many of his army veterans in Spain and North Africa. He started a public building campaign in Rome to provide work for the unemployed. Unfortunately, Caesar's success was short-lived. In 44 B.C., he was assassinated (killed) by enemies in the senate, who opposed his dictatorial rule. Caesar's assassins claimed that they were restoring the Roman republic. But the republic perished in the civil wars that followed Caesar's death. The next story describes the events that followed.

QUESTIONS FOR REVIEW

1. Describe the early settlements of Rome.
2. How did the patricians control the Roman republic?
3. Why did Marcus feel that Lucius and the other patricians had taken advantage of him?
4. What changes did Marcus and the other plebeians want to make in Roman government?
5. Why did the majority of the people lose confidence in the Roman republic?

UNDERSTANDING THE STORY

A. Write F for each statement that is a fact and O for each statement that is an opinion.

1. The Etruscans were more efficient and better rulers than the Romans.
2. Roman customs were written down in laws known as the Twelve Tables.
3. The plebeians had few rights.
4. The plebeians could have run the Roman government without the patricians.
5. Slaves were worse off than plebeians.
6. Marcus was smarter than Lucius.
7. There was no reason to have plebeian judges.
8. The plebeians wished to be able to marry into patrician families and to sit in the senate.
9. The Romans should not have destroyed Carthage.

B. The Roman republic was controlled by the upper-class patricians. Imagine that a similar situation existed in the United States. What differences would there be between our present government and one in which the average person played little part? What changes would you recommend to achieve equality?

ACTIVITIES AND INQUIRIES

1. Study the map of the expansion of Rome on page 94. Choose the term or phrase that best completes each sentence.
    a. In traveling from the city of Rome to the city of Byzantium, you would have gone (1) east (2) north (3) south.
    b. Pergamum was in (1) Asia Minor (2) Gaul (3) Numidia.
    c. An island in the Mediterranean Sea is (1) Carthage (2) Sardinia (3) Alexandria.
    d. The distance from Rome to Carthage was about (1) 300 kilometers (2) 500 kilometers (3) 1,000 kilometers.
    e. Goods shipped from Alexandria to Rome traveled to the (1) west (2) east (3) south.
2. You have read the disagreements between Lucius and Marcus. Which one had the stronger case? Why?
3. Assume that you are able to invite Lucius and Marcus to speak to your history class. What questions would you ask each of them? How might they answer your questions?
4. How do you think Marcus and Lucius would fare in a democratic society such as the United States?
5. Prepare a report on life in the Roman republic.

3. A Successful "Failure"

Julius Caesar named his 18-year-old nephew Octavian as his heir. In 43 B.C. Octavian joined with Antony and Lepidus, two of Caesar's military commanders, to rule the empire. (This three-person rule was called the *triumvirate*.) After a period, Lepidus was removed, and Octavian and Antony divided the Roman Empire between them. Antony took the eastern portion of the Roman world, while Octavian took the west.

This partnership lasted until 32 B.C., when Octavian declared war on Antony and Cleopatra, the queen of Egypt.

In 31 B.C. Octavian defeated Antony at the battle of Actium. Octavian's victory ended years of civil war. He replaced most of the members of the Roman senate with his followers from the lower and middle classes.

Octavian had promised to restore the republic. Thus, he offered to give up his dictatorial powers. The senate, however, begged him to continue as the all-powerful leader. In 27 B.C., he was given the title of *Augustus* (honored or revered one), and was also called *princeps*, or first citizen. He was the first emperor of the Roman Empire.

Augustus, the first Roman Emperor.

Augustus' decrees had the force of law. He had the legal right and power to do anything he thought was in the best interest of the empire. Augustus controlled Rome's army, its finances, and all government jobs.

Augustus was not physically strong, and constantly complained of assorted ailments. Horseback riding tired him, and he could not stand exposure to the sun. Yet his strategies defeated his enemies in battle. As emperor, he ruled fairly and efficiently for many years. Under his leadership, Rome progressed from social upheaval and economic disorder to peace and prosperity.

In our story, Augustus meets with Tiberius (the son of his second wife, Livia), a man he admires but does not love. Tiberius has just returned to Rome from a long, self-imposed exile on the island of Rhodes.

Rome   A.D. 2

"Thank you, Tiberius, for returning to Rome," said Augustus. "I haven't seen you for seven years."

"I'm glad to be back," said Tiberius. "I would have returned sooner, but I thought you never wanted to speak to me again."

"Nonsense," said the emperor. "It wasn't my idea that you leave Rome. Now, I need you. I've been ruling Rome and the empire for thirty years. I must admit that I am no longer able to do the job by myself. I'm tired and I'm sick."

"But," said Tiberius, "you must get better soon. There's so much more for you to do."

"It's no use. I've failed."

"Failed!" snorted Tiberius. "How can you say that? Think of all you have done for Rome. Before you were appointed *princeps,* Rome was a mess. Thousands of people were out of work. Many more were without enough food and decent housing. You gave them food and jobs."

"We still have unemployment."

"Not nearly as much as before," replied Tiberius. "The point is that you never stopped trying to help the needy. You went even further. You gave poor people and retired soldiers farms in the provinces."

"Rome was terribly overcrowded," replied Augustus, "but there was much unused land in our distant provinces. Anyone would have done the same."

"Not just anyone," replied Tiberius. "Your uncle, Julius Caesar, had similar ideas, but his enemies took his life. As for the others—they did nothing."

"I'll never forgive those assassins!"

"Wait—there's more. Merchants and travelers were afraid of the robbers on our roads. You provided everyone with safe travel throughout our empire by having the army wipe out the robbers. Great highways now link Rome to far-distant parts of the empire. You encouraged farmers by lending them money without charging interest. There are no restrictions on trade throughout the empire. The value of our money is stable. We have a fine postal system. Rome is a safe place, thanks to the civic guard (police)."

"You almost have me believing that I did a fairly good job," smiled Augustus.

"Look at all the new buildings and public works that have been constructed in the city—the temples, baths, theaters, public buildings, and roads. You're responsible for all of them."

"Tiberius," asked Augustus, "why do you think I asked you to return to Rome?"

"I have been waiting for you to tell me," Tiberius replied.

"I am a sick man, Tiberius. I need a successor who will be ready to take my place when I die. Therefore, I am going to adopt you as my son and heir," said Augustus.

"But why do you choose me?" asked Tiberius.

"This is something I should have done years ago. I have always admired you, though I thought you were cool and distant. You are honest, reliable, and dependable. There is no one else I can trust. You will be the emperor of Rome after I die!"

"I am surprised and honored," said Tiberius. "What shall I do first?"

"Go to Gaul and Germany and end their revolt against Rome!"

Postscript

After many battles, Tiberius defeated the Gauls and Germans. He returned to Rome in A.D. 9 and became emperor in all but name. Five years later, in the year 14, Augustus died, and Tiberius was named princeps.

With few exceptions, the next 200 years were peaceful ones. The Roman Empire was well run and its boundaries were extended in Europe, England, and the Middle East. At its height, the empire contained 70 million people of many different cultures and languages.

Some emperors, such as Augustus and Tiberius, were excellent rulers. Others, such as Nero and Caligula, were unfit for the job. Yet the empire and its people continued to enjoy a high level of prosperity.

During the reign of Augustus, events in the land of Judah—a Roman province starting in the year A.D. 6—began which would change Western society forever. Jesus and the early Christians are the subjects of our next story.

QUESTIONS FOR REVIEW

1. How did Octavian become the first Roman emperor?
2. What powers did Augustus (Octavian) gain when he became emperor?
3. Why did Augustus ask Tiberius to return to Rome?
4. How did Tiberius prove that Augustus was not a failure?
5. Why did Augustus choose Tiberius to replace him?

UNDERSTANDING THE STORY

A. Write T for each statement that is true and F for each statement that is false.

1. Octavian was not a member of the triumvirate.
2. Antony defeated Octavian at the battle of Actium.
3. Augustus had the power to do anything he thought was in the best interest of the empire.
4. Under Augustus' leadership, Rome advanced to peace and prosperity.
5. Augustus believed that he had been a success.
6. Augustus gave retired soldiers land in the provinces.

7. Augustus believed that the rebuilding of Rome was his greatest accomplishment.
8. Augustus and Tiberius were poor rulers.

B. Suppose that Augustus and Tiberius were to run for president of the United States. Which one would have made a better candidate? Why? Which one would have been a more successful president? Explain.

ACTIVITIES AND INQUIRIES

1. Prepare a report card for Augustus. Grade him in the following areas and justify each grade: (*a*) leadership (*b*) handling the Roman economy (*c*) military accomplishments (*d*) personality (*e*) new buildings for the city of Rome.
2. Prepare a report on how Augustus was able to defeat the other members of the triumvirate.
3. You are a newspaper reporter and interview Tiberius. What questions would you ask him about Augustus? What might be his answers? Now ask Tiberius how he feels about becoming the emperor of Rome.
4. Prepare an obituary (death notice) for Augustus.
5. Using the map on page 94, compare the extent and power of the Roman Empire in Europe, Africa, and Asia Minor with that of the Roman republic.

4. Meeting Terror With Love

By 60 B.C., the land of Judah (Judea to the Romans) was under Roman control. The Jewish kings and Roman governors who ruled the province were unpopular with the people. Many Jews hoped that, miraculously, a king from the House of David would descend from heaven to replace their Roman rulers. Thousands of Jews eagerly awaited the arrival of their king. They called this future king the *Messiah* (the anointed, or enthroned, one).

Jesus, a Jew, was born in the city of Nazareth in 3 B.C. He preached that people should love God and other men and women. Jesus was part of a movement within the Jewish community that preached holiness (freedom from sin). He said that people must confess their sins, and be baptized as a way to atone (seek forgiveness) for their wrongdoing. Whatever stood in the way of holiness and purity would have to be overcome.

Jesus emphasized the spirit, not the letter, of the law. He said that God cared more for people than for laws. He embraced the uneducated and the poor, and he encouraged charitable acts. Material goods were unimportant, he said, because good people would be rewarded with eternal (never-ending) life in heaven.

Since many of his followers believed that Jesus was the Messiah, he was called the Christ. (The Greek word for Messiah is *christos*.) His followers were called Christians. Many Jews denied that Jesus was the Messiah and the Son of God. The Roman rulers looked upon Jesus as a revolutionary and a threat to their government. He was executed by order of the Roman governor in A.D. 30.

In our story, Gaius, a young Roman, recalls the first time he encountered a group of Christians.

Rome A.D. 81

My friend Sulla called upon me one day and said, "Come, Gaius, let us go to the Colosseum today. I want you to see how Rome deals with its most dangerous enemies."

"Who are these enemies of Rome?" I asked.

Sulla told me that he would explain everything once we were seated inside the Colosseum. We entered the great arena, where tens of thousands of people were already gathered, and found seats.

"All right, we're here. Now, who are these enemies of Rome?" I asked once again.

"They call themselves Christians," Sulla answered.

"Go on," I said.

Late in the 1st century A.D., *the Romans sacrificed Christians to wild animals in huge public arenas.*

"The Christians teach that all men and women are brothers and sisters, and that we should strive for goodness rather than wealth and pleasure. They also believe that there is eternal life after death, and true followers of their religion go to a place called heaven when they die."

"Why then are the Christians our enemies?" I asked.

Sulla answered, "The Christians mock us. They do not accept our Roman gods, and they refuse to take part in our religious festivals. They speak out against war. The men even refuse to serve in the army. And worst of all, they are disloyal to Rome. They deny that our emperor is a god, and they refuse to worship him."

"Do they worship any gods?" I asked.

Sulla said, "They believe in just one God, whose name was Jesus. They say that he took human form during the reign of Augustus. He preached and worked miracles, such as healing the sick and providing food for the poor. The Roman leaders thought that Jesus was a troublemaker. They arrested him, put him on trial, and executed him by crucifixion."

"When did this trial happen?" I asked.

"About fifty years ago."

"Didn't his death prove to his followers that Jesus was just a human being?" I asked.

Sulla frowned. "His followers believe that he rose from the dead and went back to heaven. They say he died on the cross to atone for all the evil things that people do. They believe that his death has made it possible for all who believe in him to find eternal life in heaven after they have passed from this life."

At this moment, the mob gave a mighty roar. Men, women, and children were led into the arena. They were all dressed in the skins of wild animals. The guards left the arena, and a sudden hush descended over the crowd.

Suddenly, gates were raised and wild dogs driven mad by hunger rushed into the arena. The dogs hesitated for a moment as they spied the waiting throng of Christians. In that moment, the Christians joined hands and began to sing. The dogs now began to attack the people and tear them apart with their mighty jaws and sharp teeth.

The mob was on its feet screaming. I turned my head away from the mad spectacle before me. Even if these people were enemies of Rome, they did not deserve to die this way. I kept thinking of the courage they had shown as they faced this most horrible of deaths, and I found myself filled with admiration for them. Where did they get their courage? Did they get it by believing that the god who had died for them was a god worth dying for?

Somehow, I knew that I had not seen the last of these people called Christians.

Postscript

The Christians of Rome stubbornly continued to practice their religion. After they died, they were buried secretly in underground vaults, called catacombs. Eventually, the Christians won the admiration of a great number of Romans, many of whom decided to join their ranks. In 260 Christianity became an accepted religion in the Roman Empire. By the end of the third century, there were over 100,000 Christians in Rome. Early in the fourth century, the Emperor Constantine converted to Christianity. In 313 Constantine granted freedom of religion to all people throughout the empire. Finally, in 380 the Emperor Theodosius declared that Christianity, the once despised and persecuted religion, was to be the official religion of the Roman Empire.

QUESTIONS FOR REVIEW

1. Why did Jesus emphasize the spirit, not the letter, of the law?
2. Why did the Roman rulers consider Jesus to be a revolutionary?
3. Why did Sulla feel that the Christians were enemies of the Romans?
4. Why were the Christians exposed to the attacks of wild dogs in the Colosseum?
5. How did the Romans change their attitude toward the Christians in the third and fourth centuries?

UNDERSTANDING THE STORY

A. Write T for each statement that is true, F for each statement that is false, and N for each statement that is not mentioned in this chapter.

1. The Greek word for Messiah is *christos*.
2. The early Christians were often buried in catacombs in Rome.
3. Jesus did not believe that people should confess their sins.
4. In Jesus' time, most Romans were ready to accept Christianity.
5. Sulla said that the Christians were enemies of Rome.
6. The Christians did not accept the Roman gods.
7. Most people in the Colosseum refused to watch the wild dogs attack the Christians.

B. Suppose that most people in your community followed the moral teachings of a religious leader in their daily lives. How might their lives be changed?

ACTIVITIES AND INQUIRIES

1. Imagine that you are able to speak to the Roman emperor of the year 81. What might he tell you about Christianity?

2. Try to convince Sulla that the Christians are not a threat to the Roman government.
3. Prepare a report on the problems faced by the early Christians.
4. Assume that you are the editor of a Roman newspaper and are sympathetic to the Christians. You witness the massacre in the Colosseum. Prepare the headline and the article you would publish.
5. You are a Roman radio newscaster. Describe your meeting with a group of Christians.

5. Freedom Recalled

In the third century, the Roman Empire entered a period of grave difficulty. Less civilized ("barbarian") people such as the Goths from northern Europe were beginning to raid the empire's borders. In Rome itself, the governmental system that Augustus had established two centuries earlier was no longer secure. Rebellion followed rebellion. From the years 235 to 285, there were 19 emperors, but only two died from natural causes. The Roman army no longer fought against invaders. Instead, its leaders fought for power at home, and the soldiers stole from the peasants. Bankers stole as much as they could from the wealthy. The great Roman Empire was crumbling.

By the fourth century, the empire had become a hollow shell. Rome had been weakened by many invasions. Food was in short supply, and many people were starving. Business and trade were declining.

The free farmers who owned small plots of land were hit hard. Taxes rose higher and higher. Many of these small farmers found themselves unable to pay their debts and were forced to give up their farms. These farms were then taken over by the rich, who in turn hired the poor to work on them as tenants. At first the tenants paid the landlord with part of their crops. They also had to work a certain number of days each year for the landlord.

As the years passed, however, the tenants came under the complete control of the landlords. By the year 332, any tenant farmer who left the land could be brought back in chains. These once-free farmers had become serfs. They were part of the land. They could not be sold as individuals or as slaves. When the land was sold or changed hands, the serfs went along with the land.

In this story, we look in on two farmers who live in Carsoli, a village in central Italy located about 50 miles east of the city of Rome. The year is 350. The two farmers are surrounded by acre after acre of golden, ripening wheat. They talk of the good old days of the Roman Empire. They think back to happier times when they were young.

Ask yourself why the peasants looked to the past. How had the changes in the empire affected them?

Carsoli   350

"Why are you so angry today?" asked Horace. "It's a beautiful day. The wheat is high. We're going to have a great crop!"

"We're going to have a great crop," mocked Antonio. "Whose crop is it going to be? Not too long ago, each of us had his own land. We were citizens of Rome, and we were free! Now we're nothing but miserable tenants who can't even leave the land."

"Don't get so upset," replied Horace. "Things could be a lot worse. Our landlord isn't too bad. He protects us, and we're still working on Roman soil. Don't forget, we do get to keep part of our crops."

"Who needs the landlord?" asked Antonio angrily. "If the enemy had ever come, we could have protected ourselves. The Roman army would have rescued us from the barbarian invaders."

"There are too many barbarians around these days," replied Horace. "And you know as well as I do that we can't trust the army anymore."

"That's one point I'll agree with. We can't trust anyone," said Antonio. "In the glorious old days, things were different. Remember how powerful our armies were, and how they crushed the tribes around us? People from all over the world learned to speak Latin because it was our language!"

"Your trouble, Antonio, is that you live in the past. Times have changed. You may be right about Rome in the old days, but the world doesn't stand still. Why can't you understand that?

It's our job in life to be tenant farmers. Accept it. I don't expect you to be happy about it, but this is the way things are!"

"Maybe I do think too much about the past," said Antonio. "But what's wrong with remembering the power and wealth of our country? I'll never forget the first time my father took me to the city of Rome. There were great buildings, fountains, wide streets—all marvels of engineering. The people seemed happy. They busied themselves at their jobs. They weren't worried about barbarians."

"You mean they didn't seem worried," said Horace. "You were a child. How could you tell whether people were happy or sad, worried or carefree?"

"Child or not, I knew that Rome had great playwrights, poets, and orators who stirred the imagination of the people. I'll never forget them."

"No, don't forget any of it," said Horace, "but wasn't there another side of the coin? It wasn't all beauty and poetry and good looks. There was the cruel treatment of the Jews and Christians. And haven't you overlooked the suffering and starvation of the poor? The emperors put on big shows, but you know they weren't interested in poor people."

"You have a point there," said Antonio. "Remember when taxes got difficult, then impossible, to pay? Well, I thought of giving up the farm and moving to the city of Rome. But many people in Rome were out of jobs and begging for scraps of food. I looked at them and realized that on the farm I had always had enough to eat. I came back to my life on the land. I have suffered, but I must admit that I have never been hungry or homeless."

"Now you're starting to sound more like yourself," said Horace. "I think that you're beginning to see that we must accept our future. Our lives will be spent on the land. We'll have to work hard, but we'll live!"

"I really don't disagree with you, Horace. It was just impossible for me to accept the laws that forced us to stay on the farm even when we weren't making a living. Now this. We're tenant farmers. We're no longer free! Our lives are no longer in our hands! Is this living?"

"Calm down, please," pleaded Horace. "If some of the other farmers hear you, we may not be able to live out even this miserable existence."

"How could this happen to loyal, trusting citizens of the greatest empire in the world?" asked Antonio quietly. "Where has it all gone? Why do filthy, ragged savages roam everywhere? Where is the glory that once was Rome?"

"Try not to be so bitter," said Horace. "Perhaps some day we will be free again."

Postscript

Rome ruled the Mediterranean world for 600 years. At its peak, during the first and second centuries A.D., the empire extended from Spain to the Euphrates River and from England to Egypt. Yet by the end of the fourth century, the Roman Empire was collapsing.

The barbarian invasions and civil wars forced the emperors to spend too much money and manpower on the military. The result was a shortage of resources to provide for the everyday needs of the poor and the middle class.

At the same time that the empire was weakening at home, Roman armies were unable to subdue the invading barbarians. In 378 the Visigoths defeated a Roman army and killed the emperor. In 401 they invaded Italy. They sacked (looted and destroyed) Rome in 410, as did the Vandals in 455. Finally, in 476 Odoacer, a minor German chief, overthrew the last Roman emperor and ruled Rome until 493.

QUESTIONS FOR REVIEW

1. Why was the Roman Empire in difficulty during the third century?
2. Why were many free farmers forced to become tenant farmers?
3. Why was Antonio so angry?
4. Why did Horace feel that Antonio lived too much in the past?
5. Why did Antonio decide to stay on his farm?

UNDERSTANDING THE STORY

A. Write H for each statement that Horace made or might have made and A for each statement that Antonio made or might have made.

1. I hate my life as a tenant farmer.
2. I remember how good it was to be a free citizen of Rome.
3. The landlord protects us and lets us keep part of our crops.
4. A person should accept things as they are.
5. There were lots of things wrong with Rome.
6. Even though life can be hard for us tenant farmers, at least we don't starve.
7. How could a great empire like Rome be in such trouble?
8. Someday, we will be free again.

B. Which of the two men, Horace or Antonio, would be more comfortable living in the United States? Explain.

ACTIVITIES AND INQUIRIES

1. Go to the library and look for information on the life of women in ancient Rome. List the facts you find about Roman women. What differences do you see between the lives of women in ancient Rome and in the present-day United States? What similarities do you see?
2. Look at the map of the Roman Empire on page 94. Compare it with the map of present-day Europe on page 543. List five modern countries whose lands were once part of the Roman Empire.
3. Antonio made a difficult decision: He chose to stay on his farm. What would you have done in his place? Suppose Antonio had moved to the city of Rome. How might his life have changed?
4. Imagine yourself the emperor or empress of Rome. You see that your empire is collapsing. What steps would you take to hold the Roman Empire together? How successful do you think you might be?
5. Assume that either Horace or Antonio is your friend. What questions would you ask him? How might he answer?

6. A Time of Peace and Plenty

Shi Huang Ti (whose name means first emperor) was the first and only emperor of the Ch'in, or Qin, dynasty. This dynasty lasted only from 221 to 210 B.C. It had been preceded by many years of civil war. But the Qin period was a time of peace. The emperor was in full control of the government throughout the Chinese lands. Like the Roman emperors, Shi built a system of roads to connect the vast territories of his empire. He simplified the Chinese system of writing and set up a system of standardized weights and measures. To keep out the northern barbarian tribes, Shi extended the protective barrier known as the Great Wall, which had been started by an earlier dynasty.

After Shi died in 210 B.C., his empire held out for a short time but was finally overthrown. Liu Pang founded the Han dynasty in 202. Unlike the short-lived Ch'in, the Han held power for over four centuries, until A.D. 220. The Han had such an important and long-lasting effect on Chinese society that many Chinese to this day refer to themselves as "people of Han."

The civil service system was developed during the Han era. Candidates for jobs in the Han government were required to pass an examination showing their knowledge of the classics of literature, laws, and the writings of Confucius. All of the jobholders were men. Women did not hold government office in Chinese society.

The Chinese made important scientific discoveries in this period. Astronomers recorded sunspots in 29 B.C. and noted the orbits (paths) of the moon and the planets. The Chinese also developed an instrument to record earthquakes. They developed a waterwheel to drive water uphill and irrigate their lands.

The Chinese understood that disasters such as earthquakes and floods were the result of natural causes and were not caused by the gods. Scientists discovered that lunar and solar eclipses took place because the moon, earth, and planets were in motion, not as a result of a person's actions.

An extremely important Chinese achievement was the invention of paper. Previously, people had used writing surfaces derived from such materials as clay tablets (the Mesopotamians), reeds (the Egyptians), animal skins, and silk (the Chinese). These were usually bulky, expensive, limited in quantity, or difficult to acquire. But the availability of paper meant that

111

QIN AND HAN CHINA

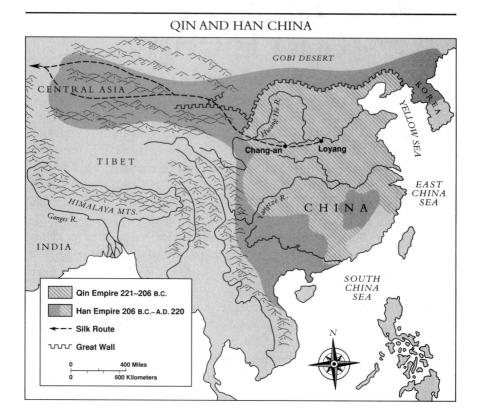

the written language could be recorded easily and transported quickly from one place to another. The written language thus became accessible to all people.

At its peak, the Han Empire rivaled Rome in the age of Augustus in its wealth and accomplishment. Caravans from China carried spices and silk across western Asia to the Middle East along the Silk Route. The goods eventually arrived at Antioch in Syria and were sold to buyers in the Roman world. In China, as in Rome, great writers and artists were at work recording and celebrating their civilization's philosophy, beliefs, and achievements.

Chinese civilization also had great influence on the cultures of Korea and Japan. China's religion, government, and written language were passed along, and they were transformed by the people who received them.

Wu Ti (140–87 B.C.) was the greatest of the Han emperors. In our story, he discusses some of his achievements with his prime minister.

Chang-an   100 B.C.

"Your Highness, I would like to ask a question," said the prime minister, "but I do not wish to anger you."

"You have served me for many years. You may ask your question," replied Wu Ti.

"These are quiet times, years of peace," said the prime minister. "Do you ever wish that once more your armies were fighting the barbarians?"

"Indeed, I sometimes do," replied the emperor. "But these days there are few places left to conquer. My armies have pushed back China's boundaries. Now, we rule Korea and lands to the south and west. It wasn't easy. But I loved the excitement of planning a battle and fighting the enemy. I remember the thrill of victory."

"I missed those days of conquest," said the prime minister. "I stayed here in Chang-an where I watched over the daily business of our government."

This cavalry figure shows the might and power of China's Han Empire.

"Thanks to you, prime minister, our government survived. But when I returned, I found that the rich were growing richer, and the poor were much worse off. I agreed with you that we could not permit the owners of the iron mines to keep their huge profits for themselves. So I ordered our government to take over these natural resources."

"Your Majesty also made the production and sale of salt and beer government monopolies. You could not allow a few persons to make such huge profits!"

"You are right!" Wu Ti exclaimed. "I couldn't tolerate the rich merchants and shopkeepers who bought and hoarded products. They refused to sell their wheat, barley, and rice until prices went sky-high—and so did their profits."

"Now, the government stores the surplus goods," said the prime minister. "We sell when prices are rising, and we buy when prices are falling. Government workers collect, ship, and deliver everything the people need throughout the empire."

"Don't overlook our income tax," Wu Ti added. "Everyone has to pay a tax of five percent. Our treasury is full."

"You never forgot the poor," said the prime minister. "Millions were unemployed, so you organized great building projects. The workers built bridges across rivers and dug canals to connect the rivers and provide water for the peasants' fields."

"I want China to be the greatest nation in the world," said the emperor.

"The people will forever be grateful for what you have done for them."

Postscript

Wu Ti's system worked for some time. Trade with foreign nations increased. Chang-an grew in population and wealth, and many people prospered. But floods and droughts raised the prices of food and clothing beyond what poor people could afford to pay. At the same time, business people objected to high taxes. Many begged for a return to the days of private business and profit. This was done, and the reforms of Wu Ti were forgotten.

In A.D. 9 another reformer, Wang Mang, went even further than Wu Ti. The lands of rich nobles were taken over by the government and distributed in equal parcels to the peasants. These lands could not be bought or sold. State control of iron and salt production and distribution was continued. Prices were set by the state, which also loaned money at low interest rates to businesspeople who needed help.

In the long run, however, Wang Mang's reforms met the same fate as those of Wu Ti. Wang Mang was assassinated, and the Han returned to power in A.D. 25. The last Han emperors were weak. After 220, the empire split into three kingdoms. Later in the third century, barbarian tribes broke through the Great Wall and conquered large areas of northern China.

QUESTIONS FOR REVIEW

1. What were the accomplishments of the Emperor Shi Huang Ti?
2. What important scientific discoveries were made during the period of the Han dynasty?
3. Why was it said that the Han Empire rivaled Rome at the time of Augustus?
4. How did Wu Ti feel about no longer leading his army against the barbarians?
5. How did Wu Ti limit the profits of the rich and help the poor?

UNDERSTANDING THE STORY

A. Write F for each statement that is a fact and O for each statement that is an opinion.

1. The Han dynasty lasted for over four centuries.
2. Many Chinese today refer to themselves as "people of Han."
3. Wu Ti was a greater ruler than any of the Roman emperors.
4. The Ch'in Empire would have survived if it had had a civil service system.
5. The Chinese knew that earthquakes were the result of natural causes.
6. The invention of paper helps to explain why the Han dynasty lasted for four centuries.
7. Chinese armies conquered Korea.
8. Wu Ti made the production of salt a government monopoly.

B. Assume that Wu Ti is a candidate for president of the United States. Do you think he would be successful? Why or why not? Write a speech that he would deliver during his campaign for office.

ACTIVITIES AND INQUIRIES

1. You visit the court of the Emperor Wu Ti. Describe what you would expect to see. What sights surprise you?
2. You speak to Wu Ti's prime minister. What do you think he will tell you about Wu Ti? What questions might he ask you?
3. The Han period was a time of great scientific discoveries in China. Prepare a chart listing these discoveries. Alongside each discovery, indicate why you think it was important for China at that time and why it remains important today.
4. Prepare a report card for Wu Ti. Grade him in the following areas and justify each grade: (*a*) personality (*b*) leadership (*c*) military ability (*d*) economic policies.
5. In a report, compare life in Han China with life in China today.

7. Beauty Is Everywhere

Japan is an island nation off the coast of the Asian mainland. There are four major Japanese islands, whose total land area is slightly less than that of the state of California. Because much of the land is mountainous, only about one sixth is suitable for farming. The islands also have limited amounts of natural resources such as coal, iron, and petroleum. The surrounding seas are a great natural resource, however.

The Japanese islands were settled thousands of years ago by people who migrated from the Asian mainland. In northern Japan live people called the Ainu, who are, descended from northern Asian people. Little is known about these first settlers, except that they were hunter-gatherers. Farming came later. Scientists have found artifacts such as tools that date as far back as 6,500 years (to about 4500 B.C.).

JAPAN IN THE SIXTH CENTURY

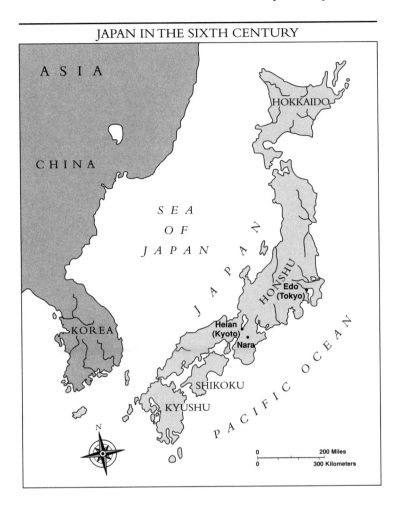

Around the year 108 B.C., the Chinese Han Empire under Wu Ti (see page 105) set up four colonies in Korea. From there, many elements of Chinese culture were transmitted to Japan. At the time, Japan was divided into more than 100 separate states, each controlled by a clan, which warred on its neighbors. The Japanese imported iron and bronze axes, knives, spears, swords, arrowheads, and mirrors. A knowledge of textile weaving was passed to the Japanese from China. Late in the first century B.C., Japan experienced a civil war, which was settled by the efforts of a priestess named Himiko, who, it is believed, ruled one of the warring states. Himiko is credited with building the Shinto shrine of Ise. Thirty separate states were created after the war. By the middle of the third century (A.D. 250), Japan had social classes, taxes, and provincial fairs where goods were *bartered* (exchanged). A few people in the upper classes were able to read and write. The Chinese ideographic system was borrowed in the mid-300s. The works of Confucius were translated into Japanese at this time.

Japan was unified sometime between the years 250 and 350. In the Yamato period (250–700), Japan had a hereditary emperor with a regal court.

Shinto, one of the two major religions in Japan, is an ancient one. Its roots are in the prehistoric period of Japan. Shinto emphasizes an appreciation for the beauties of nature. The earth, sky, sea, sun, moon, and stars are worshiped as gods (*kami*). Nature may also have superhuman qualities. The sun is worshiped as the goddess Amaterasu, ancestress of the Japanese emperors. The moon is a male god, while Mount Fuji is the mountain goddess.

Shinto festivals are held throughout the year, especially at the change of seasons in spring and fall. Ceremonies are an important part of Shinto. Shinto shrines are found all over Japan; many are in peaceful rural areas.

In the sixth century, Buddhism was introduced to Japan. Buddhism and Shinto are quite different, as you will learn. In the following story, a Shinto priest and a Buddhist monk meet and discuss their beliefs.

Kyoto   550

"Hello and welcome, stranger. What brings you to our monastery garden?" asked the Buddhist monk of the Shinto priest.

"I have come here hoping to learn about and understand your Buddhist beliefs," replied the priest.

"That may be very difficult. Our Buddhist religious beliefs are vastly different from those of you Shintoists."

"Of course they're different," answered the Shintoist. "But that doesn't mean that we can't exchange ideas and learn from each other."

"Very well," said the monk. "Guatama, the Buddha, founded our religion in India many centuries ago. He taught us how to behave properly and how to live our lives. Who started Shinto? What great man or woman do you look up to?"

The priest replied, "No one person organized Shinto. Many people who lived a long time ago were responsible for our beliefs."

At the calm seaside, a Shinto temple gate quietly beckons to worshipers.

"Perhaps you Shintoists can get along without a great founder. But who are your gods? What do you believe in? What is your code of conduct? What do you want in this life—and in the afterlife?"

"Our gods are in the objects we worship: the sun, the moon, the stars. We love them, we fear them, and we pray to them."

The Buddhist protested, "I don't understand you or your gods. How can you worship a stone, a bird, or a thunderbolt?"

The Shintoist smiled. "We worship an object in nature because a sacred spirit lives within it. This spirit is called the *kami*. It does not matter whether the thing is an animal, a tree, or a mountain. We admire and respect it because it is large, or mysterious, or strange. And, best of all, we treat the moon, or the mountain, or the stream as a living person."

"I am trying to understand," replied the Buddhist. "But we deny that anything mystical or supernatural exists. We don't worship a great many gods, as do the Hindu people. And, as for the natural world, to us trees and hills are simply trees and hills. They do not contain spirits. And surely they are not gods!"

The Shintoist asked, "Can't you see that we are standing in a beautiful garden? Can't you look at a leaf or a flower and see that it is a thing to be admired, respected, and even loved? We think that everything in nature has beauty and deserves to be worshiped!"

"I think that I am beginning to understand what you are telling me," said the monk. "You Shintoists will help us understand and admire the world around us."

"Yes, and you Buddhists will help us separate right from wrong, and show us how to become better persons in our daily lives," said the priest.

The monk said, "The world is a large place. Perhaps there is enough room in it for both Buddhism and Shinto."

Postscript

Buddhism was gradually accepted in Japan, but it never replaced Shinto. In fact, many Japanese people today are both Shintoists and Buddhists; they follow the principles of both religions. Many Buddhist temples provided space for a Shinto shrine, since it was believed that the kami were protectors of Buddhism. Later Buddhists believed that the Shinto gods were really Buddhas who had achieved enlightenment. Buddhist statues sometimes were placed in Shinto shrines, and the Buddhist priests cared for them.

Late in the Yamato period, Japan was ruled by Prince Shotoku (593–621). This enlightened ruler was a Buddhist who brought the principles of peace and salvation from Buddhism to his rule. The prince reformed the Japanese government and sent young people to study in China.

QUESTIONS FOR REVIEW

1. Describe Japan's natural resources.
2. What is the main emphasis of the Shinto religion?
3. Why do Shintoists worship objects in nature?

4. How does Buddhism differ from Shintoism?
5. What have you learned about the relationship of Buddhism and Shintoism in Japan?

UNDERSTANDING THE STORY

A. Write S for each statement that the Shintoist made or might have made. Write B for each statement the Buddhist made or might have made.

1. I have come to learn about your Buddhist beliefs.
2. Guatama founded our religion many centuries ago.
3. What is your code of conduct?
4. No one person organized Shinto.
5. We worship the sun, the moon, and the stars.
6. How can you worship a stone or a bird?
7. We worship an object in nature because a sacred spirit lives within it.
8. We do not worship many gods.
9. Can't you see that we are standing in a beautiful garden?

B. Many Japanese people practice both Buddhism and Shinto. How is it possible to be both a Buddhist and a Shintoist? What does this tell you about Japanese thinking?

ACTIVITIES AND INQUIRIES

1. Study the map of Japan on page 117. Choose the term or phrase that best completes each sentence.
    a. The northernmost island of Japan is (1) Kyushu (2) Hokkaido (3) Honshu.
    b. A country to the west of Japan is (1) China (2) the United States (3) Russia.
    c. Tokyo (Edo) is on the island of (1) Honshu (2) Shikoku (3) Hokkaido.
    d. The distance from Kyoto to Tokyo is about (1) 225 kilometers (2) 300 kilometers (3) 150 kilometers.
    e. The body of water to the west of Japan is the (1) Atlantic Ocean (2) Pacific Ocean (3) Sea of Japan.

2. Assume that you have been invited into the monastery garden and are permitted to listen to the conversation of the Buddhist and the Shintoist. Which of their ideas impresses you most? Which do you like least? Explain.

3. You speak to a Shintoist. What questions would you ask him or her? How might the Shintoist answer your questions?
4. Imagine that you are visiting Japan. What differences do you see between a Shinto shrine and a Buddhist temple? Explain.
5. How does Hinduism differ from Buddhism and Shintoism? Do you see any similarities? Mention them.

8. The Prophet Teaches His People

The Arabian peninsula is situated between the fertile areas of the Mediterranean coast and Mesopotamia. Much of the Arabian land is mountainous or barren desert. For thousands of years, Arabia has been the home of many different groups of people. Nomadic groups kept flocks of animals. Farmers lived in the fertile southern region at the mouth of the Red Sea, closest to Africa. Traders and merchants grew rich because of Arabia's strategic location between the civilizations of Africa, Asia, and Europe.

Muhammad, the founder of the religion called Islam, was born in the prosperous Arabian city of Mecca around the year 571. At the time, the Arabian people worshiped many gods. Mecca contained the religious shrine known as the Kaaba, which was dedicated to the many gods of the desert people. Many of the Arabian people traveled vast distances to worship at the Kaaba.

Muhammad studied the Biblical writings of the Jewish prophets and the books of the Christian apostles. Like the Jews and Christians, Muhammad believed in one all-powerful god. Muhammad called his god Allah. He favored strict codes of diet, cleanliness, and worship. He preached the coming of judgment day, when the world would end. All the members of humankind who had ever lived would either be rewarded for their right actions or punished for their bad deeds.

Muhammad believed that Allah had chosen him as his prophet to teach these truths to all the people. Muhammad believed that Allah was the same as the God of the Jews and Christians, and that Moses and Jesus were early prophets of Allah. Muhammad at first thought that the Jews and Christians would accept Islam. But this was not to be. Opposition from other Arabs forced Muhammad and his followers to flee Mecca in 622. This journey is called the *hegira* in Islamic history. For some years, Muhammad and his followers lived in exile in the city of Medina, where the people accepted his teachings. There, he declared that he was the representative, or messenger, of the true religion, which he called Islam. In 630 Muhammad assembled a strong army of believers and returned to Mecca in triumph.

Muhammad's teachings and Islamic law are recorded in a book known as the Qur'an, or Koran, which was compiled about 20 years after his death. To this day, it remains the prime source of Islamic faith and religious practice.

Muhammad is not regarded as a god by the followers of Islam. Rather, he is respected and honored as the messenger who brought the truth to the people. In our story, Muhammad and his wife, Aishah, discuss the history and the future of Islam.

Mecca   630

"Congratulations, Muhammad! Your armies have conquered Mecca for Islam," said his wife, Aishah. "Now you can rest."

"Thank you," said Muhammad, "but I cannot rest. There is so much more to be done. We must bring the message of Islam to all the Arabian people, not just those in the cities. Everyone must be taught that there is no god but Allah, and that I, Muhammad, am his prophet."

"Many have believed in you and Islam from the moment they met you and heard you speak, Muhammad. But can you be sure that all others will join you?"

"I can only try to convince them that our faith is the true one," said Muhammad. "If they believe in a god, I will teach them that Allah is the same as the god they worship. If they have holy books, I will accept them as divinely inspired. If they have their own wise men and women, I will accept them as people who have been touched by the divine hand of Allah."

Aishah said, "I shudder when I remember how the merchants of Mecca treated you! You preached that the angel Gabriel

Muhammad, on horseback, during the hegira from Mecca to Medina.

had ordered you to bring the word of God to the people of Arabia."

Muhammad replied, "At a time when our people believed in many gods, I taught them that there was but one. People came to Mecca from everywhere to worship the pagan gods. The merchants of the city feared for their profits if pilgrims stopped coming to worship at the Kaaba."

Aishah continued, "And so they threatened you and your followers until you were forced to flee for your lives."

"Allah watched over our *hegira* (journey) and brought me many more followers. This year, with a mighty army, we returned to Mecca in triumph. Those people who had mocked me and my beliefs have seen the wonders of Allah. Now they believe in him!

"But soon, we will go beyond the borders of Arabia. We will teach the truths of our religion to the infidel (unbeliever). Our one god, Allah, and our right way of living can do so much more for them than their pagan gods."

Aishah added, "We must tell the women of the wonderful life that awaits them under Islam. They will be able to own and inherit property. A husband may still divorce his wife, but if he does, he must return the possessions she brought into the marriage."

"True, Aishah, but we will also instruct the pagans that a wife's duties have not changed. She is still bound to obey her husband, care for their children, and manage the home."

"The pagans may like the things you tell them, but I wonder how they will react when you tell them of their obligations if they accept the new faith," said Aishah.

Muhammad answered, "Whatever their reaction, I must tell them that Muslims must purify both their spirits and their bodies so that they can prepare to stand before almighty Allah on judgment day. Thus, they are required to pray five times a day. They must be honest in business. They are forbidden to gamble. They must look upon all Muslims as their brothers and sisters. During the holy month of Ramadan, no one may eat or drink from sunrise to sunset. All must refrain from drinking wine, which will take their thoughts away from Allah, and from eating unclean foods, which will contaminate their bodies."

"Suppose that, after hearing about the requirements, the pagans decide not to accept Allah?"

"Then," Muhammad said, "I will speak of that which frightens all people: death. I will tell them that for everyone there will come a day of judgment. On that day, the dead will rise and stand before Allah to be judged. Those who believe in him and have obeyed his teachings shall find peace and happiness in a heaven beyond anyone's imagination."

"And what will you tell them about those who have led wicked lives and have denied Allah?" asked Aishah.

"I will tell them the truth. Those who deny almighty Allah will be chained and dragged into hell where they will suffer through eternity."

"And if they still refuse to listen?"

Muhammad thought for a moment. "I must do all in my power to work the will of Allah. If necessary, I will declare a holy war—a *jihad*—in order to help the infidels find the truth and save their souls. One way or another, I will teach them that there is no god but Allah, and that I, Muhammad, am his prophet."

Postscript

Muhammad died in 632. His father-in-law, Abu Bakr, was chosen as *caliph* (successor to the prophet). In less than a decade, Muhammad's followers had spread his teachings to the pagan people of Arabia and converted most of them to Islam.

Over the next century, Islamic armies conquered and converted the peoples of Palestine, Syria, Mesopotamia, Persia, Egypt, most of North Africa, and part of India. In the Mediterranean, they took over many of the islands, and the Moors (North African Muslims) became the rulers of Spain. Moorish civilization was the most advanced in Europe for many centuries. In the year 714, European armies defeated a Muslim army at Tours, in France. Muslim armies never again entered northern Europe, but for many centuries to follow they fought and sometimes conquered the lands of eastern Europe.

THE EXPANSION OF ISLAM 634–750

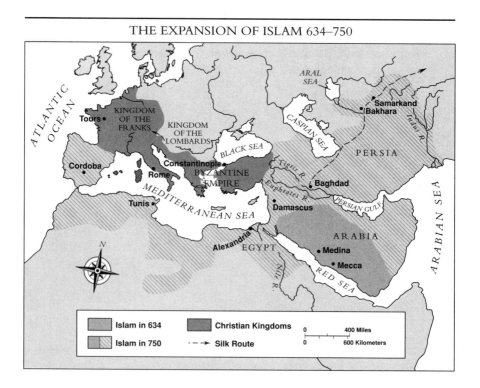

In the units that follow, we shall discuss the achievements of later Muslim societies in the Middle East and India.

QUESTIONS FOR REVIEW

1. How were Muhammad's beliefs similar to those of the Jews and Christians?
2. Why did Muhammad live in exile in Medina?
3. Why did Muhammad tell his wife that he could not rest?
4. What were women's privileges and duties under Islam?
5. How did Muhammad propose to teach the infidels (unbelievers) that there was no god but Allah?

UNDERSTANDING THE STORY

A. Write T for each statement that is true and F for each statement that is false.

1. For thousands of years, the Arabian peninsula has been the home of many groups of people.
2. Before Muhammad's time, the Arabian people worshiped only one god.
3. Muhammad studied the writings of the Hebrew prophets and the Christian apostles.
4. Muhammad believed that Allah had chosen him as his prophet.
5. For some years, Muhammad lived in exile in the city of Mecca.
6. People from all over Arabia went to Mecca to worship the pagan gods.
7. Under Islam, a husband is not permitted to divorce his wife.
8. Muslims are required to pray five times a day.
9. Muhammad did not believe that a judgment day would ever come.

B. Assume that Muhammad is living today. How might he react to the growth and development of Islam? What suggestions might he offer to Islamic leaders?

ACTIVITIES AND INQUIRIES

1. Study the map of the expansion of Islam on page 126. Choose the term or phrase that best completes each statement.

   a. In traveling from Mecca to Medina, you would be going (1) north
      (2) south (3) west.
   b. The distance from Mecca to Medina is about (1) 200 kilometers
      (2) 400 kilometers (3) 800 kilometers.
   c. The Byzantine Empire was (1) on the Atlantic Ocean (2) on the
      Red Sea (3) between the Black Sea and the Mediterranean.
   d. In traveling from Damascus to Baghdad, you would be going
      (1) west (2) north (3) east.
   e. The distance from Cordoba to Tours is about (1) 400 kilometers
      (2) 800 kilometers (3) 1,200 kilometers.

2. Outline the similarities and differences among Islam, Judaism, and
   Christianity.
3. Using the map on page 126, and other sources, prepare a report on
   the extent of Islam's expansion from the years 634 to 750.
4. Muhammad assumed that the Jews and Christians would accept his
   teachings. Why did he believe this? Why do you think they rejected
   Islam?
5. Imagine that you are preparing to write a book about the life of
   Muhammad. Prepare the table of contents. Which part of his life
   interests you most? Why?

9. A Land of Gold

Ghana, the earliest of the great West African trading empires, controlled
large areas around the Senegal and Niger rivers. From the eighth to the
eleventh centuries, Ghana's location, at the southwestern end of the caravan routes that crossed the Sahara Desert, helped make its merchants and
kings very rich. The Ghanaians exchanged gold, ivory, and slaves for
Saharan salt, Arabian horses, Egyptian cloth, and North African and
European swords.

   Salt was actually worth its weight in gold because it was not found in
central Africa. Salt was needed to preserve food. Salt merchants traveled
across the desert for many months until they reached Ghana. There, they
traded the salt for gold.

   At its height, Ghana controlled most of the sources of African gold,
and its king was believed to be the richest person in the world. This was

THE EMPIRE OF GHANA IN THE 11TH CENTURY

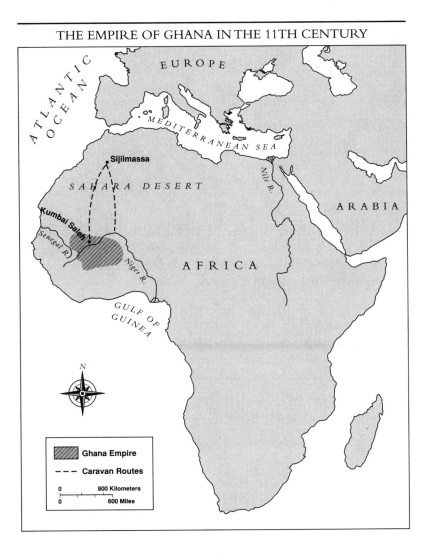

understandable, since the king levied (collected) a tax on all the gold shipped out of the country. In addition, he kept *all* the gold nuggets for himself. Only the gold dust was traded.

Kumbai Saleh 1020

King Kanissa'ai sat on the gold balcony of his pavilion (a large, tentlike building). Around the pavilion stood the king's guard of mounted horsemen. The men wore golden armor, and the horses had gold-embroidered trappings. Standing behind the king were ten pages (young people) carrying shields and gold-covered swords. Many Ghanaians had assembled to listen to the king and partake of the ample meal he had provided. It was evening. A huge fire had been built for light and warmth.

"Your Highness," whispered the prime minister, "you have many decisions to make today."

"Today is no different from any other day," said the king. "What is the most important decision I have to make today?"

"The treasurer will explain."

The royal treasurer bowed and spoke to the king. "Your Majesty, your storehouse is completely full of gold nuggets. And more are arriving every day. We have no more space to store them. What shall we do?"

The king shook his head and replied, "Treasurer, how many times have I told you to plan ahead? Build another storehouse and dig a deep vault underneath. Place the gold in the vault and guard it well. In the meantime, give one small nugget to each poor person in this audience."

"Yes, your Majesty," said the treasurer. "I will have a new storehouse built immediately."

"Fine. Prime Minister, I am ready for the next problem," said the king.

"There are several merchants here from the distant desert town of Sijilmassa," said the minister. "They are eager to speak with you."

"Gentlemen, welcome to my capital of Kumbai Saleh. How can I help you?"

A spokesperson for the group stepped forward. "Thank you, Your Highness. We have traded our salt for your gold for many years. Never have we bargained or quarreled with your traders. We have accepted whatever gold they offered. But now, we have a small request." The man hesitated.

The king gave him permission to go on.

The man seemed uncomfortable. Finally, he said, "Your Highness, not everyone in the north is happy with the gold dust your traders exchange for our salt. My people have asked us to bring home some gold nuggets."

"Absolutely not!" replied the king angrily. "Our agreement is to exchange gold for salt. There is no mention of the shape or weight. You will accept the gold dust or nothing!"

The man was about to say something, but the look on the king's face warned him to remain silent. Kanissa'ai was a great and powerful king who allowed no one to challenge his authority.

The king announced, "This discussion is closed."

The salt merchants meekly withdrew from the king's presence, bowing as they left.

Postscript

At its height, Ghana included large parts of modern-day Mali, Mauritania, and Senegal. But in 1076, Muslim people from North Africa invaded Ghana and overpowered Kumbai Saleh, and the political decline of Ghana began. The economy of Ghana was damaged by the shifting of the Saharan trade routes to the east, and agriculture suffered as water supplies failed.

In the thirteenth century, the empire of Mali emerged as Ghana's successor. We shall learn more about Mali in the following unit.

QUESTIONS FOR REVIEW

1. How did Ghana's location help make its merchants rich?
2. How did King Kanissa'ai of Ghana become very rich?
3. What did the king order when he was told the treasurer's problem?
4. Why were the salt merchants from Sijilmassa unhappy?
5. How do you explain the decline of Ghana?

UNDERSTANDING THE STORY

A. Write T for each statement that is true, F for each statement that is false, and O for each statement that is an opinion.

1. Ghana's location made trade unprofitable.
2. Salt was worth its weight in gold.
3. The king of Ghana was believed to be the richest person in the world.

4. King Kanissa'ai could have conquered Europe.
5. The king's storehouse was full of gold nuggets.
6. The king ordered that each poor person was to receive a small gold nugget.
7. The king refused to trade gold nuggets for salt.
8. The salt merchants were afraid of angering the king of Ghana.

B. If King Kanissa'ai were ruling a modern nation in West Africa today, how successful would he be? Explain.

ACTIVITIES AND INQUIRIES

1. Study the map of Ghana on page 129. Choose the term or phrase that best completes each statement.
    a. In traveling from the Senegal River to the Niger River, you would be going (1) east (2) north (3) west.
    b. In traveling north from Kumbai Saleh, you would reach (1) Arabia (2) the Gulf of Guinea (3) the Sahara Desert.
    c. Kumbai Saleh was near the river (1) Niger (2) Senegal (3) Nile.
    d. The distance from Kumbai Saleh to Sijilmassa was about (1) 80 kilometers (2) 800 kilometers (3) 1600 kilometers.
    e. The empire of Ghana was in (1) north Africa (2) west Africa (3) east Africa.
2. Imagine that you could interview the Ghanaian prime minister in the story. What questions would you ask him about the king and life in Ghana in the eleventh century? How might he answer your questions?
3. Compare the way goods were traded in Ghana with the way they are bought and sold in the United States today.
4. Prepare a report on life in eleventh-century Ghana. Cover the following areas: (a) commerce and industry (b) government (c) education (d) the role of women.
5. Suppose that you are a merchant from Sijilmassa. Describe the journey from your home to Kumbai Saleh. Explain how you expect to profit from your exchange of goods.

10. Superiority or Arrogance?

At the beginning of the thirteenth century, several Native American groups entered central Mexico from the north. In the wars that followed, the people known as the Aztec were the victors. In three centuries, they went on to conquer a large area of Mesoamerica that is present-day Mexico. In 1325 they founded their capital city of Tenochtitlán (present-day Mexico City), which at its height had a population of some 400,000 people. From the 1400s to 1521, the Aztec Empire controlled much of south-central and southern Mexico.

Military leaders were the decision-makers of Aztec society. Priests also played an important role. The Aztec worshiped many gods. They built great pyramids and temples in Tenochtitlán and other cities. Their artists created massive stone sculptures to decorate the temples. The Aztec also

THE AZTEC EMPIRE IN THE EARLY 16TH CENTURY

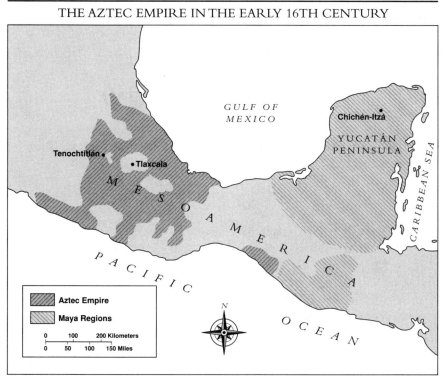

excelled in working with metals, as well as in weaving and pottery-making. They had a 365-day solar calendar. They had no written language as we know it but used a complex system of ideograms and pictograms. A few of their books remain, but they are difficult to interpret.

The sons of wealthy Aztec families went to school to become warriors or priests. Less well-to-do boys studied to become government workers, landowners, or soldiers. A small number of girls were also trained to become priests. Most women cared for homes and children. The majority of the Aztec people worked as farmers. They had a complex agricultural system based on artificial farmland islands created in Lake Texcoco.

The Aztec also extracted tribute (payment) from the people they conquered. This tribute was in the form of foods, pottery, metals, and textiles.

The Aztec, like the Maya, had complex religious beliefs and rituals. The Aztec believed that the world had been created and destroyed four times. In the final creation, the Aztec sun god Quetzalcoatl had sacrificed his blood in order to get the universe started. However, human blood was necessary to keep the universe in operation. Without it, the world would come to an end. The blood came from sacrificial victims who were the Aztec prisoners of war. Each year, the Aztec sacrificed thousands of human captives.

In our story, an Aztec soldier tells a captive about the glories of Aztec civilization and urges him to become part of it.

Tenochtitlán   1410

The scene is a long, low building used by the Aztec as a prison for captured warriors from the Tlaxcala nation. The prisoners are being pushed roughly into small holding cells. An Aztec soldier and a prisoner are overheard.

"Stop pushing!" cried the captive.

"I'll push you as much as I like," replied the Aztec soldier. "You're a captive, a slave, a person with no rights."

"You have already defeated me and humiliated me. Why do you have to be so rough with me now?"

"What difference does it make? You're going to die anyway," said the Aztec.

The captive said, "Good. I would rather die than live as an Aztec slave."

"You are a fool. Being an Aztec slave is the next best thing to being an Aztec. It's a great honor."

"I prefer to die."

"A slave's life isn't all that bad. You could live as an Aztec. You could even be *my* slave."

"Never!" shouted the captive. "You must kill me. Then, I can go to my people's heaven. I don't want to live the life of an Aztec. Being a Tlaxcalan is good enough for me."

"You don't understand what it's like to be an Aztec. We're the best! We have built huge pyramids reaching into the sky. The nobles live in great houses with many rooms. No people eat as well as we do. We always have beans and meat and tortillas."

The captive seemed uninterested.

"We Aztec protect our slaves. A person who attacks a slave is executed. Our laws are harsh but fair. Captured highway

Spanish conquistadors (left, on horseback), aided by Tlaxcalans (right), battle Aztec warriors (center). How did small numbers of Spanish soldiers defeat large Aztec armies?

robbers are executed. A thief who takes personal property must return twice the amount that he stole. If he doesn't, he becomes a slave."

"Tell me no more," grunted the captive.

The Aztec ignored him. "Look at our training and weapons. At the age of fifteen, I was taught to shoot a bow and arrow and toss a heavy javelin. My wooden club has a sharp edge of volcanic glass. Look at our hide-covered wicker shields and our body armor. We have better weapons and better protection than your people."

The captive seemed unimpressed.

"We are always prepared to fight," continued the Aztec. "Every town has its arsenal (military fort). When one of our commanders gets the order to prepare for battle, his soldiers gather in the arsenal. Before you can say 'Tlaxcala,' we are armed."

"I will admit one thing about you Aztec. You talk faster and louder than any people I've ever met," said the captive.

"I've failed to persuade you," sighed the Aztec. "The sun will rise in a few minutes. You must prepare to die!" He pushed the captive out of his cell and into the crowded courtyard. A hundred captives were waiting to be sacrificed to the sun god.

A priest cried out, "Let your heart and burning body give life to the sun god!"

The captive walked willingly to his death.

Postscript

In 1478 some 20,000 Aztec captives were executed for the benefit of the sun god. Members of tribes that did not pay tribute could be enslaved or sacrificed. Tribes sometimes rebelled when the Aztec insisted that they send more tribute and more people to sacrifice.

The Aztec were constantly at war with their neighbors. Thus, when the Spaniards under Hernando Cortés invaded in 1519, many tribes—among them the Tlaxcala—joined the Spaniards against the Aztec (see illustration, page 135). The superior Spanish weapons, combined with the assistance of the Aztec's enemies, led in just a few years to the overthrow of the Aztec Empire.

QUESTIONS FOR REVIEW

1. What were the accomplishments of the Aztec?
2. What were the differences in the education and duties of the wealthy, the less well-to-do, and women in Aztec society?
3. Describe the religious beliefs of the Aztec.
4. How did the Aztec in the story try to convince the captive that he should become an Aztec slave?
5. Why did the captive prefer to die rather than live as an Aztec slave?

UNDERSTANDING THE STORY

A. Write A for each statement that the Aztec made or might have made, and C for each statement that the captive made or might have made.

1. I'll push you as much as I like.
2. You're going to die anyway.
3. You have defeated and humiliated me.
4. A slave's life isn't all that bad.
5. I can go to my people's heaven.
6. Being a Tlaxcalan is good enough for me.
7. We have built huge pyramids reaching to the sky.
8. A thief must return twice the amount that he stole.
9. You talk faster than any people I've ever met.

B. Compare the treatment of prisoners of war by the Aztec with that of the United States.

ACTIVITIES AND INQUIRIES

1. Study the map of the Aztec Empire on page 133. Choose the term or phrase that best completes each statement.
    a. Tenochtitlán was situated (1) on the Gulf of Mexico (2) on the Pacific Ocean (3) inland.
    b. Tenochtitlán was in the (1) Maya region (2) Aztec Empire (3) Tlaxcala region.
    c. In traveling from Tlaxcala to Tenochtitilán, you would have gone (1) north (2) west (3) east.
    d. In traveling from Tenochtitlán to Chichén-Itzá, you would have traveled (1) east (2) south (3) north.

2. Compare the Aztec religion with Christianity, Judaism, and Islam.

3. Imagine that you are visiting the ruins of an Aztec city. Describe what you see. What might you learn about the Aztec from such a visit?

4. The captive in the story was offered his life if he would agree to a life of slavery. Should he have accepted? Why or why not? What would you have done if you had been the captive?

5. The Aztec warrior took great pride in his military training. Using your school or local library, compare Aztec military training, weapons, and strategy with those of a North American people before European settlement. Was the Aztec warrior's pride justified? Explain.

UNIT IV

Meetings of Cultures

This unit spans seven and a half centuries, from 690 to 1450. We move through Asia, Europe, Africa, and South America, from the Tang Empire in China to the Inca Empire in South America. We see how people of different cultures and in different eras learned from one another and often changed their views of themselves and the world as a result.

Asia. In our opening story, we learn of the achievements of China after the Han era. China's first woman ruler, Wu Chao, showed skill in running the country and keeping the people happy. During her reign, China also extended its domination to Korea.

Europe and the Middle East. In Europe, most people were kept in place

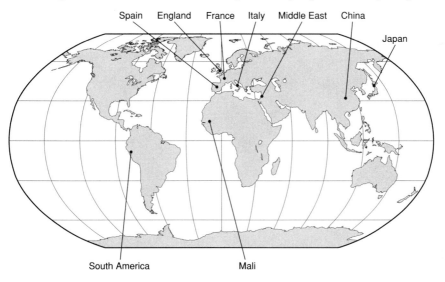

139

by a system known as feudalism, which benefited only a few. But a series of wars against a religious enemy brought Europeans into contact with a more advanced civilization, from which they learned a great deal.

Asia. Warfare was a way of life for the samurai of Japan, where a system of feudalism similar to that of Europe prevailed. Powerful military leaders controlled Japan for centuries. Japan was also influenced by China, and adapted many of its ways.

Europe. In Islamic Spain, a Muslim thinker found himself in trouble for studying and writing about the works of a Greek writer who had lived 1,500 years earlier. In England and Italy, people were finally leaving the old ways behind and seeking new lives and wide knowledge in the towns and cities.

Africa. In Africa, a North African traveler reported about a stable and rich West African society whose leader wielded great power.

Europe. In France, a young woman heard voices that told her she would lead an army to victory over foreign invaders. In doing so, she helped to increase the power of the French king but lost her life.

South America. In the Inca Empire of South America, a prisoner of war learned about his place in Inca society. He was told that all important decisions would be made for him by Inca rulers. He compared this new life to the simpler, freer life he knew among his own people.

1. An Empress Understands the People's Needs

After the Han dynasty fell in the 200s (see Unit III, story 6), China underwent nearly 400 years of invasions and civil wars. The emperors were almost powerless. China was split into rival kingdoms, with barbarians (foreigners) in control in the north. This was a dark age for China.

China was united once again under the Sui dynasty (581–618). Under the Sui, the Grand Canal, which linked the Yangtze Valley and north China, was built from 604 to 610. At one time, over a million workers were involved in the project. The Sui revised China's law codes and created a complex central government. Unpopular because of their harsh administration, the Sui were overthrown and the Tang dynasty began, with the rule of Li Yuan (ruled 618–626) and his son, Li Shih-min (ruled 627–649).

The Tang dynasty lasted until 907 and was a golden age for China. Education was encouraged. Government jobs (the civil service) were assigned on a merit basis. Those who passed the difficult exams were assigned administrative jobs according to their test scores.

The civil service examinations created a demand for books for the exam-takers. Other people wanted copies of religious writings, prayers, calendars, and stories. Each item had to be copied slowly and carefully by hand. How could this process be speeded up? The answer was the invention of block printing, which occurred in the sixth or seventh century (the exact date is uncertain). For many years, the Chinese had used pen and ink for writing. They knew how to make seals out of metal, stone, and clay. It was a short step to cutting engraved (raised) characters into a block of wood, coating the block with ink, and pressing it onto paper. Paper had been invented in China early in the second century.

Historically, China had been controlled by men. Here we turn to the story of the first woman ruler of China, the Empress Wu Chao. When her first husband, the Emperor Li Shih-min, died in 649, she was sent to a Buddhist convent, presumably to spend the rest of her life. But in 655, the new emperor, Li Che, brought her back to court as his empress. In 660 his health failed, and Wu Chao became the true ruler. After his death in 683, she became dowager empress (a widow whose title comes from her dead husband's rank) and took control of the government from her sons. In 690 she seized the throne and ruled until she was deposed in 705.

Loyang   690

"Good morning, Empress," said Lan, the royal adviser. "There are many decisions to be made today."

"And what problems have you prepared for me?" asked the empress.

"Majesty, the peasants are complaining about the great amount of labor they must give to the government each year."

"Lan, I understand their complaint, and I agree with them. The more time the peasants must spend on government projects, the more they are forced to neglect their own lands. I decree that their peasants' forced-labor time shall be cut in half. This order is to go into effect immediately."

"Thank you, Majesty," said Lan. "And now I bring you another complaint from your subjects. They say that the taxes they are forced to pay have created great burdens. They seek relief from these burdens. Majesty, what is to be done?"

Salt processing was for centuries a highly developed, government-controlled industry in China. (From right to left: quarrying, drying, packing, and finally, using salt at home.)

Wu Chao replied, "The finance minister tells me that the treasury is full. More money is coming into the treasury than we can use. You may cut taxes by one third."

"Your wishes will be carried out," bowed Lan.

"Lan, I have made another decision. I am not very happy with the caliber of some of our government workers. I don't care what a man's family background and connections are. I want you to start using written examinations to test and pick the best of the best."

Lan nodded. The empress' decrees would make a lot of people happy. He would see to it that her wishes were carried out immediately. Once again, Wu Chao had proven that she was a wise and capable ruler, and he was proud to be in her service.

Postscript

Wu Chao governed China wisely and with great skill. She saw to it that capable people were appointed to all high government positions, and she supervised them closely. Her political brilliance won her the loyalty of her advisers and officials and the admiration of the foreign rulers with whom she had dealings.

Wu Chao made many important decisions. She reorganized the army and conquered Korea (655–675). She encouraged silk production and farming and prevented peasant uprisings. Also, she encouraged the spread of the Buddhist religion. Most historians agree that she was a great ruler.

In 705 army leaders took over the government. By then, the empress was 80 years old and in poor health. Wu Chao was forcibly replaced by her son, and she died soon afterward.

QUESTIONS FOR REVIEW

1. What were the accomplishments of the Sui dynasty?
2. Why was the Tang period called a golden age?
3. Why was the invention of block printing important?
4. What did the Empress Wu Chao do to answer the peasants' complaints?
5. Why was Wu Chao considered a great ruler?

UNDERSTANDING THE STORY

A. Write W for each statement that Wu Chao made or might have made and L for each statement that Lan made or might have made.

1. What problems have you prepared for me?
2. There are many decisions to be made today.
3. Start using written examinations to find the most qualified people for jobs in government.
4. They say their taxes have created a great burden.
5. Cut taxes by one-third.
6. I bring you another complaint.
7. The peasants' forced-labor time shall be cut in half.
8. Your wishes will be carried out.

B. Imagine that Wu Chao has been elected president of the United States. What problems would she face? How might she solve them?

ACTIVITIES AND INQUIRIES

1. Go to the library. Prepare a report on the Tang dynasty.
2. Assume that you are asked to prepare a report card for Wu Chao's rule. Grade her in each of the following areas: *(a)* personality *(b)* government efficiency *(c)* military success *(d)* popularity with the Chinese people.
3. A female ruler was most unusual in China. What special problems do you think Wu Chao had to overcome? How do you explain her success as a ruler?
4. Wu Chao insisted on the selection of government officials through civil service examinations. Why do you think she did this? Do you agree? Explain your answer.
5. How do you think that Wu Chao would handle the budget and tax problems of the United States government?

2. Life on the Medieval Manor: The Feudal Arrangement

As we learned in Unit III, serfdom started in the last years of the Roman Empire. Serfdom lasted for over a thousand years in Western Europe and many centuries longer in Eastern Europe. The period of European history that followed the fall of the Roman Empire is called the Middle Ages, or the medieval period. It lasted from the fifth century (400s) through the fourteenth century (1300s).

During the Middle Ages, the serfs were under the complete control of the lord of the manor. The lord was a nobleman, a member of the upper class. He received his lands from another, higher ranking, noble, or from the king. Each noble was expected to perform certain services for the lord who ranked above him. He provided money, goods, and services to this lord. He also provided an army (usually made up of the serfs from his lands) when the lord went into battle. After the lord's death, his lands, title, and the serfs who worked on the lands were passed on to his eldest son. This social system is known as *feudalism*. Women usually could not inherit property and had few rights. There were some notable exceptions, however, of women who became powerful rulers. Often, they were the widows or daughters of powerful nobles.

The feudal manor was a sizable piece of land that was farmed by the serfs. The serfs had many obligations to the lord in return for the land they were granted. Much of what the serfs produced went to the noble lord. The serfs paid about two thirds of their crops to the lord of the manor. These payments covered rent, taxes, and services, such as the use of the lord's bake oven and wine press.

The serfs had many other responsibilities. In time of war, they were expected to serve in the lord's regiment. If the lord was captured in battle, the serfs were required to help pay his ransom. Serfs were also expected to help pay for armor and weapons when the lord's son became a knight (soldier). The lord also controlled many aspects of daily life. Serfs were treated either well or badly, according to the wishes of the noble. He could be kind or brutal, pleasant or nasty. Serfs could not leave the manor without permission. The system is known as *manorialism*. It lasted as long as feudalism.

In this story, we are in the home of a family of French serfs. It is a single room, about 15 feet long. In this small space the family cooks, eats, and sleeps. The room is dark, smelly, and smoky from the wood fire. The dirt floor is dusty in hot weather and muddy in rain and snow. The walls are mud that has been plastered over twigs and branches.

See if you can decide whether the serfs in the story should be grateful for what the noble has done for them. Do you agree with the husband or the wife? Why?

Talcy 954

"This is going to be the most exciting day of our lives," said Louis to his wife, Helene. "At last, our daughter, Estelle, is to be married, and we have our noble lord Pierre to thank."

"Thank him?" replied Helene. "You must be out of your mind. He finally did grant permission for the wedding, but the marriage tax is very high."

"I still feel we should be grateful," said the husband. "After all, he could have refused permission, as he did for our neighbor Charles' daughter. Lord Pierre might even have charged two to three times as much for the wedding tax."

"Why did he give his approval for this marriage? I'll tell you why," argued Helene. "Our daughter is marrying a man from this manor. She is going to stay right here and work alongside her husband. Later on, their children will help with the work. In heaven's name, what did our noble have to lose?"

"You forget how kind and thoughtful Lord Pierre is to us," said Louis. "He isn't nearly as cruel as some other nobles in the province. He seldom beats us. He allows us to keep part of the crops we grow. His taxes for the use of his mill, wine press, and tools aren't really too high. We have to work for him only 15 days of each month."

"Why should we have to turn over a share of our crops and work so hard for him? We have hardly anything left for ourselves. He may be better than some nobles, but the whole system is still unfair," Helene declared.

"I'll tell you why we pay," said Louis, angrily. "We couldn't get along without him. He protects us, takes care of us, and makes important decisions. We could not have had this mar-

Medieval European serfs plowing their fields, just as their ancestors had done for hundreds of years.

riage without him. It's time for the wedding. Let's all go to the chapel, and while there, let us pray for the health and happiness of our noble lord."

"You pray for him," said the wife. "I'll pray for a happy life and more freedom for our daughter and her husband!"

Postscript

Unquestionably, the serfs endured a harsh life. One season without enough rain could mean starvation. Between the years 970 and 1100, French serfs suffered through almost 60 droughts (dry periods).

The Middle Ages in Europe were, however, an age that placed great hope in the rewards to come in the next world (heaven). The sufferings that people experienced in this life were only a preparation for the joys they would experience after death. The teachings of the Catholic Church, based on the doctrines of Jesus, were the central beliefs of the time, and were held as true by people in all walks of life. Religious practices and beliefs played a central role in a person's life, from birth through adulthood to death. So deep was the faith and belief of the period that the Middle Ages have been called the Age of Faith.

In our next story, we see how faith led many people to join in a great series of battles in the name of their religion.

QUESTIONS FOR REVIEW

1. What services did a feudal nobleman perform for the lord who was ranked above him?
2. What were the obligations of the serfs?
3. What was the system of manorialism?

4. Why did Lord Pierre grant permission for the marriage of Helene and Louis' daughter?
5. Why did Helene think that the feudal system was unfair?

UNDERSTANDING THE STORY

A. Helene had strong feelings about many things. Tell which of the statements below describe her thinking.

1. We should thank our noble lord for our daughter's marriage.
2. The wedding tax is too high.
3. The noble lord had nothing to lose when he granted approval for the marriage.
4. Our noble lord is kind and thoughtful.
5. The taxes are not really high.
6. Taxes leave us little for ourselves.
7. Our noble lord protects us.
8. Pray for a happy life and more freedom for the newlyweds.

B. Imagine that Helene and Louis' lord is running for president of the United States today. Would you vote for him? Explain. Would Helene and Louis vote for him? Explain.

ACTIVITIES AND INQUIRIES

1. Use each of the following key terms in a sentence: lord   manor   serf   noble   Middle Ages.
2. Look for pictures of medieval homes and people. Bring them to class. Be prepared to talk about the differences between the lives of the nobles and the serfs.
3. Pretend that you are Louis. An old friend from another manor meets you. He tells you that his noble lord is very fair. What would you tell him about Lord Pierre? Explain.
4. Imagine that you are Helene. Would you agree with what your husband, Louis, said? Explain.
5. Helene and Louis give us different pictures of life on the manor. Which one is giving a truer picture? Explain.

3. Crusaders at the Walls

The lives of the serfs changed very little from day to day, week to week, year to year. Work followed seasonal patterns of planting, growing, and harvesting the crops and tending animals. Religious days and seasons were strictly observed. But the world of the serf was limited by the boundaries of the manor. There was no place to go.

In 1095 something happened that would bring about great changes in the lives of many serfs. Pope Urban II, the leader of the Western Christian Church, called for a Crusade. This Crusade was to be a campaign (military expedition) to capture the city of Jerusalem from the Muslim Turks. Jerusalem was a holy city for Christians, Jews, and Muslims. It was very important to Christians, since it was the city where Jesus had preached and died.

Thousands of serfs from Western Europe joined the armies of the Crusade. This was their great chance to leave their little world behind them. The Crusaders saw things they had never believed existed. They did things they had never dreamed possible. They threw away the chains of serfdom for the chance to serve in a nobleman's army. Those who lived to return to their homes would find it difficult to work in the narrow confines of the manor.

In this story, two Crusaders discuss their problems and their feelings. Ask yourself whether you would have joined this Crusade. How would you have felt as you stood before the walls of Jerusalem?

Jerusalem   July 1099

"At last, we're camped just outside the walls of Jerusalem," said John to his friend Robert. "For months we fought to capture this city, and now it's almost ours. Soon we'll be on our way home."

"Not so fast," said Robert. "We've been marching and fighting for almost four years. This is a hard life, and I'm tired of it. Suppose we capture the city. Then what will happen? We may have to stay on. I don't think we'll ever get home to see our families!"

149

"The attack has started. I told you we would be in Jerusalem very soon!"

"Why are you so discouraged?" asked John. "The city is ours. You can see the Muslims are getting weaker. They have courage, but don't forget that the one true God is on our side. The fight will be over very quickly. We'll be back home before you know it!"

"Before I know it? I'll never know it. It's all such a waste of time and human life. Even if I do get home, what useful purpose will it all have served?"

"Don't be a fool!" insisted John, his voice rising. "We have learned more in this short time than in all the other years of our lives. Our friends on the manor will never believe what we have seen and done. Think of our great adventures, the tastes of strange foods and spices. Have you forgotten the sights and sounds of different peoples, of great cities, works of art, churches?"

"True," said Robert, "but has it been worth the pain and suffering? I often wonder, Why am I fighting these people? Our leaders tell us that the Muslims are infidels who torture and kill our fellow Christians. But I don't believe that these people are guilty of all the bad things that are said about them."

"Our Savior, Jesus, died here. It is our duty to capture the city of Jerusalem for all future Christians. You must believe this," added John.

"I am sorry. I want to believe," said Robert. "But there are other things. I am very disappointed in the actions of many of the Crusaders. They seem much more interested in looting the places they visit than in capturing the Holy Land for our religion. In our travels we were often cheated by our fellow Christians. We have risked our lives, and —"

"The attack has started!" shouted John excitedly. "The enemy are fighting well, but we are pushing them back. Thousands of Muslims are running in wild panic. I told you we would be in Jerusalem very soon!"

"You're right! They are running for their lives! Bodies are piling up on the walls and in the streets. But hundreds of our men are also being killed. Their bodies fall all around. All I can smell is blood and burning flesh. I can barely hear your voice over the screams of the dead and dying! I'm going to be sick!"

"My God! The slaughter!" screamed John. "But we've won. The city is ours!"

"Would our Savior give us his blessing this day?" cried Robert.

Postscript

Many Crusaders were eager to atone for (make up for, repent) their sins by fighting for their religion. But the true religious purpose of a Crusade (to win the Christian holy places, such as Jerusalem, from the Muslims) was often forgotten. Most of the soldiers were more concerned about escaping from their hard and boring lives at home. And, for their part, many nobles were more interested in winning land and treasure.

In the First Crusade, which lasted from 1096 to 1099 and is described in our story, about 30,000 foot soldiers were led by 4,500 horsemen (knights). The Crusaders triumphed in much of the Holy Land (see map).

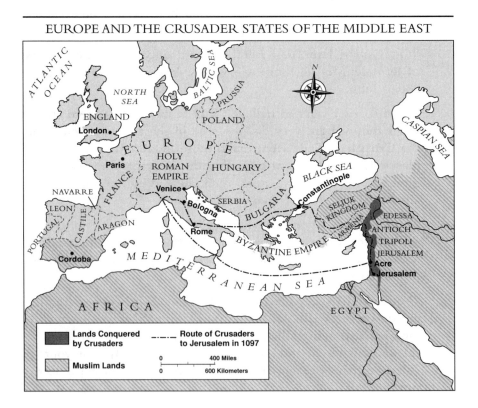

EUROPE AND THE CRUSADER STATES OF THE MIDDLE EAST

The four Latin States they founded (Edessa, Antioch, Tripoli, and Jerusalem) endured for many decades.

The Second Crusade began in 1147, after the Muslim Turks recaptured Edessa and were threatening the other Latin States. The Crusaders were defeated and returned to Europe in 1149 with little to show for their efforts.

The Egyptian-Syrian leader Saladin united the Muslims of the Middle East in 1183, and he won Jerusalem in 1187. The Third Crusade (1189–1192) tried unsuccessfully to recapture Jerusalem. But the Crusaders did negotiate the right of European pilgrims to enter the city of Jerusalem for religious purposes. In the Fourth Crusade (1202–1204), the Crusaders captured the Christian city of Constantinople and stole many of its treasures.

During the era of the Crusades, there was increased Mediterranean trade, and the Italian cities of Venice, Genoa, and Pisa prospered by outfitting and transporting the Crusaders to the Middle East. Goods from the East found their way back to Europe. Ships were improved. Navigation was made easier by the invention and use of the magnetic compass.

By the end of the 1200s, all the Latin States were back in Muslim hands, and the idea of the Crusades was abandoned. Western Europe turned from the Mediterranean to the Atlantic and exploration and trade in Africa and later the Americas.

Many thousands on both sides lost their lives during the Crusades. Some have questioned whether any long-lasting, positive results can be found in the story of the Crusades. Others have claimed that Europe was slowly waking up from the long "sleep" of the Middle Ages and would reap benefits from the Crusaders' contact with the civilization of the Middle East.

QUESTIONS FOR REVIEW

1. What was the purpose of the First Crusade?
2. Why did many serfs decide to become Crusaders?
3. What had John learned on the Crusade?
4. Why was Robert not sure that the Crusade was worthwhile?
5. What were the results of the Second Crusade?

UNDERSTANDING THE STORY

A. Tell which of the statements below are true.

1. Serfs led very interesting lives.

2. Pope Urban II asked for a Crusade to capture Jerusalem.
3. Serfs did not join the Crusades.
4. John felt that God was on his side.
5. Robert enjoyed the great adventures of the Crusade.
6. Robert and John had been marching and fighting for almost four years.
7. John said that the Crusaders would take Jerusalem.
8. Many people died in the attack on Jerusalem.

B. Imagine that John and Robert were asked to serve in a recent United States military action. Who would have served more willingly? How would the other man have felt about the war? Why? With which one of the two do you agree? Explain.

ACTIVITIES AND INQUIRIES

1. Look at the map of Europe, the Middle East, and North Africa on page 152. This map shows routes Crusaders took from France to the Holy Land. Draw the map in your notebook in outline form. On your map show the routes that a Crusader would have taken from each of the following places:
   a. England—show the route with a dotted line.
   b. Holy Roman Empire—show the route with a solid line.
   c. Venice—show the route with a broken line.

2. Pretend that you are John. You are talking to your friends on the manor about your adventures on a Crusade. Write several sentences describing these adventures. Include the exciting things you saw and did on your travels.

3. Imagine that you are Robert. You have just come home from a Crusade. Your friends have heard from John about his experiences. Now they are eager to hear from you. Write a paragraph telling of your experiences. Is your story going to be like John's? Explain.

4. Look at the illustration on page 150. Describe what is happening. Write your own title for this picture.

5. Pretend that you are a Muslim at the time of the First Crusade. List the reasons why you feel that Jerusalem should be defended against the Christians.

4. Preparing to Fight and Die

At the beginning of the Christian era, some 2,000 years ago, Japan was divided into many kingdoms or states ruled by noble families. By the third century, the Yamato were the most powerful of these families. The years 200 to 646 are known as the Yamato period.

Early in the seventh century, Prince Shotoku of the Soga family tried to establish a strong central government like that of the Sui dynasty of China. The head of the Yamato family would be the emperor. The powers of the other noble families were to be limited by the central government. The emperor of modern Japan is a descendant of the Yamato.

Actually, the Japanese government was quite different from China's. The Japanese nobles did not lose their power. Nor did the Japanese win government positions by taking tests. Those who came from powerful families were given the important government jobs. Over the years, these jobs became hereditary—they were passed from parents to children.

At first, the head of the Yamato had more power than any Chinese emperor. However, from the ninth through the twelfth centuries, the emperors gradually lost their power. They became puppets of the noble families that lived at the court. The nobles paid no taxes on their lands. The ordinary farmers, who had to pay taxes, could not afford to keep their lands and had to turn them over to the nobles. As in Western Europe, a feudal system prevailed.

The Fujiwara were the greatest of these noble families. The Fujiwara ruled Japan and used the emperor as a figurehead. The Fujiwara princes married the emperors' daughters to ensure the family's power. Government decisions were made by the Fujiwara, and the emperors followed their orders.

The ruling families were constantly at war with one another. Warrior knights called *samurai*, who were members of these fighting families, battled for control. The central government was powerless to stop them.

In 1192 the samurai leader Yoritomo Minamoto was given the title of *shogun*, or chief general. The shogun was now the real ruler. He controlled taxes, issued laws, and commanded the samurai.

In our story, two samurai of the Minamoto family talk about their lives.

Kamakura   1187

"You fought very bravely yesterday," said the samurai Ito.

"And you fought bravely too," said the samurai Yi. "I saw you drive off at least three of the enemy samurai. I'm glad that I didn't get in the way of your sword."

"We are trained to fight people and to follow orders," said Ito proudly. "The samurai's code of *bushido* teaches us to be brave and loyal to our leader."

"Yes, added Yi, "we must follow his orders, suffer pain and hardship, and, if necessary, we must die for him."

"Yi, I am not afraid to die. Sometimes, I am truly happy to fight and defeat an enemy. It is a great victory, for my enemy is a samurai, a warrior just like me."

Yi said, "The life we lead is an exciting one, Ito, but sometimes I wonder what it would be like to live as a simple peasant. I might enjoy working on the land."

Ito frowned. "I don't believe that you would prefer to change

Samurai in armor, from the Japanese medieval period (8th–12th centuries).

places with one of your peasants, Yi. I can't imagine you doing backbreaking work on your farm. Nor can I see you struggling to pay your taxes to your samurai landlord."

"You're right," said Yi softly. "I was born a samurai; I'll die a samurai."

The two samurai were interrupted by loud shouts. "Our enemies are attacking! Their samurai are at the top of the hill. Mount your horses! Prepare to fight and die!"

The two samurai looked at each other, nodded, and made ready to go into battle.

Postscript

By the fifteenth century, the stronger Japanese lords had defeated the weaker ones and taken over their estates. Thus, there was less demand for the warrior samurai. They were no longer admired and feared. Without a lord to serve, many became homeless outcasts. They wandered through the countryside attacking travelers and raiding villages.

In Western Europe, feudal *chivalry* (the code of knightly behavior) taught that upper-class women were to be looked up to and admired as superior human beings. In Japan, on the other hand, women had less freedom than in the past. Samurai wives were expected to endure hardships without protest.

QUESTIONS FOR REVIEW

1. How was the government of Japan different from the government of China?
2. How did feudalism develop in Japan?
3. What were the duties of the shogun?
4. What was the code of bushido?
5. Why was Ito sure that Yi would not like the life of a peasant?

UNDERSTANDING THE STORY

A. Write I for each statement Ito made or might have made and Y for each statement Yi made or might have made.

1. We are trained to fight and follow orders.
2. I'm glad I didn't get in the way of your sword.
3. The samurai code of bushido teaches us to be brave.
4. I don't believe you would prefer to change places with your peasants.
5. We must die for our leader.
6. I was born and will die a samurai.
7. I am not afraid to die.
8. I can't imagine you doing backbreaking farmwork.

B. Assume that you are a member of the United States armed forces. Would you like to have Yi and Ito on your side? Explain your answer. How do you think they might react to modern military discipline?

ACTIVITIES AND INQUIRIES

1. Explain each of the following names or terms and use each in a sentence: samurai bushido Yamato shogun ancestor Fujiwara Yoritomo Minamoto.
2. You are a newspaper reporter and interview Yi and Ito. What questions would you ask them? How might they answer your questions?
3. Next, you speak to the samurai's master. What do you think he would tell you about Yi and Ito? Do any of his reactions surprise you? Explain.
4. Prepare a report about life in Japan in the twelfth century, during the time of Ito and Yi.
5. Suppose that you could speak to a Japanese peasant family of this period. What would they tell you about their lives? What differences would the peasants find between their lives and the samurai's? Which would you prefer? Explain.

5. Expanding the Frontiers of Knowledge

The Arabic people brought the Islamic religion from Arabia to Palestine and Syria, to North Africa, and across the Mediterranean to Spain. In the tenth century, Muslims conquered the Indus Valley in India. The Indian Muslim rulers were called sultans. The most powerful *sultanate* had its capital at Delhi, and included much of present-day India.

Islamic nations controlled the most important trade routes between Africa, Asia, and Europe. Their fleets protected Mediterranean shipping during the Middle Ages. Islamic trade and manufacturing prospered while many Western Europeans barely made a living. The Muslims were well known for their steel weapons and textile products.

Muslim thinkers were responsible for many important advances in medicine, mathematics, navigation, and science. Doctors and pharmacists were required to pass qualifying examinations before they could practice their professions.

Muslim mathematicians studied the work of the ancient Greeks, adopted the decimal and numbering system of India, and added to the knowledge of algebra and trigonometry. They knew that the earth was round and rotated (turned) on its axis. They accurately estimated the earth's circumference. Muslim navigators took the Chinese magnetic needle and produced the compass. Their invention of the astrolabe made it possible for sailors to check their location at sea.

One of the most influential Muslim scholars of the twelfth century was Averroës. Born in Spain in 1126, he was a scientist, doctor, philosopher, and chief justice. Averroës was personal physician to two caliphs, and his work had a lasting effect on Christian philosophy as well. In our story, he has been imprisoned and placed on trial. Let us find out why.

Cordoba   1195

Time moves slowly. I think back over the years: chief justice of Cordoba, court physician, scientist, adviser to caliphs. I was respected and sought after. Now, I am in jail awaiting my fate.

159

The Muslim philosopher Averroës. Why was he accused of heresy?

I never would have believed that I would end my life in jail. I worked hard all my life. I never hurt anyone or got in trouble with the law. How could this happen to me? Yesterday, the religious court tried me as a *heretic*. They say my thinking is hostile to our religion. As Allah is my judge, I have never criticized Islam. I have always been a faithful, loyal believer.

Why, then, was I on trial? My enemies said that I could not be a philosopher, a thinker, *and* a true believer in Islam all at the same time.

"Do you deny that the Qur'an includes all the answers to the problems of the world?" asked my questioner.

"I do not deny the truth of Islam," I said. "I believe and trust in the Qur'an with all my heart. I have no differences with Islam. Its truth is my truth. My philosophy and science do not clash with our religion. My only purpose is to help shed light on the great store of wondrous knowledge that is contained within the Qur'an."

I tried to explain that the Qur'an is useful for religious and moral training. What is right and wrong? How shall a person act toward friends and strangers? What are proper punishments and rewards? A person who reads deeply into our holy book will learn that it also tells of the mysteries of the human mind and body—even the mysteries of the universe!

I had translated and explained the scientific writings of the Greek philosopher Aristotle. I tried my best to show that there was no conflict between his teachings and the religion of Islam.

"I have read," insisted one judge, "that this Aristotle is believed by some to be the source of all knowledge. This is clearly false and is opposed to our Qur'an and the words of the blessed Muhammad."

"I too have read the Qur'an," I answered, "and my understanding is that it is possible to combine both religious faith and Aristotle's thinking."

"Heresy! heresy!" shouted my accusers.

At that moment, I feared that my cause was lost. I would be found guilty. Only my punishment was to be decided.

My jailers arrived. "We find that you have taught as truths the writings of an unbeliever," one of them read. "This is your punishment. You are to lose all rank, honors, and titles. You are exiled from this country for the rest of your life."

I had been judged to be guilty of heresy. But deep down I knew that I was innocent. I would go to my grave believing that those who claimed my ideas were an attack against the Qur'an did not fully understand the holy book they were trying to protect.

Postscript

Averroës did not go into exile. His judges' verdict was overturned by the caliph, and Averroës was restored to his high rank.

Averroës wrote a complete summary of Islamic law. His encyclopedia of medicine was used in Europe for centuries. His commentaries on (explanations of) Aristotle were studied in European universities for many centuries. Most of his works in Arabic were lost, but Jewish scholars preserved them in Hebrew translations.

QUESTIONS FOR REVIEW

1. What were the contributions of Muslim mathematicians?
2. How did the work of Muslim navigators encourage exploration?

3. Why did the Muslim religious court rule that Averroës was a heretic?
4. What did Averroës say were the most important uses of the Qur'an?
5. What was Averroës' contribution to science?

UNDERSTANDING THE STORY

A. Write F for each statement that is a fact and O for each statement that is an opinion.
1. Averroës was the greatest philosopher of his age.
2. Islamic fleets protected Mediterranean shipping.
3. Averroës should have denied his interest in Aristotle.
4. Muslim mathematicians knew that the earth was round.
5. The astrolabe made it possible for sailors to learn their location at sea.
6. Averroës would have done a good job as caliph.
7. Averroës translated the works of Aristotle.
8. Averroës should not have been put on trial.

B. The Nobel Prize is one of the world's highest awards. It is given each year for achievements in science, mathematics, economics, and literature. Assume that Averroës is living today, and that you are a member of the Nobel Prize awards jury. Would you award him a Nobel Prize? Why or why not? In what field would you grant this award? Explain.

ACTIVITIES AND INQUIRIES

1. Explain each of the following key terms and use it in a sentence: sultan navigation decimal algebra trigonometry circumference magnetic compass astrolabe.
2. You are a reporter at Averroës' trial. How might he answer these questions: Why has this court put you on trial? Why did you spend so much time studying Aristotle's philosophy? Wouldn't you have avoided this trial by not writing about Greek philosophy?
3. Assume that you are one of the judges at Averroës' trial. What would have been your decision? Explain.
4. Prepare a report on Muslim contributions to science, medicine, and navigation.
5. Compare the contributions of Averroës to those of a major present-day scientist or philosopher.

6. A New Life in the Town

During much of the Middle Ages, as we have seen, European life was very orderly and predictable. Many thought that the arrangements between serfs and nobles would last forever. But there were also challenges to the great powers of the nobles. Serfs were unhappy and restless. As the Crusaders learned, there was another world outside the manor. Serfs now looked to the towns. In the thirteenth century, these towns became magnets for many serfs. Some serfs bought their freedom. Others simply ran away from the manor. All were looking for a new life.

Former serfs were attracted by the openness and variety of the jobs offered in the towns. However, the great differences between life on the manor and that in the town could be both exciting and terrifying.

In this story, a serf who has bought his freedom faces the dangers and pleasures of the new life in any English town. Ask yourself whether he made the right decision in leaving the manor and going to the town. Would you have stayed in the town under the conditions he describes?

Leeds 1230

Has it only been seven days since I left the manor to come to Leeds? Everything seems such a blur. So much has happened in one short week. I paid the lord of the manor for my freedom, and I had such strange feelings. It was odd that he was happy to accept a little money from me after so many years of work and service. Perhaps he won't miss my crops and tax payments.

Night is falling. It is the worst time for me. I am afraid. The room is hot and stuffy. I feel as though I am choking. I'd like to go outside for a walk, but I don't dare to. People warned me that there are robbers hiding in the shadows. There is no one to protect me. I have no friends yet, and I can't afford to buy a weapon to protect myself.

I thank God when daylight comes. I like to walk through the crowded marketplace and watch the people working at their trades. I see them making helmets, saddles, coats of armor,

163

"I like to walk through the crowded marketplace and watch the people working at their trades."

spurs, and swords. Others are dyeing cloth or melting gold and silver and making cups and jewelry. There's a fair almost every day. People come from all over to buy these wonderful things. I have asked many people for a job. Today a cloth merchant told me to come back to his shop tomorrow. I hope he will take me on as an apprentice. Then he will teach me about the cloth trade. I will be part of his family and live in his house. I will be safe and have many new friends.

The manor was never this interesting, but I was safer there. Often, I long for the sights and smells of the land and the harvest. My home was small, but I never felt shut in. I miss my friends and relatives. How I wish I had someone to talk with!

Enough of this dreaming. I must stop thinking about days past. The way of life on the manor is dying; there's nothing there for me. This is where I am going to stay. There is excitement and liveliness here in Leeds that I never saw on the farm. There are thousands of people doing great things. There are people to meet and people to know. I will make friends with many of them; I will find a woman to love.

I am going to learn a trade and earn enough to live well. When I marry, I am not going to have to ask Lord Cecil for his approval. My children will be free. I am not afraid any longer. There is much more life than death here.

I will live and die a free man.

Postscript

Towns and cities grew up during the feudal period on easily defended heights, at road crossings, along rivers, or on national borders. At first, the feudal nobles owned and ruled the towns. But, over the years, the town merchants bought—and in some cases, fought for—their freedom. In England the kings won the support of towns against the nobles by giving the towns charters granting them limited self-government. By the end of the twelfth century, the towns of Europe were no longer controlled by feudal nobles.

During this time, more and more people were attracted to the towns. Before long, many towns had grown into good-sized cities. 1200 Paris had 100,000 people; by 1300 there were 150,000. In 1200 London had a population of 20,000. There were more than 35,000 people by 1300. In 1300 Venice, Milan, Florence, and Siena each had 100,000 people.

Each city had many churches and often had a cathedral in the central area. A castle stood atop a hill or flanked a river. Thatched cottages and shops were crowded together. Streets were narrow, winding alleys. In a few cities, streets were paved with cobblestones. In most places, however, the streets were unpaved and unsafe for walking.

As you would guess, there were many fires, which often swept unchecked through a city or town. People fought the fires with buckets of water but they were seldom successful. They used long hooks to pull down a building if nearby houses were threatened.

People often kept small gardens alongside their houses. They also kept livestock. In London, pigs were supposed to be kept inside the house, but this law was not usually obeyed.

QUESTIONS FOR REVIEW

1. Why were many serfs unhappy and restless?
2. Why were serfs attracted to the towns?
3. Why was night the worst time for the former serf in the story?
4. Why was the town an exciting place for a person from a manor?
5. Describe a typical English town of this period.

UNDERSTANDING THE STORY

A. Compare life in a town in the Middle Ages with life in your city or town today. Write S for each statement that is similar to life in your town and D for each statement that is different from life in your town or city.

1. There is a fair almost every day.
2. People come from all over to buy the goods that are made here.
3. No one protects the people from robbers.
4. People are afraid to go out at night.
5. Many people come to the town to study or learn trades.
6. The town has crowded marketplaces where people work at their trades and sell goods and services.

B. If you had a choice, would you live in a big city or on a farm? Explain. If you had lived during the Middle Ages, would you have chosen life in a town or on a manor? Why?

ACTIVITIES AND INQUIRIES

1. Look at the illustration on page 164. Describe what is happening. Write your own title for this picture.
2. Imagine that you are standing on the roof of the tallest building in Leeds during the Middle Ages. Make a list of what you see.
3. Bring to class pictures of your town or city. Compare these with pictures of a medieval town. Does your town or city have anything in common with the towns of the Middle Ages? Explain.
4. Imagine that you are a health inspector. List all the dangers to health and safety that you find in a town in the Middle Ages. Compare these with the dangers in your city or town today.
5. Pretend that a former serf asks your advice about staying in the town or going back to the manor. Write down what you would tell her or him.

7. School Life

In the 1100s and 1200s there was a revival of learning in Western Europe. For many centuries, learning and literature other than religious writings had been only for the wealthy nobility. Books were copied by hand and studied by monks (religious people) who lived far away from the world of the serfs and the tradespeople of the towns.

Now people began once more to be interested in the writers and philosophers of the ancient world. Europeans were influenced by what they had seen in the Middle East and in Constantinople, and by the Islamic civilization of Spain. Europeans began to realize that they had much to learn about medicine, science, law, and philosophy. Here, a student tells his father of the difficulties and rewards of attending a great Italian university.

Bologna 1260

Dear Father,

I really appreciated the advice you gave me when I left for school. I do try to study hard and stay out of trouble. I keep myself clean and avoid the cold and damp air. But surely you can't believe that life here at the university is easy and full of fun. You write that you would rather study here than run your business. You seem to think that all we do is make life difficult for our teachers and annoy the people of Bologna with our singing and pranks.

Don't you think that we should have the best teachers? Shouldn't our teachers come to class on time? Shouldn't their lectures be interesting and helpful? Yes, the professors know that they can lose their jobs if their lectures are dull and boring. This keeps them on their toes. You would be surprised at the number of professors who are eager to get jobs here under these conditions.

It is not true that we waste time and fool around. I get up at four o'clock each morning—hours before you do. Can you imagine taking notes at a lecture at five in the morning, before you have had breakfast? All day, I have classes, debates, recitations, and lectures. That's not all, Father—I have a recitation most evenings after supper. I still have to find time for study at night to memorize my lecture notes. Believe me, by the time I crawl into bed at night, I have had a full day and an evening of hard work.

No, this is not like living in a fancy inn. I wonder how you would feel sitting on the floor of a cold classroom for hours at a time. I strain my eyes reading hand-copied books. At times, I can just about stay awake. Yes, if you would like to learn speech, logic, arithmetic, geometry, astronomy, music, and many other subjects, you could join me here. There are some men your age studying at the university.

I am sorry, Father, if I sound disrespectful. I want you to understand the life I lead here. Please don't think that I'm discouraged. The life is hard, but it's worth it to me to suffer a bit and get my degree. I have learned a great deal, and I have

Medieval Bologna University: How is this scene similar to a present-day classroom? How is it different?

started to ask questions and think for myself. I don't always agree with my professors, but I realize that I still have much more to learn.

I know that you do not like to think of a university as a place where people argue with one another. But I am trying to find the answers to many puzzles. You have faith in things as they are. I recognize your beliefs, but I must know more. I must find new paths, and I must understand.

Father, please realize that I am very grateful for your sending me to a university that teaches me to disagree with you. Please give my love to my mother and my sisters and brothers. I look forward to seeing them during the winter recess.

Your loving son,
PIETRO

Postscript

A few girls from well-to-do families went to convent schools. Boys had a better chance for schooling, but it was difficult for the son or daughter of a serf to get an education. Religious doctrine and practical information were taught at home. Specific work skills for trades were learned from master craftspeople.

There were no entrance examinations for a medieval university. A student was required to know some Latin, and had to pay a small fee for each class. In the year 1300 there were 7,000 students at the University of Paris, 6,000 at Bologna, and 3,000 at Oxford, in England.

Students did not have to follow a specific dress code. They could go without shoes only if their student robes reached to the floor. The masters or professors wore a red or purple cape and hood, and a square cap.

At the University of Paris male students had all the privileges of the clergy (priests). They were excused from military service and taxes. Married people could continue as students, but lost their privileges and could not receive degrees.

QUESTIONS FOR REVIEW

1. Why were Europeans in the 1200s interested in the writers and philosophers of the ancient world?
2. What advice did his father give Pietro before the student left for school?
3. How were the professors at the University of Bologna kept "on their toes"?
4. Outline Pietro's schedule at the University of Bologna.
5. What were the requirements for admission to a medieval university?

UNDERSTANDING THE STORY

A. Write T for each statement that is true, F for each statement that is false, and N for each statement that is not mentioned in the story.

1. Students at the University of Bologna wanted the best teachers.
2. Pietro, the student in the story, never had evening classes.
3. All the students did their homework every night.
4. Pietro's father said that he preferred work to study.
5. All the professors at the University of Bologna were at least 40 years old.

6. Pietro often sat on the floor of a cold classroom for many hours.
7. Students at the University of Bologna studied music, astronomy, geometry, and many other subjects.
8. Pietro always agreed with what his professors said.

B. Imagine that Pietro is a visiting student in your school. What would he say is similar to his school in the Middle Ages? What would he say is different about his school?

ACTIVITIES AND INQUIRIES

1. Write down your daily school program. Compare your school day with that of Pietro by writing his program alongside yours. Would you trade any part of your school day for his? Explain.
2. Pretend that you are a student at the University of Bologna in 1260. Your friends write to you and ask if they should become students there. What would you write back?
3. Imagine that you are Pietro's father. Write a letter to Pietro answering the one in the story, which you have just received from him.

8. A Ruler With Tremendous Power

In the fourteenth century, Mali was the richest and most powerful nation in West Africa. It had taken over the caravan routes and cities that Ghana had ruled. As you have learned, Ghana controlled the gold trade. However, Mali controlled both the gold and the salt trade.

At its height, Mali was larger and wealthier than Egypt. In fact, at one time, it was the second largest empire in the world. Only the Mongol Empire in Asia was larger.

Mali stretched from the Atlantic Ocean as far east as present-day Niger, along the northern coast, and included most of present-day Senegal and the Gambia, Guinea, and Mali. It ranged from the Sahara in the north

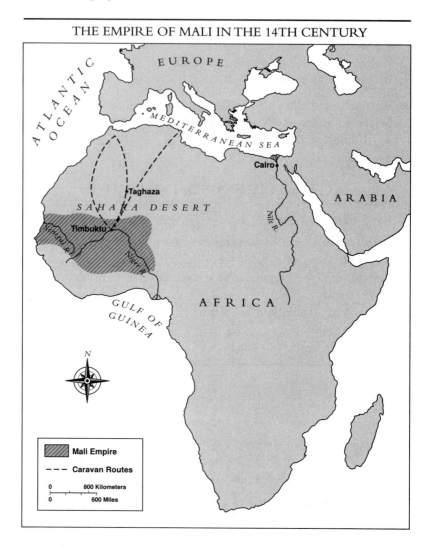

THE EMPIRE OF MALI IN THE 14TH CENTURY

to the forests and grasslands of the south. Travelers of the time said they needed many months to travel through Mali's territory.

The Niger River was and is the life blood of the country. It connects the north and south and provides water for agriculture. On land, large caravans of camels and donkeys carried gold and salt across the Sahara. Timbuktu, the capital of Mali, had 6,000 houses, several mosques (Muslim houses of worship), and many Islamic schools. Its people were merchants and workers. The city had a reputation for learning throughout the Muslim world. Students traveled long distances to study law and the Islamic religion with famous teachers at the university. Some of the teachers' writings are still studied in religious schools today.

Ibn Battuta was a North African Muslim who traveled throughout West Africa. He was full of curiosity about how the people of different regions lived. But he did not always like the things he saw.

Timbuktu   1352

My Dear Friend Ali,

Timbuktu is the most impressive city I have seen in all of West Africa. This is a completely safe place in which to live. The city has many charms and attractions. There are many beautiful mosques. Most of the people are well off and live in attractive houses. I stayed with friends of my family. They treated me well and told me many interesting stories about their country.

Mansa Musa, of Mali (right), with a map showing his travels. Taghaza (see page 174) is above left of the king's raised hand.

When the emperor of Mali appears in public, he puts on a splendid show. One day, I watched him leave his palace. First came many musicians playing gold and silver two-stringed guitars. Then came the emperor wearing a red velvet coat and a golden skullcap. Drums and bugles sounded while he climbed a platform to his throne.

People accused of crimes were brought before him. Those who were found innocent were acquitted and set free. Those who were found guilty received harsh but fair justice. I was told that no one who commits a crime goes unpunished. Travelers in Mali have nothing to fear from thieves; the roads are safe. The strict laws have freed Mali of the highway robbers who plague other lands. Besides, there are plenty of jobs paying good wages for those who are willing to work hard. Why bother with illegal and dangerous activities?

I was told stories about the great emperor Mansa Musa, who lived about 50 years ago. He was a ruler of tremendous power and style. When he traveled to Mecca in 1324, he was escorted by 60,000 soldiers and 500 slaves. Each slave carried a bar of gold weighing four pounds! If Mansa Musa had wanted to, he could have bought whole kingdoms as he traveled!

Not all of West Africa's towns and cities are as civilized or as attractive as Timbuktu, however. I must tell you of my visit to Taghaza, in the Sahara Desert. It is the bleakest place I have ever seen. There are no trees or grasslands. It is burning hot during the day but freezing cold at night. And everything is covered with sand. All over the town there are deep pits where the people dig for salt. Thick slabs of salt lie on top of one another all over the village. I asked whether their straight edges had been shaved by hand. No, I was told, this was how the salt looked as it was removed from the pit.

Perhaps the strangest feature of Taghaza is the appearance of its buildings. Imagine houses and mosques built of blocks of salt! For protection against the rain, the roofs are covered with camel skins.

That's enough for now. I expect to tell you much more when I see you in Cairo (Egypt) in two months. Until then, I am

Your friend,
IBN BATTUTA

Postscript

Toward the end of the 1300s, Mali was divided by struggles over which group would rule the country. The central government lost control of the country. In 1468 Sunni Ali, the rebel leader of a breakaway area of Mali, captured Timbuktu. This was the end of the great West African kingdom of Mali. It marked the beginning of the rise of the kingdom of Songhai, which we shall study in the following unit.

QUESTIONS FOR REVIEW

1. Describe the geography of Mali.
2. Why was the Niger River called the lifeblood of Mali?
3. Why did Ibn Battuta like Timbuktu?
4. Describe the system of criminal justice in Mali.
5. Why did Ibn Battuta dislike Taghaza?

UNDERSTANDING THE STORY

A. Write T for each statement that is true and F for each statement that is false.

1. Timbuktu was an unsafe place in which to live.
2. People accused of crimes were brought before the emperor of Mali.
3. Mansa Musa was a very powerful emperor of Mali.
4. Many who were found guilty of crimes were set free.
5. The buildings in Taghaza were made of salt blocks.
6. Mali was free of highway robbers.
7. In Timbuktu, there were very few good jobs, and even those paid low wages.
8. When Mansa Musa traveled to Mecca, each of his slaves carried a gold bar.

B. Imagine that you are given the opportunity to live and work in four-teenth-century Timbuktu. Would you accept the offer? Explain. Assuming that you do, describe your life in Timbuktu.

ACTIVITIES AND INQUIRIES

1. Imagine that you are with Ibn Battuta when he meets his friend, Ali, in Cairo. What questions might Ali ask him about his travels? How might Ibn Battuta answer Ali?

2. You return to Timbuktu with Ibn Battuta. What sights would you especially like to see? What differences do you notice between the buildings of Timbuktu and your hometown?
3. While in Timbuktu, you watch the emperor dispensing justice to his subjects. What are your reactions to his decisions?
4. Prepare a report comparing Mali in the fourteenth century with present-day Mali.
5. As a reporter, you are permitted to interview the emperor of Mali. Why are you surprised that he is willing to speak to you? What questions would you ask the emperor?

9. Joan of Arc

By the 1300s, European wars were no longer local affairs between feudal nobles fighting for territory. Entire nations were involved in endless killing. The war in this story was fought between England and France and was called the Hundred Years' War. It dragged on for 116 years, from 1337 to 1453. First the French, then the English, looked like the victors.

In the last part of the war (1421–1453), the English had the French on the run. Fortunately for the French, a peasant girl, Joan of Arc, heard voices. Only she could hear these voices, and their message was clear. Her voices told Joan that it was her duty to lead a French army against the English and bring the rightful French king to the throne. Joan, who was born in the village of Domrémy in 1412, was 15 or 16 years old when she began to hear the voices.

Joan faced many problems. How could she convince the French leaders that her voices spoke the truth? How could she get them to permit her to lead an army into battle? Would the soldiers follow her? What would be her plan of battle? What would happen if she lost? Somehow, she convinced the French of the truth of her voices. She, the uneducated young girl, was given an army to lead.

In 1429 Joan's army defeated the English and ended their siege of Orleans. The English were driven from north central France. In 1430, however, Joan was captured by the Burgundians (enemies of the French king) and was turned over to the English.

Joan of Arc was held prisoner in a small tower in the city of Rouen,

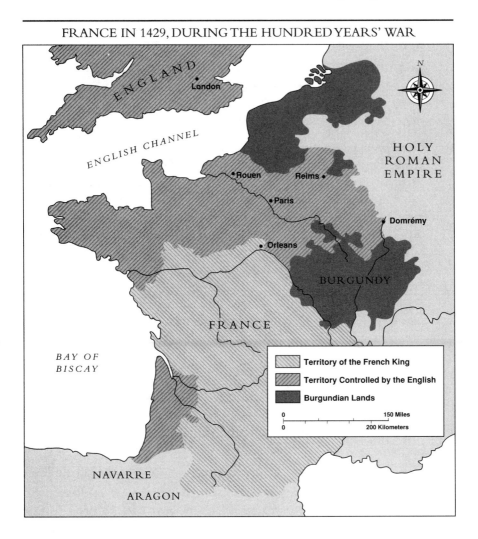

FRANCE IN 1429, DURING THE HUNDRED YEARS' WAR

about 90 miles northwest of Paris. She was burned at the stake in the city square. The ungrateful king of France, Charles VII, did not try to save her.

As you read, ask yourself whether you would have followed this young, untrained girl into battle. How did Joan's actions encourage the French to be more loyal to their nation?

Rouen   May 1431

The English are in an ugly mood today. They curse and wave their fists at me. Now rough hands take hold of me and tie me to the stake. Soon my executioner will set fire to the straw. I will be burned alive!

As I silently pray to my maker, my whole life passes before me. How strange that I, a peasant girl who cannot read or write, was chosen by God to achieve a miracle. How strange that I was chosen to save France!

How well I remember those difficult days. For nearly 100 years, England and France had been locked in a bitter war. Most of France had already fallen into English hands. There was talk that the king of England would soon be crowned king of France. This would happen when the English captured our city of Orleans. Most French people expected the city to fall at any moment. It was then that I first heard the voices— voices that urged me to lead the French to victory at Orleans. I remember trying to run from those voices because they made me afraid. But no matter how I tried, the voices continued to speak to me. Finally, I asked for a meeting with the French leaders.

How they howled with laughter when I explained my mission! "You, a girl, are going to lead an army of men against the English?" said one. "Go home and milk your cows," said another. "We men will protect you." But the voices would not let me go home. Finally, the leaders decided that I should be given a chance.

How amused the army captains were to see me dressed in a man's armor and riding a horse. But the common soldiers loved me, and they swore to risk their own lives to protect mine. Soon we grew from a small band into an army. When the smoke of battle had cleared, we had chased the English from Orleans.

Now those who once had mocked me stood in line to congratulate me. I was asked to be at the king's side in the cathedral in Reims as he was crowned king of all of France. My voices had not deceived me after all.

But just as my Savior had once carried his cross, mine was also being prepared. The English put me on trial, made fun of my voices, and condemned me to death. My followers have all deserted me in my hour of need. Yet I stand before my maker unafraid, and not quite alone.

Victorious Joan of Arc leads her army into the city of Orleans.

The flames are now beginning to rise. The pain is unbearable—I bite my lips to keep from crying out. In my last moments on earth, I beg forgiveness for my torturers. My life is about to begin.

God save France.

Postscript

Joan of Arc could not read or write, and she knew nothing of military tactics or strategy. But she was intelligent, resourceful, and a convincing speaker. She knew that an army should attack wherever its enemy had an unfortified position.

Joan was tried by a French court and was sentenced to life imprisonment for witchcraft and heresy. The English were furious and insisted upon the death penalty. After her execution, Joan became a legend, a heroic woman who had given her life to the cause of the French nation.

Joan's case was reopened in 1455. All now agreed that her trial had been unfair and she had been unjustly treated. The church court reversed the earlier decision. Over four and a half centuries later, in 1920, the French parliament ordered that the second Sunday in May be celebrated as a national festival day in her honor. In the same year, Joan of Arc was canonized: She became a saint of the Roman Catholic Church.

QUESTIONS FOR REVIEW

1. What did the voices tell Joan of Arc to do?
2. What was Joan's major achievement?
3. Why were the common soldiers willing to follow Joan?
4. What crimes was Joan accused of committing?
5. What was the result of Joan's trial?

UNDERSTANDING THE STORY

A. Write T for each statement that is true and F for each statement that is false.

1. The Hundred Years' War lasted for 116 years.
2. Joan's army defeated the English at Orleans.
3. Joan of Arc fought to save England.
4. Joan of Arc was burned at the stake by the French.
5. Joan of Arc could neither read nor write.
6. The common soldiers would not follow Joan into battle.
7. Joan was at the king's side when he was crowned king of France.
8. Joan died bravely.

B. Would the president of the United States let a 16-year-old who hears voices lead an army? Explain your answer. Would you follow Joan of Arc into battle? Why or why not?

ACTIVITIES AND INQUIRIES

1. Look at the map of France on page 177. In your notebook, draw an outline of the map. On your map mark the places where Joan (*a*) was born (*b*) defeated the English (*c*) saw the king crowned (*d*) died.
2. Imagine that you are a French soldier who fought at the side of Joan of Arc. What was there about Joan that made her a great leader?
3. Pretend that your class is going to hold the trial of Joan of Arc. You are her lawyer. Prepare her defense.
4. Now imagine that you are Joan's accuser. Prepare the case against her.
5. Assume that you are visiting Rouen today. You talk to a few of the residents of Rouen. What might they tell you of Joan of Arc and her heroic deeds?
6. As a reporter, you interview King Charles VII of France. Ask him how he felt about letting Joan lead the French army. Then ask him why he failed to help Joan of Arc when she was on trial for her life.

10. Should a Government Make All Decisions?

A third major civilization of the Americas was located in South America. There, in the 1400s, people known as the Inca began the conquest of the west coast. By the early 1500s, their empire stretched along some 2,500 miles of the Pacific coast and westward into the Andes Mountains. The Inca Empire had an area of almost 400,000 square miles and a population of about 12 million people. Included in this area were lands that are now the countries of Ecuador, Peru, Bolivia, Chile, and Argentina.

The vast Inca Empire was divided into provinces ruled by governors. It was connected by thousands of miles of roads. As with the Maya and

THE INCA EMPIRE IN THE EARLY 16TH CENTURY

ancient Egyptians, the ruins of Inca temples, pyramids, and sacred roads are all that remain of this civilization.

The Inca worshiped the sun god. The Inca's leader was thought to have descended from the sun. The Inca called themselves "people of the sun."

In the Andes, the Inca grew potatoes; along the Pacific coast, they grew maize (corn). Because of the lack of rain, Incan farming depended on irrigation. The Inca built complex terraces (walls) on mountainsides to create level, protected areas that could be farmed.

Unlike the Maya and Aztec, the Inca did not have a written language. But their spoken language is still used by many South Americans. The Inca kept track of business affairs and records by means of a device called a *quipu*, a cord with knotted strings of different colors and lengths. The knots were spaced to show specific sums. The Inca used *oral history*. Adults would memorize important events and the persons involved and pass on the information to their children. They, in turn, would do the same for their offspring. Only upper-class young men and specially chosen women received a formal education.

Like all the other people of the Americas, the Inca did not have the wheel or knowledge of how to work with iron. They used wood and stone tools. However, they did make objects of copper, tin, and gold.

In our story, an Inca farmer meets with a Chilean who has been relocated from his home to the mountains of Peru.

Cuzco   1450

"Hello, stranger," said the Inca farmer. "What are you doing here?"

"My people were given a 'choice' by your army commander," the stranger replied angrily. "Join and become part of the Inca empire or else die! We were outnumbered. We knew that we couldn't win, so we agreed to join the Inca."

"But how did you get to Cuzco?"

"After we surrendered, we were told that we would not be permitted to stay in our home village in Chile."

"Where were you told to go?" asked the Inca.

"We were given a 'choice': Go to a new Inca colony in the eastern territories or come here to Cuzco. In the east we would have been pioneers. We would have cleared the forests, built homes and roads, and farmed the lands. We chose instead to come here and try to make a life for ourselves among your people."

"You have made a good choice," said the Inca. "If you like, I can tell you some things about our people and our customs that might be helpful to you."

The Chilean nodded in agreement.

The Inca began. "Do you see that great palace in the distance? That's where our supreme ruler, the Great Inca, lives. He is both a god and our king. His word is law. Never disobey an order of the Inca or his nobles."

The Chilean replied, "We weren't ruled by a king. We had a chief, and he was elected by the elders (older persons) of the tribe. If the chief made too many mistakes, he lost his job. And he didn't live in a fancy house or tent."

The Inca continued. "Those attractive houses near the palace belong to the nobles who help the Great Inca run the country. Close by are the smaller houses of our warriors, or fighting men. The warriors are necessary for our defense (and to help us build our empire), but are not as powerful as the nobles."

"It seems to me that you Inca have a society of many castes, or classes. In my tribe, there are no social classes. Everyone is equal. Of course, we look up to the chief and the elders. By the way, what is your place in this society?"

"I am a farmer and am on the lowest rung of the Incan social ladder," said the Inca. "We farmers do not own or rent our land. It all belongs to the government. The government decides where I farm, and how much and what crops to grow. But I know that what I do is important. Without my labor, people would starve."

"You are a farmer, but the important decisions are not yours to make," said the Chilean. "Doesn't this upset you?"

"There are reasons why the government makes decisions for us. We need water, and the government builds an irrigation system for us. We need level land to farm, and the state builds terraced fields for us. We may have too many potatoes, beans, or peanuts one year. Our farm experts send the excess to storehouses and save it for a time when we (or other parts of the country) need it."

"This sounds like good planning. But what if I wanted to be a craftsperson instead of a farmer?"

"Men are needed to work in the fields much of the year," answered the Inca. "An average worker can be drafted into the army or put to work on road building at any time. Stay on the land, and you won't be given too many other jobs."

"I am married," said the Chilean. "How will my wife be treated?"

"Your wife will get special training in our religion and will be taught how to be a good Inca wife and mother. It is good that you are married. An unmarried man must find a wife—otherwise, a wife will be found for him!"

Postscript

Like the Maya, the Inca also were interested in astronomy. They knew about anesthetics (painkillers) and performed brain surgery. The Inca were well organized and industrious. They transported huge stone blocks long distances to build their temples and palaces. The stones were shaped to fit perfectly without using cement.

In 1522 a Spanish soldier (conquistador) named Francisco Pizarro landed with 200 soldiers in Inca territory. We will tell the story of his conquest in the following unit.

QUESTIONS FOR REVIEW

1. Describe the Inca's agricultural methods and crops.
2. How did the Inca keep track of their business affairs?
3. How did the Inca use oral history?
4. Why did the Chilean decide to go to Cuzco rather than to a new colony?
5. Why did the Inca farmer feel that it was an advantage to have the government make decisions for him?

UNDERSTANDING THE STORY

A. Write C for each statement that the Chilean made or might have made and I for each statement that the Inca made or might have made.

1. We had to choose between becoming part of the Inca Empire or losing our lives.
2. You have made a good choice in coming here.
3. Our chief didn't live in a fancy house or tent.
4. In my tribe, there are no social classes.

5. The warriors are necessary for our defense.
6. Important decisions are not yours to make.
7. An average worker can be put to work on road building.
8. An unmarried man must find a wife.

B. What are the differences between the farming methods of the Inca and those in the present-day United States? Would farmers in the United States approve of the federal government making all decisions for them, as the Inca government did for its farmers?

ACTIVITIES AND INQUIRIES

1. Suppose you were the Chilean farmer. Would you have chosen to go to Cuzco rather than Bolivia? Explain.
2. The Chilean believed that the Inca had a caste society. Do you agree? Why? Had the Chilean really lived in a classless society? Explain.
3. Using your library as well as this chapter, prepare a drawing of the city of Cuzco. What things do you see that are very different from your city or town?
4. According to the story, what was the role of women in Inca society? Compare this with women's role in our society.
5. Referring to the story about the Maya in Unit II, prepare a chart comparing them with the Inca. Use the following headings: Science Astronomy Mathematics Agriculture Role of Women Architecture.

UNIT V

New Empires, New Ideas

In this unit, we study five empires that flourished in the years from 1275 to 1650. We travel in Asia, Asia Minor, Africa, Europe, and the Americas. And we will also look at several important ideas from that period which changed the course of human thought and expression.

Asia. The Mongol Empire of Genghis Khan and Kublai Khan in China dominated Asia in the 1200s. A young Italian named Marco Polo traveled to the court of the great khan and learned of Kublai's thirst for knowledge.

Asia Minor. The Ottoman Turks captured the Christian city of Constantinople in the mid–15th century and went on to create a mighty

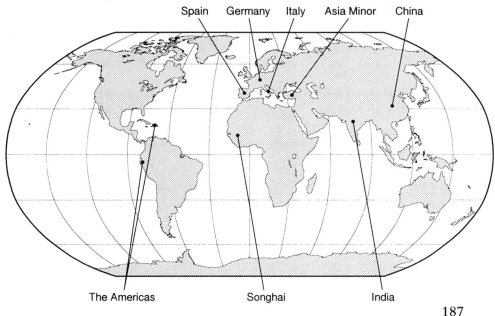

empire. Their leader, Muhammad II, was equally at home in the arts as he was in battle.

Africa. In the Songhai Empire of Africa, the city of Timbuktu became an important center of learning. What was there to study? An aspiring student discovered that there was almost too much to learn.

Europe and the Americas. In Spain, the Christian rulers defeated the Muslims. Next, they set their sights on trade with India and China. A daring sea captain proposed a plan to reach these eastern lands by sailing west. Despite strong opposition, the queen of Spain backed the voyage of Christopher Columbus. His discoveries set the stage for a mighty Spanish Empire. But the rise of this new empire also meant the end of two empires in the Americas.

Also in Europe, radical new ideas challenged the authority of the leaders and changed the ways in which people viewed themselves and the universe. A German monk who protested against the old ways set in motion forces that created a new religion. An Italian scientist proved that the earth was not the center of the universe, but he was forced to declare that he was wrong or lose his life.

In South America, a Spanish soldier defeated the Inca of Peru. He had so much Inca gold that he believed he had found El Dorado—a land of limitless wealth. But the quest for riches exacted a terrible price from the Spaniards and the people they conquered.

India. In India, the Mughal Empire controlled much of the vast subcontinent. Its ruler built lavish monuments and cared for the welfare of the people. Secretly, he mourned a loved one and worried about the fate of the empire when he could no longer rule.

1. A Ruler Attempts to Conquer Knowledge

In 1206 the great Mongol warrior Temujin was named the *Genghis Khan*—Universal Ruler. His armies had defeated their foes in Mongolia, North China, Central Asia, Persia, and Russia. Even the Great Wall of China did not keep out the Mongol cavalry. By the time Genghis Khan died in 1227, the Mongol Empire extended from east China to the Caspian Sea. His successors invaded Korea, Russia, Hungary, and Poland.

Genghis' grandson, Kublai Khan, conquered South China (the Sung Empire) in 1279. Kublai began the Yuan Dynasty, which ruled all of China until 1368. At first, Kublai did not trust the Chinese. But he later grew fond of Chinese culture and allowed Confucian ceremonies. In fact, non-Mongol religious groups were spared from paying taxes.

THE MONGOL (YUAN) EMPIRE OF KUBLAI KHAN IN 1280

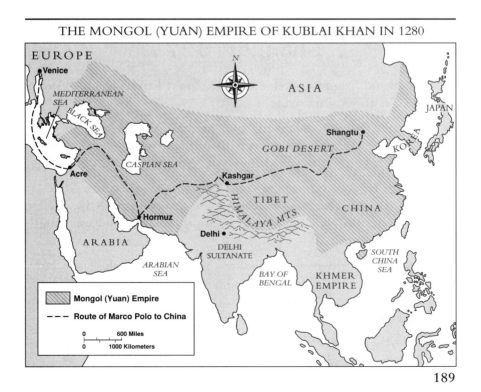

Kublai understood that the Mongols needed help from the Chinese people to govern the vast country. Therefore, he appointed many Chinese to all but the upper-level government offices and organized his state along Chinese lines. However, Kublai refused to permit civil service examinations. Perhaps he feared that the Chinese might win the high-ranking jobs from the Mongols.

Kublai was eager to learn and sought the help of experts from all over the world. He surrounded himself with Confucian scholars, Muslim financial experts, and Christian advisers.

Kublai moved the Chinese capital north to Beijing. He extended the Grand Canal to that city so that food could be shipped in more easily from the south. China's postal system and roads were expanded. Artists and architects were encouraged and paid to create. All of this cost a great deal of money. When high taxes failed to raise enough funds, Kublai turned to printing paper money to pay his growing debts. He even hired foreigners to act as fundraisers.

In 1271 two Venetian merchants, Maffeo and Niccolò Polo, together with the latter's son, Marco, age 17, started a journey eastward across Asia to China. Marco was 21 when the Polo family finally reached Kublai Khan's court. Our story tells of Marco Polo's first audience (meeting) with the khan.

Shangtu   1275

"Niccolò, Maffeo—welcome back," said Kublai Khan. "And who is this young man?"

"Your Highness, this is my son, Marco," replied Niccolò. "He is eager to see the wonders of your land, which we told him about when we returned home to Venice."

"I am happy to greet the son of my Venetian friends. Marco, you have a great deal to learn about my country. Now, Maffeo and Niccolò, you two must explain the reason for your long-delayed return."

"Sire, you sent us on a mission to Rome to speak to the Holy Father, Pope Clement IV," said Maffeo. "We were to ask him to send a group of educated Christians to China to teach you, and members of your court, about Christianity."

"I'm aware of what I asked you to do. Tell me, without wasting more words, why you took so long."

Kublai Khan (left) greets Marco Polo and his father on their arrival in China.

"Sadly, Pope Clement died soon after our arrival in Rome. A year passed and a new pope had not been named," added Niccolò. "We grew weary of waiting and returned to Venice. After all, we had not seen our home and family for ten years."

"Go on," said the khan impatiently.

"My wife had died," added Niccolò, "and Marco was no longer a boy. We decided to bring him with us and return to China."

"I accept the reasons for your delay. But what happened to your mission to the pope?"

"The new Pope, Gregory the Tenth, is a personal friend. He promised to send to your court the Christian scholars Your Highness requested."

"Fine. All is forgiven," smiled Kublai Khan. Then he turned to Marco.

"Marco, tell me all that you saw and did on your journey from Venice to my court."

"We traveled from Venice to the Holy Land, then to Persia, and across many mountains and deserts," replied Marco. "Here, Highness, let me draw a map for you. We traveled from Acre to Hormuz. Next, we went northeast to Kashgar. Finally, we crossed the Gobi. The days were long, but the lonely nights were even longer."

"I am very impressed with your son, Niccolò," said the khan. "*Now*, at last, I understand why your return trip from Venice to China took almost four years."

"Highness, I would like to ask you one question," said Marco Polo with some hesitation. "Why are you interested in the beliefs of people who live far from here?"

"Excellent question, Marco. You see, I am very curious. I must know about everything that exists in this world of ours. Before I die, I must be sure that there are no puzzles left to solve, no secrets that are unknown to me."

Postscript

Marco Polo became one of the khan's most trusted advisers. He was sent to many parts of the empire to study problems and report back to Kublai. Marco was even given the task of governing cities and provinces. As a spokesperson for the khan, he traveled on missions to many countries: India, Japan, Sumatra, Myanmar, Thailand, and beyond.

Kublai Khan found all three Polos so interesting and useful that he kept them in his service for 17 years. Finally, in 1292 they were permitted to leave China. They were asked to escort a Mongol princess who was to become the bride of the Persian ruler.

The Polos returned to Venice after an absence of 24 years. At first, their family and friends did not recognize them. According to the story, the Polos then threw back their worn oriental robes and ripped open the linings. Hundreds of emeralds, rubies, and pearls fell all over the floor. Now their friends and family remembered the Polos!

Marco Polo later wrote a book about his journey and adventures in China and east Asia. The book, *Description of the World*, told about the lands and cultures of the East. Europeans were amazed. It became one of the most celebrated and widely read books of the age.

QUESTIONS FOR REVIEW

1. What was the extent of Genghis Khan's Mongol Empire?
2. How did Kublai Khan enlist the help of the Chinese people?
3. How did Kublai use the talents of foreigners?
4. How did the Polos explain their delayed return to China?
5. How did Marco Polo describe his trip from Venice to China?

UNDERSTANDING THE STORY

A. Write K for each statement that Kublai Khan made or might have made and P for each statement that the Polos made or might have made.

1. You have a great deal to learn about my country.
2. You sent us on a mission to Rome.
3. Pope Clement died soon after our arrival.
4. I'm aware of what I asked you to do in Rome.
5. Tell me all that you saw and did on your journey to China.
6. We decided to bring my son with us.
7. I am very impressed with your son.
8. The days were long, but the nights were even longer.
9. Tell me why you are interested in people who live far away.
10. I am very curious about everything that exists in this world.

B. Suppose the president of the United States followed the example of Kublai Khan. The president decided to appoint his advisers and cabinet from among the world's greatest scholars and financial experts. These men and women were brought to the United States from all corners of the globe. How would this differ from the usual manner of choosing government appointees? Do you approve? Why or why not?

ACTIVITIES AND INQUIRIES

1. On the map of Kublai Khan's empire, on page 189, trace Marco Polo's route from Venice to China. Compare the trip during the 1200s with a trip you would take to China today.
2. Kublai Khan felt that he had to know about everything that existed in the world. Are you that sort of person? Why or why not? Assume that you are as curious as the khan was. How might your life change?

Is it possible for one person to know all there is to know about everything? Explain.

3. Imagine that you are with the Polos at the khan's palace. Describe the sights and sounds. How would your days be different from those you normally experience in this country? How would they be the same?

4. Assume that you interview the khan and the Polos for a local television program. You ask the khan why he wants the Polos to stay in China. Next you ask the Polos how they feel about staying in China. What are their answers? Would you expect Niccolò and Maffeo to have a different reaction than Marco? Why?

5. Pretend that Marco Polo tells you that he would like to return to the United States with you. What is your reaction? Do you think that Marco would enjoy living in this country? Explain.

2. A Warrior With the Heart of a Poet

At the beginning of the 1300s, the Ottoman Turks (named for Osman, the first ruler of the lands where the empire had its start) replaced the Seljuks as the major power in the Middle East. In 1345 the Ottomans invaded Eastern Europe. During the next hundred years, they conquered the Balkan kingdoms. In 1453 the Turks captured Constantinople (Istanbul), and the Byzantine (eastern Roman) Empire collapsed. The Turks now controlled the Middle East and the Balkans.

The Ottoman Empire was divided into provinces. Each was ruled by a governor. The central government, however, controlled each province. At the head of the government was the sultan.

The Ottomans, who were Muslims, did not accept the people of other religions as their equals. But they did give the Christians and Jews in conquered lands the right to live peacefully and practice their own religions and govern themselves under their own religious leaders.

The sultans relied on the defeated Christians of Eastern Europe to provide soldiers for their armies. Every four years, youths between the ages of ten and twenty were taken from Christian villages in the Balkans and sent to special schools to become Muslims. The best students were trained for government service. The others became soldiers, who were known as Janissaries. In the 1400s they were the best fighting group in Europe.

Our story begins outside of Constantinople (Istanbul). The Ottoman army of 150,000 soldiers, led by Sultan Muhammad II, has been besieging (attacking) the city.

Constantinople   May 29, 1453

"Your Highness!" shouted the Turkish general. "Our cannons (artillery) have breached (smashed) the city's wall! Our men are fighting in the city streets. The enemy is on the run. Nothing can stop us."

"Good work," said Muhammad. "You followed my battle plan perfectly."

"We mustn't forget your suggestion that we order new cannons," said the general. "I said it was impossible because the cannons would be too heavy and too long (15 feet) to ship.

Turkish Sultan Muhammad II, great warrior and poet.

You replied, 'Then, let's have them made right here at the gates of Constantinople.' Today, the cannons blasted enormous holes in the city walls!"

"Thank you, general. Now, we must be very careful. We must not let our enemy escape. Look at this map: There are gates here, here, and here. Send a company of Janissaries to each gate. They'll know what to do with anyone who tries to get out! And be sure to tell them that I want Constantine, the Byzantine emperor, captured, not killed."

"It's too late for that, Highness. Constantine died fighting. Now the eastern Roman Empire is yours. You are the Sire (king) of Victory. The Black Sea is now your domain."

Constantinople   1460

"Do you know what the people are calling you?" asked Mahmud Pasha, the Sultan's grand vizier (adviser).

"I can guess," replied Muhammad II, "but I doubt that it's Sire of Victory. I haven't led our army into battle for some time."

"You're right about that, Your Highness. These days they are calling you the 'Father of Good Works.'"

"I know what they mean, but I'm not sure I like being called the 'father' of anything but my children," smiled the sultan. "The point is that the ruler of a country is supposed to help the people. I'm just doing what is expected of me."

"Ah, but you are doing so much more than any other ruler," replied Mahmud Pasha. "You have established colleges all over the country for our young people. You have built more mosques than any other ruler. You are very generous in help-ing the poor."

"True, but any other sultan would do as much."

"I must disagree with you, Sire," said the vizier. "But here's more proof of your goodness. No one loves writing and art as much as you. No other ruler gives pensions to so many Turkish poets. You even send gifts to poets in India and Iran."

"Everything you say is true," said Muhammad. "I can't decide which I'd rather do: read a beautiful poem or lead my army to glorious victory in battle."

THE EXPANSION OF THE OTTOMAN EMPIRE 1453–1566

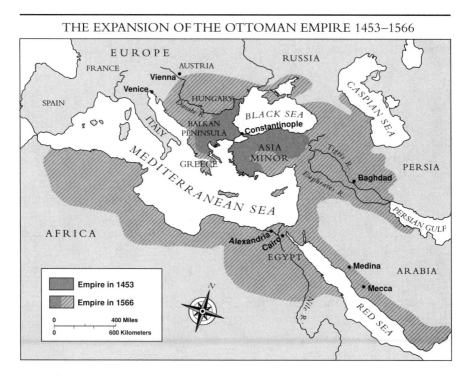

Postscript

Muhammad II was only 21 years old when he directed the siege of Constantinople. An expert in mathematics and engineering, he spoke and read five foreign languages. His military skills earned him the title of "conqueror." He is regarded as the founder of the Ottoman Empire. Muhammad's armies conquered Syria, Egypt, and southeastern Europe. In Russia, they set up a ring of vassal (dependent) states around the Black Sea.

The Ottoman Empire increased in size until almost 1700. Under the great leader Suleiman, the Turks conquered most of Hungary between 1526 and 1543, and in 1529 they threatened to capture Vienna, the capital of Austria. Also in the 1500s, the Turks gained control of coastal North Africa, Mesopotamia, and western Arabia.

By 1700, however, Ottoman power was in decline. Hungary was lost, and the Turks were forced out of many of their Black Sea vassal states. The empire lived on until the end of World War I in 1918.

QUESTIONS FOR REVIEW

1. How did the Ottoman Turks treat people of other religions?
2. Who were the Janissaries? How were they chosen?

3. How did the sultan's plan help bring about the fall of Constantinople?
4. Why was the sultan called the "father of good works"?
5. Why did Mahmud Pasha say that the sultan did more for the people than any other ruler?

UNDERSTANDING THE STORY

A. Write T for each statement that is true, F for each statement that is false, and O for each statement that is an opinion.

1. At the beginning of the 1300s, the Seljuk Turks replaced the Ottomans as the major power in the Middle East.
2. The Ottomans did not accept the people of other religions as their equals.
3. The Ottomans were the brightest people of the fourteenth century.
4. Most of the men in the Ottoman Empire wanted to become Janissaries.
5. The Turkish general followed Muhammad's battle plan at Constantinople.
6. Turkish cannons blasted holes in the walls of Constantinople.
7. The Emperor Constantine survived the battle for his city.
8. Muhammad II built many mosques and colleges.
9. Turkish colleges were far superior to those in Western Europe.
10. Muhammad II spoke and read five languages.

B. According to the story, Sultan Muhammad II was a great military leader. Suppose he was offered the job of chief of staff of the military forces of the United States. Would he accept? Explain. If he accepted, would he be a successful military leader in this country?

ACTIVITIES AND INQUIRIES

1. Study the map on the Ottoman Empire on page 197. Choose the term or phrase that best completes each statement.
   a. Constantinople is on the (1) Black Sea (2) Red Sea (3) Persian Gulf.
   b. A river that flows through central Europe is the (1) Euphrates (2) Nile (3) Danube.
   c. In traveling from Constantinople to Baghdad, you would be going (1) north (2) east (3) west.

    d. The distance from Vienna to Constantinople is about (1) 600 miles (2) 400 miles (3) 100 miles.

    e. In traveling from Constantinople to Alexandria, you would be going (1) east (2) south (3) north.

2. Prepare a report on what the fall of Constantinople meant to Western Europe and the Ottoman Empire.

3. Using written or oral descriptions and drawings, show how the sultan's tactics resulted in the fall of Constantinople.

4. As a reporter, you interview Muhammad II. You ask him whether he would rather be known as a military leader or a scholar. How might he reply? Select the leader of a country today. How might he or she reply to your question? Explain.

5. Compare the treatment of Christians and Jews in the Muslim Ottoman Empire with the treatment of Jews in Christian Europe.

3. An African City Becomes a Center of Learning

Songhai began as a small trading kingdom east of Mali in West Africa. By the 1400s, Songhai had grown powerful. It defeated Mali in many wars and replaced it as the most powerful state in the region. Songhai's generals used cavalry as well as foot soldiers effectively. Some 3,000 horsemen provided them with a major advantage over their enemies.

Songhai had an efficient banking system, a workable public education system, and a complete code of laws. Inspectors checked on the use of proper scales in local markets. Cheating of any kind in buying and selling was severely punished.

Neighboring states were required to pay Songhai tribute (money, or ransom). Those that refused were attacked, and their people were sold into slavery. By 1500 Songhai ruled a large empire. The empire was divided

THE EMPIRE OF SONGHAI IN THE 16TH CENTURY

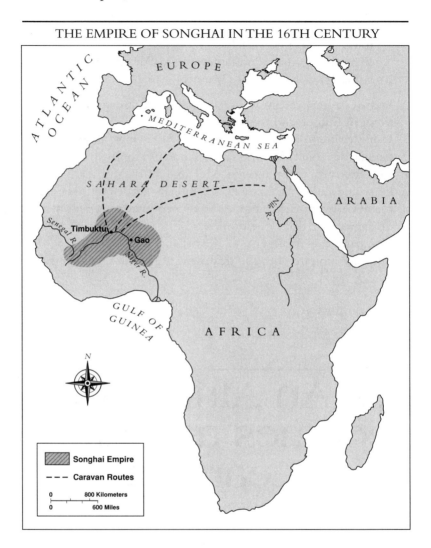

into provinces, which were governed by trusted officeholders. They controlled trade, farming, and the law courts.

Like Mali, Songhai prospered because it controlled the trade routes in gold and salt. At the time, the nations of Western Europe believed that their wealth depended on possessing a large supply of gold. Songhai supplied a considerable part of that gold.

We have described the city of Timbuktu in Unit IV. Under King Askia Muhammad, Timbuktu became an even more important center of learning. Here, a young man tells his friend about his visit to Timbuktu.

Gao   1510

"Akbar, I'm glad to see you after all these months," said his friend Ahmad. "What did you think of Timbuktu?"

"I don't know where to start," said Akbar. "Gao is so different from Timbuktu. Gao is a trading city—the people here buy and sell almost everything. Most of the people I know here are merchants. They grow rich by exchanging their products for gold. Others travel long distances on the Niger River to exchange their gold for articles they will sell to others."

"I know all about Gao," said Ahmad impatiently. "Tell me about Timbuktu."

"It's wonderful! I visited the University of Sankore. Its beautiful buildings and vast library were very impressive. I've never seen so many books in my entire life."

"Do you still plan to study law?" asked Ahmad.

"I don't know," said Akbar. "I'm more confused than ever. In Timbuktu there were so many wonderful people from all over the world. First, I met a medical student from Spain. Naturally, he urged me to study medicine. Then I visited with an Egyptian woman who was studying law. She almost convinced me that law would be my best choice."

"All right, then, Akbar, there's your answer. You always wanted to be a lawyer."

"Not so fast, Ahmad. I spoke for a long time with a cleric from Ghana who was studying for a higher degree in Islamic studies. As you would guess, he tried to convince me to follow his way of life."

"I understand your problem," said Ahmad. "But you don't have too much time left to make your decision. Did you speak to any of the professors?"

"My mistake was that I spoke to professors of law, medicine, and religion. Then, too, there were doctors, and lawyers, and more scholars than you could find in any other place. All were studying. All were excited with what they were learning. No wonder I can't make up my mind!"

"All right, Akbar, Timbuktu has a great university. But you haven't said very much about the city itself. You'll be hundreds

A 19th-century rendering of Timbuktu. Where might the university have been located?

of miles from here. You'll hardly see your family and friends during the next few years. What is there in Timbuktu besides the university that would encourage you to leave Gao?"

"Well," replied Akbar, "I never thought that Gao was a great place to live. The houses are unpleasant and almost all alike. If I had the nerve, I'd call Gao ugly!"

"Does that make Timbuktu beautiful?"

"No, Ahmad. But there are many attractive buildings. As for food, the markets there have many things that we don't have here in Gao. But I think that our markets have much more bread and meat than those of Timbuktu. And you can't beat Gao's melons, cucumbers, and pumpkins. And I know I'll miss my family and friends. My father has offered to help me get started in business if I stay in Gao."

"Does that mean that you might decide to give up your studies and stay home?" asked Ahmad.

"No, it doesn't," replied Akbar. "I may decide to become a doctor, or a lawyer, or, perhaps, a cleric. But whatever I decide to do, the University of Sankore in Timbuktu is the place where I'll make my decision."

Postscript

In the time of Akbar and Ahmad, visitors to Timbuktu reported that it had a magnificent royal palace. There were many shops run by African craftspeople, and the markets sold European goods. The city was a center of learning. Students from all over the Muslim world studied at the university. Its teachers of law, literature, medicine, and religion were admired throughout the Islamic world.

In 1591 the Moroccans of northwest Africa defeated the Songhai army. The empire of Songhai was destroyed. Today, Timbuktu is a small town in Mali, far away from most traveled roads. There is nothing about present-day Timbuktu to suggest that it was once a city of great wealth and scholarship.

QUESTIONS FOR REVIEW

1. How did Songhai become powerful?
2. Why was Songhai prosperous?
3. Why did Akbar think that Gao was different from Timbuktu?
4. Why was it difficult for Akbar to decide what to study at the university?
5. According to Akbar, how was Gao superior to Timbuktu?

UNDERSTANDING THE STORY

A. Write T for each statement that is true and F for each statement that is false.

1. Songhai had an efficient banking system and a code of laws.
2. Songhai failed to control the trade routes in gold and salt.
3. The market scales in Gao were inaccurate because they were not checked by government inspectors.
4. In Gao, the people bought and sold almost everything.
5. Akbar did not speak to any university students in Timbuktu.

6. Akbar thought that the city of Gao was ugly.
7. Akbar's father offered to help him get started in business if he stayed in Gao.
8. Timbuktu was never a center of learning.

B. Compare the University of Sankore (Timbuktu) with a college or university in or near your city or town. Include the following: (*a*) courses offered (*b*) campus (*c*) where students come from (*d*) degrees offered.

ACTIVITIES AND INQUIRIES

1. Assume that you are a high school senior and are applying for admission to a number of colleges. Would you apply to the University of Sankore? Why or why not?
2. Prepare a table comparing the cities of Timbuktu and Gao in the following areas: (*a*) commerce and industry (*b*) housing (*c*) food (*d*) center of learning or culture.
3. Assume that you are a student at the University of Sankore. How would you convince Akbar that he should join you in your subject area?
4. Akbar's father wanted his son to start a business in Gao. What can the father say to convince Akbar that he should change his mind about studying in Timbuktu?
5. Imagine that you are a businessperson from another country. What is there about Songhai that encourages you to trade there?

4. Europeans Sail to the Americas

While people like the Polos were traveling east to the lands of Asia, others had a dream about traveling in the opposite direction. They believed that by sailing west from Europe, they would reach India and China, and the Spice Islands.

Christopher Columbus and other European sea captains sailed to the west, hoping to make that dream come true. But the continents of North and South America blocked the way to the riches of the Orient. Instead, Columbus landed on islands in the Caribbean Sea. He thought that he had reached India, however, and therefore called the people "Indians." Actually, the people Columbus "discovered" in the Americas were the descendants of migratory people from Asia who had arrived thousands of years earlier. He never found the gold, silver, spices, and precious gems of the Orient. But his explorations made his four trips worthwhile.

In this story, Queen Isabella of Spain thinks back over her years as ruler. She has vivid memories of Columbus and his dreams. See if you agree with her selection of the most important act of her reign. Was she really responsible for the creation of the Spanish Empire?

Seville   1504

The other night, my son Charles asked me what I thought had been the most important or best act of my service as queen of Spain. I brushed him aside with a brief remark about there having been so many good things. Actually, though, I simply was not prepared to answer at that point.

Now I wonder. This is the twentieth year of my reign as queen. So many things have happened. Marrying Ferdinand was important and exciting. We did many good things for Spain. Who can deny the importance of driving the Jews and the Moors out of our country? We united Spain and made it into a truly Catholic country. The Inquisition keeps it that way. We have ruled firmly and well. The nobles may not be too happy, but our nation is strong.

Yes, we have done so many things for Spain. In my mind, though, one thing always seems to come first. I am proudest of my support for Christopher Columbus. When he first came to see us in 1486, I knew that he was a man to believe in. He was a most convincing charmer. He could make a believer of almost anyone. He insisted that by sailing about 3,000 miles to the west from Spain, he would come to the gold, silks, and spices of India, China, and the Spice Islands.

I believed in him from the beginning, even though my commissioners would not accept his plan. They insisted that the ocean was too wide to sail across to Asia! Anyway, with the

Columbus (left) tells Queen Isabella and King Ferdinand of Spain about people and lands that Europeans never knew existed before his westward voyages.

war going on against the Moors in Granada, there simply wasn't money for expeditions.

Columbus never gave up! He returned five years later, and I believed in him even more strongly this time. But what demands he made upon us! I think that if it had been anyone but Columbus, I would have had him thrown into jail without another thought.

The nerve of Columbus! There he was begging support for his

voyage to the unknown, but still insisting that he be named "Admiral of the Ocean Sea"! He wanted 10 percent of all of the profits and had to be viceroy of all islands he discovered. That ridiculous man went on and on. In April 1492 I finally agreed to what he wanted. Why did I do it? He wanted too much. But somehow I knew that he would make some great discoveries. And he was such a charming man!

He never found the Spice Islands or China and India. He never found much of the wealth he promised either, but he discovered people and lands that we Europeans never knew existed. All were claimed in the name of Spain.

THE FOUR VOYAGES OF CHRISTOPHER COLUMBUS 1492–1504

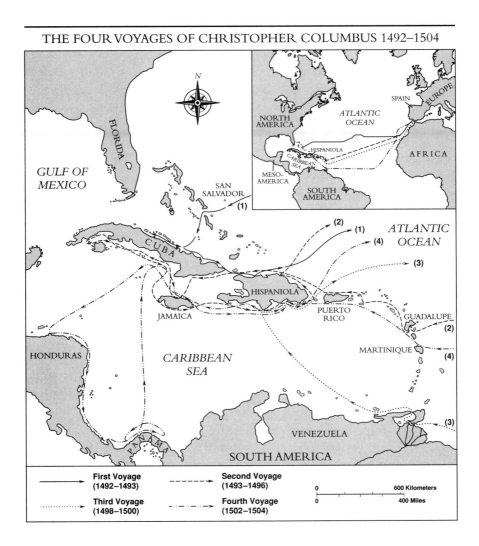

	First Voyage (1492–1493)		Second Voyage (1493–1496)
	Third Voyage (1498–1500)		Fourth Voyage (1502–1504)

I read his detailed letters with pleasure and worry. His food was poor; the crew was hard to control. He often wrote that the people were hostile or the climate was bad. But I always knew that he would succeed, and he did. We gave him a hero's welcome on his return to Spain!

Four times he sailed from Spain. He found many islands and the coast of South America. He even named a colony after me on the island of Hispaniola. Yes, he did much for Spain and the world.

Why then did I approve of his arrest and imprisonment after his third voyage? Why did I believe the stories told by jealous liars? Perhaps he wasn't the best leader in the world, but why should that be so important? What if he did not find all the gold he had promised? Was there ever a man more dedicated to his purpose and to his queen?

I am so happy that he was given a fourth chance to sail to the Americas. I wonder what great stories he will tell me when he returns this time. What new wealth will he bring back for me? For his sake and mine, I pray that he finds a passage to India. Even if he finds nothing, I will welcome him. Please God, have him hurry back to Spain. I want so much to see him again. I know that I do not have too many months left on earth.

What have I, Isabella, accomplished in a lifetime? I am the mother of the empire of Spain.

Postscript

In the 1490s and 1500s, many other explorers followed the lead of Columbus. John Cabot, sailing for the English king in 1497, explored the east coast of Canada and claimed it for England. Three years later, Pedro Cabral, sailing for Portugal, arrived in Brazil. Also in 1500, Vicente Pinzón explored the Brazilian coast and reached the Amazon River.

Amerigo Vespucci also explored the coast of Brazil, for Spain, in 1501–1502. This voyage convinced Europeans that the lands which were being explored were not Asia but part of a new, previously unknown continent. The Spanish monarchs rewarded Vespucci with the title "master navigator." His first name, Amerigo, was used as the basis for calling the Western Hemisphere the Americas.

In 1513 Vasco Balboa marched across the Isthmus of Panama until he came to a vast body of water. He named it the Pacific Ocean and claimed it for Spain. In 1519 the Portuguese navigator Ferdinand Magellan sailed with a fleet of five ships from Spain to South America. In 1520 he sailed around the southern coast of South America and crossed the Pacific to the East Indies. Magellan was killed in a battle in the Philippines in 1521, but his ships continued across the Indian Ocean and around Africa. One remaining ship reached Spain in 1522. Magellan's expedition is honored for having proved that the world is round.

Both Spain and Portugal claimed the same lands in the Americas. The pope was asked to settle the dispute. He drew an imaginary line in the Atlantic Ocean between the North and South poles. The lands to the west of the line were to be Spain's; those to the east were Portugal's. This meant that in South America Portugal could claim Brazil. All the rest of the Americas belonged to Spain.

QUESTIONS FOR REVIEW

1. Why was Columbus unable to reach India and China by sailing west from Spain?
2. Why did Isabella think that her support of Columbus was her most important achievement?
3. What did Columbus ask of Isabella before he would sail?
4. Why was Isabella eager to see Columbus upon his return to Spain after his fourth voyage?
5. What were the accomplishments of other explorers in the 1490s and 1500s?

UNDERSTANDING THE STORY

A. Tell which of the following statements are true.

1. Columbus believed that the earth was round.
2. Columbus at first thought that he had sailed to India.
3. Columbus married Queen Isabella.
4. Ferdinand and Isabella united Spain.
5. Isabella never trusted Columbus.
6. Columbus was given the title Admiral of the Ocean Sea.
7. Columbus arrived at islands in the Caribbean instead of India.
8. Columbus had excellent food and good crews on all of his voyages.

B. Imagine that Columbus is alive today. He wants the government of the United States to pay for his exploration of the planet Mars.

Would you want the government to pay for his trip? Explain your answer. Would you go along? Why or why not? Which do you think takes more courage: the voyage to the Americas or the exploration of Mars? Explain.

ACTIVITIES AND INQUIRIES

1. Look at the map of Columbus' voyages on page 207. Copy the map in your notebook. Draw a line showing the route you would have followed from Spain if you had been Columbus. Compare your route with the ones that Columbus took.
2. Pretend that you are Columbus at the court of Queen Isabella of Spain. Write a letter to the queen. Explain why you want her to help you make your voyage to the Indies. In your letter underline the ideas that you think would be most convincing.
3. Pretend that you are Queen Isabella. Write a letter to Columbus. Tell him what you think of this idea of sailing west.
4. Go to the library. Read more about Columbus' voyages. Be prepared to talk about one of them in class.
5. Imagine that you are one of the crew sailing with Columbus on his first voyage. Make a drawing of your ship. Write a diary describing your experiences on one or two days of your voyage.

5. A Monk Rebels

This unit is concerned with change. We have seen how explorers opened new worlds. Old ways of thinking were challenged, and many questions were asked.

In Europe, the Catholic Church was being challenged during this period. The pope and other Church officials often had to yield to the power of strong kings. Some people even began to ask serious questions about the role of the clergy.

Martin Luther was a monk who seriously felt that many things in the Church were wrong and had to be changed or reformed. For example, he said that the sale of indulgences (pardons for sins) should be stopped. He believed that one could not substitute indulgences for the faith of the people. Finally, he could stand it no longer. In October 1517 he nailed 95 theses (ideas to be debated publicly) to the door of the church at Wittenberg, Germany. These theses were printed and read all over Europe. People were excited and upset. The authority of the Church was challenged. Perhaps the Church did not have absolute control over everything that was right and true. Those who complained and wished to make changes and reforms in the Catholic Church were called protestors, or protestants. This movement was called the *Protestant Reformation*.

In the letter that follows, Martin Luther expresses to a friend his feelings about religion and the Church. See if you understand and agree with Luther's feelings about the Church. Do you think that he was really trying to reform the Church? Or was he eager to become a very powerful man?

Wittenberg 1526

Dear Kurt,

I am terribly sorry that I have not been able to answer your letter of several months ago until today. You can guess that I have been very busy.

You ask me many questions that are very difficult to answer. Why did I leave the Church and become its enemy? There is so much to say and so much to explain that I would never finish this letter to you. I know that you are unhappy with what I have done, but they left me no choice. Believe me, Kurt, when I say to you that all I wanted to do was to make a few changes. My Church had strayed from the path of true religion. My job was to reform it, to bring it back to its real purpose. All I wanted was that people be saved from sin and find salvation by having faith in God. Faith was the answer, but they would not listen to me, a poor monk!

I write to you, Kurt, as my oldest and dearest friend. I will never forget the fun and good times of our childhood. It was a simple life; we were very poor. But our fathers worked hard in the mines to feed and clothe us. There was always food on the table; that and the fresh air and the mountain beauty were all we needed to live. Remember how we loved the snow and hated and feared the fog? Remember how we talked of the future? We decided to leave our beloved mountains and study law.

In those early days, I honestly had no desire to follow the religious life. Then it happened! In July 1505 I was thrown to the ground by a bolt of lightning! For the first time, I saw death. I was afraid that this was the end for me. I cried out, "Saint Anne, help me! I will become a monk." That moment of intense fear passed as death went on its way.

That promise to my father's saint saved my life. I could not back away. I had to become a monk. My father and your father protested—they cried and argued. It was no use. I had to do it! So I joined the Augustinians.

I was happy with the simple, harsh life of the monastery. I thought it was God's will that this was where I would spend the rest of my days. But it was not to be. I was ordered to teach Bible classes at the University of Wittenberg. What of it, you might very well ask. When I started preparing my lectures, I began to understand what God meant in his Bible.

Now I saw that the Bible was the written record of our God. There were his words for all to see. I asked myself, How can the people read and understand his divine words? They are written in Latin! Most people cannot read Latin. The answer came to me at last: Translate the words of God into the language of the people. I knew than that I must rewrite the Bible in German! Each person must be able to read and explain the meaning of the stories of God's Bible as he or she wishes. No one needs the help of a priest to understand the Bible!

I knew something else. I knew that God did not want the money or the lands of sinners. I do not have to tell you that salvation cannot be bought. I saw Tetzel selling indulgences, and I exploded. What right did he have to sell salvation? What right did he have to speak for the pope and the Catholic Church? Then I realized —Tetzel was their appointed representative!

I understood then that people do not need priests to speak to God for them. God speaks and listens to all. Why should a person ask forgiveness for sins through a priest? Worst of all, why should we pay someone to be forgiven by God? This is not the way of God! You cannot sell religion!

I went up to the church and hammered a list of 95 theses onto the front door. You did not approve; you felt that I was going too far too fast. I must disagree with you, dear friend. The

"I went up to the church and hammered a list of 95 theses onto the front door."

holy Church and its leaders had gone too far. They had lost sight of the true meaning of God and religion. They forgot that they must be absolutely pure, honest, and sincere.

Now we come to your question about the "good life." You think that I am in favor of a dull, boring existence. Not so! Give away your fancy clothes, your foreign spices, and your profits from business. This will force you to think more of

God. Your life will not be dull. You will be much more aware of the world around you, just as you were when we were young. Stop all of this overeating and drinking. Think more of other people's needs!

Put a stop to wanting so much that we do not need and we will stop war and senseless killing. You write that my attacks on the Church have led to war and bloodshed. You wonder how I can justify all of this fighting when I say that I am a man of peace. This is an excellent question about a situation that I hate. You know that I detest killing. The fighting must and will stop. First, princes and kings will have to stop hiding behind the pope and the Church. They must stop using the Church as an excuse for fighting against the Protestant nobles. These Catholic princes want the Protestants' land and money. Soon, I hope, all people will understand the importance of the simple life. Fighting will stop, and peace will be with us.

No, I do not feel that I am a revolutionist. All I want is a church that will help people to develop faith in our God. Some day, the Catholic Church will realize that it is not the only voice of God. There are other voices and other ways.

My wife, Kathie, joins me in sending our sincerest wishes for your peace and happiness.

Your friend,
MARTIN LUTHER

Postscript

Martin Luther's protests had wide influence. His followers insisted that they should have the right to explain the Bible and choose their own priests. Others joined them, for religious, political, or economic reasons. The absolute authority of the Church over the lives of the people was questioned in many lands.

The German peasants had many grievances against their noble lords. Taxes were high, and the peasants had to work on the lords' lands as well as their own. Much of the richest land was owned by the Church or the nobility. The peasants could not hunt or fish on these rich lands. In 1524 the peasants revolted, but Luther refused to support them after they burned castles and monasteries. The peasants' revolt was crushed, but about half of the German nobility became Protestants.

Luther's ideas spread across Europe. Over the years, Lutheranism became the state religion of Scandinavia. In about half of Switzerland, John Calvin's form of Protestantism replaced Catholicism. In Scotland, Calvinists were known as Presbyterians; in England, they were known as Puritans. In the Netherlands, Calvinists founded the Dutch Reformed Church.

Most of northern Europe was Protestant by the year 1600. Catholicism remained the accepted religion of Spain, Portugal, France, Italy, Poland, the southern Netherlands, southern Germany, and half of Switzerland.

QUESTIONS FOR REVIEW

1. Why did Martin Luther insist on stopping the sale of indulgences?
2. Why did Luther translate the Bible from Latin into German?
3. Why did Luther hammer his list of 95 theses (arguments or reasons) onto the door of the church at Wittenberg?
4. Why did Luther tell his friend Kurt to stop thinking of his own wants?
5. What were the grievances of the German peasants against their noble lords?

UNDERSTANDING THE STORY

A. Martin Luther had strong feelings about many things. Tell which statements Martin Luther made or might have made.

1. Salvation cannot be bought.
2. People need priests to speak to God for them.
3. People need priests to ask God's forgiveness for their sins.
4. While all priests cannot be saints, they must be honest, sincere, and decent.
5. People should think more of God.
6. People should dress in fancy clothes and live and eat well.
7. Religion must help people think more of God and others' needs.
8. The Catholic Church should not be the only Christian church.

B. Martin Luther dared to challenge and change the Catholic Church. Suppose that Luther were alive today. Would he challenge religion in America? Why? If your answer is "yes," how would he do it? Do you think he would succeed? Explain.

ACTIVITIES AND INQUIRIES

1. Look at the illustration of Martin Luther at Wittenberg on page 213. What do you think would be a good title for this picture? Why? What does it tell you about the type of man Martin Luther was?
2. Make a list of the things in your life that you think should be changed. Give reasons for your choices.
3. Go to the library. Prepare a report on another Protestant reformer of the 16th century. How was his thinking similar to that of Martin Luther? How was it different from Luther's thinking?
4. Imagine that you are Martin Luther's friend Kurt. You are a loyal Catholic. Answer Luther's letter.

6. The Blood-Stained Road to Gold

The Portuguese took the lead in exploring the unknown parts of the globe in search of people, places, and goods to buy and sell. Their ships, called caravels, were faster and safer than those of their rivals. The voyages of Vasco da Gama and Bartolomeu Diaz proved that long sea voyages to remote new lands were possible. The way was open to explore and settle the continents that Columbus had found. In 1500 Pedro Cabral, while en route to India, reached the shores of what is now Brazil. The vast country was to become Portugal's South American kingdom.

Spain soon became the leader in American explorations, however. Vasco Balboa discovered the Pacific Ocean after crossing the Isthmus of Panama in 1513. Three years later, Juan Díaz de Solís explored the Rio de la Plata in South America.

Spain gained control of much of Mesoamerica and South America (except Brazil) because of the efforts of explorer–adventurers called *conquistadors* (conquerors). These were men looking for gold and fame. (Some also were eager to convert the Native Americans to Christianity.) For example, Hernando Cortés, with 550 men, 16 horses, and a few cannons, conquered the Aztec Empire of Mexico. In 1523 the Spanish king, Charles V, named Cortés governor and captain-general of New Spain.

Francisco Pizarro, unlike Cortés, was uneducated and poor. He was a fearless and brutal conquistador who could not sign his own name. He had been with Balboa when he discovered the Pacific Ocean. In the 1520s Pizarro was living quietly in his home in Panama, when he heard rumors of great treasure to be found in the land of the Inca (present-day Peru). He was then almost 50 years of age, an elderly man in those times, but nothing could keep him from his dream of finding a great fortune. In 1524 he began the series of explorations that culminated in the conquest described in the story. (See the Inca Empire map on page 182.)

Cajamarca 1533

"Diego de Almagro, I'd almost forgotten about you," gasped Francisco Pizarro. "Where are the men you were supposed to bring?"

"Is this how you greet your long-time partner?" replied the exhausted Almagro. "You can see them in the distance. I rode ahead to get here as quickly as possible. Tell me all that has happened."

"We spent almost two years struggling to get from Panama to this valley of Cajamarca," said Pizarro. "Suddenly, facing us were thousands of howling Inca warriors led by King Atahualpha. What chance of success did my little army of fewer than two hundred have?"

"What did you do?'

"I sent my horsemen to call on Atahualpa," said Pizarro. They did some trick riding in front of his house. The Inca were stunned and frightened by the horses. Then, I invited the king and his followers to visit us the next day."

"Wasn't that dangerous?"

"Perhaps, but we had to be brave and pretend that we were in control," answered Pizarro. "At noon, Atahualpa appeared on a golden throne, surrounded by thousands of his men. I knew we couldn't fight them face-to-face. Surprise was the only solution. I gave the signal. My horsemen rode among the Inca. The Inca were frightened and ran wildly in all directions.

Their spears, bows, and arrows were no match for our cannon. We slaughtered most of them and took Atahualpa prisoner."

"What's the point of holding him?" Asked Almagro.

"He thinks he can buy his freedom in exchange for gold. For two months his Inca warriors have brought their gold treasures to us. You won't believe this, Almagro, but we now have enough gold to fill a huge room."

Pizarro took Almagro to see the gold-filled room.

"How are you going to move those bulky things back over the mountains?" asked Almagro. "And how are you going to give each of us his proper share of the loot?"

"Easy," smiled Pizarro for the first time. "I'm having the Inca goldsmiths melt down everything and cast it into gold bars.

The Inca ruler, Atahualpa (center), meets the Spanish conquistador, Pizarro (left), in the city of Cajamarca.

One-fifth goes off to Spain. The rest is for us—and our men."

"You are generous," grinned Almagro. "I congratulate you. You have discovered El Dorado (the country of gold), which all the conquistadors have been seeking. We must thank God for our good fortune."

"I agree, let us thank God. But we must also not forget to thank our horses. We could never have defeated the Inca without them!"

Postscript

Pizarro had the Inca ruler executed for "treason" in 1533. He then pushed on to the Inca capital of Cuzco and stripped that city of its gold. He understood that Cuzco was too far inland to be the center of his Spanish government. Thus, in 1535 he built the seacoast city of Lima, "the city of kings."

In 1537 Almagro returned from a long, useless trip across the Andes and the Chilean desert to find that Pizarro was in complete control of the new empire. Learning that he was no longer Pizarro's "partner," Almagro rebelled. But his army was defeated, and in 1538 he was executed. Several years later, Almagro's men avenged his death by killing Pizarro in his own city of Lima.

Other Spanish conquistadors added to Spain's empire. Francisco de Orellana crossed the Andes from Ecuador to the Brazilian jungles. He and his small group then explored more than 2,000 miles of the Amazon River to the Atlantic Ocean. They were the first Europeans to explore this great river. In 1541 Pedro de Valdivia built the city of Santiago, in Chile.

In the Americas, the conquistadors conquered an area twice the size of Europe. It was almost 100 years before the English would begin their conquests in North America.

QUESTIONS FOR REVIEW

1. Why were the Portuguese able to take the lead in exploration?
2. Outline the achievements of the sea captains who sailed for Spain.
3. How did the conquistadors create a Spanish Empire in the Americas?
4. How was Pizarro able to defeat the huge army of Atahualpa?
5. Why did Almagro tell Pizarro that the latter had discovered El Dorado?

UNDERSTANDING THE STORY

A. Write P for each statement that Pizarro would have agreed with and N for each statement he would have disagreed with.

1. I had Atahualpa, the Inca ruler, executed.
2. Almagro will always be my trusted partner.
3. It's too bad that we did not bring our horses with us to the Americas.
4. We faced thousands of Inca warriors.
5. My horsemen did some trick riding.
6. I wish the Inca had had some gold to bring us.
7. We will melt down the Inca gold and cast it into gold bars.
8. It took us less than one month to get from Panama to Cajamarca.

B. Pizarro was a fearless explorer. Imagine that he was given the opportunity to become an astronaut. Would he have accepted? Why or why not? Assume that he became an astronaut. Would he have been successful? Explain your answer.

ACTIVITIES AND INQUIRIES

1. Assume that you are a radio commentator. You interview Atahualpa. What questions would you ask him about Pizarro and the Spanish soldiers? How might he reply?
2. Next you interview Pizarro. What questions do you ask him about the Inca? What are his answers?
3. Did Pizarro treat Almagro unfairly? Explain. Should Almagro have known what to expect? Explain. Imagine that Pizarro is on trial for Almagro's execution. What would be Pizarro's defense?
4. Make a table listing the names of the Spanish conquistadors in column A. In column B, indicate the accomplishments of each. In column C, tell whether this was a plus or minus for Spain and for the rest of the Western world.
5. Draw a map of Central and South America, or copy the map on page 245. Point out Spanish and Portuguese possessions. Show which conquistador was responsible for the conquest of each area.

7. A Scientist Challenges the Past

During the European Middle Ages, people had been taught that life on earth was not as important as life after death. By the 1300s and 1400s, however, this outlook was changing. Many people were living better. They were looking forward to a good life on earth rather than later.

The Italian writers Petrarch and Boccaccio, who were called *humanists*, stressed the importance of life for human beings. The humanists got many of their ideas from the writers of ancient Greece and Rome. The ancient authors had said that people should be the measure of all things. In their excitement, the humanists felt that they and their world were being born again. This rebirth or revival of interest in people and the writings of the past is called the *Renaissance*.

At the same time, Renaissance artists such as Leonardo da Vinci, Raphael, and Michelangelo painted and sculpted men and women as living creatures, not as dull, blank figures. The artists of the Renaissance studied the human body and learned a great deal about how people moved. They sought to show how people looked when they were happy, sad, or tired.

So too in the 1500s and 1600s, daring scientists had new ideas about how to study and understand the world. They challenged what the ancient writers and the Catholic Church had said about the earth and the sun. These scientists looked around them. They observed nature, saw how people lived, and learned that the earth moved around the sun.

They asked questions and searched for answers. Sometimes they found the answers. If they did not, they kept searching. One of these searchers for truth was Galileo Galilei, who made several important discoveries.

In the selection that follows, Galileo is about to appear before the Inquisition to explain his discoveries. This court seeks to uphold the teachings of the Church. Galileo will be given a choice of life or death. If he insists that the earth moves around the sun, he will die. If he denies what he knows to be true, he will live. Given these same choices, what would you have done? How can Galileo be so sure that he is right and that the teachings of the Church are wrong?

Rome   1633

To think that I have come to this! If I do not admit that I am wrong, I will be executed! I will be remembered for all time as a heretic who denied the truth of the teachings of the Church. Yet I, Galileo Galilei, have always been faithful to my Church and to the discoveries of science. Now I am told that I cannot believe in both science and God.

The Church says that the earth is the center of the universe. I know better. I have read and tested the theories of Copernicus. A hundred years ago, he proved by mathematics that the earth moves around the sun. I made my own telescope because I wanted to test his ideas. People asked how the astronomy of the Bible could be wrong. It was an insane idea to think that the teachings of the Church have been false for so many centuries. But my eyes did not betray me. Copernicus was right. The earth is not the center of the universe. How excited I was when I saw the rings of Saturn, the moons of

"In my heart of hearts, I know there is much to be discovered and explored. We must experiment and experience as much as we can."

Jupiter, and the countless stars of the Milky Way. These were my eyes, my telescope, making my discoveries!

We know the things we can see and prove. Is there any other possibility? There cannot be. Perhaps I was wrong to think that I could know more than the great scholars of my Church. If it is true that we are made in God's image, then we must be at the center of the universe. Are there not mysteries and spirits that we cannot understand? Only God knows all. The leaders of his Church can explain the meaning of life to us.

That is what I am supposed to believe. But in my heart of hearts I know that there is much to be discovered and explored. No one, not even the holy Church, knows the answers to all the mysteries!

If we are to find the answer to the riddle of the universe, we must never stop looking. We must experiment and experience as much as we can. Blind faith is not my way of life. I cannot accept whatever I am told simply because it has been said by the Church.

When I wanted to find the speed of falling objects, I dropped some weights from the top of the Leaning Tower of Pisa. I experimented, I saw, and I made my conclusions.

The other day I heard an argument in the street. Five grown men were arguing about the number of teeth in a horse's mouth. The horse was standing right there, but no one thought of opening the animal's mouth and counting its teeth. In fact, no one even looked at the horse! This argument went on for over an hour. I suggested checking the horse's mouth, and I was rewarded by being pushed rudely aside. There was no conclusion to the argument. The people went away confused and angry. Is this the way to learn the answers?

Enough of these wandering thoughts! I must make up my mind. I know that I can have faith in my God and still search for answers. The Church fathers do not agree. They say I must give up my search for learning, destroy my book, agree that the sun moves around the earth. They want me to stop my experiments and accept the ways of God and of the Church.

I don't want to accept blindly, but if I am to see another sunrise, I must give in. I must pretend to believe. I wonder—is it better to live a lie than to die and face the unknown?

Postscript

To save his life, Galileo told the judges of the Inquisition that the earth was the center of the universe. However, as he left the courtroom, he whispered, "All the same, the earth does move." Galileo was placed under arrest at his home in Arcetri, near the city of Florence, and remained there until his death in 1642.

Many agree that Galileo, more than any other person, deserves to be called the founder of modern science. His work on the laws of motion was extremely important, as were his discoveries of sunspots and the moons of the planet Jupiter. He discovered that the Milky Way was a vast array of stars. Galileo's experiments were skillful, and his measurements were highly accurate.

QUESTIONS FOR REVIEW

1. How did scientists in the sixteenth and seventeenth centuries challenge the ideas of the past?
2. What was the achievement of Copernicus?
3. Why did Galileo find it impossible to believe that the earth was the center of the universe?
4. Why was Galileo upset about how the crowd he encountered decided on the number of teeth in a horse's mouth?
5. Why did Galileo tell the Inquisitors that he was wrong, and the earth was the center of the universe?

UNDERSTANDING THE STORY

A. Write T for each statement that is true and O for each statement that is an opinion.

1. Galileo was the greatest scientist of all time.
2. Galileo looked through his telescope to see planets and stars.
3. Galileo should not have looked beyond the earth.
4. The Inquisition should not have tried Galileo.
5. Galileo studied the speed of falling objects.
6. A scientist should do whatever he or she thinks best.
7. Galileo wondered why he had to lie to the Inquisition.
8. No one should drop weights from a tall building.

B. Imagine that you are Galileo. You are accused of heresy by the

Church. Would you act in the same way that Galileo did? Explain your answer. Are there people today who, like Galileo, are placed on trial for their ideas? Explain.

ACTIVITIES AND INQUIRIES

1. Make a drawing of Galileo sitting in his prison cell. What is he thinking? Make up a title for your drawing.
2. Imagine that you are a lawyer. Would you rather defend or prosecute Galileo? Prepare your case.
3. Go to the library. Prepare a report on another scientist of the Renaissance. Why was this person not placed on trial?
4. Pretend that you are Galileo. You have been arrested by the Inquisition. Write a letter to a friend explaining why you are in prison.

8. A Ruler Builds a Great Tomb

For over 500 years, waves of Muslim invaders from Turkey, Persia, and Afghanistan marched into India to seize territory. Their goal was to gain control of the capital city of Delhi and its surrounding areas. The ruler of Delhi was called the sultan. The governors of the provinces were supposed to obey the sultan's orders, but generally they ruled as they pleased.

Princes and governors made many attempts to overthrow the Delhi sultans. The sultans' lives were in constant danger. Throughout India, local rulers battled one another. There simply was no one leader who was powerful enough to rule more than a small section of India at any given time.

This changed when the Mughals swept into India from Afghanistan in 1526. Their empire lasted over 200 years. Babar, the first Mughal emperor, was a descendant of the Mongol conqueror Tamerlane, who had captured Delhi in 1398. (Tamerlane did not stay in Delhi, but left the deserted city to return to Samarkand.) Babar ousted the Delhi sultans and gained control over northern and central India. Unlike Tamerlane, Babar stayed in Delhi.

Babar's grandson Akbar continued the conquest of India. He also conquered Afghanistan. Akbar was in power for nearly 50 years (1556–1605). Although he was a Muslim, he married a Hindu woman. He repealed the tax that all non-Muslims were forced to pay. Akbar also encouraged both Hindu and Muslim artists.

Akbar brought peace to the country for the first time in over a thousand years. The Mughals never conquered all of India, but they ruled more of the subcontinent than anyone since Alexander the Great (see Unit II).

The Mughal emperor we meet here is Shah Jahan, who ruled from 1627 to 1658. We find him thinking back over his years as ruler.

Delhi   1650

I know I shouldn't be annoyed by the questions that visitors ask me. But I hate it when all they want to know is why I built the Taj Mahal. They never ask about the other great buildings erected during my reign, such as the Hall of Private Audience, with its Peacock Throne, in the Red Fort here in

The Taj Mahal.

Delhi. Nor do they have any questions about how I built and ran this vast empire. I, at least, think it was a job well done.

"Why did you build something so beautiful for just one of your wives?" they ask. "Why did you have to use white marble and all those precious stones? And that beautiful garden: There's nothing like it in all of India!"

My answer is always the same. "Mumtaz Mahal was my favorite wife. Here she has a tomb worthy of a great empress." To myself, I add: She was my one true love.

Perhaps I should tell those fools that there are many other beautiful tombs built by past rulers. They are all over northern India, especially in Delhi and Lahore. They are not quite as handsome as the Taj. But in most of them you approach the tomb in a similar way: through a narrow gateway. The pools in front of the Taj reflect the onion-domed tomb. Few tombs have four narrow minarets (towers) reaching to the sky, as the Taj does. And how many are made entirely of marble?

It took over 15 years and a good portion of my treasury to build this tomb. Over 20,000 people worked on the building. How the peasants complained about the high taxes! But the

Shah Jahan: "The Taj Mahal will be admired for centuries. Doesn't that make the labor and the expense worthwhile?"
Do you agree?

Taj will be admired for centuries after my death. Doesn't that make the labors of the people and the expense worthwhile?

I am very proud of another achievement. Thanks to the wealth of our empire, I am able to give large amounts of money to the holy places of Medina and Mecca. The money is then used for charity and good works throughout the world of Islam. People everywhere thus profit by the riches of our kingdom.

But I still have a number of worries. First and foremost, who will succeed me when I am gone? Each of my four sons thinks that he should rule the empire when I am no longer able to do so. I fear that they will start a civil war among themselves to gain power. I fear great bloodshed and suffering. I hope that I am wrong.

Postscript

In the late 1650s, Shah Jahan's fears came true. He became ill, and the fight to succeed him began. After a long series of battles, the shah's favored sons lost power, the shah was imprisoned, and his son Aurangzeb took the throne. After his death in 1666, Shah Jahan's remains were placed in the Taj Mahal, next to Mumtaz's coffin.

Aurangzeb taxed the Hindu people heavily and destroyed many of their temples. His wars against other rulers gained territory but weakened the Mughal Empire. After his death in 1707, the Mughals were no longer able to protect their traders against their Hindu enemies in the south. The Mughal Empire split in two: the Nizam of Hyderabab became the most powerful ruler in central India, while the Mughals still held on in the north.

In 1738 the Persians destroyed the city of Delhi, but they did not stay in India. And the Mughal army was defeated by the Afghans in 1760 at Panipat. As a result of these events, no one group was in control in northern India. India was ripe for yet another invasion—by tradespeople and then armies from Europe. We will discuss this European "invasion" in Unit VIII, Imperialism.

QUESTIONS FOR REVIEW

1. How did the Indian government change when the Mughals entered India in 1526?

THE MUGHAL EMPIRE IN 1650 AND 1700

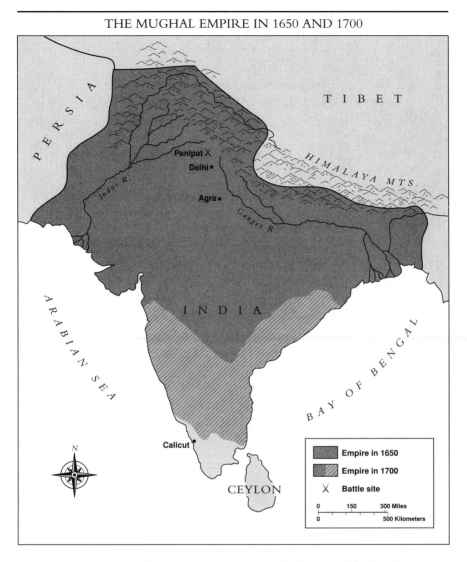

2. How were conditions in India improved during Akbar's rule?
3. Why did Shah Jahan build the Taj Mahal?
4. Describe the Taj Mahal.
5. How did the Mughal Empire change in the early 1700s?

UNDERSTANDING THE STORY

A. Write T for each statement that is true and F for each statement that is false.

1. For over 500 years, waves of Christian invaders marched into India from Turkey and Persia.
2. Throughout India, local rulers battled one another.
3. Akbar conquered Afghanistan.
4. The Taj Mahal was the only great building erected by Shah Jahan.
5. Mumtaz Mahal was Shah Jahan's beloved wife.
6. All the royal tombs in India were decorated with four narrow minarets.
7. Shah Jahan did not believe in helping others through charity.
8. Aurangzeb, Jahan's son, taxed the people heavily.

B. What would Shah Jahan think of modern skyscrapers, your local city hall, the White House, the Washington Monument, and the Lincoln Memorial? Explain your reasoning.

ACTIVITIES AND INQUIRIES

1. Visit your school or local library. Prepare a report on the Taj Mahal. Include: (*a*) architectural design (*b*) comparisons with several famous buildings in this and other countries (*c*) explanations of why these other buildings were erected.
2. Suppose that you were given the contract to design a tomb for a very wealthy person. Prepare a plan and tell about your ideas for the building.
3. What can you learn about India and its rulers from studying the Taj Mahal?
4. Akbar encouraged both Hindus and Muslims, and he married a Hindu woman. Why was this unusual? Suppose this policy of religious toleration had continued throughout the centuries. Might it have helped to avert later struggles between Hindus and Muslims in India?
5. Imagine that you are an architect. You are asked to design a building that will be a duplicate (copy) of the Taj Mahal. Would you accept the assignment? Why or why not? What problems would you face if you took the job?

UNIT VI

Absolutism Versus Freedom

This unit spans nearly six hundred years, from 1215 to 1812. We witness the rise and fall of absolute rulers and their empires in Europe, South America, and Asia. We see wars and revolutions and the sowing of the seeds of modern democratic government. We learn of a man's struggle for freedom in the United States against seemingly overwhelming odds.

Europe. Our first story takes place in England, in the year 1215. An unpopular king was forced to give up some of his absolute powers. The document he signed became a landmark in the history of free people.

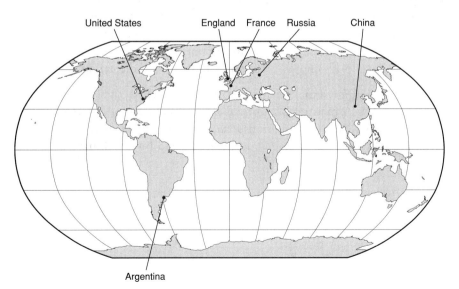

Three centuries later, in the mid-1600s, an English king stubbornly maintained that he could rule as he pleased because he answered only to God. But the English Parliament insisted that the king seek its approval and support for his actions. Our story tells of the outcome of the struggle.

South America. Spain extracted great wealth from the colonies in its South American empire. But some people in Argentina in the 1600s were beginning to rebel against Spain's restrictive policies. They sought the freedom to make their own decisions and run their lives.

Asia. In China, also in the 1600s, a non-Chinese people, the Manchus, took control. They imposed their own laws and customs on the Chinese people. But history had a strange twist of fate in store for the Manchus.

Europe. In 17th-century France, a powerful ruler made all the decisions about how the country was run. His followers worshiped him and called him the Sun King. But the very traits for which the king was admired would help bring about the downfall of his successors.

Nearly a century later, in July 1789, France suffered from many problems, but the king did little to help. By committing an outrageous act, a Parisian mob sent a strong message to the king: A revolution had begun.

Five years later, revolutionary battles were being fought inside and outside France. Fear and distrust were everywhere. A leader of the revolution saw that his violent acts had turned against him. A few years later, a young army general saw that the time was ripe to seize power in France. He took a chance and succeeded. By the year 1812, the general had taken control of France, defeated many of its enemies, and created a new French Empire. But the general took on an opponent that was stronger than any nation, and the outcome was a bitter one for him and for France.

North America. For our final story, we travel to the young United States, in 1793. A man recalls a brutal act of his childhood: Taken by force from his native land, he was transported across the ocean to be sold as a slave. He tells how he survived and finally gained his freedom.

1. Forcing a King's Hand

In Unit V we saw that many changes were taking place around the world—in the sciences, in religion, and in relations among nations. People wanted to know more about themselves and the world around them. They looked and studied and realized how little they really knew. There was so much more to discover. For example, how should large numbers of men and women be governed? Should people accept the decisions of their rulers merely because they were kings or queens? Should any one person on earth be all-powerful?

In the early thirteenth century, England was ruled by King John. We should not be surprised that he didn't care about the average man and woman. His control was total. A person lived or died because of a nod of the head or a wave of the hand by John. Even the nobles, or upper classes, were afraid of the king. He was unpredictable. His ideas changed from day to day. The nobles' lives, lands, and fortunes were in the king's hands.

In 1215 the English nobles refused to stand any longer for John's mistakes and taxes. They insisted that there must be limits to what an English king could do. They forced John to sign the Magna Carta, the Great Charter. The powers of the king were no longer absolute.

In this story four English nobles and a French traveler discuss King John and the Great Charter. Ask yourself why King John agreed to sign away some of his powers. Did he do the proper thing? How did the Magna Carta help the common people of England?

Egham   1215

(A French traveler enters the dining room of an English inn. The room is hot and noisy. The traveler hesitates for a moment, then walks over to a table where four English nobles are eating dinner.)

PHILIPPE. Good evening, noble lords. May I join your group?

BARON HOWARD. Yes. Please sit down. Your speech and clothes tell us you are French. It isn't often that English barons have a chance to speak to a Frenchman. Join us for dinner.

PHILIPPE. Thank you very much. Tell me, what's this I hear about your good King John?

BARON ROGER. What do you mean, "What's this I hear?" He's done so many things. Who knows where to begin with our king? If we wanted to talk—

PHILIPPE. I meant about John and the Magna Carta. What is it all about?

BARON ROGER. A better question might be, What's King John all about? He's dug himself into a deep hole. He did too many things unworthy of a king. John *had* to sign the Magna Carta.

PHILIPPE. Well, what did he do?

BARON REGINALD. You name it and he has done it. Murder? He did away with his nephew! Divorce? He's your man! Why not marry someone else's fiancée?

BARON ROGER. Yes, and the man he took the woman away from was his best friend. How do you like that?

PHILIPPE. I don't like it one bit. But shouldn't kings have more power and rights than people like us?

BARON EDWARD. Maybe kings should have more power, but there have to be limits on what anyone can do. Because a man is a king is no reason to let him do whatever he pleases. He had no right to raise so many taxes and try to force us to pay them.

PHILIPPE. But didn't he need the money to fight his wars?

BARON ROGER. Yes, he needed money, so that he could lose more land and more soldiers to your French armies.

PHILIPPE. Your King John doesn't sound like a wise ruler. Why didn't you just get rid of him?

BARON ROGER. Careful, Frenchman! He is our king. We are pledged to support him. But he went too far. He had to understand that there is a higher law. There are certain things that even kings cannot do!

BARON REGINALD. We had to show him that we have rights. If he had not agreed, then we would have gotten rid of him.

PHILIPPE. But how does the Magna Carta put the king in his place?

BARON HOWARD. I'll try to explain. Let's take taxes. Taxes can be ordered only by the king's Great Council, not by the king himself. He can ask for taxes, but the Council must approve them. And the barons are the Council.

PHILIPPE. Suppose the king controls the Council?

"John had to sign the Magna Carta."

BARON ROGER. The Magna Carta takes care of that too. We have made certain that every one of the barons will be called to meet at a certain time in a certain place for a definite purpose. We will meet 40 days after getting the call for the meeting.

PHILIPPE. Is that all?

BARON ROGER. If we are to be fined, only people of our own class—our peers, or equals—can fine us.

PHILIPPE. Sounds great, but haven't you forgotten the common people?

BARON REGINALD. Absolutely not! There's something for them too. Suppose merchants, free peasants, or even serfs do something wrong. Now they may be fined only according to how serious their crimes are. Their neighbors will decide on the fines. But no one can take a free farmer's land or a merchant's goods. Nor can they take a serf's farm tools.

PHILIPPE. That's a great step forward! Let the punishment fit the crime. But don't take away a person's means of support.

BARON REGINALD. Wait, there's more. Trials will be held as soon as possible. And free peasants cannot be sent to jail without being tried by their equals.

PHILIPPE. Is there more?

BARON HOWARD. A great deal more! We have just mentioned only a few things. But these few give all English people more liberty as well as protection from an evil tyrant like King John.

BARON EDWARD. Wait, don't forget that a widow does not have to marry again if she does not want to.

PHILIPPE. And local government?

BARON EDWARD. The king may not interfere with the running of our great city of London!

PHILIPPE. I have to admit that I am impressed. You have come a long way toward freedom. One thing, though: I still don't agree with you about keeping King John. He's no good—

BARON EDWARD. You still don't understand! John could easily have been pushed off his throne. But then, what would we have had? We would have had total war. This way we have peace and we have our king in a corner. He wants his throne. We want our rights. We both have what we want.

BARON HOWARD. If John goes too far, we have our Magna Carta to straighten him out. It's all written down to keep him in his place. We have him where we want him.

PHILIPPE. I am not so sure. Suppose he does not keep his word? What then?

BARON ROGER. He will not dare break his written promises to the English nobles. But if he does, we will march against him—even if it means civil war. Don't worry about us.

BARON HOWARD. We may have trouble. But I know that many years from now people will remember the Magna Carta.

Postscript

There was still no assembly of people to discuss and pass laws in England. In 1265, the nobleman Simon de Montfort brought together, for the first time, an assembly of representatives of the nobility. This group was called a *parliament*.

In 1295 King Edward I assembled a group that was later called the Model Parliament because it became the example for all later English parliaments. The Model Parliament included bishops, barons, knights, and townspeople. Bishops and barons formed the upper house (now called the House of Lords). Knights and townspeople made up the lower house (now the House of Commons).

The parliaments used the Hundred Years' War with France (1337–1453) as an excuse to increase their powers. Members insisted that the kings must have their approval before they collected new taxes or raised old ones. Of course, the kings needed a great deal of money for their armies.

The Hundred Years' War was followed by a bloody civil war for control of England between the houses (families) of York and Lancaster. This was called the War of the Roses (1455–1485) because the House of York used a white rose as its symbol; the House of Lancaster used a red rose. In 1485, when the victorious Henry Tudor became King Henry VII, the power of Parliament was once again limited by a strong ruler. During his last 20 years, Henry called a meeting of Parliament only once! Parliament had become a rubber stamp. Henry VII controlled it completely.

Elizabeth I was the last of the Tudors. During her rule (1558–1603), England grew powerful and prosperous. The arts and literature flourished. Elizabeth was a very powerful ruler who had the good sense to ask for the approval of Parliament for her actions.

Elizabeth was followed by James I, the first of the Stuart kings. At first the people liked James, but his popularity faded when the people saw that he was a weak and ineffective king.

QUESTIONS FOR REVIEW

1. How was King John affected by the Magna Carta?
2. Why did King John have to sign the Magna Carta?
3. How were conditions for the common people improved by the Magna Carta?
4. How was the Church affected by the Magna Carta?
5. How did the English parliaments use the Hundred Years' War to increase their powers?

UNDERSTANDING THE STORY

A. Which statements show how the Magna Carta started England on the road to democracy?

1. The king alone could not order new taxes.
2. Every baron had a chance to become king of England.
3. The size of fines to be paid was decided by the guilty person's peers.
4. Trials of accused people were to be held as soon as possible.
5. The king could break any contract as he pleased.
6. English people were given freedom and protection from evil kings.
7. Widows could be forced to marry again.
8. People would be tried by members of their own class.

B. The English are very proud of the Magna Carta. It limited the powers of the king. Does the United States need a Magna Carta to limit the powers of the president? Explain.

ACTIVITIES AND INQUIRIES

1. Imagine that you are one of the barons responsible for writing the Magna Carta. Your job is to make a list of the powers of the king that hurt the people. List these powers.
2. Look at the illustration on page 235. Describe what is happening. Write your own title for the picture.
3. Imagine that you interview King John. Ask him what he thinks about the Magna Carta. What are his reactions? Then ask him whether he intends to abide by the charter.
4. Ask Philippe what he thinks about the Magna Carta. Ask him to justify his opinion.
5. There are a number of free peasants and serfs nearby. Ask them for their reactions to the Magna Carta. How might their opinions differ from those of the nobles?

2. A King Is Executed

When James I died in 1625, few English people were sorry. Many hoped that his son, Charles I, would be a successful replacement. Charles worked long hours, did not waste money (as his father had), and even looked like a king. But the job of being a successful king was simply too much for him. Before long, the people knew that he could not and would not understand them.

Charles could not stand anyone who opposed him. He fought constantly with Parliament. For their part, the members of Parliament did not trust him. Charles' wife was a Catholic, and Parliament was afraid that Charles would convert to Catholicism and possibly turn England away from the Protestant faith.

For a period of 15 years, Charles struggled with Parliament. It refused to obey him. In return, he did not permit it to sit. In fact, for 11 years, he did not call Parliament at all. He ruled on his own, without the approval and support of Parliament. But he was able to raise enough money to keep his government going, fight wars, and live the way kings were expected to live.

By 1640 Charles was forced to turn to Parliament for money. In return for taxes, he agreed that the Parliament would meet at least once every three years. It could not be dissolved (sent home) unless it agreed. But Charles would sign anything without the slightest intention of keeping his word. He even personally tried to arrest the leaders of the House of Commons who were against him. Parliament now knew that Charles would not obey the law. Promises were empty words.

In the English civil war that followed (1642–1645), the majority of the nobles were aligned with the king. On the other side, the parliamentary army was composed mainly of merchants, tradespeople, and small farmers. The king's followers were called Cavaliers because of their fancy clothes and their custom of letting their long hair fall over their shoulders. The supporters of Parliament were called Roundheads because of their close-cropped hair.

At the beginning of the war, Oliver Cromwell, the leader of the Roundheads, understood that he could not win with his untrained parliamentary army. He insisted on recruiting only very religious people to fight in his army. He said that those who prayed best fought best. Swearing and drinking were punished severely. Cromwell's soldiers went into battle singing psalms (religious songs), and they fought fiercely.

Cromwell's forces defeated those of the king. Charles was captured, placed on trial, and condemned to die.

In this story, we find the king preparing to face his executioner. Ask yourself whether Charles really had to die. What, if anything, was accomplished by his execution? Was Charles really a martyr (a person who dies for a noble cause)?

The Tower of London   January 1649

"What time is it, Father?" asked King Charles.

"We have plenty of time," said the priest. "Have no fear."

"Fear!" replied Charles. "I am the king of England. I am not afraid. I am God's representative on earth. God walked beside me; he guided me."

"We are all human," said the priest. "We all make mistakes."

"You are right, Father. Perhaps I have made a few mistakes,"

Charles replied. "But do I belong in jail because Parliament would not agree with me?"

"Sire, you knew that Parliament represented the English people. Why couldn't you give in—at least some of the time?"

"Perhaps I was too sure of myself," said Charles. "Perhaps I kept myself too much apart from my people. But then I could never get too close to anyone."

"Think of how you might have changed your feelings about Parliament," suggested the priest. "Could you not have tried to get along better with some of the members? Could you not have understood that all people are jealous of their rights? Would you be feeling the ax if you had been willing to give in a little here and there?"

"But, Father, I gave and gave. I promised and promised. Did I not agree to the Petition of Right?"

"Yes, and it was the high spot of your rule as king. Was it so difficult to agree to these things?"

"Of course not," said Charles. "I agreed with Parliament. I would never order a man imprisoned without a fair trial. But they would not believe me! They would not trust me! They would not accept my promise to do these things. They had to write it all down and take those powers away from me! Why did they have to make a long list of the rights of English people? Habeas corpus, where an accused person must be charged in open court, sounds important. But is it necessary? Bail or freedom for a prisoner brought to court on a writ of habeas corpus? Ridiculous! All that does is encourage more crime. Steal and be free! Is this to be the basis of English law?"

"Do you really mean all that, Your Highness? I'm sure that you know as well as I do that these are guarantees that must be given to all free English people. Innocent persons must be kept out of jail; all accused persons must be given a fair trial. This is a nation of laws, not of individuals. Your promise was not enough! People come and go. They say and do different things from year to year, from day to day. The law remains. Parliament must see that our laws are obeyed."

"But the members of Parliament are power grabbers," said the king. "They fought me and I fought back. Would I be here if they weren't out to steal my powers? Who are Cromwell and all the others? Did they fight me to protect English people? No sir, they are rebels, traitors! They are mad for power. They have overthrown the king, the monarchy, the representative of God on earth!"

"Your Highness has a way of turning things around. You signed the Petition of Right. You knew very well it said that tax bills had to be passed by Parliament. How then could you expect to raise money when you dismissed Parliament? You would not let it meet for years."

"I refused to meet with traitors," said the king.

"But you promised," replied the priest.

"I promised Parliament what it wanted to believe."

"Sire, you are the king. You will do as you wish," said the priest wearily. He got up to leave the cell.

Suddenly, there was a harsh shout from outside the cell. "Get ready, Your Highness! Your time has come!"

Charles looked at the priest. "Will you stay with me, Father? I am cold and weary."

"I will stay, if you wish."

Postscript

Soon after Charles I was executed, the monarchy and the House of Lords were abolished. The government of England was changed to that of a free *commonwealth*. In theory it was a republic, but in reality the army was in control. Oliver Cromwell was the head of the army. Therefore, he was the ruler of England. He was the man who had crushed and executed Charles because he was a tyrant. Now Cromwell turned around and did some of the things for which Charles had been put to death. Cromwell became the Lord Protector—a military dictator. He believed, as the English kings had, in his divine right to rule. He felt that God had called upon him to rule England.

After Cromwell died, the people were happy to see a king once again. Charles II, the son of Charles I, became king. Parliament went back to its usual pattern of struggling with the king about money matters.

Charles II was followed by his brother, James II, in 1685. He was sincere and honest, but also narrow and stubborn. He was very much like his father, Charles I. He had no idea what people wanted and never tried to find out. He had decided to become an absolute ruler and restore the Roman Catholic Church to England. But the English people would not agree to be ruled by an all-powerful Catholic king.

Leaders of Parliament felt that drastic steps had to be taken. In 1688 they asked William of Orange (the Netherlands) to come and rule England. William was married to James' Protestant daughter, Mary, and was acceptable to the English people. When William landed in England, the soldiers in James' armies deserted, and James was forced to abdicate (give up the throne). William and Mary were offered the English crown as equal rulers. This marked a very important step in the march of English democracy. Parliament had shown that it had the right to remove the crown of the country's rulers. This great change in the English system of government is called the *Glorious Revolution*.

QUESTIONS FOR REVIEW

1. Why did King Charles I refuse for many years to let Parliament meet?
2. Why did Charles have to turn to Parliament?
3. Describe the opponents in the English civil war of 1642–1645.
4. Why did Parliament insist that the rights of English people be written down?
5. Why did Charles call Cromwell and his followers traitors?

UNDERSTANDING THE STORY

A. King Charles and the priest have many different points of view. Decide who made or might have made the remarks that follow. Write KC for each statement that the king made or might have made and PR for each statement that the priest made or might have made.

1. I am not afraid to die.
2. We are all human and make mistakes.
3. Parliament represented the English people.
4. Members of Parliament are power grabbers.
5. You should have tried to get along better with Parliament.
6. All accused persons must have a fair trial.
7. Habeas corpus encourages crime.

8. Keep innocent people out of jail.
9. Cromwell is a rebel and a traitor.

B. Some people today say that we have so much crime because our leaders are too weak. They are said to worry more about the rights of accused criminals than the rights of the victims. Would Charles I serve as a good model for the leaders of our country in the fight against crime? Explain your answer.

ACTIVITIES AND INQUIRIES

1. Use each of the following key terms in a sentence: bail   Parliament writ   habeas corpus   petition.
2. Go to the library. Prepare a report on either the Cavaliers or the Roundheads. Would you be willing to fight for that side? Explain.
3. Look for pictures of Cavaliers and Roundheads. Bring them to class. Be prepared to talk about why their clothing and appearance were so different from each other.
4. Imagine that you are present at the trial of Charles I. You are Charles' lawyer. Prepare his defense. Now pretend that you are Charles' accuser. Prepare the case against him.
5. Suppose Charles had been told that his life would be spared if he agreed to certain things. Write down what you think those things might be.

3. One Government Too Many

The pope's division of the Western Hemisphere awarded Portugal the huge territory of Brazil—a land almost equal in size to the United States. The majority of Brazil's colonists settled along the northeast coast. Even today, more than three-quarters of Brazil's people live within 100 miles of the Atlantic Ocean. Most of the early settlers grew sugarcane for export to Europe. Later, they also grew tobacco, cacao, and cotton.

The typical Brazilian settlement included a number of sugar plantations grouped around sugar mills. The mills were usually situated near a river and ran by waterpower. There were too few Native Americans to provide the necessary workforce. Instead, black African slaves were the main source of labor. They were imported by the thousands from Portugal's African colony of Angola.

In contrast to the Portuguese, the Spanish built their settlements both along the coasts and in the interior. The conquistadors also felt very strongly that life in these settlements should be centered around cities. Farms would come later.

Thus, by 1550, most of Latin America's major cities had been founded. For example, Mexico City was built atop Aztec ruins in 1521. Quito in Ecuador, Lima in Peru, Asunción in Paraguay, and Bogotá in Colombia all date from the 1530s. In Argentina, Buenos Aires was settled in 1536 but abandoned for a few years because of Indian attacks. Sucre, La Paz, and the silver-mining town of Potosí were all built at high altitudes in the Andes Mountains of Bolivia before 1550.

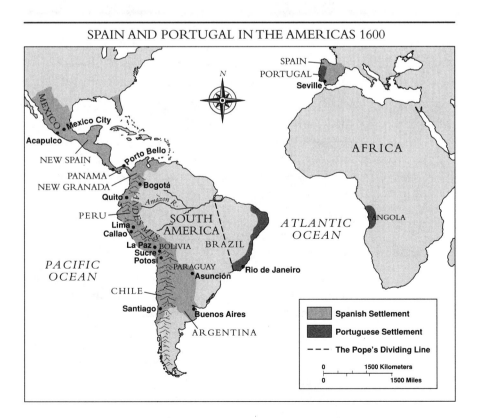

SPAIN AND PORTUGAL IN THE AMERICAS 1600

The Spanish used black slaves from Africa as well as Native Americans as laborers. The treatment of the Native Americans was harsh and cruel. They worked in silver mines and on cacao plantations under miserable conditions. The Native Americans were often sick, poorly fed, and barely clothed. Over a period of 100 years, the population fell from 15 million to 4 million.

The Spanish did not permit other Europeans to settle in their colonies. They also barred anyone who did not follow Catholic beliefs. The Spanish rulers were determined to keep the riches of the colonies for themselves and fellow Spaniards.

In our story, a Spanish couple discuss their business problems.

Buenos Aires   1610

"Inez, I'm fed up with my life as a merchant in South America," said Ramon bitterly. "I work sixteen hours a day arranging for shipments to Spain. But what happens? Either they never arrive or they're months late! And who gets the blame? I do!"

"The people in Spain depend on you," replied Inez. "You can't disappoint them. Besides, we love it here. We have a beautiful house, servants, and many good friends."

"*We* don't love it here; *you* love it! You just don't know how the business is killing me! Suppose I have to ship a big order of cacao, wool, and quinine to Seville. I must race around, buy the goods, and have them brought to my storehouse. Then I have my workers place the goods into neat crates, and my shipment is ready to go to Spain."

"Then what are you complaining about?" wondered Inez. "You filled the order and you sent it off. Now, you have to hope that the shipment arrives safely."

"It's not so simple, Inez. My goods don't go directly to Seville. First, they are put onto ox-drawn carts and taken on mule-back over the Andes to the port of Callao in Peru."

"Fine. Then they go by ship to Seville," said Inez.

"Not exactly," replied Ramon. "First the ship lands on the west coast of Panama. Next my goods are taken overland once again to the east coast to Porto Bello."

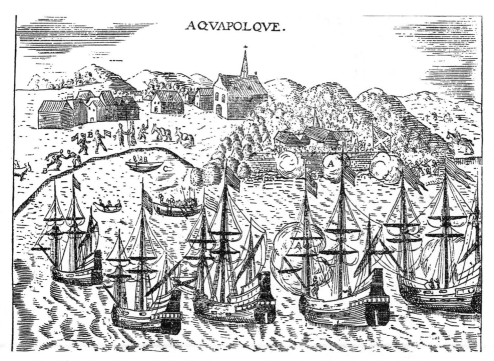

AQVAPOLQVE.

Spanish trading ships at the Pacific Ocean port of Acapulco, Mexico, in the 1600s.

"*Then* they must go aboard ship to Seville."

"Exactly, Inez. Now do you understand how I feel? This is a loser's business. None of my buyers' orders can possibly reach them on time."

"That's nonsense, Ramon. Your customers must know what's involved in shipments from Argentina to Spain. No merchant's goods will arrive much faster than yours. By the way, I have been talking to a few of your friends about shipments to Spain. I'm not as ignorant as you think."

"Please, Inez, no arguments. I've always said you knew a great deal."

"All right, then, this is what I learned," smiled Inez. "The seas are dangerous; there are enemies of Spain all around. But Porto Bello is well defended. And that's not all. Your ship will sail in a convoy, with many other ships. The convoy will be protected by Spanish warships."

"Absolutely right," said Ramon grimly. "And there's another reason why all the overseas trade goes through Porto Bello. The government of Spain checks on every shipment and collects high taxes on the goods we ship. We pay dearly for the right to do business."

"I see your point, Ramon. And what do you plan to do, besides complain to me?"

"My plan was to leave here and return to Spain. But you won't go. I have no other suggestion," said Ramon.

"I'll say it again: I will not return to Spain to a life of hardship and dreary dullness—a life that you hated more than this one! Ramon, let me tell you what I would do. First, start selling the products that are shipped *from* Spain. There's a big demand here in Buenos Aires for silk and woolen clothes, farm tools, and whatever else they send over. By selling Spanish goods, you can double your business."

"I can try to do that," said Ramon.

"Now, for the most important thing. There are ships that sail *directly* to and from Spain. These ships never go anywhere near Porto Bello. *Use them!* You can avoid sending goods over the Andes to Peru, and you will stay far away from the Spanish tax collectors."

"What you are suggesting sounds like treason," replied Ramon. "I would be breaking Spanish law; I would be a smuggler!"

"Ramon, Spain is interested only in the well-being of Spain. We in Argentina must take care of ourselves."

Ramon nodded. "Yes, Inez, you are right. We must think first of the happiness and prosperity of the people of Argentina. After all, they are *our* people now."

Postscript

The illegal trading that Inez described expanded over the years. Ship captains had many ways of avoiding Spanish regulations and taxes. Claiming that their ships had been driven off course by storms, they would sail into West Indian ports far from Spanish control. Or ships supposedly sailing from South America to Europe would turn about and return to South America.

Spain's policies slowed the development of its American colonies. This was not unusual, since colonies, it was believed, existed for the benefit of the country that controlled them. Spain did achieve its goal of importing vast amounts of gold and silver from the mines in the Americas. In the long run, however, these riches harmed Spain. They caused inflation (rising prices) and encouraged lavish spending, and they discouraged the development of Spanish industry.

The time came when Spain could no longer supply the colonists with the manufactured goods they wanted. They had to turn to other countries to meet their needs. Then Spanish restrictions on American trade and business were forgotten.

QUESTIONS FOR REVIEW

1. How did Spanish and Portuguese settlements in the Americas differ?
2. How did the Spanish and Portuguese labor forces differ?
3. Why was Ramon so discouraged with life in Argentina?
4. What problems did Ramon have in shipping his goods to Spain?
5. What were Inez' suggestions for solving Ramon's business problems?

UNDERSTANDING THE STORY

A. Write I for each statement Inez made or might have made and R for each statement Ramon made or might have made.

1. I work 16 hours a day here.
2. The people in Spain depend on you.
3. You filled the order and you sent it off.
4. *We* don't love it here: *You* love it!
5. No merchant's goods will arrive in Spain much faster than yours.
6. The Spanish government collects high taxes on the goods I ship.
7. My wish is to leave here and return to Spain.
8. There are many ships that evade Spanish-controlled ports.

B. Inez appears to know a great deal about trade and commerce in Argentina. Assume that she is offered the position of secretary of commerce in the cabinet of the president of the United States. Do you think that she is qualified? Why? Could she handle the job effectively? Explain. Would Inez accept? Justify your answer.

ACTIVITIES AND INQUIRIES

1. Copy the map of Latin America in 1600, on page 245. On your map, mark the following cities: Mexico City   Quito   Lima   Asunción   Bogotá   Buenos Aires   Sucre   Potosí   La Paz.
2. On the same map, draw the route followed by Ramon's shipments from (1) Buenos Aires, Argentina, to (2) Callao, Peru, to (3) Porto Bello, Panama, to (4) Seville, Spain. Can you explain the reasons for this long, roundabout journey? If you were Ramon, would you take Inez' advice and ship goods directly to Spain? Why or why not?
3. Assume that Ramon has made up his mind to move back to Spain with or without Inez. Try to convince him to stay in Argentina. How might he reply to your arguments?
4. Use your school or local library to prepare a report on present-day United States trade policy with Latin America. Do you agree with this policy? Explain.
5. Compare Inez and Ramon's everyday life in Spain with their life in Argentina. How do you explain their different feelings about returning to Spain?

4. Civilization Conquers the Conqueror

The Yuan (Mongol) dynasty of China became weaker in the years after Kublai Khan. Finally, a Buddhist monk, Chu Yuan-chang, led the native Chinese in battle against the Mongols. He captured Nanking in 1356 and Beijing in 1368. By 1371 Chu controlled all of China.

This new dynasty was called the Ming, and it ruled China until 1644. To overcome the Mongols' neglect, roads and bridges were restored, city walls were repaired, and new tombs and shrines were built. All signs of the Mongols' influence were erased from the legal system. The goal was to return China to the Chinese.

During the Ming period, China was once again ruled by a native dynasty. However, while the Ming government grew weaker, another non-Chinese people, the Manchus, were waiting in Manchuria.

The Manchus took advantage of China's weaknesses. They invaded from their strongholds in the north and broke through the Great Wall. Their advance was made easier by Chinese peasant revolts and by the Ming's feeble leadership and poor military equipment. The Qing or Manchu dynasty ruled China from 1644 to 1912.

In 1644 Chinese and Manchu armies fought on the same side against Chinese rebels, who had captured the city of Beijing. In our story, a Chinese soldier and a Manchu soldier compare their experiences fighting a common enemy four years earlier. They also speak of the changes that have since taken place in China.

Beijing 1648

"Li, I hardly recognized you," said Shu, pleasantly surprised.

"We all change over the years," replied Li with a smile. "Anyway, I'm glad to see that you and I are still friends—even though I am Manchu and you are Chinese."

"That never was a problem," said Shu. "We faced danger together in the battle for this city. We were both frightened, but we tried not to show it. I fell; you stopped and helped me up."

"And you bandaged my wounded arm. It is strange, but I haven't thought about the battle for several years."

"I used to wonder," added Shu, "whether we would have won without that violent dust storm. Somehow, the enemy was more confused than we were."

"Wasn't it strange that a Chinese general asked us, the Manchus, to help him against a Chinese army?" said Li. "True, the enemy were rebels, but how could he be sure that he could trust the Manchus? After all, we were invaders from the north."

"The general certainly took a big gamble," smiled Shu. "And, in spite of our friendship, I must tell you that he made a serious mistake! The Manchus were supposed to help us and then leave Beijing. Instead, they broke their promise and occupied the city."

The Great Wall of China: In the 1600s, Manchu armies broke through the wall to invade China and crush the Ming dynasty.

"Let's take it one step further," grinned Li. "After the battle, we sent for our emperor. He said he loved the city. Now, Beijing is and always will be *our* capital."

"I don't think that is funny," said Shu grimly. "You say that we are friends. But how can I forget that you Manchus are the conquerors and occupiers of my country?"

"Now, you're being unfair," replied Li. "True, the Manchus are the rulers of China, but let's look at the facts. Half of all the top jobs in government are held by native Chinese people. And more than three out of every four jobs are given to Chinese."

"I know that sounds fair to an outsider. But you and I know

that there are many more of us Chinese than there are of you Manchus. Besides, the Manchus could not run this government without help from the Chinese."

"I disagree with you," said Li. "Anyway, here's another example of the Manchus' fairness. We made a rule that no Manchu can win first place in any civil service examination."

"Granted, Li. But do you think that it's fair that all Chinese men must shave their heads, grow a ponytail, and wear Manchu-style clothes? I look and feel terrible."

"You don't look bad at all, Shu. You will be uncomfortable for a while longer. But you'll get used to our way of doing things. In a few years, you'll be proud of your clothes and hair."

"That's very nice of you to say," replied Shu, sarcastically. "Wouldn't it be better if you Manchus didn't behave like our conquerors? We're Chinese. Why do we have to dress and act like you Manchus?"

"We are trying our best to get along with you Chinese," said Li. "We accept some of your ways. You in turn must accept ours."

"That's the problem," said Shu as he walked away. "You *may* adopt some of our customs; we *must* accept yours."

Postscript

Actually, Shu was wrong. Over the years, the Manchus lost touch with their own customs and language—and eventually lost their fighting skills as well. In the long run, the Manchus became as Chinese as the Chinese.

By the beginning of the 1800s, the Qing dynasty was in serious trouble. Corruption in government was very grave. Favorites of the emperor robbed the treasury and enriched themselves. China's policy of isolation cut the nation off from the growth and changes resulting from the European Industrial Revolution. (See Unit VII, stories 5 and 6.) Canton was the only Chinese port allowed to receive foreign trade. A small group of Chinese merchants had total control of China's foreign trade. This situation would not change until the 1840s.

QUESTIONS FOR REVIEW

1. How did the Manchus take advantage of the Chinese government's weaknesses?
2. Why were Chinese and Manchu armies fighting on the same side?
3. Why did Beijing become the Manchus' capital?
4. Why did the Manchus decide that no one of them could place first in Chinese civil service examination?
5. Why was it said that the Manchus became as Chinese as the Chinese?

UNDERSTANDING THE STORY

A. Write T for each statement that is true and O for each statement that is an opinion.

1. The Chinese were more cultured than the Manchus.
2. The Manchus were more intelligent than the Chinese.
3. The Manchus broke through the Great Wall.
4. Li and Shu faced danger together.
5. Shu knew more than Li.
6. Chinese men were ordered to wear Manchu-style clothes.
7. Li felt that the Manchus were treating the Chinese fairly.
8. Shaving their heads and wearing ponytails was the best thing that happened to Chinese men.

B. It has been said that "the enemy of my enemy is my friend." What does this mean? How does this apply to Shu and Li? List as many wars as you can in which former enemies fought on the same side. Is this kind of alliance unusual? Explain.

ACTIVITIES AND INQUIRIES

1. You interview Li. What questions would you ask him about the Chinese? How might he reply?
2. Next you speak to Shu. What questions would you ask him about his future in a society controlled by the enemy? What might he tell you about his plans? What advice would you give him?
3. Prepare a library report on the Manchus.
4. As you walk around the city of Beijing, following your interviews with Li and Shu, you speak to a number of Chinese people. Many seem satisfied with their lives. What do they tell you? Others are unhappy. What are the reasons for their unhappiness?

5. How does a civil service system operate? What are its advantages and disadvantages? Compare the operation of the Chinese civil service system with the method of choosing government officials in your town or city.

5. The Sun King

One result of the Glorious Revolution of 1689 was that the English king could not rule without the help of Parliament. The kings and queens of England were no longer the sole (only) rulers of their country. Death and taxes were too important to be decided by one person.

In France, the absolute power of the French king was challenged by the Parisian Parlement (parliament) during the seventeenth century. Actually, the Parlement had little power. It was not representative of France, as the English Parliament was representative of England. But the French also were eager to limit the king's power to set taxes. Wars cost a great deal of money, so taxes were very high.

A revolt against the French monarchy was fought from 1648 to 1653. The revolt was called the Fronde. The name means slingshot. It was taken from the gadget that children in the Paris slums used to toss mud at passing coaches. The mud annoyed the noble riders in the coaches, but it never stopped them from using the streets of Paris. So too the revolt of the Fronde was annoying, but it did not stop the kings of France from doing as they pleased. The Fronde was a failure. No limits were to be placed upon the absolute powers of the kings of France until the end of the eighteenth century.

In 1643 Louis XIV, a child of five, became king of France. For the next 18 years, the real ruler of France was Cardinal Mazarin. When he died in 1661, the people were shocked that Louis XIV himself took control of the French government. He decided that he would be his own prime minister. For the next 54 years Louis XIV was at the center of Europe, its wars, its life. In fact, this period has been called the Age of Louis XIV.

Louis was the greatest of the absolute monarchs. (Absolute monarchs had total control of their countries' affairs.) Louis was called the Sun King.

He looked and acted like a king. He loved praise and flattery and was very fond of pictures and statues of himself. He believed he was the greatest of all rulers—a king of kings.

Louis insisted on moving the French court ten miles from Paris to Versailles. Louis disliked Paris. He hated the narrow streets and was afraid of the crowds of people. He never forgot his fears during the Fronde, when he was at the mercy of the mob. He had to get out of Paris, no matter what the cost.

At Versailles, he built a palace worthy of a sun king. It was the finest palace in the world. It took over 30 years to build, and as many as 35,000 people worked on it at one time. No one knows how much Versailles cost. Louis made sure that he destroyed the records of expenses before he died.

In this story two young nobles meet at Versailles. They talk about life at the court. We can see how everything revolves around the thoughts and actions of the king.

Ask yourself why most of the nobles of France were at the court of Versailles. Why was Louis called the Sun King? Did he deserve the title?

Versailles   1691

"Count Chaumont!" called Count Rideau as he recognized a familiar face in the crowd that filled the great Hall of Mirrors. "I see that Louis finally forced you to come here. How do you like it?"

"It's good to see you again, Rideau," said Chaumont as they greeted each other. "It's been three years since you left our province of Normandy to come live here at Versailles. I've been here only three days, and already I wish I were back home!"

"Chaumont, now you realize that everything they say about Versailles is true. You can be happy here only if you can learn to do exactly as you are told," said Rideau.

Chaumont said, "Tell me, do you see the king very often? Are you at all close to him now? Will he talk to me?"

Rideau answered, "Only the most powerful nobles are close to the king. That doesn't include people like you and me. I haven't even reached the high position of handing the king his shirt or pants. The best I've been able to do so far is watch him wash his face a few times. Oh, and once I saw him put on his wig. Only his favorites may actually hand him his food. I have never gotten that close."

"I'm sorry," said Chaumont, "but I must confess that I just don't understand what you're talking about. Who wants to watch the king eat or bring him his food? We're not servants, we're nobles! This is ridiculous!"

"Chaumont, you have to understand that Louis isn't just the king of France. He is the sun and the moon and the stars! He is the center of everything in our world. We nobles are here to honor him, to do everything to make him happy."

"Does being waited on by his nobles make him happy?" asked Chaumont.

"You'll find out," answered Rideau. "There is a set way of doing everything at court. These things please the king. He likes doing exactly the same thing at the same time each day. This is his life. You'll see. Someday you'll be happy to do things you now think are so silly for the king. Who knows, someday he may even speak to you! But don't expect it; he's not a great talker. Some claim he says so little because then he won't have a chance to say the wrong things.

"Do you know that he has been his own prime minister since Mazarin died? He tries to do too much. Not even the 'Great Monarch' can run a country as large as France all by himself. He wants to know everything, sign everything."

"With all the parties and games going on around here, when does the king find time to govern?" asked Chaumont.

"Don't let appearances fool you," said Rideau. "Yes, he loves all the parties and rituals of Versailles. But he spends many hours a day on the business of running the country. Believe it or not, he is a hardworking king."

"Isn't he afraid of making mistakes?" asked Chaumont.

"My dear Chaumont, the king makes no mistakes. He is the all-powerful ruler. He is the image of God on earth. He thinks of himself as the greatest of men—and we nobles agree. That's why he took the sun as his emblem. Our King Louis XIV is the source of our light and life!"

Versailles, France: Louis XIV (center), surrounded by courtiers and advisers, meets the playwright Molière (seated at right). What does this scene tell you about the king?

"But that's blasphemy!" cried Chaumont. "That's disrespect for God—to compare Louis with God!"

"Chaumont," said Rideau coolly, "what I said is what the people at court are saying. Those are not my ideas."

"I want to be able to be myself, to express my own ideas," Chaumont said. "Should I ask for permission to go home?"

"Ask, but you are now a member of this court. There is not much chance that you will be given permission," answered Rideau. "You may visit your home, but this is where you will spend the rest of your life!

"Since you have just come here, chances are that you know much more about what's going on in the rest of France than I do. Tell me what you know."

"Well," said Chaumont, "Louis is a great spender. Taxes are very high. People say that the money goes in and out of the royal treasury faster than you can say 'Sun King.' But the spending isn't all personal. Let's not forget all of his wars. It's hard to think of a time when France, or should I say Louis, was not at war! First he wins some land and then he loses some land. He is bleeding our country to death!"

"Louis fights for the glory of France," replied Rideau. "We will not let any nation push us around. Why should we? We are great!"

"Yes, but does he have to fight the world?" responded Chaumont. "Doesn't France have enough land of its own? Don't we have enough problems?"

"What you are saying about our king makes sense to you as a newcomer to Versailles," said Rideau, speaking quietly once more. "But wait. The king will soon become the center of your world. You will accept whatever he does and whatever happens here."

"But what will happen to France and Europe after Louis dies? Who will pay for all of his waste, for his extravagance? Who will account for all the people's suffering?" asked Chaumont.

Rideau thought for a moment. "In the end, we will all pay, I suppose."

Postscript

Louis XIV's extravagance (wasteful spending) and 50 years of war emptied the French treasury. Louis spent far more than his government took in in taxes. As a result, he was obliged to borrow money from bankers, force well-to-do citizens to "lend" the country money, and raise taxes. Many nobles managed to avoid paying these taxes without being punished. However, the peasants who could not afford to pay taxes were sent to prison.

It was said that 10 percent of the people were begging, and 50 percent were almost starving. By 1708 many farmers did not have the money to buy seed to plant their crops. In 1709 the very severe winter weather added to their suffering. As a result, food riots occurred in many cities, where starving mobs broke into bakeries and other food stores.

The king should have known that the people were suffering. As he drove from Versailles to Paris, his carriage was surrounded by people crying "Bread! Bread!" But Louis did not seem to care what happened to the poor.

QUESTIONS FOR REVIEW

1. How did Fronde affect the French monarchy?
2. Why was Louis XIV called the Sun King?
3. What was life like for nobles at the palace of Versailles?
4. Why was it difficult for the king to act as his own prime minister?
5. Why was it unlikely that Chaumont would ever receive permission to return home?

UNDERSTANDING THE STORY

A. Which statements show that Louis XIV had complete control over France?
  1. Louis XIV always asked the peasants for advice.
  2. The revolt called the Fronde did not affect Louis' actions.
  3. Louis liked being called the Sun King.
  4. Louis spent as little money as he could.
  5. Most French nobles were forced to live at Versailles.
  6. Louis believed in democratic government.
  7. Louis was his own prime minister during much of his rule.
  8. Louis felt that he was the image of God on earth.

B. Imagine that Louis XIV is alive today. How would life be different for all of us if Louis were president of the United States? What changes would Louis have to make to be a successful United States president?

ACTIVITIES AND INQUIRIES

1. Imagine that you are Chaumont. Write a letter to a friend. Describe how you feel about your new life at the palace of Versailles.
2. Pretend that you are Rideau. You have found Chaumont's letter. You know that the king sees all mail before it is sent from the palace. What changes would you make in the letter to protect your friend Chaumont?
3. Look at the illustration on page 258. Describe what is happening.
4. Suppose that you were able to spend a day at the palace of Versailles in the time of Louis XIV. Write a diary describing the sights and events of your day at Versailles.

6. The Revolution Begins

Louis XIV was a great king in name and in deed. He ruled as he wished. Who would dare to tell him that he was wrong? He was followed by his great-grandson, Louis XV, who ruled from 1723 to 1774. He tried to continue Louis XIV's system of government but had little success. He sat at councils, yawned a great deal, and often dozed. He was not interested in doing the work of a king. In fact, just about everything bored him! The government of Louis XV was weak, corrupt, and divided. Yet somehow the monarchy survived.

The people of France were growing more and more dissatisfied, however. Average people played no part in government, were taxed unfairly, and were looked upon as inferior to the so-called upper classes. France was a nation of inequality and privilege. French society was divided into three classes, or estates: the high clergy (First Estate), the nobility (Second Estate), and the remainder of the people (Third Estate). The Third Estate included peasants, workers, professional people, the lower clergy, and members of the middle class.

The first two estates made up about 2 percent of the people but controlled the lives and fortunes of the other 98 percent. The high clergy and nobles had little in common with the average French person. They were exempt from the worst of the direct taxes, were tried in special courts, and were even given different punishments. This system was called the Old Regime (old way).

The vast majority of the French people were peasants. True, they were better off than peasants in Germany, Italy, Russia, Poland, or Spain. But the French always worried about famine. A poor harvest would bring with it hunger, illness, and death. Hardly a year passed without a shortage of grain in some part of France. It was difficult to ship extra grain from one part of the country to the area in need. Taxes on the peasants were extremely high and unfairly collected. Many nobles decided to collect feudal taxes that had been overlooked for generations. All in all, the peasants felt exploited (used).

When Louis XV died, it was obvious that France needed a king with the ability and personality of a Louis XIV. Louis XVI was not that king. He was timid and slow. He was more interested in hunting and locksmithing than in learning how to rule France. He too slept through many council meetings. He could not get himself to give a definite opinion and stick to it. His opinions were often those of the last person he had spoken to. He neither looked nor acted like a king. Obviously, he was not the man to deal with an emergency.

The emergency was real. There had been a series of bad harvests. Bread was scarce, and prices were high. When factories closed, many French workers lost their jobs. In 1789 Louis XVI found himself badly in need of money and decided to call the Estates General, the representatives of the three estates, into session. Many people expected great things from these representatives. Petitions (lists of grievances) were drawn up. There were demands for equal taxation, freedom of speech and press, and the abolition of special privileges and feudal dues.

A major question was how the three estates would vote. The Third Estate insisted that each person was to be given one vote. The nobles said that each estate was entitled to exactly one vote. But the Third Estate had its way. It met by itself and said that it was now the National Assembly—the representative of all of France!

In this story, we find that the people of Paris were determined to storm and capture the vast and frightening prison called the Bastille. The Revolution was under way.

Ask yourself why the people felt that it was so important to capture the Bastille. What should Louis XVI have done about its capture? Why were the people of France justified in staging a revolt against the French monarchy?

Paris   July 14, 1789

"What's it all about? I've never seen the streets so crowded," said Jeanne. "Where's everyone running to?"

"Haven't you heard?" George replied. "We're going to capture the Bastille!"

"Capture the Bastille? How can you possibly imagine yourself doing such a thing? It's not just a prison—it's a fortress. Soldiers are defending it. Those thick walls with cannon on top have to be too much for a mob without guns. You'll all be killed—and for what purpose? What a waste!"

"We won't all be killed. What you say is plain nonsense," said George impatiently. "I am not fool enough to want to die. I say that we can take the Bastille. There are thousands of us against a few hundred of them. We know what we want, and nothing will stop us. Besides, when those soldiers see all of us coming at them, they'll give up without a fight! Don't be surprised if they come over to our side."

"Come over to our side?" asked Jeanne. "I don't understand. What is *our* side? People are running around screaming and yelling. 'Hurray for the Revolution!' 'Liberty and Equality' are on everyone's lips. What's it all about? I'm completely confused!"

"Jeanne, where have you been during the last few months? Haven't you heard about the Revolution? Don't you understand that everything in France is going to be changed? Things will never be the same again!"

"Change...revolution...things will never be the same," repeated Jeanne. "I do my work, take my few francs, and try to survive. I've always felt that government was for the king and the nobles. I am a worker, a member of the Third Estate. I was born poor and I will die poor. That is my destiny. Money and privileges are for the nobles. They are born to have good things. I am born to—"

"Born to what?" cried George. "To starve, suffer, and die! And for what? So that those nobles can enjoy life? They all have a great time—at your expense! Doesn't it bother you that you are treated unfairly? Don't you care that, no matter how hard you work and slave, you will always be poor? Aren't you ashamed always to be under someone's heel? Do you enjoy bowing to and being pushed around by the nobles? Aren't you as good as they are? Don't you want to be free?"

"George, I see your point. Of course, I am not happy with my life. But I always thought that this was the way things had to be. I never dreamed that things could be changed. I never realized that it wasn't fair."

"It's not a matter of fair or unfair. This is a case of absolute right and wrong. This is a case of crude privilege. Those people live off your suffering. They laugh at you. They spit at you. Sorry, Jeanne, there goes a group of my friends on the next street. I've got to be with them."

Close by, people were shouting—"On to the Bastille!"; "Save the political prisoners!"; "Kill the nobles!" George started to leave but changed his mind.

"Oh, what's the difference? I'll go along with the next bunch. Perhaps you'll join me. You have to realize what they have been doing to you. By the way, how do you like the taxes you pay?"

"No one likes to pay taxes," answered Jeanne, "but everyone does. It's a part of living."

"No, Jeanne, not everyone pays taxes. Even when they do, some don't pay all of their share. Do you realize that the nobles and the higher clergy don't even pay a land or an income tax? They get away without paying the poll tax (a head tax paid per person). And those privileged people pretend that they never heard of other taxes too! It's a great life, isn't it? The people with the least money pay the most taxes. Those vultures of the upper classes use us!"

"Perhaps they would pay their fair share if asked," said Jeanne.

"It's not that simple, Jeanne. There's more. Do you know why I came to Paris from my little farm a few years ago? I just couldn't survive. Do you have any idea what the peasants have to sacrifice to work their land? Do you realize how unfair their tax burdens are? How would you like to neglect your own crops to help the noble with his harvest? How would you feel having to work on his roads? And when he went hunting, I was supposed to smile when his horses trampled my crops! I sold my land five years ago. Would you believe that I had to pay the noble almost one quarter of what I got out of it? For what!"

"I knew that peasants had a hard life, but I didn't realize it was anything like that," said Jeanne. "I thought that feudalism had been done away with in most of France."

"True," said George, "but no one ever thought of wiping out feudal taxes and services. These taxes stayed and broke our backs. Do you know that I had to have my bread baked in the noble's oven? My grain was ground in his mill. My grapes were pressed in his wine press. I had no choice. He taxed us and he taxed us until there was almost nothing left for us to give." He started to walk away.

"Let me walk with you toward the Bastille," said Jeanne. "A lot of things in France have been wrong. Many nobles have been treating us unfairly. We poor people have been in a bad spot. But what are we going to do about it? Capturing the

Bastille isn't going to stop the nobles from pushing us around. It won't cut our taxes."

"Wrong again, Jeanne. It will all help. We have to show those loafers that we mean business. We are going to the Bastille because it is a symbol of the rotten government of France, the Old Regime. It is the place where they put away the political prisoners. When the Bastille falls, the government and the king will know that things must change. They must make changes or they will die—their blood will flow through the streets of Paris! You will see!"

"I don't understand what you mean by 'political prisoners,'" said Jeanne.

"The king can put anyone in jail for as long as he wants. There's no hearing, no trial, and no sentence. People are sent to the Bastille to rot. Their only crime is that someone in power doesn't like them!"

"Aren't you exaggerating?" asked Jeanne. "Don't you think that most of the prisoners in the Bastille are really criminals? Perhaps a few are what you call political prisoners. Why free these convicted men? They may be dangerous."

"I've heard that there are dungeons far underground where hundreds of innocent people are rotting away," George said. "I have also been told that there is a storage place where thousands of guns have been hidden away to be used against us. I am telling you for the last time that this place, this Bastille, must fall tonight!"

"George, I'm with you. Let me stay with you," said Jeanne. "But what about the king? Why don't we tell him about the things we don't like and ask him to make changes?"

"We've begged and we've begged," said George breathlessly, as he slowed down his pace. "He won't listen. Believe me, after the Bastille falls, he'll listen, or off goes his head. Here's the Bastille now."

"Look!" cried Jeanne, "there are thousands of people here! They have all kinds of weapons. But I still say that they are no match for the trained soldiers of the garrison. Look, the draw-bridge is down. Our people even have cannon. Everyone is rushing into the Bastille."

"Everyone is rushing into the Bastille! The Bastille is ours! The Revolution has begun!"

"Victory! The Bastille is ours! Jeanne, we have won! I told you that we could capture it! The Revolution has begun! Let's show the nobles what we think of them. Kill the soldiers!"

Shouts of "Kill them all!" "Show no mercy!" "They drew the first blood!" "Let their blood join ours!" are heard.

"I wonder who really won tonight?" thought Jeanne.

Postscript

The revolutionists found seven prisoners in the Bastille: four counterfeiters, two lunatics, and an alcoholic. Only one of the seven was a political prisoner.

King Louis XVI tried to cool the anger of the French people. On July 17 he visited Paris. He wore a tricolor ribbon of red, white, and blue, the emblem of the new revolutionary government. He was pleased when many in the crowd cheered him.

Louis believed that he could stay in power if he accepted, or pretended to accept, the great changes that were taking place in France. However, many of the higher nobility, including the king's brother, no longer felt safe. They fled the country. Queen Marie Antoinette remained in France with her husband.

Outside Paris, because of food shortages, there were peasant uprisings weeks before the fall of the Bastille. After July 14, there were reports that nobles were coming with an army to kill those who supported the revolution.

The army of nobles never came, but armed peasants continued to roam the countryside. They demanded that the nobles give them the rolls (lists) of feudal dues owed by the peasants. If the nobles refused, their manor houses were burned down. Peasants thought that if they destroyed the rolls, they would no longer have to pay their feudal dues.

QUESTIONS FOR REVIEW

1. Describe the three estates (social classes) in 18th-century France.
2. How was Louis XVI different from Louis XIV in ability and personality?
3. Why was the Parisian crowd eager to capture the Bastille?
4. Why was George sure that the mob would capture the fortress?
5. Why did George feel that the poor were taxed unfairly?

UNDERSTANDING THE STORY

A. Write T for each statement that is true, F for each statement that is false, and N for each statement that is not mentioned in the story.

1. Louis XIV was a great king.
2. Louis XV was also a very successful king.
3. The taxes paid by the French people in the 18th century were as high as those of today.
4. There were three estates, or social classes, in 18th-century France.
5. Most of the people of France were peasants.
6. The voting in the Estates General was fair: Each person had one vote.
7. The Third Estate included most of the people of France.
8. French peasants used good-quality seed and farm tools.

9. Louis XVI called the Estates General because he needed money.
10. Most French peasants were as bright as most French nobles.

B. Read the first paragraph of the postscript once again. Many would say that the people of Paris did not have good reason to storm the Bastille. Do you agree? Explain. How would George answer this question? What reason would he give?

ACTIVITIES AND INQUIRIES

1. Imagine that it is 1789. You were a political prisoner in the Bastille in Paris. The revolutionists have set you free. You are asked to write a newspaper article telling why you were in prison and what prison life was like. Write the article.
2. Bring to class pictures of buildings and streets of 18th-century Paris. Draw a picture of the streets of Paris, including the Bastille and surrounding areas.
3. Draw a picture of what you think the inside of the Bastille looked like.
4. Imagine that you are George. Write a letter to your former lord. Tell him why you feel that he did not have the right to collect taxes from you. Pretend that you are the noble. Write a letter answering George.

7. The Reign of Terror

The French Revolution was well on its way. Which path would it take? Could Louis XVI live through the changes it would bring? Could the revolutionists live with the British solution, both a Parliament and a king?

At first it seemed that Louis would be able to keep his crown. He said that he accepted the revolutionists' Declaration of the Rights of Man, which was inspired by the United States Declaration of Independence. All men and women were to be considered equal. The class lines created by birth were to be erased. The constitution of 1792 ruled that the king would stay on his throne. But the real power was to be in the hands of a legislature—a lawmaking body.

Those were great days in the lives of the French people. The surprise was that so much had been done with so little bloodshed. The Revolution seemed a great success. Then in 1792, the scene changed. France was thrown into a war with the great powers of Austria and Prussia. The new French government was in deep trouble.

Louis XVI did not really accept his new role as a not too powerful king. He hoped that European kings would win the war against France and rescue him. This was an idle dream. The French government was overthrown by the more radical (extreme) group called the Jacobins. Louis was found guilty of treason—plotting with the enemies of France.

The new Jacobin government was in a very dangerous situation. It was fighting a war against powerful enemies. At the same time, it was fighting its enemies within France. It felt itself surrounded. It trusted no one—including its own members. The Jacobins' answer was to start the Reign of Terror (rule of death). Over 500,000 French people were accused of being traitors. They were thrown into the overcrowded jails. From 3,500 to 4,000 were executed at the guillotine. Others were shot to death or were drowned on boats that were sunk in the Loire River. What were their crimes? They were suspected of not being completely loyal to the revolutionary government of the Jacobins.

In this story it is five years after the fall of the Bastille. We meet Robespierre, who planned the Reign of Terror. Now he himself has been sentenced to die by the same blade that had killed so many other "enemies" of France. He writes in his diary of his days of glory. He recalls the people he worked with and against whom he plotted.

Ask yourself why Robespierre felt that the Terror was necessary. Did the leaders of the Terror destroy themselves? Could there have been a French Revolution without the Terror?

Paris   July 27, 1794

What a ridiculous way for Maximilien Robespierre to end his life! A few days ago I was the leader of the revolutionary government. I was the head of the Committee of Public Safety. Now the "head" will lose his head. And for what? My enemies never understood what I was trying to do. They insisted that I wanted nothing but power. They even had the nerve to say that I wanted to become a dictator. What nonsense! They forget that in the National Assembly I was the champion of democracy. I was the one who worked to win the vote for all French people!

My dream was to make France a republic that would be fair, honest, and just. But I found that people had to die so that France could live. Life is sacred to me. It hurt me to send people to the guillotine. But I had to do it. France had to be cleansed and purified of all those who stood in the way of fair government! All the people who were not with us were against us. They were the suspects; they were the guilty ones! It was the only way I knew to make the Revolution live. Yes, people had to die for a better life for the good people of France. The end justifies the means!

Thoughts race wildly through my mind. I am perspiring. Can it be that I, the great Robespierre, am afraid? How will I act when I climb those stairs to the guillotine? Will I be able to make it on my own? I remember how the king behaved. There was a man who never looked or acted like a king during his lifetime. He was timid, always afraid. He never made a decision on his own. He was a slow thinker and doer! I thought they would have to carry him to the scaffold. But no, this was his greatest moment! Imagine, Madame La Guillotine bringing out the best in our King Louis!

I can see Louis now. He refused to let the soldiers take off his outer clothes. He would not even let the soldiers tie his hands. Yes, he died bravely. He had a strange dignity in death that he never had in his lifetime. I can still hear the mob screaming, "Long live the nation! Long live the Republic!" Then a soldier held up the king's head for all to see. For a moment, I wondered whether his life might have been spared. Was it a mistake to kill the king? No, that was no mistake. The king had to die. He stood for all the evils of the absolute monarchy. He *was* the Old Regime in all of its evil ways.

Soon I will join those who gave their lives for the cause. I wonder whether Marat would have defended me. Would he have taken my side? Or would he have joined the rest and sent me to the guillotine?

I know the answer. He hated everyone in authority. He thought of himself as a great scientist and felt that no one recognized his talents. Too bad! He was no democrat. In his own way, he wanted to help the poor people, but he would not have given them any power. I have to laugh now, in spite of my troubles, when I think of people calling me cruel and ruthless. They do not remember when Marat called for 270,000 heads! He would solve all problems by killing and killing and killing. Too bad that he did not have the honor of dying by losing his own head to Madame La Guillotine! Stabbed to death while taking a bath! What a poor way to die!

There is one other I think of often. I remember meeting Danton before the Revolution. What a kind man he was. And he was one of the strongest men I have even known. He had a neck like a bull, with a head to match! And those piercing eyes: They seemed to look right through you! No wonder they called him Hercules and Atlas!

Danton was the best speaker I have ever heard. He could turn an audience upside down. Ah, how the Revolution changed him. A good man became cruel and harsh. I admit that I was afraid of him. He challenged me. I was afraid of losing my head as well as my job. I accepted his challenge. I sent him to the head chopper before he could get to me. Yet he was not all bad. He tried to help the poor. He worked hard to get feudal dues abolished.

I was too clever for him. I accused him of making secret deals with the nobles and get-rich-quick types. I wonder now if he really did those things.

Danton, I laughed when you said that you would break that guillotine before long, or you would lose your own head to it. I guess that you were tired of all the killing. I knew then that you were a dead man; you had to lose your head. But I did not laugh as I watched you climb the stairs to the knife. I admired the way you stood there and said, "Show my head to the people. It is worth it!" You were right; I can admit this now in my secret diary. I was shaken when you shouted, "Robespierre will be next!"

How right he was. That was only four months ago! I, Maximilien Robespierre, was called the "apostle of terror" by the people who should have known better. I, who hated and feared death, became a killer. Now I am about to die by the same instrument I used to save France.

"Soon, I will join those who gave their lives for the cause. I am about to die by the same instrument I used to save France."

I cannot stop my mind from wandering. I see myself in a tumbril (cart) carrying those condemned to die to the Place de la Revolution. I see the scaffold with the guillotine. It looks hideous, monstrous! The crowd is huge. People are screaming for my head! Why do they hate me so? I am afraid. I am weak. O Lord, please do not let me faint. I must be strong.

Somewhere I have read, "Those who live by the sword will die by the sword!" Now I understand the truth of these words.

Postscript

As Robespierre feared, the crowd screamed and cursed him as he rode to the guillotine. Windows overlooking the execution had been rented at high prices. People wore their fanciest clothes. After the guillotine had done its work, Robespierre's head was held up high. The crowd roared in delight.

The people who sentenced Robespierre to death were afraid of him. They believed that they saved their own heads by cutting off Robespierre's. As for the Terror, they would have preferred to continue the killings. But they had no choice. The people had had enough of the slaughter. Trials and executions continued, but in ever-decreasing numbers.

QUESTIONS FOR REVIEW

1. What did Louis XVI hope would happen to save his throne?
2. Why did the Jacobins start the Reign of Terror?
3. What were Robespierre's dreams for France?
4. What did Robespierre think of King Louis XVI?
5. What did Robespierre think of Marat and Danton?

UNDERSTANDING THE STORY

A. Write T for each statement that is true and F for each statement that is false.

1. The Reign of Terror was a time of peace and quiet.
2. Louis XVI died bravely on the guillotine.
3. Robespierre sent many people to the guillotine.
4. Robespierre felt that it was a mistake to execute the king.

5. Marat was stabbed to death in his bathtub.
6. Danton was a poor speaker.
7. Robespierre was afraid that he would not die bravely.
8. Robespierre believed that the end justifies the means.

B. Pretend that Robespierre is alive today. Once again, he wants to become a leader of a country. Which country today might welcome his leadership? Why?

ACTIVITIES AND INQUIRIES

1. Go to the library. Prepare a report on a modern-day revolution anywhere in the world. What similarities do you see to the French Revolution? What differences do you see?
2. In the library find material on the part played by women in the French Revolution. Tell the class about your findings.
3. Look at the illustration on page 272. Describe what is happening. Write your own title for this picture.
4. Imagine that you are admitted into Robespierre's prison cell prior to his execution. He assumes that if he impresses you favorably, his life will be spared. What does he tell you?
5. Try to convince Robespierre that he and his followers should not have started the Reign of Terror.

8. Napoleon's Rise to Power

We have seen how France lived in fear of the guillotine. But the Terror could not last. The people turned against violence and the radical Jacobins. The government became less extreme. It fell into the hands of the middle class. But many French people were still not satisfied. They felt that they should go even further and bring back a king. The Royalists (those who favored the king) were especially strong in Paris.

During October 1795, the Royalists of Paris were ready to make their move against the democratic government of France (called the Convention). Paul Barras, the president of the Convention, asked a young Corsican general to defend the government. The young general was Napoleon Bonaparte. He quickly ended the Royalist revolt by firing artillery shells into the crowd at close range. The streets were filled with the dead and wounded.

From this time, Napoleon was the man to watch in France. He was a man of action, one who seemed to know what to do in difficult situations. He was counted on to crush the enemies of France in foreign lands. Why not let him do the job in France?

In this story, Barras and Lucien Bonaparte talk about their plan to make Napoleon Bonaparte the first consul, or leader of France. You will see how the *coup d'état*, the plot to put him in power, almost failed.

Ask yourself why they felt that Napoleon could be a successful ruler of France. Were they right in turning to one man to rule their country? Why did Lucien Bonaparte talk of the possibility of a Jacobin takeover?

Paris   November 9, 1799

"Barras, this is it!" said Lucien Bonaparte excitedly. "This is the day we have been waiting for."

"If all goes well," replied Barras, "your brother, Napoleon, will be the first consul of France. He will control the government."

"What do you mean, 'If all goes well'?" asked Lucien. "We're putting him in control, and that's that! You are not backing down at this point. We need your help, but this is no time for weaklings! Do you have any doubts?"

"Lucien, you forget very quickly. I gave your brother, Napoleon, his first push into power. I asked him to come to Paris in 1795 to put down the rebellion. I put him in charge of the army."

"Yes, Barras, and he rewarded our trust by crushing the rebellion. He stood up to the mob! He was not afraid to shoot them down! He's a brilliant organizer. He is brave and fearless. Remember how he drove the British army from Toulon in 1793? Do you know any other 24-year-olds who have been made brigadier-general?"

"True, Lucien. But remember that I was the first who saw his talents. I sensed what he could do, even though people thought that he was a revolutionist. You forget very quickly that your brother, Napoleon, was a Jacobin! He was a friend of Robespierre."

"I know, I know," replied Lucien, impatiently, "but that was a long while ago."

"Lucien, you are wrong. It was only five years ago. He was in jail right after Robespierre was executed. People knew that Napoleon was a Jacobin—a radical! His name was crossed off the list of French generals in September 1795. He could just as easily have lost his head! I rescued him by giving him his big chance against the Parisian mob. I had faith in him. I knew that he could be trusted. His radical days were long past. Wasn't I the one who introduced him to his wife, Josephine? Would I have done that if I didn't really trust him?"

"Barras, I trust no one, not even you, where money and power are concerned!" said Lucien Bonaparte.

"How can you talk that way to me?" said Barras angrily. "I am as honest as any other person in politics!"

"All right, Barras, you gave Napoleon his big chance in spite of a few mistakes he had made in his younger years. But many others also saw that he was going to be a great leader. Look what he did in Italy. He won brilliant victories in the north, while other French generals were losing to the Austrians."

"Why stop there?" continued Barras. "Remember how easily he beat the Austrians in 1797? We gained control of Belgium and the left bank of the Rhine. I could go on and on. He is a military genius! There's no doubt about it. He isn't afraid to try new battle plans. People are happy to fight and die for him. He is a natural leader!"

"Good," said Lucien excitedly. "We agree. Napoleon will be first consul. You'll see. There will be no trouble."

The following day

"What's the problem, Lucien?" asked Barras. "I thought that things were going well for us."

"They are not going too well, Barras. At first, everything seemed almost too easy. The Council of Elders went along with the plan, and Napoleon was made commander of the soldiers of Paris. But now the Council of 500 looks doubtful."

"I don't understand," said Barras. "You are the president of the council. Keep control. Don't let them spoil our plan. Don't lose your nerve."

"I'll do my best. Watch me," said Lucien Bonaparte.

Lucien took his seat in the council chamber.

"I recognize Napoleon Bonaparte. He has a few words to say to you."

Several deputies rose and began shouting: "Don't let him speak! He's a liar! He's a traitor! Down with the tyrant! Death to Napoleon Bonaparte! Throw him out of here! Throw him out of France! Kill the dictator! Outlaw him!"

Deputies rushed at Napoleon. He fainted. At Lucien's order, soldiers rushed in, surrounded Napoleon, and carried him out of the building. When Napoleon recovered, he spoke to the assembled soldiers. He was nervous and unable to control his emotions.

"Soldiers of France," said Napoleon, "our country is in great danger! We must protect France from the Jacobins. Otherwise, once again, death and destruction will tear apart our beloved France! I beg you, help me to save our nation. Together, we can make our France even greater—"

Napoleon's face was bleeding where he had nervously scratched it with his fingernails. Lucien Bonaparte rejoined Napoleon. He realized that his brother's speech was having no effect upon the soldiers. He then decided that he must speak to them.

"You know me. I am the president of the Council of 500. I am Lucien Bonaparte, Napoleon Bonaparte's brother. I tell you he is right. We need a new government, a government that can be trusted. I know that many of the deputies are plotting against us. They refuse to let us speak. They insist on running things in their own corrupt way. I ask you, soldiers of France, to protect us from those traitors! Clear them out of the hall! Give Napoleon a chance to lead you, to show you what he can do!"

Paris, 1799: Napoleon watches as soldiers clear the council hall of deputies who opposed him. His takeover of the government was a success.

Lucien pointed his sword at his brother. "I swear I will kill my own brother if he attacks the liberty of the French people!"

"A great speech, Lucien," said Barras. "You've done it! The soldiers are rushing into the council hall! They're throwing the deputies out! The deputies are running from the bayonets! Look, some of them are jumping out the windows! We've won! We've won!"

"Yes," said Lucien, "we will have a new government for France. The Revolution is finished!"

Postscript

Barras resigned from the council to smooth the way for Napoleon's takeover of the government. Napoleon never gave him another job.

Whether he was on the battlefield or in the drawing room, Napoleon was always working on his plans. He thought nothing of getting up to work in the middle of the night. Eating was almost a waste of time to Napoleon. He never spent more than 12 minutes at any meal, no matter how elegant it was.

Napoleon suffered from many ailments and drank only barley water or warm lemonade. He said that he was never tired and could work for 14 hours at a stretch without a break. He exhausted those who were appointed to work with him. Some of the unlucky ones died from overwork. Those who survived left his service after a short time.

When Napoleon was working on a plan or project, he would continue until he found the solution. He had an excellent memory and a logical mind. His military plans seemed to cover every possible emergency.

In his early years in power, Napoleon was kind and generous. Later, he became strict and harsh. Sometimes, he even lost control of himself, and would hit or kick an aide who failed to carry out his orders exactly.

In 1804, as the pope watched, Napoleon crowned himself emperor of France. His political control of France was complete. Next he sought to dominate Europe, and he nearly succeeded.

QUESTIONS FOR REVIEW

1. Why did Barras pick Napoleon to defend the government?
2. How did Barras give Napoleon his "big chance"?
3. Why did many deputies oppose Napoleon?
4. What did Lucien Bonaparte tell the soldiers to convince them that Napoleon should be their leader?
5. Why did Napoleon feel that eating was a waste of time?

UNDERSTANDING THE STORY

A. Tell which statements show that Napoleon was a great general.

1. Napoleon fired artillery shells at a crowd of Royalists in 1795.
2. Napoleon drove the British army from Toulon in 1793.
3. Napoleon had been a radical Jacobin.
4. Napoleon defeated the Austrians in 1797.
5. Napoleon was a great leader of soldiers.
6. Napoleon was a friend of the Robespierre family.
7. Napoleon knew what to do in difficult military situations.
8. Soldiers were happy to fight and die for Napoleon.

B. Imagine that Paul Barras and Lucien Bonaparte are running for political office in the United States today. Which one would you vote for? Why? Which one has a better chance of winning? Why? Would you trust either of them? Explain.

ACTIVITIES AND INQUIRIES

1. Use each of the following key terms in a sentence: Jacobin first consul tyrant radical *coup d'état* dictator royalist traitor.
2. Imagine that you are a member of the Council of 500 in 1799. You are against Napoleon's taking over as first consul. Prepare a short speech against Napoleon.
3. Prepare an answer in favor of Napoleon's being given the job.
4. Napoleon never gave Barras another job. Imagine that Barras goes to Napoleon and asks him for a government position. What might Barras say? How might Napoleon answer him?
5. Napoleon's speech obviously did not impress the soldiers. Why? What might he have said that would have been more effective? (Do not include any of Lucien's remarks.)

9. "General Winter" Beats Napoleon

In 1805 Napoleon secured a brilliant victory over Austrian and Russian armies at Austerlitz (in the present-day Czech Republic). France's major European enemies were crushed. After Austerlitz, Napoleon continued to beat his enemies. At his peak, Napoleon controlled an empire that extended from the North Sea to the Mediterranean. (See map.) His brother Joseph was king of Spain, brother Jerome was king of Westphalia (Germany), and brother-in-law Murat was king of Naples (Italy). Only Britain remained unbeaten.

Napoleon thought that he had a clever idea to defeat the British. He

NAPOLEON'S EMPIRE IN 1812

would not allow their goods to enter any port on the continent of Europe. This was called the Continental System. Naturally, the British made some rules of their own. They insisted that no neutral ship (a ship from a nation not at war) could enter a European port unless it stopped first at a British port. Before long, European countries were losing trade and business. Across the Atlantic, the young United States was caught between the rules of the British and the rules of the French. By 1812 the United States would be drawn into a war with the British.

Most countries found Napoleon's Continental System too hard to follow. They closed their eyes to the smuggling and the chances of losing their ships. Napoleon was disturbed and angry, but Russia's complete disregard for his system enraged him. Czar Alexander I was supposed to be his ally. Napoleon decided to teach the czar a lesson. He would invade

Russia with a large army and crush the Russian forces. In June 1812 Napoleon crossed the Russian border. He hoped for a quick victory, but the Russians had other ideas.

In this story, we see how Napoleon's dreams of empire were smashed by Russia's plans and the freezing weather. Two French officers on the battlefront near the city of Vilna tell what they think went wrong.

Ask yourself why Napoleon wanted to invade Russia. Was the Russian invasion a mistake? Would the empire of Napoleon have lasted if Napoleon had not insisted on invading Russia?

Vilna   December 1812

"Stop!" shouted the French soldier on guard duty. "Who goes there?"

"Captain Menton, Ninth Dragoons."

"Give the password," said the guard.

"I don't know the password," said Menton, shivering. "I've lost my soldiers. I've lost everything. If you don't believe me, shoot me. I have nothing to live for."

At that moment Captain Darcy rode up. "It's all right, corporal. I know this man. I will be responsible for him." The two men recognized each other immediately. Darcy led Menton to a small tent. It was little shelter from the below-zero cold and high winds.

"Am I glad to see you again!" said Menton, still shaking. "How long has it been?"

"It seems a hundred years ago," replied Darcy. "Actually, it's been five years since I last saw you. It was at the Battle of Friedland."

"Those were glorious days," said Menton, now warming up a bit. "How happy we were! Napoleon took us from one victory to another. I honestly had a strong feeling that we could never lose as long as Napoleon was our emperor!"

"How little we knew what was going to happen to us," said Darcy thoughtfully. "Who would have thought that Napoleon and the great armies of France could be crushed by the Russians?"

"Not crushed by the Russians, Darcy. We were beaten by

'General Winter.' Napoleon had never fought under these conditions. How could he have known what the weather would be like? All I can remember are my men freezing to death. Every morning, at dawn, I'd see a dozen men I thought were still asleep. I'd try to wake them up. But their bodies were frozen stiff. They were dead! But it wasn't Napoleon's fault!"

"Not his fault?" said Darcy angrily. "You forget that Napoleon is the great leader, the great planner. He is supposed to know everything about war. He must be prepared for every possibility. He should have known about the weather. Surely he could have learned the facts about the Russian winter!"

"That may be true," replied Menton with some hesitation. "But he could not have known that the Russians would not fight battles. How could he have predicted that they would retreat and retreat into this huge country? At last we fight a battle at Borodino. We win, and—"

"We lose," finished Darcy. "Napoleon doesn't cut off the Russian retreat. The rest of their army gets away. We had lost

Russia, 1812: Napoleon leads his battered army from the frozen wastes of Russia.

150,000 troops to 'General Winter.' Perhaps we lost fewer soldiers than the Russians in the fighting, but how could our dead and wounded be replaced?"

"What a great speech Napoleon made to us at Borodino," continued Menton, as though he were alone. "I can still hear him saying, 'Soldiers, here is the battle you wanted. Victory depends on you. We need one victory—'"

"To make up for all my past mistakes," finished Darcy once more. "I will say it again: Napoleon did not prepare for this Russian war. He should have realized that the Russians might retreat. He should have planned for feeding and supplying an army that could not live off the land. He should have had enough soldiers to replace the sick and wounded. If he could not do these things—and I say that he could not—he should never have come to Russia. A great leader must know that there are certain things he cannot do. Napoleon thought that nothing was impossible for him."

"I suppose that you are going to blame him for the Moscow fire," said Menton.

"Menton, what difference does it make? It's a terrible mistake that we are here. It is not my fault, and it is not yours. Yes, it was our leader's responsibility to care for his soldiers. He didn't do it because he couldn't. The fire is just the worst example of his weaknesses! Fire is a weapon of war."

"We came to Russia for the greater glory of Napoleon and France," muttered Menton. "The Russians starved us, froze us, and burned us out of the shelter of Moscow!"

"There's not much glory in our starving and freezing to death, Menton. I wonder how many of us are left? Where are they all now? Dead—and for what? Did we have to be used to feed Napoleon's dream? Did he have to try to conquer the world? Didn't we have enough?"

"Ah, but what a dream," said Menton. "All of Europe would have been Napoleon's. Europe would have belonged to France—to us! The world could have been ours!"

"Be thankful that you are still alive," answered Darcy thoughtfully. "Empires, like dreams, fade away—and die."

Postscript

Following the defeat in Russia, Napoleon was still able to raise a new army. Unfortunately for him, most of the soldiers were very young (about 17). They were brave but inexperienced fighters. Napoleon won the next few battles, yet his "victories" cost the lives of far too many soldiers. Finally, in 1813 at Leipzig (the Battle of the Nations), the best part of his army was either killed or captured. After three days, Napoleon ordered his remaining forces to retreat.

After the Battle of Leipzig, Napoleon's empire collapsed. His armies were forced out of Prussia and other German states, Austria, the Netherlands, Italy, and Spain. As the final blow, the allied armies of his enemies attacked and captured his capital city of Paris. Napoleon still refused to give up, but his generals convinced him that further fighting was useless.

Napoleon was banished to the island of Elba, in the Mediterranean. But his military career was not over, as we shall see in Unit VII.

QUESTIONS FOR REVIEW

1. What was the purpose of Napoleon's Continental System? How did the British respond to it?
2. Why was Napoleon hostile to Czar Alexander?
3. Why was Menton surprised by what happened to Napoleon and his army?
4. Why was Darcy certain that Napoleon was unprepared for the war with Russia?
5. Why was Darcy so bitter about Napoleon's losses in Russia?

UNDERSTANDING THE STORY

A. Tell which item in each sentence makes each statement correct.

1. Napoleon's empire at its height extended from the North Sea to (a) the Mediterranean (b) Finland and Poland (c) Sweden and England.
2. To defeat the English, Napoleon tried (a) the Continental System (b) an invasion of Russia (c) an invasion of England.
3. A country that was drawn into the fight between England and France was (a) Mexico (b) the United States (c) Canada.

4. In 1812 Napoleon and his army invaded (a) England (b) Austria (c) Russia.
5. In Russia, Napoleon and his army were beaten by (a) rain and fog (b) "General Winter" (c) bad supplies from France.
6. The Russians used fire as a weapon of war when they burned (a) Moscow (b) Leningrad (c) Kiev.
7. Napoleon's dream was to (a) conquer Europe (b) become president of the United States (c) put the son of Louis XVI on the throne of France.
8. The person in the story who thinks highly of Napoleon is (a) the corporal (b) Menton (c) Darcy.

B. General William Sherman, a famous American Civil War leader, said, "War is hell!" Would Napoleon have agreed with him? Explain. If war is "hell," why do we continue to fight wars?

ACTIVITIES AND INQUIRIES

1. Pretend that you are Captain Darcy. Write a letter to your family in France. Tell how you feel about Napoleon.
2. Imagine that you are Captain Menton. Write a letter to your family in France. What would you tell them about Napoleon?
3. Adolf Hitler invaded Russia in 1941, many years after Napoleon. Write down the lessons that Hitler should have learned from Napoleon's invasion of Russia.

10. A Voyage to Slavery

Slavery began in the ancient world. The Egyptian, Greek, Roman, and African empires all held slaves. And slavery occurred and was accepted in Biblical times. During the European Middle Ages, white Christians were enslaved by other Europeans. These slaves were prisoners of war, criminals, or debtors.

In ancient times, slaves were often protected by law and custom. In some countries, slaves would be freed after a number of years of faithful service. Most were excused from work on the Sabbath, the seventh day of the week. In Africa before the European traders arrived, slaves were not looked upon as property. They were working members of a tribe, but their standing was lower than that of the free men and women. Slaves could advance through work or good fortune, and the children of slaves were not considered slaves.

When Europeans became involved in the African slave trade, conditions changed completely. It all began in 1442, when ten Africans were brought to Prince Henry of Portugal. In 1501 Spain approved the shipment of African slaves to its American colonies. European colonists needed cheap labor to work in the mines and fields of the Americas. In Africa they found people who knew farming and were accustomed to hard work.

Black Africans were captured by white and black slavemasters. The Africans were taken from their homes in chains and forcibly packed into rotting, leaking slave ships. The slave traders sold the survivors of the terrible voyages across the Atlantic to the Americas for handsome profits.

European and American merchants were sometimes denounced for enslaving other human beings. They pointed out that Africans were not Christians. Enslaving non-Christians was therefore acceptable to them, and the African slave trade became a major part of the commerce of the Western world.

Gustavus Vassa was born in West Africa, in 1745. When he was 11 years old, he was forced aboard a slave ship and taken to the colony of Virginia. There many years later, he tells the story of his capture and the voyage to the Americas.

Alexandria   1793

I was 11 years old when I was taken from my home by African slavers. I was tied up, beaten, and forced to march many miles with dozens of other captives to the seacoast. There was a broken-down, filthy ship tied up at the dock. "Get on that ship," they ordered. I was so terrified I couldn't walk. Strong men carried me on board. They tossed me around to check on my strength and health. This, I thought, is the end. They are going to kill me!

I cried, but they paid no attention. Before long, they threw me below deck. Everyone was crying. The smells were unbearable.

Two white men offered me some food, but I was too frightened and sick to eat. They absolutely would not accept my refusal. One tied my feet, while the other beat me countless times with a huge stick. This time, I was sure that they would kill me. But at last, they stopped beating me.

When I awoke, I talked to some of the men near me. Each one was chained so that he could scarcely move. "What's to become of us?" I asked. "Where are we going?" One replied, "We are being taken far away, to the white people's country to work for them." Somehow, I felt relieved. Perhaps they wouldn't kill me because they needed my labor.

There were too many people in the hold. Cargo filled every available inch of space not occupied by a human. The heat was unbearable; I couldn't breathe. All I heard were the shrieks of the women and the groans of the sick and dying. Finally, I was so sick that they let me stay on deck. Would they allow me to stay in the fresh air without chains unless I was about to die?

One day, two Africans jumped overboard. Another soon followed. They preferred death to a life of pain. Many more tried to follow, but the sailors held them back. Others set out in the rowboat to pick up the three jumpers. Sadly, two had

Gustavus Vassa, a freeman, in later years. What questions did he ask himself about the slave ship and its other passengers?

drowned, but the third was "rescued," thrown on deck, and beaten almost to death.

I and all the Africans aboard the ship lived through many more days of this torture until we landed in Barbados. Fortunately for me, I was then shipped to Virginia, where I was sold to an English sea captain named Michael Henry Pascal. Captain Pascal was very kind to me and taught me a great deal about the merchant shipping business. I spent most of my time working on ships in the West Indies, taught myself to read and write, and became a Christian.

But that wasn't all. I was paid for my services and bought and sold many goods. Over the years, I earned enough money to buy my freedom from my last owner. I became a free man! I lived well, and I prospered. I also worked to improve the conditions of those still held in bondage. But what of all the others who sailed with me on that miserable slave ship? I never saw one of them again. Would they have been better off dying at sea?

Postscript

In the Spanish colonies, keeping Africans in slavery was difficult. Many slaves fled to live among the Native Americans and were not recaptured. Colonists who were slaveholders lived in constant fear of slave uprisings. In the Portuguese colonies, some runaways began their own settlements. The largest was Palmares in northeastern Brazil, with 20,000 former slaves. In English North America, from New England to Georgia, all slaveholders were alert for attempted escapes. Slaves ran away from all kinds of owners, no matter how well they were treated.

Slaves were treated differently in Latin America and North America. In Latin America the Church encouraged owners to free the slaves who became Christians. Also, marriages between blacks and whites were permitted.

In Latin America, slaves were not considered inferior beings. Slaves who were severely mistreated could protest in court and might even win their freedom. In Brazil, slaves could buy their freedom by paying their owners the original purchase price. In Cuba, slaves could buy their freedom by making payments over a period of time. But in North America, no church or other organization dared tell the slaveowners how to treat their slaves.

Before the coming of European traders, the African slave trade had existed on a small scale. When the African chiefs became involved with Europeans, they had no idea what effect it would have on their countries. Huge numbers of African people were captured and sold. Whole tribes were lost. Over the years, it is estimated that Africa lost from 18 million to 24 million of its best and strongest people.

QUESTIONS FOR REVIEW

1. How did conditions in the slave trade change when Europeans became involved?
2. How did Europeans and American merchants justify slavery?
3. How was Gustavus Vassa treated aboard the slave ship?
4. Why was young Vassa so sure that his captors were going to kill him?
5. What were the differences in how slaves were treated in Latin America and North America?

UNDERSTANDING THE STORY

A. Write T for each statement that is true, F for each statement that is false, and N for each statement that is not mentioned in the story.

1. Slavery began in North America.
2. Gustavus Vassa came from a large family.
3. European colonists needed cheap labor in the Americas.
4. Black Africans were captured by white and black slave masters.
5. Conditions were better on some slave ships than on others.
6. There were too few people in the slave ship's hold.
7. None of the Africans attempted to escape from the ship by jumping overboard.
8. In Latin America, the Church encouraged the slave owners to free those slaves who became Christians.

B. Slavery has been called a form of imprisonment in a different type of jail. What does this mean? Suppose that the people who ran the slave ship were given the job of running a modern prison. How successful do you think they might be? Explain your answer.

ACTIVITIES AND INQUIRIES

1. Assume that you are traveling as an observer on the slave ship with Gustavus Vassa. Describe the scene aboard the ship. Describe your feelings.
2. As a reporter, you interview Gustavus Vassa after he has been freed by his master. What questions will you ask him? What answers might he give you?
3. Prepare a report on the differences in the treatment of slaves in Latin America and North America.
4. The United States Constitution forbids cruel and unusual punishment. Why then was slavery permitted? How did the slave owners justify slavery?

UNIT VII

Nationalism and the Industrial Revolution

This unit spans nearly 100 years, from 1780 to 1871. We visit South America and several nations in Europe. Politically, a new world order was being born, and the process was a painful one. Some people tried to turn back the clock of history to an earlier age. Others set out to make a new world. An invention helped bring about a revolution in the way goods

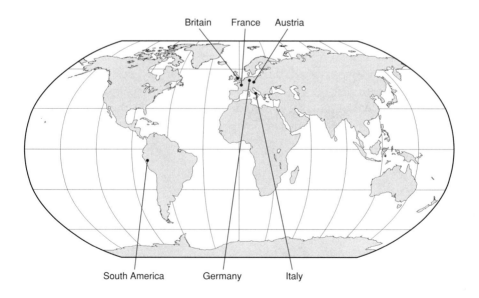

Britain France Austria

South America Germany Italy

were produced. Millions of people would enjoy better lives as a result. But the same revolution also destroyed lives and altered the face of the planet forever.

Europe. Our first story takes place in Vienna, Austria, in 1815. The French Revolution and the Napoleonic Era had brought many changes to Europe. The rulers of Europe feared these changes. Their ministers met in Vienna to redraw the map of Europe and return to the days before 1789. But the idea of nationalism had been set in motion by the French Revolution, and it was a force that some knew would be impossible to contain.

South America. In our second story, we move across the ocean to South America. It is 1822. The winds of freedom had blown from Europe and the United States. Revolutions had occurred in the Spanish Empire. Two heroes of these revolutions met for the last time. Their difficulties show us why the life of a revolutionary leader was only for the very few.

Europe. In our third story, we meet an Italian revolutionary who had dedicated his life to fighting for his country's independence. He paid a high personal price, but his zeal was undiminished.

Our fourth story takes place at a European peace conference in 1871. A national leader had used trickery and deceit to start a war that unified his people. But the forces released by this war would bring about more warfare in the next century.

For our next story, we turn to Great Britain in the late 1700s. A man invented a machine that would help change the face of the world and the lives of everyone. Our final story, set in the 1800s, shows some of the results of the inventor's work. His machine was in use everywhere. But not everyone agreed that the changes the machine had brought about were for the better. Two women expressed different views about these changes, and each made a strong case for her viewpoint.

1. The Plot to Turn Back the Clock

Napoleon had been defeated. In 1814 he was shipped off into exile on the island of Elba. His enemies hoped that this would be the end of Napoleon. But somehow he escaped in 1815, and for a time known as the Hundred Days, he won battle after battle. His moment as the great conqueror had passed, however. The Battle of Waterloo was his final defeat. This time, he was sent far away, to the island of Saint Helena in the South Atlantic Ocean. There he spent the rest of his days.

Now that Napoleon was gone, the scene shifted from the battlefield to the meeting room. Kings and ministers of the major powers of Europe met in Vienna, Austria, from 1814 to 1815. They redrew the map of Europe. Their goal was to "turn back the clock" to the "happy days" before the French Revolution and Napoleon.

Let us see how they proposed to return to those "good old days." Here, we sit in on a meeting of Czar Alexander I of Russia, Prince Metternich of Austria, Viscount Castlereagh of Great Britain, and Talleyrand of France. They are discussing the past and the future of Europe.

Ask yourself why they wanted to turn back the clock. Do you think that it was possible to turn back the clock? How did they try to prevent the rise of another Napoleon?

Vienna   July 1815

CASTLEREAGH. There is one thing we can all agree on. Things have changed in Europe.

TALLEYRAND. Things—I'm not so sure I know what you mean. Aren't we back where we started before the Revolution? Haven't we turned back the clock to the good old days? Change has been wiped out!

CASTLEREAGH. Don't be a fool, Talleyrand. (*He raises his voice slightly.*) Things will never be the same. We can try, but the French Revolution and Napoleon will always be with us.

295

METTERNICH. Don't say that! Thank God, Napoleon is gone. We've shipped him off to Saint Helena. I could not sleep if he were as close as Elba. Put the man on a battlefield and you never know what might happen. He took boys and gave them guns. Somehow he won ten battles in twenty days! That man is dangerous!

TALLEYRAND. I still dream of his escaping and rallying the mobs around him once again. What a nightmare! Never again will a man rise from nowhere and become an emperor, as Napoleon did. Only those born to the throne may be rulers!

(Czar Alexander enters the room. He listens to Metternich.)

METTERNICH. You are right for once, Talleyrand. It was clever of us to choose old Louis, the dead king's brother, to sit on the throne of France. There is no question about his being the legitimate ruler. It was a blessing that there was at least one real Bourbon left in France.

ALEXANDER. Not clever, Metternich—we were not clever at all. We are lucky that Louis happened to be available. The clever thing was to make it look as though the French people were calling Louis back to the throne. What fools they were! Now he is Louis XVIII. Stupidly, he thinks that he was made king of France by the grace of God!

METTERNICH. He looks like a fool and acts like a fool. But he is the king of France. And that's it! Revolutions are over! There will be no more changes in the governments of Europe. The common people will never rule our nations. They will never be given a chance to get control. We must keep the mob in its place! Legitimacy—inherited rank and privilege—is the answer! We must never forget that!

CASTLEREAGH. I repeat: You cannot turn back the clock! We can *try* to hold back the hands of the clock. We can *try* to prevent changes. But gentlemen, the world is not the same. It can never be!

METTERNICH *(angrily)*. Wrong again, Castlereagh! We are going to keep things exactly the way they are. We will insist upon it! Everything we have done here in Vienna has one goal: Keep things as they are. The present order will remain forever. We have made revolutions impossible!

The Congress of Vienna, 1815: After the Napoleonic Wars, diplomats planned to return political power to those who had controlled Europe before the French Revolution.

TALLEYRAND *(places a map of Europe on the table).* Look at this map of Europe. The countries of our continent are all locked in. There is simply no room for change. No new nations can ever rise. Notice how Italy is broken up into many states; each is weak and helpless. And don't forget how cleverly we've divided Germany! There are now 38 weak states, and they're really controlled by Austria. No, there will never be a united Germany!

CASTLEREAGH. I wonder—are we really all that clever— Belgium ruled by the Netherlands, Norway ruled by Sweden? Do you honestly think that all of this is going to last forever?

ALEXANDER *(in a commanding voice).* Gentlemen, I have a simple suggestion that will make all of this last forever. We must protect our thrones through definite action. I hear too much talk about how things will never change. To prevent revolutions, I propose a Holy Alliance of the kings and queens of Europe. Let the people try to revolt. We will crush them without a second thought! We must be sure of ourselves. We must work together. We must fight together to keep things from changing!

(Talleyrand and Metternich seem pleased and excited by Alexander's suggestion. Castlereagh's expression does not change.)

CASTLEREAGH. You once said that kings and queens were put on their thrones because God wanted them there. Then why do you need an alliance?

METTERNICH. Castlereagh, you know better than that. God helps us, but he does not fight our wars. We must never permit the world to be ruled by people like Napoleon. This is the best of all possible worlds for us! Let us keep it that way! My government will support Czar Alexander's proposal for a Holy Alliance!

CASTLEREAGH. England cannot become part of your alliance. It is not to our advantage to support one side or the other.

EUROPE AFTER THE CONGRESS OF VIENNA

ALEXANDER. Nonsense! Who suffers from change? We who have created legitimate governments are the ones who must pay. Look what happened to your own country, Great Britain, during your American Revolution! Those little colonies made the great British empire look almost idiotic! And have you forgotten what the Americans did during the last years of the wars with Napoleon? What did they call it?

CASTLEREAGH. The War of 1812. Your Highness, no one likes to lose. But we have to face the facts. The world changes no matter what we try to do. We cannot stop the movement of time. It is not in England's best interest.

METTERNICH. Tell me, Castlereagh, if your king and queen lost their throne, what would you do? Would you whine and complain? Wouldn't they be better off having all the other rulers of Europe help them?

TALLEYRAND. Do you think that those who have once tasted freedom will forever be satisfied with rule by others? We must always be alert and prepared!

CASTLEREAGH *(for the first time his face reddens with anger).* Enough of this talk of freedom and revolution! Britain may help, but it will not be part of your plan! *(He quickly walks out of the room.)*

ALEXANDER. He simply does not understand. God's will is that the governments are not to be changed. We must protect our rights! If we do not help each other, we are lost!

TALLEYRAND. I wonder—is it too late? Can we keep the seeds of nationalism and freedom from growing forever?

Postscript

The purpose of the Congress of Vienna was to return Europe to the political system that existed before the days of the French Revolution and Napoleon Bonaparte. Change and reform were rejected. People were expected to live under governments that severely restricted their freedoms. But many people refused to conform.

In 1819 German university students demonstrated for more freedom and German unification. Metternich's response was the Carlsbad Decrees.

Newspapers and magazines were strictly censored. Political comment against the government was forbidden, and a committee watched for "revolutionary" activity. No protests were permitted.

Also in 1819, a crowd gathered in Manchester, England, to hear speeches on voting and parliamentary reform. A cavalry troop was ordered to charge into the crowd. Several people were killed, and hundreds were injured. This event was called the Peterloo Massacre.

In spite of Metternich, power was shifting in Europe. The upper middle classes were now in control in England and France. Louis XVIII, who understood this, died while king of France. His successor, Charles X, who refused to accept middle-class leadership, was driven from his throne by a revolution in 1830. He died in exile.

In the United States, the common people achieved more democratic rights. In 1832 the election of President Andrew Jackson represented a shift in political control from the rich, industrial northeast to the poorer, agricultural west. In Canada, an uprising led England to grant more political freedom.

QUESTIONS FOR REVIEW

1. What did the European leaders at Vienna hope to accomplish by "turning back the clock"?
2. What did Castlereagh mean when he said that the world would "never be the same"?
3. Why was Louis XVIII chosen to be the king of France?
4. Why was Talleyrand so sure that the new map of Europe would not change?
5. Why did Czar Alexander propose a Holy Alliance?
6. How did the Carlsbad Decrees limit freedom?

UNDERSTANDING THE STORY

A. Write T for each statement that is true and F for each statement that is false.

1. Napoleon was exiled first to the island of Elba and later to the island of Saint Helena.
2. Most of the leaders at the Congress of Vienna felt that everyone, rich or poor, should benefit from the French Revolution.
3. Many of the leaders at the Congress of Vienna wanted to turn back the clock of history.

4. Metternich and Talleyrand worried that Napoleon might return to Europe.
5. Metternich said that the common people should rule.
6. Castlereagh said that the world would never be the same.
7. "Europe must change" is a remark that Talleyrand might have made.
8. Czar Alexander proposed the Holy Alliance.
9. Castlereagh said that England would not join the Holy Alliance.

B. Imagine that Germany and Britain go to war. Britain is defeated. Germany now attacks several other countries and also defeats them. The United States then goes to war against Germany and wins. Should the United States use the ideas of the Congress of Vienna in dealing with Germany? Write a peace treaty between Germany and the United States. Use the ideas of the Congress of Vienna.

ACTIVITIES AND INQUIRIES

1. Look at the map of Europe after the Congress of Vienna, on page 298. Copy the map in your notebook. Now look at the map of present-day Europe on page 543. Make a list of countries that were not free in 1815 but later became independent.
2. Pretend that you are an American newspaper reporter at the Congress of Vienna in 1815. Interview Czar Alexander. Write a newspaper article telling why the czar feels he must have a Holy Alliance.
3. Interview Castlereagh. Write an article on why he is against the Holy Alliance.
4. Use each of the following key terms in a sentence: exile   reactionary   Holy Alliance   reaction   legitimacy   nationalism.
5. Castlereagh stands alone several times in our story. He does not agree with the other three men. Tell which statements Alexander, Talleyrand, and Metternich would accept, but Castlereagh would reject.
   a. We must have a Holy Alliance.
   b. We must turn back the clock.
   c. It is not in Britain's interest to join an alliance.
   d. The world will never be the same.
   e. There will be no more revolutions in Europe.

2. Unfinished Dreams

At the beginning of the nineteenth century, there were only two independent nations in the Western Hemisphere: the United States and Haiti. Spain had controlled its colonies in the Americas for 300 years. However, beginning in 1808, during the Napoleonic Wars, the Spanish Empire was threatened by colonial wars of independence. The leaders of these revolutions were inspired by the American, French, and Haitian revolutions, as well as by Napoleon's rise and invasion of Spain.

Each of the uprisings in the Americas was local, unconnected with the others. There was no movement for union among the Spanish colonies as there had been among England's 13 American colonies. Nor was there a master plan, or a unified command. There were 17 separate colonial nations.

In 1810 Argentina declared its independence from Spain. In 1811 Venezuela followed. Its leaders wrote a republican constitution, based on the French and American documents. In 1811 a revolutionary army fought its way to the Pacific and moved south to Peru. Other armies were equally successful. The Spanish Empire was breaking up.

King Ferdinand of Spain refused to accept the loss of his colonies, however. The Spanish army and navy overthrew all the new governments, with the exception of Argentina. The Spanish colonial system was restored, but it would not last long.

In 1817 José de San Martín marched from Argentina across the Andes to defeat a royalist army at Chacabuco, Chile. Bernardo O'Higgins had led the main cavalry charge, and in 1818 was rewarded with the leadership of the republic of Chile. In 1822 Simón Bolívar created the Republic of Great Colombia, which included present-day Colombia, Panama, Ecuador, and Venezuela. By 1825 only Puerto Rico and Cuba were left of Spain's once-great Latin American empire.

José de San Martín and Simón Bolívar were two of the great heroes in the fight against Spain. In 1822 they met in secret conference in Ecuador. As we shall see, their goals were quite different.

Guayaquil   July 26, 1822

"Well, San Martín, you asked for this meeting," smiled Bolívar. "What can I do for you?"

"You have your facts slightly twisted," replied San Martín grimly. "The question is, how can we help each other?"

"That's not true, San Martín," said Bolívar. "I know that you are in trouble. The people of Peru are not too happy being ruled by a foreigner from Argentina. And you know very well that a strong Spanish army is waiting in the mountains to attack you."

"Your information is partly correct," San Martín admitted. "But the Peruvians are beginning to accept me. As for the Spanish army, I'll defeat it easily. All I'd like from you, Bolívar, is a little help. I need more money for guns and supplies."

"San Martín, I have very little money, I'm sorry to say. The best I can do is lend you a few hundred soldiers. I'm afraid you'll have to defeat the Spanish forces on your own. Anyway, I don't approve of the way you propose to govern Peru. How can you believe that monarchy is the best way to run a country? And you want to invite a European prince to rule on this continent. Have you lost your mind?"

"Bolívar, the people can't or won't rule themselves. They need a king to tell them what to do."

"And are you that king?" grinned Bolívar.

"Certainly not!" snapped San Martín. "And I'm not happy with *your* views on government. You ramble on about the wonders of democracy, yet you want the wealthy upper class to do your governing."

"That's only temporary," replied Bolívar. "Remember, we had a marvelous democratic constitution in Venezuela in 1811. It was based on the United States Constitution and the French Declaration of the Rights of Man. It was a federal system. Each province was supposed to govern itself. But the average person wasn't ready for self-government."

"Admit it, Bolívar, you just don't trust the common people," said San Martín.

"You're wrong," said Bolívar grimly. "I do trust them. But in this case the people had no experience in running a country. They wasted money by paying themselves salaries for jobs they didn't perform. And they put their lazy friends in office. Then they tried to solve their money problems by printing worthless paper currency. They have a lot to learn."

Simón Bolívar (left) and José de San Martín. On what principles did they agree? What did they disagree about? Who do you think was right?

"We all have a lot to learn," snapped San Martín. "I learned that the best government for our new nations of South America is a monarchy. No, I do not want an all-powerful one like Napoleon Bonaparte's. I prefer a king whose powers are limited."

Bolívar shook his head. "I disagree with you completely, San Martín. A federal government with equal rights for each state is a perfect choice—but not for now. What each new South American country needs *at first* is a well-trained army and a strong, centralized government. True democracy will come later. Now, let's stop our bickering."

"We seem to disagree about everything," said San Martín.

"Perhaps. But why not look at the facts? You've conquered Chile, but your position in Peru is very shaky. I have successfully created the new nation of Great Colombia out of New Granada (Colombia). Of course, I still have to conquer Ecuador."

"No, Bolívar! Ecuador will be *my* conquest."

"You are too late, San Martín. I have just made Ecuador part of the territory of Great Colombia."

Postscript

On the night of July 27, 1822, a ball was given in honor of San Martín. As usual at these affairs, Bolívar enjoyed himself, but San Martín was distant and unhappy. He told his aides that he wanted to leave because of the noise. Unobserved, he left the building, returned to his ship, and set sail for Lima.

San Martín arrived in Lima too late. A revolution had taken place while he was away, and his government had been thrown out of office. Completely discouraged, he refused to fight the rebels. He left Peru and

CENTRAL AND SOUTH AMERICAN INDEPENDENCE
IN THE 19TH CENTURY

never returned. He took no further part in South American politics. José de San Martín died in France in 1850.

Simón Bolívar was exhausted from 12 years of war. But he would not stop. He went into the high Andes, to Cuzco and Arequipa (Peru), and gave orders on how to improve living conditions. He visited La Paz and Potosí in Bolivia, viewing the ruins and poverty. He wrote a constitution for Bolivia, but it was unworkable. All the while, his dream country of Great Colombia was breaking up into its several parts: Colombia, Venezuela, and Ecuador went their separate ways.

Bolívar had hoped to create a federation, or union, of the South American nations, but geography made it impossible. There was little trade or exchange of views among the separate countries. In 1826 he called for a conference at Panama. Only four nations attended, and the conference was a failure. Exhausted, Bolívar died in 1830 at the age of 47. But his dream of international friendship and cooperation did not die.

In the meantime, other nations were concerned about events in Latin America. Freedom from Spanish rule led to a great increase in England's trade with the new nations. The British granted loans to several new countries and were awarded mining leases.

In the United States, there was pressure for recognition of the former Spanish colonies. President James Monroe delayed because he was dealing with Spain for the purchase of Florida. He was also afraid of war with the European powers. In 1822 Monroe finally recognized Argentina, Chile, Peru, Colombia, and Mexico.

In 1823 France invaded Spain to help Ferdinand VII. Many thought that a Franco-Spanish invasion of South America would soon follow. The British were alarmed and suggested to the United States that they jointly oppose the invasion.

Instead, the United States government issued its own warning—with British support. In the Monroe Doctrine, the United States said that there could be no outside (foreign) interference with the nations of the Western Hemisphere. Nor could there be any new colonies. France and Spain did not invade South America.

QUESTIONS FOR REVIEW

1. How were the uprisings in Spain's Latin American colonies different from those in England's North American colonies?
2. How did José de San Martín and Simón Bolívar work to achieve Latin American independence?
3. Why did San Martín ask for a meeting with Bolívar?

4. How did San Martín's views of government differ from Bolívar's?
5. What did Bolívar think the new South American governments needed at that time?

UNDERSTANDING THE STORY

A. Write B for each statement that Bolívar made or might have made and S for each statement that San Martín made or might have made.

1. You have your facts twisted.
2. I know that you are in trouble.
3. The best I can do is lend you a few hundred soldiers.
4. The people need a king to tell them what to do.
5. The average person wasn't ready for self-government.
6. We all have a lot to learn.
7. We seem to disagree about everything.
8. Your position in Peru is very shaky.

B. You have the opportunity to vote for either Bolívar or San Martín as your country's leader. Which man would you choose? Why? The leader of your choice offers you a cabinet position in his government. Why might you refuse the offer?

ACTIVITIES AND INQUIRIES

1. Prepare a report on the life and personality of Bolívar or San Martín.
2. On a map of South America, trace the military campaigns of Bolívar and San Martín. Then write about their military and political successes and failures.
3. Imagine that Bolívar and San Martín appear on your radio or television interview program. What will they tell you about their preferences in government? What points might they agree on? What disagreements would you expect them to have?
4. Prepare a report card for San Martín in each of the following areas: (*a*) personality (*b*) government leadership (*c*) military leadership (*d*) major accomplishments.
5. Now prepare a report card for Bolívar in each of the same areas.

3. The Dream That Would Not Die

We have seen how the seeds of nationalism and revolution were planted by the French Revolution and Napoleon. The diplomats at the Congress of Vienna thought that they could uproot these ideas. They tried to turn back the clock, but they failed. Progress stopped for a few years, but that was all. Europeans were to have their own nations and would not be ruled by foreign kings. They insisted on the right of self-government. The people remembered the words of the American Declaration of Independence and the French Declaration of the Rights of Man. Governments could not be forced upon people; they must be allowed to make their own choice.

The changes made by the Congress of Vienna were supposed to last forever. How wrong the diplomats were! Within a few years, nations that had been imprisoned within the boundaries of others were fighting for their freedom. Here is the roll of honor:

1821   Greece: Revolution failed, but independence from Turkey was granted in 1829.

1830   France: July revolution overthrew King Charles X. This led to rule of Louis Philippe, "the bourgeois king."

1830   Belgium: Gained independence from the Netherlands.

1848   France: Louis Philippe abdicated (resigned) under pressure. Louis Napoleon elected first president of the Second French Republic.

1848   Austria and Hungary: Revolutions broke out in Hungary, Bohemia, and Vienna itself. (Metternich's home in Vienna was burned.)

The revolutions were crushed, but the peasants were finally freed from feudal taxes.

Italians also were struggling for independence. An uprising in Naples in the 1820s was crushed by Austria. In 1848 King Charles Albert of Sardinia attacked the Austrian armies. Eventually, he was badly beaten, and he abdicated as king. Revolutionists led by Giuseppe Mazzini and Giuseppe Garibaldi were successful at first in Milan and Venetia, but were not strong enough to keep control.

In this story, Garibaldi writes about his experiences and feelings as he fought around Rome in 1849. Ask yourself why Garibaldi and Mazzini felt so strongly about Italian nationalism. Why did they want to create an Italian nation? How did the views of Garibaldi and Mazzini differ on the subject of Italian nationalism?

A ship off Sardinia   August 1849

DEAR MAZZINI,

My dear friend, what can I tell you at this point in our lives? How can I ever forget your words when you left Rome? You realized that all was lost, even though I insisted that I would stay awhile and fight on. How right you were when you said, "I feel rage rising within me at the triumph of brute force over right and justice!" What else is there to say? What else is left to do but think of fighting still another day!

I am sure you heard that we were crushed and scattered by the soldiers of France. I never thought that Louis Napoleon would order his soldiers to fight against my Red Shirts in the streets

"We must continue to fight. Let's gain our independence! Liberty and equality will follow!"

of the Holy City. But Pope Pius IX called for help, and
Napoleon answered. He turned our fight to build an Italian
nation into a holy war to protect the pope. He forgets that the
pope is not merely the head of the Catholic Church. He is the
ruler of the Papal States—of states that must belong to the
Italian nation and people!

My Red Shirts fought bravely. Many gave their lives without
complaint for the cause of the Italian nation! Was it a waste? I
do not really know! We fought off the French soldiers for
over two months. Finally, their numbers and training were just
too much for us. I was lucky and escaped capture. But Anita,
my beloved wife, is dead! The whole business was too much
for her. She was completely exhausted. She could stand no
more punishment. Perhaps she is better off.

Giuseppe, I swear by all that is holy to both of us that I will
avenge her death! There is only one way. There is only one
reason for my living now. I must free the people of Italy from
their slavery. We Italians will have our own nation, our own
rulers. Let's throw out the Austrians! The pope must give up
the Papal States! We must do something about Louis
Napoleon! It will be soon, Giuseppe, soon! Do not be discouraged by our failure. I will win! I will win for Anita and
the people of Italy!

I am sure that you agree that we must continue the fight. We
cannot give up—we cannot stop now! I know that you are as
dedicated as I to the cause of Italian freedom. But there is one
thing I do not understand about your thinking. You keep saying that Italy must be free and independent. Then you go on
to say that it must have a democratic government. Let the
people rule, you say. Fine—but what if the people are not
ready to govern themselves? What if the people know nothing
about making their own laws at this time?

How many successful democracies do you see in Europe?
What difference does it make what kind of government Italy
has, as long as it is Italian? Charles Albert of Sardinia was a
good king and a fair man. But he has been forced to abdicate.

Enough of Charles. Let's talk about his son, the new king,
Victor Emmanuel. Will you agree to support him? Can't you
see that we must have someone in a high office to whom we
can turn? Victor Emmanuel can be the head of a united Italy!

Encourage all Italians to rally to the flag and crown of Sardinia!

Giuseppe, back in the old days, you were the fighter, the conspirator! Nothing bothered you. You had one purpose in life: the creation of the nation of Italy. Remember your slogans: "Unity and independence"; "Liberty, equality, and humanity." Remember how you swore an oath to your brotherhood of Young Italy? Your life was to be given to the cause of Italian independence. Here's our chance, Giuseppe; let's gain our independence first! Liberty and equality will follow!

I know that you are discouraged. You have a right to be. But please, don't give up the fight now. Do you remember how you talked about remaking the map of Europe? It's not too late. You will still have your chance. Italy and Anita need you! Join with me once again in the fight to make Italy free!

I have no idea when we will meet again. But I pray that it will be on an Italian battlefield!

Italy will live again!

Your friend in freedom,
GIUSEPPE GARIBALDI

Postscript

Garibaldi did return to Italy to lead the forces for Italian independence. In battle, Garibaldi was not afraid to tell his soldiers, "We are going to die, but Italy will win the day. *Viva Italia!*" On one occasion, he was slightly wounded, and several bullets passed through his clothing. He refused to take the time to have the wound treated. His only complaint was that he wished that he had another pair of pants. Soldiers followed him without hesitation into battle. With his colorful, reckless style, Garibaldi was by far the most popular man in Italy.

In 1860 Garibaldi conquered the Kingdom of the Two Sicilies (the island of Sicily and the kingdom of Naples on the mainland). He could have become the ruler of the kingdom. Instead, he encouraged the people to vote to join Sardinia. In 1861 the Italian parliament named King Victor Emmanuel of Sardinia the king of Italy.

Later in life, Garibaldi was unhappy with the government of his newly united nation. There was a written constitution and a parliament, and the

THE UNIFICATION OF ITALY 1859–1870

powers of the king were limited. However, the parliament was chosen by a limited number of male voters. Very few citizens—only about one in 30—had the right to elect representatives to the lawmaking body.

QUESTIONS FOR REVIEW

1. Why were the diplomats at the Congress of Vienna wrong about the changes they made?

2. Why was Garibaldi surprised that Louis Napoleon ordered his soldiers to fight against Garibaldi's Red Shirts?
3. How did Garibaldi plan to avenge his wife's death?
4. Why was it important that Mazzini supported King Victor Emmanuel?
5. Why was Garibaldi unhappy with the government of the newly united Italian nation?

UNDERSTANDING THE STORY

A. Write T for each statement that is true and O for each statement that is an opinion.

1. Garibaldi worked to create an Italian nation.
2. Garibaldi was the greatest Italian leader who ever lived.
3. The diplomats at the Congress of Vienna failed to turn back the clock.
4. Garibaldi's Red Shirts fought bravely in Rome.
5. Garibaldi should not have taken his wife along when he went to fight in Italy.
6. Mazzini wanted a democratic government.
7. Mazzini believed Italy had to be free and independent.
8. One of Mazzini's slogans was "Liberty, equality, and humanity."

B. Imagine that you are fighting for the independence of a state or province somewhere in the world today. Would you prefer your army to be led by someone like Garibaldi or someone like Mazzini? Why? Which person, Garibaldi or Mazzini, would be more successful as president of the new country? Why?

ACTIVITIES AND INQUIRIES

1. Look at the map of Italian unification on page 312. Draw this map in your notebook. Indicate on the map the territories mentioned in the introduction and the story.
2. Go to the library. Prepare a report on one of the following: Cavour Victor Emmanuel Young Italy the Carbonari the Red Shirts.
3. Imagine that you are Mazzini. Answer Garibaldi's letter to you. Tell him how you feel about the future of Italy.
4. Draw a cartoon showing Mazzini and Garibaldi working to turn a group of Italian states into an Italian nation. What is the title of your cartoon? Why are Mazzini and Garibaldi having such a hard time?

What advice would you give Mazzini and Garibaldi to help them build the Italian nation?

5. Assume that Garibaldi is talking to King Victor Emmanuel. What is the most important part of their discussion? Why? What does the king ask Garibaldi to do? What is Garibaldi's response? How would you have answered?

4. Iron and Blood

By 1870 Italy was a unified nation. The dreams of Mazzini, Garibaldi, and many others had come true. The Germans had a similar dream. But there was a difference. There was not even a hint of democracy in the vision of Otto von Bismarck. This master planner of the German nation believed that the people should be ruled with an "iron hand." The state of Prussia would lead and the other German states would follow.

In this story, we learn that Prussia has just defeated France in the Franco-Prussian War (1871). The leaders of the two countries—Louis Napoleon (Napoleon III) of France and Prince Otto von Bismarck of Prussia—meet at Sedan, France, after the final battle.

Ask yourself why Bismarck wanted Prussia to fight a war against France. What difference do you see in the personalities of Napoleon III and Bismarck? Why was German unification so important to Bismarck?

Sedan   1871

(Louis Napoleon thinks to himself before meeting Bismarck on the battlefield.)

Where did I go wrong? What a fool I was to let myself be dragged into war with Prussia! That Bismarck! He had only one thing on his mind: Prussia must win. Prussia must be all-powerful, no matter what the cost! I didn't understand what he meant by "iron and blood," but, alas, now I do. Nothing must stand in his way. Bismarck will stop at nothing. War and death are his tools. Whoever gets in his way is crushed!

I felt that he was pushing France into war, but how could I do anything about it? Was I supposed to look like a coward? Could I be a weakling? I should have known that his Ems Dispatch was a trick to force me to declare war against Prussia. The scoundrel cleverly changed the words of the telegram. We French thought that our ambassador had been insulted by the king of Prussia. At the very same time, the Prussians thought that the French had insulted their king! How could Bismarck fail to create a war?

It's all so clear now. We were used. The war against France brought all the German states rushing to Prussia's side. Now I see that Bismarck used me to bring them together!

Now it's done and I'm the loser. How could I have been so stupid? My dreams of greatness are all down the drain! Where did I get the idea that I could build a great French empire? Why did I have to try to copy my uncle, Napoleon I? I was a Napoleon—how could I fail? I would show the world what a Napoleon, an emperor, could do! The people of France would believe in me. They would follow me wherever I led them! I was the great man. Failure was impossible. Today, France; tomorrow, the world!

I could have been the greatest leader of this century. I knew all the mistakes my uncle, Napoleon Bonaparte, made. I was going to avoid them. I made up my mind never to fight all the strong countries of Europe, as he did. I would pick a weak country here, a soft one there. It worked for a while. I built up France's empire in West Africa, Asia, and the South Pacific. I was doing well. It was all so easy.

But there were also some glorious days in Europe. When I led the 1856 conference ending the Crimean War, we made those Russians squirm! What a moment of greatness! France was once again the leader of all Europe!

But after that, things went downhill. I have a peculiar feeling that I might have been better off if that Italian assassin's bullet had killed me in 1858! I would not have become involved in war in 1859 with Austria. Imagine *me* fighting on the side of little Sardinia! I got out of that war fast! And I would not have become involved in Mexican affairs in 1863. How the United States objected to the presence of French troops in Mexico! I was forced to withdraw my soldiers. What a disgrace!

Louis Napoleon (left) and Bismarck meet at Sedan, in 1871. Why was Bismarck's plan for unifying Germany successful?

Here comes Bismarck now! How stuffy and coarse he looks! Look at that ridiculous uniform! I must pull myself together. I must not let him see that I am bitter and unhappy. I am a loser, a dreamer of broken dreams. But I must act the part of the emperor of France. I will give him nothing! He will have to kill me first!

(Bismarck thinks to himself before he meets Louis Napoleon.)

This has to be the greatest day of my life! Louis Napoleon and France have been crushed by my Prussian war machine. I have the backing of every German state. Now nothing stands in the way of the unification of Germany. It has taken me many years, but Germany will be a nation at last. The king of Prussia will be the king of all Germany. And I did it!

To be more honest, I did it with the help of Louis Napoleon. He's a fool trying to act like an emperor. Did he really think that he was a great man and a great leader? Did he imagine that he could defeat Bismarck and Prussia on the battlefield?

Yes, Germany owes Louis Napoleon a great deal. His greed and dreams of empire made him a pushover for me. I changed the Ems telegram to make it read as though the Prussian king, William, had snubbed the French ambassador. I knew that Louis Napoleon would have to uphold the honor of France. I knew that he couldn't allow himself time to think.

Weaklings are sensitive about their honor. Fools are easily insulted. Louis Napoleon was very touchy and willing to fight. Perhaps he was afraid that people would find out the truth about him. Well, it's too late for you now, Louis Napoleon. They know what you are—a boastful, hollow shell. Yes, I pushed him into war; yes, I used him. But I had to do it for the greater glory of a united Germany.

It was a bloody war. We lost many soldiers, but it was worth it! General von Moltke did a great job of leading our army. His organization and planning were excellent. Louis Napoleon's battle plans were out of date. He was finished before he started!

This is the end of the trip. The goal, a German nation, is in sight. It has taken me a long time to get to this point. Iron and blood, iron and blood—that was the way to do it! Nothing could stop me!

Yes, Louis Napoleon, I've crushed you. Now, I'm going to make you pay! You must suffer. I'll teach you that no Frenchman can stand up to a Prussian.

Here he comes now. Look at him in his fancy uniform with all those medals. Look at that mustache! He must spend hours in front of a mirror! Yes, he's a fool all right—a clumsy fool! Why doesn't he look at me? His eyes are blank. He's staring at the sky.

"Ah, Prince Bismarck," said Napoleon III, "you have never looked better. This situation is a little unpleasant, but I am very happy to see you."

"Your excellency," answered Bismarck, "it is a pleasure to see you. I have been looking forward to this meeting for quite a long time!"

Postscript

Bismarck succeeded in unifying Germany and in dominating neighboring countries. However, at home, he was worried about the industrial workers who had recently been given the right to vote. Was it possible that they might replace him by voting for the Socialist Party? (*Socialism* is a system in which the government owns or controls much of the way that goods and services are produced.)

Bismarck decided to win the workers' votes by offering them *social insurance*: health care and medical coverage for sickness and accidents, and pensions in old age. These were also the major demands of the Socialist Party. Bismarck made the Socialists' program his own.

Bismarck believed that a person who expected to receive an old-age pension and other benefits would be a happier and more productive worker. "It may be state socialism," he said, "but it is necessary."

Bismarck went one step further. He also felt that the government

THE UNIFICATION OF GERMANY

must take care of orphans and the poor. It was important that the propertyless poor be treated decently. Otherwise, there was always the chance that they might turn against the ruling government.

By the twentieth century, similar social insurance programs had been adopted by Great Britain, France, Belgium, and Italy.

QUESTIONS FOR REVIEW

1. How did the dreams of Garibaldi and Bismarck for their nations differ?
2. What did Bismarck mean by "iron and blood"?
3. How did the Ems Dispatch force Louis Napoleon into war against Prussia?
4. Why did Louis Napoleon feel that he might have been better off had the assassin's bullet killed him?
5. Why did Bismarck feel that this was the greatest day of his life?

UNDERSTANDING THE STORY

A. Decide who made or might have made the remarks that follow. Write LN for each statement that Louis Napoleon made or might have made and B for each statement that Bismarck made or might have made.

1. I could have been the greatest leader of the century.
2. Iron and blood are what I used to win.
3. He is a fool trying to act like an emperor.
4. I know that I'm the loser. How could I have been so stupid?
5. Why couldn't I be a great general?
6. I pushed him into war.
7. It was a bloody war, but it was worth it.
8. I built up our empire in Africa and Asia.

B. Imagine that Bismarck and Louis Napoleon are running for president of the United States. Which one would you vote for? Why? Suppose that you refuse to vote for either of them. What sort of person would you seek for this job? Explain your reasons.

ACTIVITIES AND INQUIRIES

1. Look at the map of unified Germany on page 318, and the map of Germany after the Congress of Vienna, on page 298. Make a list of the differences in the two maps.

2. Imagine that you are Bismarck. Write a letter to the king of Prussia. Tell him about your victory at Sedan. What does this mean to German unification? What does this mean to the king of Prussia?

3. Pretend that you are the king of Prussia. Write an answer to Bismarck's letter.

4. Imagine that you are a reporter at the battle of Sedan. Your job is to interview Louis Napoleon and write an article for your newspaper. Write the article.

5. Many historians believe that Bismarck was a great leader. Make a list of the abilities you believe a great leader should have. Alongside each, indicate whether Bismarck met this requirement.

5. The Steam Engine

We saw how the English and French revolutions changed people's views about government. Ordinary people were not willing to be ruled by those who were born to power. They began to believe in themselves. They felt that they should select their own rulers. But these new rulers would stay in power only as long as the people wanted them. And life would be freer for all people. Each person was as good as any other.

In the eighteenth century, another revolution got under way. It too made great changes in the way people worked and lived. The *Industrial Revolution* began in England and spread to many other countries. It was not a revolution of battles or wars, of land or nations. It was a revolution of how and where things or goods are made.

At the beginning of the 1700s, England was a nation of farmers. Only one person out of every four lived in cities. Products such as cloth were made in the farmers' cottages. The entire family took part in manufacturing. The wife and children combed and spun the wool or cotton. The husband did the weaving. (The spinning wheel and hand loom had been used for centuries.) This work-at-home production was called the *domestic system*.

By the end of the 1700s, however, farm families were no longer spinning and weaving in their homes. Cloth was made in factories by machines. But there still was a problem: where to find the power to run the machines. The solution was found in the steam engine that James Watt constructed in 1769.

In this story, James Watt writes a letter to a person who does not understand what steam power can do. Ask yourself whether Watt had good reason for being angry. Was the Industrial Revolution possible without the steam engine?

Birmingham   1790

DEAR GEORGE,

I have heard that you are telling people that England could have existed without James Watt. "What did he do? He was no inventor. He built a steam engine, but anybody could build a steam engine. What was wrong with Newcomen's steam engine? It puffed; it had lots of power. All Watt did was copy Newcomen."

George, let's be honest. I never said that I alone invented the steam engine. You know as well as I do that the ancient Greeks made a steam engine. But it was a toy; it could not make a machine run. Yes, Tom Newcomen made an engine many years before I did—and, by God, it worked! But all it could do was pump water out of the mines. That's where I did my part. I took Tom's engine and made change after change! No matter what you think, it wasn't easy. I worked on the steam engine until it had the power to drive the machines in the factories. I used coal to power the steam engine. And you know how rich England is in coal! We have enough coal to power millions of machines.

What did I do for England, George? I made it possible to use steam. I gave factories the power they needed to make cloth and iron. Yes, I made it easier and cheaper to run the coal and copper mines.

Do you remember what it was like when factories used the rushing waters of a river or a pond to drive the machines? What did you do when there wasn't enough water? What happened when there was no rain? Did you bring your own buckets of water when the wheels would not turn?

Perhaps you would like to go back to the old days. Hitch up your horses and let them turn the power wheel. Find out what

James Watt's Soho Engineering Works, at Birmingham, England. Watt manufactured steam engines here from 1775 to 1800.

it means to depend on horses. How much cloth do you think the machines run with horsepower can produce?

You simply do not understand that steam is always there. You never have to worry whether there is enough water. You don't have to build your factory near water. My steam engine never gets tired, as your horses do. It never gets hungry. Do you know that my engine has the power of 20 horses? In fact, I have even made a few engines with the power of 80 horses! Imagine having 80 horses indoors for each of my engines! Can you see what this means?

My engine never sleeps. It makes those factory wheels turn faster and faster. Each turn of the wheel means more goods and cheaper goods! That means money for the factory owners. It means lower prices for the buyers. It means more money for all of us. England's wealth is greatly increased. And don't forget the jobs the engine creates for all the workers in the new factories!

Yes, George, England could have survived without me. But

could we have had an Industrial Revolution without my steam engine?

Someday, you'll see. They may well call my steam engine the greatest invention of all time.

Your friend,
JAMES WATT

Postscript

As Watt claimed, the steam engine made possible a vast increase in the production of goods. However, it was still very difficult to bring raw materials to factories and to ship finished products to buyers. Most goods were shipped on slow-moving pack horses over rutted, rugged roads. As roads were improved, horse-drawn wagons replaced the pack horses. Also, rivers were deepened, and thousands of miles of canals were dug.

The movement of goods remained a slow process until Watt's steam engine was put to use. In 1807 the American engineer Robert Fulton, using an engine designed by Watt and Matthew Boulton, built the first successful steamboat. By 1812 the first British steamboats were running regularly.

At the same time, other inventors were working to create a steam locomotive. In 1803 Richard Trevithick demonstrated his engine, but it was much too heavy for the rails. In 1829 George Stephenson built his lighter, faster "Rocket" to win a competition among locomotive builders. He proved that the steam locomotive was faster and cheaper than horses or stationary engines whose cables pulled the cars uphill. Stephenson's locomotive opened the way to the development of railroads and the rapid movement of goods and people.

James Watt's steam engine may or may not have been "the greatest invention of all time," but it ensured the success of the Industrial Revolution.

QUESTIONS FOR REVIEW

1. Describe the domestic system of manufacturing.
2. What changes did the Industrial Revolution bring about?
3. What was wrong with Newcomen's steam engine?

4. What are the disadvantages of using water power to drive machines?
5. What are the advantages of using steam power to drive machines?

UNDERSTANDING THE STORY

A. Which statements show how the Industrial Revolution changed the lives of the English people?

1. Most cloth was now made in factories.
2. The spinning wheel and hand loom were widely used.
3. Steam power rather than water power turned England's machines.
4. Horses turned the power wheels in England's new factories.
5. Factory owners made higher profits.
6. The prices of goods made in factories were always higher than the prices of goods made at home.
7. There were many jobs for workers in the new factories.

B. Imagine that James Watt did not develop the steam engine. Neither did anyone else. Imagine too that the Industrial Revolution never took place. Write a short paragraph telling how different your life would be if there had never been an Industrial Revolution. List some of the items you use every day that were made possible by the Industrial Revolution.

ACTIVITIES AND INQUIRIES

1. What does the illustration on page 322 tell you about the steam engine? How could one steam engine be more powerful than 20 horses?
2. Go to the library. Prepare a report on another inventor whose machine helped make the Industrial Revolution. Among those you might choose from are John Kay, Richard Arkwright, Samuel Crompton, Edmund Cartwright, Eli Whitney, and James Hargreaves.
3. Make drawings of one or more of the inventions you listed above. Be prepared to explain how the invention works.
4. Prepare an article for your local newspaper on inventors in the fields of electronics and computers. Compare their accomplishments with those of James Watt.
5. Describe your experiences with present-day uses of steam power. You may cover such areas as transportation, cooking, and heating.

6. Farm or Factory?

As we have seen, before the Industrial Revolution, people made goods by hand and with hand-powered machines at home. This was called the domestic system. Then the work shifted to factories with machines. Farm people flocked to the factories in the towns and cities. No special skills were necessary to work in those early factories. The workers repeated the same operations over and over, thousands of times each day.

Factory workers in cities often lived in filthy rooms in overcrowded slums. They worked in dark, airless factory rooms, where they were in constant danger from the unguarded machinery. They worked as long as there was light. Often, they could barely see what they were doing. The pay was low, but it was more than they could earn on the farm. Many of the workers in these factories (and in the mines) were women and children.

In this story a young girl of 14 returns to her family home on an English farm. Ask yourself whether she should stay on the farm. Did she make the right decision? What would her life have been like if she had stayed on the farm?

Harrowgate 1842

"Susan, welcome back from Manchester," said Joyce. "It's great to see you again. Are you going to stay home with us for a few months?"

"I'm glad to see you, too," said Susan. "It's been such a long time since I left home. No, I'm just visiting for a short time. I am not going to stay here."

"Why not?" asked Joyce. "You look terrible. You're as skinny as a stick. Your clothes hang on you as though you're a scarecrow!"

"Stop it, Joyce," said Susan angrily. "I've been sick for the past few weeks. How do you expect me to look?"

"Please don't be angry, Susan. I just want you to be well and look healthy. Stay with us for a few weeks, and you'll be yourself again."

"I am myself. This is the real me," answered Susan quickly. "I have no intention of staying for more than a few weeks. I never want to feel the way I felt when I lived here on the farm. My mind was a blank. My life was empty. I was so lonely and sad! All that I had to look forward to were the endless days and nights on the farm. There were chores to be done from before sunrise to after sunset. Chores and more chores every day—365 days a year. There was no end to my work. And I was so bored!"

"It may be lonely here," said Joyce quietly. "Yes, you may do the same things all during the year on the farm. But the farm isn't at all like a factory. You don't repeat the same movements minute after minute, hour after hour, day after day. Talk about being bored!"

"Joyce, you just don't understand," said Susan. "The thing that's so great about factory work is that it is not boring for me. I like it!"

Joyce said, "Susan, look around you. It's clean here. The air is sweet and pure. The blue sky is up there to see—not just to

Two 19th-century factories: (below) Western woolen textile-making; (facing page) Chinese silk-making. These products were major exports of their regions. How are the two scenes similar? How are they different?

dream about. It's not blotted out by the smoke from hundreds of factory chimneys. The water is good. There are no epidemics here in the country. You may not make any money, but I guarantee you that you will live twice as long!"

"Joyce, you will die of boredom on the farm. The city may not be clean, but it has life. There are lights, good times, excitement. There are people—real people. We can talk, go out, have fun. I'm alive in the city, Joyce. "I'm dead here!"

"Look at you, Susan. You tell *me* that you're having a good time! I feel sorry for you. You look as though you're just this side of the grave. Face it. That factory work is killing you! How many hours do you work a week: 72, 84, 104? When do you have time for all that fun you talk about? You have less time off than you had on the farm. Do you think we don't know what goes on in those factories? Do you think we don't know what happens to girls who work in the cities?"

"Stop preaching at me!" interrupted Susan.

"No, I won't," continued Joyce. "Do they let you work at your own pace? Do they beat you if you slow down? Is there light and air? Who pays the doctor if you get hurt on those dangerous machines? Don't you try to tell me that there's excitement and pleasure in working in a filthy room—100 girls squeezed into a space where 15 would be a crowd! What happens when you try to talk to another girl? And suppose they did let you talk. Could you hear anyone over the clatter of the machines?"

"Wait a minute," interrupted Susan. "I never said that the factory was paradise. Sure it's hard work, and there are dangers. But we work only 60 hours a week. Life in the factory is much easier now. They hardly ever beat us. There's more light in the factory than you think. Anyway, we usually stop work when the sun goes down. Yes, some girls do get hurt, but don't accidents happen on the farm? I'll never get hurt if I am careful. Girls get hurt because they get careless. They forget to keep their eyes on the sharp blades and the rough edges. You have to be alert every second. And, don't forget, I get two free meals a day!"

"What do they give you to eat?" snorted Joyce. "Garbage, that's what—and not too much of that! How much time do you get to eat: 15 minutes? Every extra minute spent eating means less cloth made by your beautiful factory. The bosses aren't going to lose profits so that you can eat your food in peace and quiet. Free meals? You know as well as I do that those meals come out of your pay. If they don't, they come out of your hide!"

"You still miss the point," continued Susan, refusing to give in. "Things are getting better every day. Besides, I'm away from home. I can earn money and I can save some. I'm on my own. A woman with money finds it easier to get a husband. You should know that!"

"No, Susan, I don't know! What are you earning? Is it one penny or two pennies an hour? How much can you save from all of that? You are living in a world of make-believe. You'll never have any money. Do you think you'll get a husband? What will you look like in a few years? What man will have you with or without money?"

"Let's not talk about good looks," said Susan angrily. "I suppose that you're going to tell me that working on a farm makes a girl better looking!"

"Maybe not, Susan, but at least I won't choke to death. I'll always have plenty to eat. I can get a good night's sleep after being out in the fresh air all day. I may not meet too many people, but the ones I do meet will be honest and trustworthy. I know that I won't be robbed walking down some dark, crooked alley in a filthy city."

"You won't be robbed," said Susan, "because you won't be going anywhere. Someday you may learn that people really live in the city!"

Postscript

The factory system revolutionized the production of goods. It brought new machines and procedures under one roof. Newly introduced farming methods also greatly increased production. Soil preparation, cultivation, seeding, and sowing were improved. New varieties of long-standard crops were developed. Crop rotation and the use of soil–enriching crops also helped greatly to increase farm output. Through the years, improved farm machinery also led to vast increases in crop yields.

A problem in the past had been how to feed farm animals in the winter. This was solved in the 1700s by growing crops such as clover and turnips. Clover meant better summer growth and more hay for the winter. Turnips proved to be an excellent cattle conditioner. At the same time, larger and stronger domestic animals were developed by careful breeding. Cattle and sheep were no longer thin and spindly. These new animals provided more and better-quality meat, milk, and wool for a growing population.

Fewer and fewer people were needed on the farms to produce these larger crops. In the long term, many farm workers migrated to the cities where they provided an ever-growing supply of labor for the factories.

QUESTIONS FOR REVIEW

1. Describe the living conditions in nineteenth-century English slums.
2. Why did Susan object to farm life?
3. Why did Joyce object to factory work?

4. What was Joyce's objection to the free factory meals?
5. How did the Industrial Revolution change women's job opportunities? Did it change their responsibilities at home? Explain. How did the Industrial Revolution open the way to women's equality with men?

UNDERSTANDING THE STORY

A. Susan and Joyce have different ideas about many things. Decide who made or might have made the following remarks. Write S for each statement that Susan made or might have made and J for each statement that Joyce made or might have made.

1. I'm not going to stay here. There's too much work on the farm.
2. A woman with money can always find a husband.
3. The air is pure and you can breathe here on the farm.
4. The city is full of excitement, fun, and people.
5. They don't give you enough to eat at the factory.
6. You don't repeat the same job endlessly on the farm.
7. It's hard work, but we work only 60 hours a week in the factory.
8. You will live twice as long on the farm.
9. I never said the factory was paradise.
10. I won't be robbed walking down a dark street in a filthy city!

B. Pretend that you have just graduated from high school. You are offered a choice of jobs. You can work on a farm in the country or you can work in a factory in the city. Which would you choose? Why? What differences would you expect to find between Susan's factory and your factory? What differences would you expect to find between Joyce's farm and your farm?

ACTIVITIES AND INQUIRIES

1. Imagine that you have the job of preparing a report card on the working conditions in Susan's factory. Grade each of the items below pass or fail. Write a sentence explaining the reasons for each grade. How can the failing grades be raised to passing grades? How can the passing grades be raised to excellent grades?

wages or pay	light and air	living quarters
hours of work	space in the factory	labor by women
safety of ma-	vacations and	and children
chinery	holidays	air pollution

2. Pretend that you are a member of the British government in the 1800s. Write a report telling how working conditions in the factories can be made better.

3. A newspaper reporter visited a typical factory in 1842, the year our story took place. Read the description and answer the questions that follow.

> There are 1,500 people working in the factory. Most are under 15 years of age. Some, not yet seven years old, are barefoot. All start work at 5:30 A.M. They do not finish until after 7:00 P.M. The children are small for their age. They are weak looking, and many are crippled. They are beaten with a heavy strap by the foreman. This makes them work harder. They have never been to school.

Imagine that you are a health inspector. You visit the factory. Make a list of all the violations you find. Why do you suppose parents sent their children to work in factories like this one?

4. Visit a factory. Compare this factory with the one you read about in question 3.

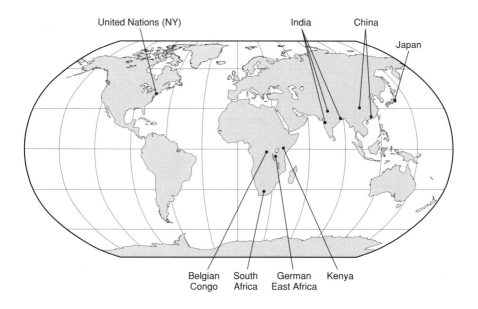

United Nations (NY)   India   China

Japan

Belgian   South   German   Kenya
Congo   Africa   East Africa

UNIT VIII

Imperialism

Beginning in the eighteenth century, but mainly during the nineteenth, many European nations rushed to gain control of large areas in Asia and Africa. When a strong nation takes control of a weak one, this act is called *imperialism*.

Why were Europeans prepared to spend fortunes and go to war to bring these areas under their control? There were several reasons. First, Europeans needed Asia and Africa to supply them with raw materials, cheap labor, and markets for their manufactured goods. Second, Europeans feared if they did not gain colonies, they would become weak and lose the respect of other countries. Third, many Europeans also claimed that a sense of duty drove them to take control of many lands and people in Africa and Asia. As a "superior" people, the Europeans said, it was their duty to bring Western civilization to the "backward" areas of the world.

The West would certainly bring great changes to Africa and Asia. Many nations would be modernized, whether they wished to be or not.

Asia. In our first story, we visit China in 1839. Convinced of their superiority, the Chinese were preparing to fight a war with England, one of the most powerful nations in the world. The Chinese did not know it, but their way of life, which had endured for thousands of years, was about to undergo severe stress and enormous change.

In our second story, almost 60 years passed. The Chinese had tried to overthrow the European imperialists by finding answers in the "old ways," but they succeeded only in binding themselves more firmly. New answers had to be found, and new problems had to be overcome. This story details the difficulties that awaited those who sought new answers.

Our third story takes place in China, in 1945. Two men had come forward in a bid to lead China. Both believed that China had to become a modern nation, but they disagreed on how this was to be done. One man would emerge the victor. The loser would learn that victory demands more than money and material resources.

In our fourth story, we are in Japan in 1853. The Japanese received an unwelcome visit from representatives of the United States government. But the Americans brought gifts that would help the Japanese open the door to the modern world.

Africa. From Japan, we move to Africa in 1871. An explorer and newspaperman was in search of a great story. He was looking for a famous missionary who had disappeared. The newspaperman found his story.

Next we visit the Congo, in Africa, in 1903. Europeans had taken control, and stories had been received in the outside world that terrible acts had been committed there. The story will show whether or not the rumors were true.

Our next African story takes place in Kenya, in 1974. Africans had become increasingly opposed to European rule, and many dreamed of independence. Some Africans believed that they had to learn modern ways before they could reclaim their countries. But others believed that violence would make their dream come true.

We move to South Africa in 1977. A young black leader had privileges that were denied to most black people. But he knew that he would not have real freedom until all his people had the same rights. He would risk all for his beliefs.

India. We next visit the Indian subcontinent. The land and people were under the control of the British. Some Indian people were grateful to the British for all they had brought to India, but many others resented them for taking over their country. An Indian who had praised the British discovered something that made him change his mind.

Our next story is about an Indian leader who was determined to free his country from British rule. Pledged not to use force and violence, this leader developed other tactics that were so powerful they forced the British to grant independence to the Indian people.

Now we look at India in 1948, a nation that had just won its independence. The leader who preached against violence would become one of its victims. Many ancient hatreds were unleashed by independence, and the new Indian government faced many difficult challenges.

Our final story takes place at United Nations headquarters, in New York City. We listen to a conversation between an African delegate and several European delegates. The Europeans tried to convince the African that independence was a mistake for the African people. The African delegate's answers gave the Europeans much to ponder.

1. A Dance of Death

For centuries Europeans had shown great interest in China. China's beautiful cities, vast natural resources, great wealth, and its porcelains, silks, and teas had powerful appeal for Europeans. (See Unit V, story 1.) China appeared to be very powerful, and the Europeans were careful not to push the Chinese too far.

In the nineteenth century, little was really known about Manchu China, however. Europeans did not know about China's vast problems. China was crippled by poverty, illiteracy, disease, and overpopulation. Laws favored the rich and hurt the poor. Secret terrorist societies plotted to overthrow the government, which was weak and corrupt.

The Chinese had another picture of themselves. They saw themselves as the proud bearers of the world's finest civilization. The Chinese agreed to trade with the Europeans only after the latter had begged for the privilege. The Chinese showed little interest in European goods. They were even less interested in the steam power-driven machinery that was making the Western nations so strong. The Chinese believed that anything foreign was not worth having.

At first, the European traders exchanged silver for Chinese goods. Later, they discovered that the Chinese would accept a new "currency": opium. The opium trade was outlawed. The Chinese government became alarmed when Europeans began bribing corrupt Chinese officials to help them smuggle opium into the country. The Chinese people were being harmed. The Manchu government finally acted and destroyed a large opium shipment. It was time to rid China of the Europeans.

Our curtain rises on China in 1839. The Chinese people are preparing to defend themselves against a British attack.

Canton 1839

I am a Chinese official. I fear for my country. Giant ships, all of them flying the British flag, are coming closer to the shore. Soon my people and those foreign devils will lock together in a dance of death. We must teach those barbarians a lesson they will never forget!

How I hate those foreigners! The Europeans lie, they curse, and they stink from the evil odors of the things they smoke

The Opium War: British ships bombard the Chinese city of Canton.

and drink! We Chinese are a far more refined and civilized people than they are.

Yet I fear these people. We invited them to leave our country. They refused to go. We told them that we had no interest in their barbarian goods. We had everything we needed under the sun. Still, they begged to trade with us. We called them inferiors and made fun of their clumsy ways. They ignored our insults!

They protested that they had come here in the name of peace. But they brought ugliness with them. These British smuggled opium into China. They made many of my people suffer so much that they begged to die. But the Chinese people will no longer allow these foreign devils to bring their poison into the country. That is why the English have declared war against us.

The ships draw closer. Some of our soldiers are shouting cries of victory before the battle has even begun! I will wait awhile before I join them.

Postscript

Badly organized and poorly equipped, the Chinese were defeated in battle after battle in the Opium War. The war continued for three years (1839–1842) and ended when the Chinese asked for peace and gave in to British demands.

The British received the island of Hong Kong, and the Chinese were forced to open the ports of Amoy, Fuchow, Ningpo, and Shanghai to foreign trade. British subjects in these areas were to be governed by British, not Chinese, laws. They were also to be tried in British courts. This practice by which foreigners are not being subject to the laws of the nation where they reside (live) is called *extraterritoriality*. In the next few years, other nations forced China to sign similar agreements.

Many Chinese people, especially the peasants, became increasingly upset with their government. China faced a famine that was made worse by the flooding of the Hwang Ho River. The resulting crop failures forced many poor peasant farmers to sell their lands for a fraction of their worth. At the same time, Chinese officials were accused of accepting bribes and growing rich at the expense of the people.

Some of the Chinese people began to take action. Secret antigovernment societies were formed, and rebellions broke out. One such revolt, the Taiping Rebellion, lasted from 1850 until 1864. The movement called for ridding China of the Manchu government, dividing the land equally among all peasants, and granting full equality to women. Fearing they would lose their special privileges if the rebellion succeeded, many wealthy Chinese supported the Manchu government and helped put down the Taiping Rebellion. The government was spared for the moment, but the internal rebellions and attacks by the foreigners had done much to weaken it. The 200-year rule of the Manchu dynasty was coming to an end.

QUESTIONS FOR REVIEW

1. Why was nineteenth-century China far less powerful than it appeared to the Europeans?
2. What was the Chinese attitude toward Europeans?
3. Why did China go to war with England in 1839?
4. How was China affected by the war with England?
5. Why did many Chinese people become upset with their government? How was the Taiping Rebellion an attempt to bring changes to China?

UNDERSTANDING THE STORY

A. Write T for each statement that is true and F for each statement that is false.

1. Until the nineteenth century, Europe was not interested in China.
2. The Chinese believed that they had the greatest civilization in the world.
3. The Chinese did not want "barbarian goods."
4. The Chinese were fond of the British.
5. The Chinese wanted to trade with the British.
6. The British smuggled opium into China.
7. The Chinese believed that they had everything they needed and trade with foreigners was unnecessary.

B. The United States has a drug problem today. A large percentage of the illegal drugs sold here come from abroad. How might the Chinese official in the story advise the United States government to deal with the problem?

ACTIVITIES AND INQUIRIES

1. Use each of the following key terms in a sentence: superior barbarian   opium   inferior   culture.
2. Pretend that you are a British sailor spending some time in China in the 1840s. Write a letter home describing what China is like.
3. Imagine that you are Chinese. You are writing to your cousin who has never seen a Westerner. Describe what Westerners are like.
4. Below is part of a letter written by a Chinese emperor to King George III of Great Britain. Read it carefully. Then answer the questions that follow.

> Yesterday your ambassador asked permission to trade in new areas of China. This cannot be done. I remind you that we have no need of your goods. We have everything we need within our own borders. You, on the other hand, need our teas, silks, and porcelains. Do not take advantage of our good nature. Be happy that we let you trade in the city of Canton. Tremblingly, obey!

What did the Chinese emperor think of the British? Why do you think he felt this way? Imagine that you are King George. Answer the emperor's letter.

5. Look at the map on page 340. Locate Canton and the treaty ports Amoy, Fuchow, Ningpo, and Shanghai, which the Chinese were forced to open to the British as a result of the Opium War. Now locate the island of Hong Kong, which the Chinese were forced to grant to the British.

2. Sun Yat-sen

The Chinese came to hate their new conquerors. Westerners who committed crimes in China were put on trial in their own courts under Western laws and were usually found innocent or given light sentences. Chinese laborers were paid far less than European workers. Westerners grew rich even as many Chinese people continued to sink into helpless poverty.

The Chinese also resented their own leaders. They said the Manchu government was weak and corrupt, and they blamed it for China's backwardness, poverty, and high crime rate. People became even more upset when China declared war against Japan in 1894 and was defeated.

The Manchu dynasty, led by an aging empress, decided that China's problems could best be solved by driving out the foreigners. A group of Chinese who called themselves the Society of Righteous and Harmonious Fists (the Boxers) organized for just such a purpose. The Manchu rulers supported the Boxers.

The Boxers were determined to rid China of all foreign ideas and people. They used terror and violence in their effort to drive foreigners out of China. Some 240 foreigners were killed. The Boxer Rebellion began in 1900 and was finally brought to an end by a combined army of 20,000 British, American, Japanese, German, and Russian troops.

The Manchu rulers became very nervous since they had supported the Boxers. In desperation, the Manchus tried to save themselves by introducing some reforms. They built Western-style schools and modernized the army. But it was too late. The Chinese people were looking elsewhere for leadership.

It would take a very special person to awaken the Chinese and give them the will to face their terrifying problems. The Manchu government would stop at nothing to crush such a man.

IMPERIALISM IN ASIA 1900

RUSSIA

SAKHALIN IS.
(Rus.)

MANCHURIA

MONGOLIA

Vladivostok

Beijing

KOREA (Ja.)

SEA OF JAPAN

JAPAN

CHINA

Seoul

Tokyo

TIBET

Shanghai
Ningpo

EAST
CHINA
SEA

Fuchow

Amoy

Canton

FORMOSA
(Ja.)

PACIFIC
OCEAN

INDIA

BURMA

Hanoi

Hong Kong

SIAM
(Indep.)

SOUTH

Manila

BAY OF
BENGAL

FRENCH
INDO-CHINA

Saigon

CHINA
SEA

PHILIPPINES (U.S.)

N. BORNEO
BRUNEI

MALAYA

SARAWAK

SUMATRA

Singapore

CELEBES

MOLUCCAS

NEW
GUINEA

(GER.)

DUTCH EAST INDIES

JAVA

(Port.)

INDIAN
OCEAN

British Possessions

French Possessions

Dutch Possessions

Amoy Treaty Port

0	1000 Kilometers
0	500	1000 Miles

London   1895

I am Sun Yat-sen. I love my country, but I fear for its future.
Every day, foreigners insult my people. These outsiders grow
rich on Chinese soil while my people can barely make a living. My country has been invaded and disgraced because
China is governed by corrupt people. These officials have
stopped every attempt to reform our laws and bring China up-
to-date. They do not understand that the old ways are dying,
and they are doomed to die with them.

I went to London to raise money for my cause. My followers and I had decided that we must rid China of the Manchu rulers. We had to move China forward. For this, the government had put a price on my head. I was thousands of miles from home, but I knew that dangerous enemies were close at hand.

I prepared to leave my apartment. There was a knock on the door. "Enter," I said. Two men burst into the room and grabbed me. I was pushed into a waiting carriage and taken to the Chinese embassy. I was dragged to the basement and tied to a chair.

Later, a man appeared at the door. I had seen him before. He was the Manchu's ambassador to Great Britain. He walked up to me, looked into my eyes, and slapped me hard across the face. "You are the worst kind of traitor," he said. "You throw mud in your country's face while strangers attack it. You travel around the world and tell unspeakable lies about us. You are more dangerous than the barbarian!"

"One man was left to guard me. He stared at me for a long time. Was he my executioner?"

I spoke out through puffed lips. "One day, my people will again command the respect of the nations of the world. A true Chinese government will help them to grow strong and will free their minds. Your empress is not that government!"

The ambassador now whispered something to one of the men. Suddenly, all but one rose to leave. One man was left behind to guard me. Was he my executioner? He stared at me for a long time. At last he whispered, "I can get word to someone who will help you!" He loosened the ropes so that I could escape. He too had seen a glimpse of China's future. He was willing, as I was, to risk his life for it.

Postscript

The revolution began in 1911 and encountered little resistance from the exhausted Manchu government. The Manchus vacated the throne in 1912 mostly because they could not survive modernization and change. Over two thousand years of rule by dynasties had finally come to an end in China.

When Sun Yat-sen founded the Nationalist People's Party, he made no secret of his goals for China. He wanted the Chinese people to develop a feeling of national unity, which he believed could be accomplished only if the Manchus were overthrown and all foreign powers left China. Sun also wanted to educate the Chinese people about how to live under a democratic form of government. Finally, Sun hoped to buy land from the landlords and distribute it to the peasants who had none. He also believed that the government should help industries so that China would be less dependent upon foreigners.

Sun realized that in order for the revolutionary government to survive, it had to have the support of the army. To gain that support, Sun placed the presidency in the hands of army leader Yuan Shih-kai.

Unlike Sun Yat-sen, Yuan was interested only in gaining power for his personal benefit. Yuan made himself so powerful while in office that in 1915 he was able to name himself emperor of China. But he died a year later and left China in chaos. To fill the void, powerful Chinese warlords, who had armies of their own, began to carve up sections of China for themselves.

Throughout these years, Sun Yat-sen tried desperately to bring order and unity to China. He died in 1925 still dreaming of a unified, democratic China. It was a dream that seemed a long way from fulfillment.

QUESTIONS FOR REVIEW

1. Why did the Chinese come to hate those who had conquered them?
2. How did the Boxers propose to solve China's problems? Did they succeed? Explain.
3. Why did the Manchus hate and fear Sun Yat-sen?
4. What were Sun Yat-sen's goals for China?
5. Did Sun Yat-sen live to see his goals accomplished? Explain.

UNDERSTANDING THE STORY

A. Write T for each statement that is true and O for each statement that is an opinion.

1. Chinese officials stood in the way of reform.
2. China would suffer as long as it followed the old ways.
3. The Chinese government believed that Sun Yat-sen was its enemy.
4. Sun Yat-sen was accused of telling lies about China.
5. A government run by the empress would never have been able to command respect from the nations of the world.
6. One of Sun Yat-sen's captors helped him to escape.
7. The man who helped Sun Yat-sen escape believed that Sun would become a great Chinese leader.

B. Imagine that Sun Yat-sen is visiting the United States today. List the things that he would like about this country. List the things that he would want China to copy. List the things that he would not want China to copy.

ACTIVITIES AND INQUIRIES

1. Pretend that you are a reporter. Your assignment is to interview Sun Yat-sen. List the questions that you want to ask him. Write down the answers that you think Sun would give you.
2. Imagine that you are interviewing a Manchu government leader. List the questions that you would like to ask. Write down the answers that you think the leader would give you.
3. Suppose that you are a follower of Sun Yat-sen. Draw a poster that will help explain some of Sun's ideas.
4. Sun Yat-sen has come to you for advice. He wants to know how he can begin to make China a more modern country. Write down your ideas.

3. Civil War: Chiang Versus Mao

After the 1912 revolution, two groups began to compete for the leadership of China. One group, the Nationalists, was headed by Chiang Kai-shek, a conservative general. The other group, the Communists, was led by Mao Zedong, a man from a peasant family. At first, these two groups worked together to unify China. But in the 1920s, Chiang broke with the Communists and declared war on them. Watching this carefully, Japanese military leaders decided that this was the time to acquire Chinese territory. In 1931 the Japanese invaded Manchuria, in north China, and set up a "puppet" state there which they called Manchukuo. (See Unit XI, story 1.) Chiang agreed to stop the war against the Communists and join with them in fighting the Japanese. But both sides continued to oppose each other while they fought the Japanese.

As the war dragged on, the Nationalists faced serious problems. They had to print paper money to pay for the war. This caused the value of money to drop and the price of goods to rise. People began to charge that the Nationalist government was corrupt. Officials could be bribed to do favors for the wealthy. The government took food from the people and forced them to pay high taxes. The people became restless, confused, and unhappy under the Nationalist government.

In the meantime, the Communists were winning the support of the people by lowering land rents and aiding the peasants. The Communists also gained the reputation of being fierce fighters against the Japanese.

When the war with Japan ended in 1945, people wondered how long it would be before the Nationalists and the Communists would be at each other's throats. As our story opens, Chiang and Mao are meeting in a last-minute effort to prevent a civil war. See if you can guess whether or not war will break out between these two and their followers.

Chungking 1945

Chiang entered the room. He was well-groomed. His uniform was hand-tailored, and his chest was covered with medals.
Next Mao entered. His uniform was simple and badly in need of a pressing. He wore no medals.

Chiang Kai-shek (left) and Mao Zedong, foes who could never be reconciled.

The two men glared at each other. For 19 years they had been locked in a fight to the death. Both had bitter thoughts at the moment. At last, the two began to bargain.

Chiang said, "Now that the Japanese have been defeated, there is no need for you to keep your armies. You must send your soldiers home and turn their weapons over to China's real government, the Nationalists."

Mao replied, "I will be happy to join my army with yours if you give me and some of my generals a place in your government."

Chiang spoke quickly. "This I will not do!"

"All right, then," said Mao, "don't take me into your government. But I insist that you hold free elections and give up the powers that have turned China into a dictatorship!"

Chiang would have none of this. "My voice is the voice of the Chinese people. I govern in their name. For this reason, I consider my government to be a democratic one."

Both men were silent. Chiang thought: "Mao is a dangerous man. He kills the landlords and gives their lands to his followers. He encourages his people to steal from property owners. Soon no one who owns property will be safe from these jackals. If Mao has his way, those who have become rich by use of their wits and hard labor will be chased from China. The country will become a land of peasants!"

Mao stared at Chiang. Mao thought: "Look at the way he dresses. How many mouths could be fed for a year with the money that uniform cost? While people starve, he and his wife sleep on silk sheets! How can he understand China's problems when he surrounds himself with landlords and bankers? But time is on my side. Chiang may have larger armies than I do, and, thanks to the United States, he will soon have the newest equipment. But his government is rotten. The Nationalists will be destroyed because they are their own worst enemies!"

The meeting was over. The two men faced each other. Mao filled his glass with wine. He raised the glass in Chiang's direction. With a half-smile he said, "Long live China!"

Chiang filled his glass, raised it, smiled, and said nothing. The two men drank their toasts in silence.

Postscript

In 1945, despite efforts by the United States to bring Mao and Chiang together, the Nationalists and the Communists once again declared war on each other.

The Nationalists began with more troops and equipment and the backing of Western nations. But the Communists had a better-organized army with higher morale. The Communist troops also were better disciplined, and they defeated the Nationalist armies decisively. Chiang's troops began to defect to the enemy. Tired of war, many Chinese people threw their support to the Communists. The people believed that the Communists would win the war, and they hoped this would bring the needed changes to China.

On October 1, 1949, the Communists captured the Nationalists' capital city and gained control of mainland China, which they named the People's Republic of China. The Nationalist forces fled to the island of Taiwan, 90 miles off China's coast.

QUESTIONS FOR REVIEW

1. Why did the Nationalist government face serious problems during China's war with Japan?
2. How did the Communists try to gain the support of the Chinese people?
3. What did Chiang and Mao demand of each other when they met in 1945?
4. Why were the Communists able to defeat the Nationalists?

UNDERSTANDING THE STORY

A. Write C for each statement with which Chiang Kai-shek would have agreed and M for each statement with which Mao Zedong would have agreed.

1. A leader should always be dressed well.
2. Leaders should dress as their followers do.
3. The Communists should turn their weapons over to the Chinese government.
4. Communist generals should be given positions in the Chinese government.
5. Free elections should be held in China.
6. People should take goods from property owners.
7. Landlords and bankers are useful people to have around.
8. The Chinese Nationalist government is corrupt.

B. Imagine that a number of Chinese people have asked you for advice. They want to know which leader they should follow, Chiang or Mao. What advice would you give them? Why?

ACTIVITIES AND INQUIRIES

1. Go the library. Prepare a report on either Chiang Kai-shek or Mao Zedong. Be prepared to tell the class how he rose to power.
2. Pretend that you are a reporter. Interview Mao Zedong. List the questions you would ask. Write down the answers that you think Mao would give to your questions.
3. Imagine that Chiang has read your interview with Mao. How would he answer Mao's charges?

4. Pretend that you are an American reporter and are present at the meeting between Mao and Chiang in 1945. Write a newspaper article about your impressions of the two leaders.

5. Now imagine that you are a Chinese person who is present at the meeting between Chiang and Mao. Write down your thoughts about the two leaders. Be prepared to defend your ideas.

4. East Meets West

European sailors and merchants began to visit Japan in the sixteenth century. Many Japanese people welcomed these foreigners and were eager to learn from them. But the Japanese rulers, the Tokugawa shoguns, feared that foreigners would bring unwanted changes to Japan. They forced most of the foreigners to leave the country. Some Dutch traders were allowed to remain, however, and they helped to keep alive the desire of the Japanese for knowledge of the outside world.

By the nineteenth century, the Tokugawa were beginning to lose their hold on Japan. People began to resent the Tokugawa rulers. Many Japanese wanted the emperor to rule. They also wanted more economic and personal freedoms. Some outside pressure was needed to help bring about change. This pressure was on the way.

In our story, Commodore Matthew Perry of the United States Navy has just arrived in Japan with four ships. He is there on an important mission. How will the Japanese deal with Perry? Will his mission be successful?

Tokyo   1853

"Commodore Perry, a Japanese noble and his guards are here. He and his party want to come aboard ship and meet with you."

Perry gave orders for the Japanese group to be escorted to the bridge. An interpreter was sent for.

"May I ask the purpose of your visit?" said the Japanese noble, perhaps a bit too politely.

"By all means, sir," answered Perry. "I am here to ask you to stop torturing and putting to death shipwrecked American sailors."

To this, the Japanese noble said nothing.

"In addition," Perry continued, "my government asks that you open your ports to American ships so that our two countries can trade and become good friends."

"Perhaps," said the Japanese noble, "we will become even better friends if we do not trade with one another. We have our own way of life, and we do not wish to see it disturbed by outsiders!"

"But I believe that we have much to offer one another," Perry replied. "My government asks that I present you with gifts for your emperor. We think that these gifts will convince you that we can be of service to your people."

The Japanese noble waited for Perry to offer his gifts. Perry nodded his head, and sailors brought out a sewing machine and a large model of a railroad steam engine.

A Japanese artist's rendering of Perry's command ship, in 1853. The inset (top, left) shows Perry, at right, and one of his crew. Why were the Japanese interested in the details of Perry's steam-powered ship?

"We will show you how to use these things," said Perry, smiling. "You see," he repeated, "we do have much to offer you!"

The Japanese noble spoke in hard tones. "Once before—long before my time—foreigners came to our shores. At first, they too wished only to trade. Later, we learned that many of our people were being taught to pray to a false god. So we ordered the foreigners to leave. We see no reason to change that policy now!"

Perry looked uncomfortable. "I hope that this is not your final decision. My government understands that you must have time to think things over. I am returning to the United States, but I will come back soon. Perhaps by then you will have changed your mind."

The Japanese noble greeted this statement with silence. Suddenly, he stood and bowed politely. It was the signal that the meeting was over.

Perry watched in silence as the Japanese party left the ship. He had strong doubts that the Japanese would change their minds. But as he turned back to his cabin, Perry saw some papers that had accidentally been dropped by one of the Japanese group. Every sheet of paper was covered with drawings of parts of Perry's ship.

Perry relaxed and smiled. He would have good news for his government after all.

Postscript

Perry returned to Japan in 1854, and the Japanese agreed to a treaty. Soon, other nations knocked on Japan's door, and the Japanese signed treaties with them as well. Many Japanese complained about these treaties, however. Cheap foreign goods were driving Japanese industries out of business. The shogun was blamed and was forced to step down.

A new group of nobles came to power in Japan. They demanded the end of the shogunate in Japan and the restoration of the emperor to power. In 1867 they forced the last Tokugawa shogun to give up his powers so that they could be transferred to the emperor. The young emperor took the name Meiji. This period in Japanese history is known as the Meiji Restoration.

The ruling nobles believed that Japan must become a modern nation in order to stop the West from taking over the country. They decided that Japan would borrow the best ideas from the West. They modeled Japan's government, army, navy, and industries after those of Western countries. There was a two-house legislature and a written constitution granting men the right to vote. However, the ruling nobles did not actually transfer power from the shogun to the emperor. Instead, they kept most of the powers that had been taken away from the Tokugawa shogun. Once again, the emperor ruled in name only. The Japanese government was really an oligarchy in which a few made decisions for the many.

QUESTIONS FOR REVIEW

1. Why were many Japanese people becoming unhappy with their rulers in the nineteenth century?
2. Why did Commodore Perry visit Japan? What did he accomplish?
3. What changes did the powerful nobles bring to Japan?
4. How did the new Japanese government hope to prevent the West from taking over Japan?
5. Did this new government model itself after the Western democracies? Explain.

UNDERSTANDING THE STORY

A. The following statement shows how the Japanese felt about Perry's visit. Read it carefully. Then choose the item that makes each of the sentences that follow correct.

> If we were to go to war with a foreign country today, we would face a very tough enemy. The enemy would come with many ships and surround our shores. They would capture our ships. No matter how many of their ships we destroyed, the enemy would fight on.
>
> Japan cannot afford such a war. Our people would suffer many hardships and grow tired of fighting. Let us, therefore, have contact with foreigners. Let us learn from them. Let us study their science and inventions. Perhaps one day we shall be strong enough to wage wars with foreign countries and take land from them. We will give the land to our people.

1. The Japanese believed that foreign countries might one day (*a*) declare war against Japan (*b*) sell them their products (*c*) torture shipwrecked Japanese sailors.
2. The Japanese thought that foreigners were probably (*a*) cowards (*b*) very rich (*c*) great fighters.
3. In case of war with a foreign country (*a*) the foreign country would suffer more (*b*) Japan would suffer more (*c*) neither would suffer great hardships.
4. Foreign ships were (*a*) better than Japan's (*b*) not as good as Japan's (*c*) not as fast as Japan's.
5. The person who wrote the statement on page 351 believed that Japan should (*a*) not have any contact with foreigners (*b*) have little contact with foreigners (*c*) have much contact with foreigners.
6. The Japanese should (*a*) stick to their own ways (*b*) learn the ways of foreigners (*c*) follow the religions of foreigners.
7. The Japanese should be prepared to (*a*) live in peace with foreigners (*b*) teach foreigners Japanese ways (*c*) go to war with foreigners.

B. Imagine that a spaceship has landed in your country. People from another planet step from the ship. They ask that your country open its cities to the people of the other planet. These people also bring wonderful gifts, which no Earth person has ever seen before. Should your country open its cities to these people? Explain your answer.

ACTIVITIES AND INQUIRIES

1. Go to the library. Prepare a report on Perry's trip to Japan. See if you can find pictures of nineteenth-century Japan.
2. Imagine that you are a United States sailor aboard Perry's ship. Write a letter home describing the Japanese people.
3. Pretend that you are a Japanese official who has just come from a visit aboard Perry's ship. Write a report about everything that you saw.
4. Assume once again that you are a Japanese official. The emperor wants your advice. He wants to know if Japan should open its ports to the United States. Advise the emperor, and explain why you advised him as you did.

5. The Riches of Africa

By the nineteenth century, thanks to three centuries of exploration, Europeans knew much about Africa's coastal areas. Little was known about Africa's vast interior, however. Most people were afraid to explore the interior. They feared diseases, unfriendly people, wild animals, jungles, swamps, and deserts. They also believed that anyone who dared explore the African interior would perish. For these reasons, Africa became known as the *Dark Continent*. It was widely believed that the African interior was populated only by people who used all of their energies just to survive in the hostile environment.

As we learned in earlier units, Africa had been the birthplace of a number of highly developed civilizations. They had governments, laws, economies, religions, strong family ties, literature, arts, and other social traditions. In the nineteenth century, there were a number of complex African cultures, but it would take years before outsiders recognized them.

In the meantime, Europeans built trading posts along Africa's west coast where they bought gold, ivory, and spices from African traders. Europeans were eager to explore the treasures of Africa, but fear kept them back.

In 1865 a British missionary and explorer named David Livingstone went on an expedition to central Africa. Over the next few years, little was heard from Livingstone, and rumors of his death soon spread throughout the Western world. Henry Stanley, a British reporter for the New York *Herald,* was sent to Africa to search for Livingstone. The following are some highlights from Stanley's diary of the trip. (See map, page 359.)

Zanzibar   January 6, 1871

Here I am in Africa. What do I do now? I must organize an expedition. James Bennett, my publisher, has given me unlimited funds, but I don't know where to begin! I'm sure that this will be my toughest newspaper assignment.

January 10

I have made great progress. At the advice of some American and Arab traders, I have begun to organize the expedition. I must buy thousands of yards of cloth, thousands of different colored beads, and several hundred pounds of brass wire. I will use these items to trade with the people in the interior. I also need food, pots and pans, boats, donkeys, horses, guns and ammunition, medicine, and porters. I'd better get busy!

Bagamoyo   March 21

Ready at last! I left Zanzibar on February 4 and sailed for Bagamoyo, 20 miles away. My party is now 192 persons, 22 donkeys, 12 goats, two horses, and a watchdog. We carry six tons of material and supplies. Now the adventure begins!

April 3

The journey is turning into a nightmare. We are bogged down in rain and mud. Sickness is everywhere. The porters are coming down with malaria. Luckily, we have quinine. My horse became infested with stomach worms and died. We are moving through a jungle. The smells are sickening. The bush slows us and tears our equipment loose from the backs of our donkeys. I can't wait to leave this place behind us.

April 24

We have had good luck. A friendly chief sent us food in return for some of our cloth. The rains have stopped and we are moving nicely again. The scenery is beautiful. We are dazzled by wildflowers, sugarcane, Indian corn, cucumbers, eggplants, and beautiful trees against a background of giant mountain ranges. Best of all, I met an Arab trader who told me that he lived next to a white man in Ujiji. He said this man was old and had just recovered from a serious illness. I'm sure this man is Livingstone, and I am more determined than ever to find him.

Makata River Valley   May 9

Bad luck again! The rains started once more. The porters are tired. We can cover only a few miles a day. Someone in the group is stealing from us. I have had bad attacks of chills and fever. The donkeys keep getting stuck in the mud. They are beginning to die. My faithful watchdog has also died. Each day, more come down with the chills. When the rains stopped, they were followed by blazing heat waves. The temperature rose to 128 degrees Fahrenheit! One man died and another's legs were so badly swollen that he couldn't move. Perhaps we'll find better luck in the next village.

Mpawapwa   May 22

Thank heaven for Mpawapwa! The food is delicious and we are well rested. My only complaint is about insects. They are in my tent, my cot, my clothing, and in my hair. We are joining two Arab caravans and moving on.

Tabora   June 23

What an adventure! We have traveled through 30 miles of desert. Then we passed through the lands of the Wagogo people. The Wagogo chiefs were greedy and demanded much wire, cloth, and beads before they would let us pass on. My porters tried to turn back and I had to threaten them with my pistol and my whip before they would move on. At last we reached Tabora. We have been traveling for three months and two days and we have come 525 miles from the coast.

Malagarasi River   October 25

We have narrowly escaped death. The road to Ujiji was blocked by a bandit chief named Mirambo. He made war on the Arabs at Tabora, and we were stranded there for many weeks. We have finally decided to take our chances and move toward Ujiji. I have 54 porters left. Some deserted. Others fell sick. We stumbled into a grassy plain where we saw many wild animals. Herds of buffalo, zebra, giraffe, and antelope ran past us. At the riverbank, I was about to dive into deep water for a refreshing swim when I saw a giant crocodile swimming beneath me! We stocked up with food and pushed forward. We have seen lions, leopards, elephants, and rhinos. Will we ever reach Ujiji?

November 3

Great news! I met two men who had been in Ujiji eight days ago. They said they saw a white man dressed like me. His beard was white and he was elderly and seemed ill. It must be Livingstone! He is alive! We have packed our supplies and are about to complete the last leg of our journey. Next stop, Ujiji.

Ujiji   November 10

We have made it! We completed a journey of 800 miles in 236 days. The men were overjoyed. We marched into the village and greeted the chief. My heart was pounding. I asked

"I saw an elderly white man. I removed my helmet and in a trembling voice said, 'Doctor Livingstone, I presume?'"

the chief if a white man lived in the village. He nodded and pointed toward a hut.

I saw an elderly man wearing a blue cloth cap and gray tweed trousers. I walked toward him. I was now face to face with him. I wanted to hug him, but I was afraid that I would frighten him. I removed my helmet and in a trembling voice said, "Doctor Livingstone, I presume?" He looked at me for a moment and smiled.

Postscript

Henry Stanley's newspaper accounts of his adventures in Africa aroused tremendous interest around the world. Stanley told of great quantities of ivory, copper, cotton, copal, and many other resources. Europeans made a mad rush to explore and colonize the interior of Africa.

As for David Livingstone, he refused to leave the jungle with Stanley. He chose instead to continue working in his beloved Africa. A year after Stanley found him, Livingstone died.

QUESTIONS FOR REVIEW

1. Why were most Westerners afraid to explore the interior of Africa?
2. What was the truth about Africa's history?
3. Why did Stanley go to Africa?
4. How did Stanley prepare for his expedition?
5. How did Stanley's expedition help lead to the colonization of Africa?

UNDERSTANDING THE STORY

A. Tell which statements by Henry Stanley encouraged Europeans to colonize Africa.

1. Many of the porters became ill with malaria.
2. I was dazzled by the sugarcane, Indian corn, and eggplants.
3. The temperature rose to 128 degrees.
4. There are large amounts of ivory and metals.
5. The Africans traded valuable goods for our cloth, beads, and brass wire.
6. There are many dangerous animals.

7. Many of the African people are very friendly to us.
8. There are bandits who rob and kill travelers.

B. Imagine that you have a choice. You can go to Africa with Stanley to search for Livingstone, or you can stay at home. What would you do? Why?

ACTIVITIES AND INQUIRIES

1. Use each of the following key terms in a sentence: Dark Continent missionary   expedition   reporter.
2. Go to the library. Prepare a report on Stanley, Livingstone, or another African explorer.
3. Pretend that you are Stanley. You are looking for Livingstone but have not yet found him. Write a news report telling about your experiences.
4. Now assume that you have found Livingstone. Send a report to your newspaper telling how you found him.
5. Look at the map of Africa on page 359. Follow Stanley's journey to find Livingstone by locating Zanzibar and Ujiji. Using the scale, determine the approximate distance between them.

6. Africans Learn About Obedience

After reading Stanley's journals of his African exploration, Europeans raced into Africa's interior. Countries sent agents to explore and claim territory. Often, several countries went after the same territories. Tempers flared, and threats were exchanged. Britain and France almost went to war over a desert in the Sudan.

The Europeans finally decided that it was both foolish and dangerous to fight over Africa. Meeting in Berlin in 1884 and 1885, they set rules for the colonization of Africa. They tried to settle their disagreements and divide Africa in a fair manner. They also tried to provide for free trade on African rivers. The only people not represented at the conferences were

IMPERIALISM IN AFRICA 1913

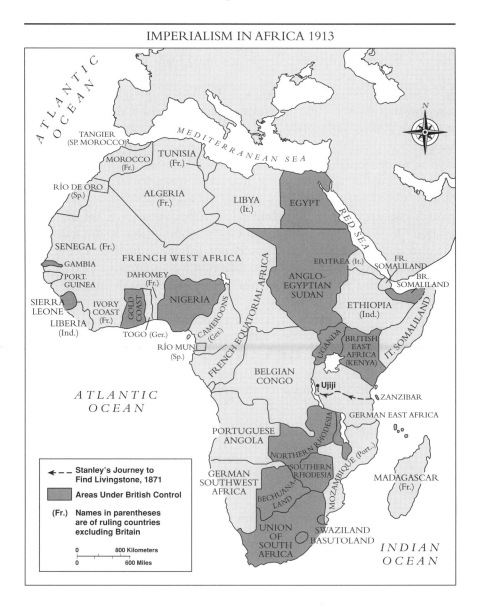

the Africans themselves. By 1913, except for Liberia and Abyssinia (Ethiopia), Africa had been divided up among the countries of Europe.

The Europeans took much from Africa, but they brought a number of good things as well. They built schools, hospitals, roads, and railroads. They installed telephones and telegraphs, provided jobs, and put an end to the slave trade. Agriculture was modernized, and industries were developed. But these things had to be paid for. The Africans paid with their hard work. They provided the cheap labor needed to make profits. They also paid taxes from their wages. In addition, African chiefs were told to provide laborers to help clear jungles and build roads and highways. These workers had no choice.

Some European colonists treated the African people decently, but others treated them cruelly. The worst colony was the Congo Free State, or Belgian Congo, which belonged to King Leopold of Belgium. Leopold was concerned with just one thing: making money. There were great profits to be made from African ivory and rubber. Leopold hired companies to gather the rubber and ivory. He instructed them to use forced labor. Africans were beaten, crippled, tortured, and even killed for not gathering enough rubber. Women and children were held hostages until the men returned. Men were forced to spend long periods of time in the forests in order to gather rubber. Some could not gather enough to satisfy the Belgians and ran away. Others were killed by wild animals or died of disease. In our story, African rubber workers are protesting the terrible conditions they are forced to endure.

Belgian Congo   1903

"Mr. Hendricks, please come quickly. We have a terrible problem!"

"Yes, Smith, what is it?"

"Five men are refusing to go to work. They are just sitting together, and the others are watching them. I don't like it one bit!"

Hendricks quickly pushed through the crowd of Africans, and Smith followed. He approached the five men, who suddenly stopped speaking to one another and looked up. Their mouths were set defiantly, but there was a trace of fear in their eyes.

"All right, men, rest time is over! It's time to go to work. Pick up your baskets and move out!"

One man stood and faced Hendricks. He was obviously the leader of the group. He nervously cleared his throat and prepared to speak.

"Sir, we do not wish to make trouble. We have tried to please you by working hard and you only force us to work harder. Each time you send us out for rubber, you ask that we bring back more. It takes us many days and much hard work to fill these baskets. We must sleep away from our families, and it is lonely and cold. We only ask that you—"

"Seize that man!" Hendricks cried. The man was immediately set upon by three armed men who tied his hands behind his back. The man began to scream with fear.

At Hendricks' command the man was pushed into a hut. The others gathered around. Frightened, they waited and listened.

They heard the man pleading and moaning. Suddenly, there was a horrible cry! Then another! Then silence. The workers picked up their baskets and ran off to the forest. The work stoppage was over.

Hendricks looked down at the dead man. He smiled and said to Smith, "Well, I gave him his wish. He'll never have to gather rubber again!"

Postscript

Under pressure because reports of atrocities were beginning to reach the rest of the world, the Belgians began to introduce some reforms. They made some improvements in housing, education, roads, sanitation, and health. But Africans were not allowed to hold important positions in the government, and until 1952, they were not allowed to attend universities in Belgium.

The Africans began to demand a voice in government and an end to high unemployment. The Belgians responded by arresting the most outspoken among them. Riots broke out, and many Belgian settlers began to leave the country. The Belgian government finally agreed to independence, and general elections were held. Independence was declared in June 1960.

There was much disagreement over what form the new government of the Congo should take. Some people wanted a strong central government, while others wanted the provinces to retain much of the power. Many people were more loyal to their tribes than to the central government. And Europeans, with their technical, business, and political skills, still controlled most of the country.

Two weeks after independence, civil war broke out. Many were killed, including a number of European settlers. Europeans began to flee from the Congo. The United Nations attempted to bring about peace, but several years of unrest followed. Finally, peace was restored in 1965 when Joseph Mobutu, an army officer, took control of the government. After Mobutu was elected president in 1971, he changed the name of the country to the Republic of Zaire. When Mobutu fell from power in 1997, the country's name was changed back to Congo.

Today, Congo continues to suffer from poverty and many of its earlier problems. Some people hope that the development of Congo's natural resources, which include copper, cobalt, gold, silver, manganese, and uranium, may one day bring peace and prosperity to its people.

QUESTIONS FOR REVIEW

1. What changes did the Europeans bring to Africa? How did the Africans pay for them?
2. How were Africans treated in the Congo Free State?
3. How did the African people of the Congo gain their independence?
4. Why did the newly independent Congo face many serious problems? What were some of these problems?
5. What might bring peace and prosperity to the people of Congo?

UNDERSTANDING THE STORY

A. Tell which item makes each statement correct.

1. This story takes place in (*a*) the Congo (*b*) Egypt (*c*) South Africa.
2. The Europeans got the Africans to work harder by (*a*) being kind (*b*) using force (*c*) paying them more money.
3. Some Africans refused to work because they (*a*) wanted more money (*b*) thought the work was too hard (*c*) wanted a five-day week.
4. Hendricks wanted to teach the workers (*a*) how to collect rubber (*b*) how to speak English (*c*) to obey.
5. The African colony where the people were most exploited and ill-treated was (*a*) Algeria (*b*) Cape Colony (*c*) the Congo.
6. The workers complained that when they worked hard (*a*) they were made to work harder (*b*) they were paid less (*c*) nobody talked to them.
7. When Hendricks spoke to the workers (*a*) they did not listen (*b*) they were afraid (*c*) they refused to obey because he was a European.
8. After Hendricks killed the workers' leader, they (*a*) ran away (*b*) rushed back to work (*c*) refused to work.

B. Pretend that you are the owner of a rubber plantation in Africa. Would you hire Hendricks as your manager? Explain. You are a worker. How would you like to work with Hendricks as your boss? Explain.

ACTIVITIES AND INQUIRIES

1. Study the map of Africa in 1913 on page 359 and answer the following questions.
    a. France controlled (1) Nigeria (2) Equatorial Africa (3) South Africa.
    b. Cameroon was a possession of (1) Germany (2) Italy (3) Great Britain.
    c. Egypt was a possession of (1) Great Britain (2) Germany (3) France.
    d. Portugal controlled (1) Mozambique (2) Madagascar (3) Angola.
    e. An independent African nation not controlled by a European country was (1) Liberia (2) Somaliland (3) Gold Coast.
    f. Which country did *not* control lands in Africa in 1913? (1) France (2) Denmark (3) Spain.
2. The caption of a cartoon based on the story is: "This will teach them to obey!" Draw the cartoon.
3. Imagine that you are a Belgian. Your government has sent you to the Congo. Write a report describing what Hendricks did. What action would you recommend that the Belgian government take? Why? If none, explain why.
4. Assume that Hendricks is being tried for murder. You have been named the prosecuting attorney. Prepare the case against Hendricks.
5. Suppose that you were assigned to defend Hendricks. Prepare his defense.

7. Jomo Kenyatta

World War II (1939–1945) forced the European colonial powers to use Africans as soldiers or factory workers in Europe. These Africans came in contact with Europeans and learned from them. They listened to speeches about freedom. They saw African Americans in uniform, bearing arms. Most of all, they watched Europeans fighting among themselves. The Africans came to realize that the Europeans were not all-powerful. The Africans were profoundly changed. They returned home with new ideas and goals. They wanted what the white colonists had in Africa: good schools, jobs, and decent salaries. Most of all, they wanted to be free people in their own countries.

Jomo Kenyatta (1890(?)–1978) was one of those African people who returned to their countries after having lived in Europe. Here is his story.

Nairobi 1974

You are Jomo Kenyatta and you believe that the price of freedom comes very high.

As a boy growing up in Kenya, you would cry with tears of anger because your tribe, the Kikuyu, were no longer what they used to be. They and the other African tribes were pushed aside by European settlers, who took the best lands for themselves. A few thousand white farmers produced four times as much farm goods as Kenya's entire black population of 8 million. Secretly, you admired the Europeans. They had worked hard to conquer crop and livestock diseases, insects, and dry spells. But you hated them as well. They and the settlers from India controlled your country. They owned the best land and most of the industry. They ran the government. You swore that someday you would help your people to become the rulers of their own country.

You spoke often and well. People began to listen. You became a leader of the Kikuyu tribe. Soon money was collected to send you to England. Your backers hoped that you would win some rights for your people from the British government.

You stayed away from your homeland for 15 years. You lived in England and traveled to other European countries. But you

Jomo Kenyatta, prime minister of Kenya.

never forgot Kenya. You spoke, you pleaded, you demanded a greater share of government for your people. The British turned a deaf ear.

You returned to Kenya in 1946. Once again you became a leader of your people. You demanded the vote, the end of racial discrimination, and the return of some of the best lands to Africans. While you talked, many of your followers took an oath to kill Europeans or frighten them into leaving the country. These people called themselves the Mau Mau. They terrorized both blacks and whites. They spilled the blood of women and children. Throats were slashed. They burned entire villages to the ground. All who did not go along with them were the enemy. Years of pent-up rage were now drenching Kenya with the blood of its children.

The Mau Mau never attacked you. This made the police suspicious. They decided to arrest you. You maintained your innocence but did not resist. You were sentenced and imprisoned for seven years.

The war went on. It would last for almost ten years. At last the African fire burned itself out. The Mau Mau had killed 30 white civilians, almost 2,000 Africans, and 38 British security people. The Mau Mau dead totaled over 7,800.

The British got the message. They began to prepare Kenya for independence.

You were released from prison in 1961. Your party, the Kenya African Union, immediately chose you as its leader. Elections were held in 1963, and for the first time the people were given the right to vote. When all the votes had been counted, you learned that your party had won. You became prime minister of Kenya. You thanked the people for their support by declaring, "I have snatched you out of the lion's belly!" Your people understood.

You decided that it would be best to forget the bitter past. You kept close ties with the British. You believed that your country still had much to learn from them. You tried to teach your people that independence is a responsibility. Independence means hard work. You invited all races to work together for Kenya's future. Your people listened.

You are Jomo Kenyatta, and you believe that the price of freedom comes very high. You were not afraid to pay that price!

Postscript

Jomo Kenyatta remained president of Kenya until his death in 1978. He left Kenya a legacy of democratic institutions, as evidenced by the national elections that are held every few years. He also left the legacy of a powerful national leader. Despite this, Kenya, with its rich farmlands and world-famous wildlife preserves, has been plagued by ethnic violence and economic problems similar to those in other African countries.

QUESTIONS FOR REVIEW

1. How did World War II help to plant the seeds of independence in the minds of many Africans?

2. What did Kenyatta admire about the Europeans?
3. Why did Kenyatta also dislike the Europeans?
4. How did Kenyatta deal with the British after Kenya won its independence? Why?
5. What was Kenyatta's legacy to Kenya?

UNDERSTANDING THE STORY

A. Tell which statements are true.

1. Africans resented Europeans for having taken their best lands.
2. All Africans were against using violence.
3. Kenyatta secretly admired Europeans.
4. Kenyatta spent many years away from his homeland.
5. The Mau Mau attacked Kenyatta.
6. The Mau Mau killed more whites than blacks.
7. The Mau Mau used terror tactics against both blacks and whites.
8. As prime minister, Kenyatta threw the British out of Kenya.

B. Pretend that your government is doing certain things that you feel are wrong. How can you make your feelings known to your government? What action would you expect to be taken as a result of your efforts?

ACTIVITIES AND INQUIRIES

1. Go to the library. Prepare a report on the Mau Mau movement.
2. Pretend that you are a writer. Your assignment is to prepare a motion picture or television script on an African nation's struggle for independence. Who would your main characters be? Describe some of the major scenes in your script.
3. Go to the library. Prepare a report on the life and work of the leader of an African nation's independence movement.
4. Imagine that you are a British soldier who is fighting against the Mau Mau. Write a letter home describing your feelings about them. Why do you think they are so violent?
5. Study the table on page 368 of lives lost in the Mau Mau conflict and answer the questions that follow.

Casualties in Kenya in the Mau Mau Conflict

	Persons Killed			Persons Wounded and Captured		
	Africans	Asians	Europeans	Africans	Asians	Europeans
Mau Mau	7,800	0	0	7,850	0	0
Security forces (soldiers)	470	2	38	400	12	62
Civilians	1,315	20	30	0	0	0

a. The table shows losses in the Mau Mau conflict in (1) Europe (2) Africa (3) Kenya.

b. Most of those killed in the fighting were (1) Africans (2) Asians (3) Europeans.

c. The number of civilians killed in the fighting was (1) smaller than the number of soldiers killed (2) much larger than the number of soldiers killed (3) about the same as the number of soldiers killed.

d. The smallest number of those killed, wounded, or captured were (1) Asians (2) Europeans (3) Africans.

e. The number of Europeans killed and wounded in the fighting was (1) much smaller than the number of Africans (2) much larger than the number of Africans (3) about the same.

8. The Minority Rules

In 1652 the Dutch East India Company set up a trading post at the Cape of Good Hope, located at the southern tip of Africa. Dutch settlers (Boers, or farmers), soon began to move in the Cape Colony area to grow crops and raise livestock. The African people were driven off their lands and forced either to flee or work for the Boers. The Boers looked down upon the African people. They thought themselves superior and believed that Africans existed only to work as laborers for them.

In 1814, following the downfall of Napoleon Bonaparte, the British took control of the area. But the Boers did not want to live under British rule, so in 1836 they left the colony and moved farther north. There, they encountered the Zulus, a Bantu-speaking people, and fought with them for control of the land. The fighting was fierce, but in the end, the Boers' superior weapons brought them victory.

In the 1870s and 1880s, diamonds and gold were discovered in areas controlled by the Boers. British settlers moved into these areas, and in 1899 war broke out between the British and the Boers. By 1902 superior British weapons had prevailed over the Boers. The British also fought and defeated the black Zulu kingdom. All black South Africans were now ruled by whites.

In 1910 the British and Boer lands were joined to form the Union of South Africa. To make the Boers more comfortable, the British allowed them to decide how the African people should be treated.

Over the years, the white-controlled South African government enacted stricter and stricter segregation laws. Black South Africans were required to carry passes at all times. The penalty for not doing so was a fine or jail term. Blacks were not allowed in certain buildings, parks, theaters, or libraries. They were also forced to live in areas separate from whites and obey curfew laws. Their ability to travel around the country, or even to move to and from their jobs, was severely limited. This policy of racial separation is known as *apartheid* (apartness). Education, while free, was usually inferior to that which white children received. Blacks were not allowed to vote in elections or hold high government jobs.

Many people predicted that there would be an explosion in South Africa. The first one came in 1960. Thousands of blacks left their passes at home and walked to the police stations to surrender for arrest. They hoped to force the government to stop demanding that they carry passes. The police fired on the marchers, killing or wounding a number of them. The government, however, was unwilling to give up its tight control of the black people. Nor would it give them the right to vote.

In 1976 black Africans protested once more, this time against low pay and discrimination. Workers walked off their jobs. Again, the police shot and killed a number of protesters. Black leaders were arrested and kept in prison without trial. Our story is about a young South African black leader who was imprisoned at this time for fighting for what he believed in.

Port Elizabeth   1977

My name is Stephen Bantu Biko. I am a black South African who is prepared to die, if necessary, so that his people can live in freedom.

As a young man, I had certain advantages that were denied to all but a handful of black South Africans. I attended medical school and had a large number of white friends. I even joined the National Union of South African Students. This organization was mostly white, but it allowed black students to become members.

But I was troubled. I asked myself how I could accept these special privileges while my black brothers and sisters continued to be oppressed. I withdrew from the students' organization, and I promised myself that I would use all of my energy fighting for freedom.

I helped found the South African Students' Organization and was made its president. Our goal was to raise black consciousness and develop pride in our culture and history. We would call attention to the inferior education that black South Africans received. We would awaken our young men and women, and together we would march on our enemies and demand all that had been unjustly denied to us.

But I and other student leaders were rounded up and arrested under the Terrorism Act. We were held in prison for 16 months without trial for the crime of creating black pride. Finally, nine of us were placed on trial.

My friends and I knew that we would not get a fair trial. At our trial we showed our defiance by singing freedom songs and raising clenched fists. This was our way of alerting the world that a terrible thing was going on in South Africa. It was also our way of telling our people to take heart and have courage. When the verdict was announced, all of us were convicted as terrorists.

Students rose in protest. Thousands marched and demonstrated in peace and were met by armed forces. The world was shocked to read that hundreds of students had been fired upon and wounded or killed during what had started as a peaceful demonstration.

The prison authorities hate me and fear me. They think that I have helped to unleash a force that will one day destroy their country. They keep me in chains and beat me. My head hurts, and I am in constant pain. I am growing weaker with every passing day. But I know that through my torture and pain I am teaching the world about the oppression of blacks in South Africa. Perhaps my ordeal will bring my people closer to freedom. This is what gives me the strength to go on.

Postscript

Suffering from head wounds and critically ill, Stephen Biko was taken to Pretoria. He died there on September 12, 1977, at the age of 30. Prison authorities claimed he had died during a hunger strike. Twenty years passed before two South African policemen admitted to beating Biko to death in prison.

Many nations criticized South Africa's racial policies. The United Nations passed resolutions condemning South Africa. A growing number of South African whites also were critical of their government. These people were usually silenced by prison terms or house arrest.

In Unit XII, we will return to the story of the fight for freedom in South Africa.

South African woman holds up a picture of Stephen Biko as she protests his death in jail.

QUESTIONS FOR REVIEW

1. Why was the Dutch settlement of South Africa costly to the African people?
2. How did the white minority in South Africa try to maintain control over the black majority?
3. What was the policy of apartheid?
4. How did South African blacks react to the government's racial policies?
5. How did the students' organization founded by Stephen Biko fight to improve the lives of black South Africans?

UNDERSTANDING THE STORY

A. Tell which statements show how life in South Africa was dominated by the white government's fear of the black population.

1. People could not be arrested unless they were accused of committing a crime.
2. The police refused to fire on black demonstrators.
3. Blacks and whites were not permitted to mix socially or in the workforce.
4. The policy of apartheid aimed at improving the conditions of blacks.
5. Black South Africans had to carry passes at all times.
6. Blacks did not get the education or training that would enable them to hold better paying jobs.
7. Blacks had to obey strict curfew laws.
8. If blacks left South Africa without government permission, they were forbidden by law to reenter.

B. Imagine that you are a member of the United States Congress. A bill has been introduced that will authorize the imprisonment of any person who makes people angry by publicly criticizing the government. It is your turn to speak either for or against the bill. Prepare the speech you will give to the Congress.

ACTIVITIES AND INQUIRIES

1. The caption of a cartoon is: "Take pride in your culture and history!" Draw the cartoon, using the ideas in the story.

2. Imagine that you are an American newspaper reporter who is covering the trial of Stephen Biko. Write your story.
3. Now imagine that members of the South African government have intercepted your story. What changes will they want you to make before they allow you to wire the story to the United States?
4. Look at your local newspaper. Clip out a picture that you feel would not have been permitted in a South African newspaper that supported the government's apartheid policies. Explain your reasons.
5. Read the following selection. It was written by Chief Albert Luthuli, a South African, who was awarded the Nobel Peace Prize in 1960. Then answer the questions by telling which item makes each statement correct.

> Here in South Africa white supremacy is worshiped like a god. The government claims that white men built everything that is worthwhile in the country. They are the only ones who can plan and build the cities, the industries, and run the farms and mines. Only they, the whites say, are fit to own and control these things. Black people are only temporary visitors in the cities. They are supposed to be fit only for the dirtiest, least important jobs. Blacks are not fit to share in political power. These ideas survive in South Africa because the people who support them profit from them.

    a. The author of this selection wrote about (1) England (2) South Africa (3) West Africa.
    b. According to many white South Africans, the only ones who could build the cities were (1) the blacks (2) the whites (3) members of special tribes.
    c. Black people were considered (1) good city planners (2) the best politicians (3) fit only for the least important jobs.
    d. White supremacy was (1) insisted upon by both races (2) insisted upon by the blacks (3) insisted upon by the whites.
    e. White rule survived in South Africa because (1) the United Nations approved of it (2) its supporters profited from it (3) black people preferred it.

9. Indian or English?

The West brought great changes to the East. The nations of the East were Westernized (modernized) whether they liked it or not.

India was once a powerful empire. As we saw earlier (Unit V), in the sixteenth century, India had been invaded by Muslims from central Asia, who established the Mughal Empire. The first Mughal rulers unified the country and extended religious toleration to the Hindu people. (See Unit V, Story 8.) These rulers governed wisely and fought well. They were able to expand the empire as well as unite the many different peoples and religions within the area.

But as time passed, the Mughals became increasingly intolerant of the Hindus. The Hindus resented these rulers and began to rebel. In the 1600s, the empire began to break up into independent states, each with its

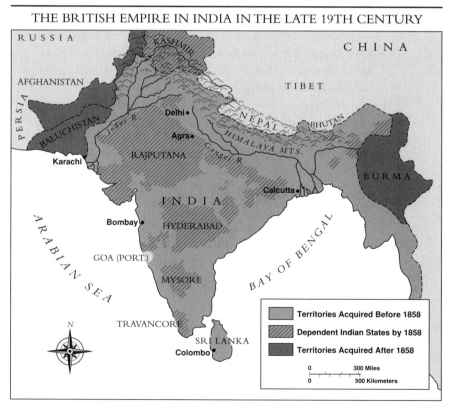

THE BRITISH EMPIRE IN INDIA IN THE LATE 19TH CENTURY

own ruler. By the end of the 1700s, the Mughals had lost most of their former territory.

European explorers in the late 1400s had discovered a direct sea route around Africa to India. European merchants established trading centers in India. In the mid-1700s, England and France, the two most powerful European countries, went to war in part to determine which would have more influence in India. The British defeated the French in 1761, and the British East India Company began to take political control over a weak and divided India.

The Indian people began to resent the British East India Company, even though it brought modern ideas to India. The people resented being ruled by outsiders who did not understand their ways and who treated them like inferiors. They rose in rebellion in 1857 and were defeated a year later. To avoid further rebellions, the British government abolished the East India Company and took control over all British territories in India.

The British made huge profits from India. They used some of these profits to introduce changes in the country. Schools were built, and the English language was taught. A civil service was created. Indians who knew how to speak and write English could get government jobs.

Our story is about an Indian who is a successful civil servant (government employee). He is proud of the fact that he is a loyal British subject. But he has just learned something that disturbs him very much.

Bombay 1911

I, Akbar, am a native-born Indian, but everything I am I owe to the British. As a child, I was educated in British schools here in India. As a young man, I was sent to England to study law. Today I hold a good position in the Indian government, and I am paid very well.

Some Indian people are unhappy that we are not ruling our own country. They often complain to me. I listen for a while. Then I remind them that, thanks to the British, Indian widows are no longer burned according to the old practice of suttee. The Indian people are healthier, and we live longer. Can my people forget that the British have brought law, order, and industry to our country? In spite of my arguments, people usually look at me, shake their heads slowly, and walk away.

Yesterday, a woman listened to me and said, "Your face is Indian, but your heart is British."

I thought this over all day. Finally, I had to admit to myself that I knew far more about the history and customs of the British than of my own India. Feeling a little ashamed of myself, I decided to buy some books on Indian history. I visited five bookstores, but there were very few books about Indian history. I am beginning to understand the feelings of other Indian men and women.

Postscript

A group of Indian people who were unhappy with British rule established the Indian National Congress in 1885. The Congress demanded a greater voice in government and better job opportunities for the Indian people. These demands were not met. Only the British continued to hold high positions in the government, and the major businesses remained under their control. Frustrated and angry, some of the leaders of the Indian National Congress came to the conclusion that India had no choice but to seek self-government and independence.

QUESTIONS FOR REVIEW

1. Why did the once-powerful Mughals eventually lose most of their territory?
2. Why did the Indian people begin to resent the British East India Company?
3. Why did Akbar at first speak highly of the British?
4. What made Akbar change his mind about the British?
5. Why did many Indians decide that they had no choice but to seek self-government and independence?

UNDERSTANDING THE STORY

A. Complete each of the following sentences.

1. Akbar had a position in the _____ government.
2. The British said that they had brought _____, _____, and _____ to India.
3. Thanks to the British, the Indian people were _____ and _____.

4. The British abolished the Indian custom of burning ———.
5. Akbar was told that his ——— was Indian, but his ——— was British.
6. Akbar knew more about the ——— and ——— of the British than he did of his own country.
7. Akbar could find very few ——— on ——— history.

B. Imagine that Akbar approaches you for advice. He asks you to tell him why his fellow Indians dislike him. He also wants to know what he should do to win the respect of other Indians. Answer his questions.

ACTIVITIES AND INQUIRIES

1. Go to the library. Find pictures of nineteenth-century India. Also find pictures of Britain in the same period. Study the two sets of pictures. How are they alike? How are they different?
2. Imagine that you are a British soldier stationed in India. Write a letter home telling about your life in India.
3. Pretend that you are an Indian who has been sent to Britain to study. Write a letter home telling about your life.
4. The caption of a cartoon reads, "Your face is Indian, but your heart is British." Explain the caption. Is this meant as a compliment or an insult? Draw the cartoon that goes with the caption.
5. Study the map of India on page 374. Tell which item below makes each statement correct.
   a. After 1858, British control of India (1) increased (2) decreased (3) stayed the same.
   b. A territory acquired after 1858 was (1) Mysore (2) Baluchistan (3) Nepal.
   c. An area not under British control was (1) Bombay (2) Goa (3) Bengal.
   d. A city under British control was (1) Delhi (2) Rajputana (3) Travancore.
   e. An island off the southern coast of India is (1) Sri Lanka (2) Bhutan (3) Madras.

10. The Supreme Crime

Unlike Akbar in the previous story, there were many Indians who disliked the British. These Indians were angry that high positions in Indian government were filled by the British. Indian schools taught European rather than Indian history. Many industries were owned and run by the British. The Indians accused the British of practicing racism by keeping Indians out of certain clubs, parks, and neighborhoods where only white British people were admitted. They charged that the British had caused much poverty in India by exporting the country's wealth.

The Indian people began to demand a greater voice in government. Soon they would ask for total independence. But how could the Indian people hope to force the British to leave India? The British had a strong army with modern weapons. At the same time, the Indian people were still struggling with some ancient ways, such as the caste system. (See Unit II.) This system divided Indians according to skin color, jobs, and social class. It prevented the Indian people from becoming united and strong.

Our story is about an Indian lawyer named Mohandas Gandhi, who managed to shape the Indian people into an army so powerful that even the mighty British were forced to respect it. How was it possible for him to do so much with so little?

Calcutta   1932

I am the chief secretary to the governor-general of India. Last week, the governor-general and I were waiting for the Indian leader, Mohandas Gandhi. In the past few years, Indians have talked of no one else but this man. They say that one day he will free them from British rule.

The governor-general was pacing back and forth. He was nervous about this meeting. Because of Gandhi's teachings, Indians were refusing to work in British factories or to pay their taxes. Some threw themselves across railroad tracks and tied up our trains. Our jails were filled with the rebels. We did not know how to deal with them.

Mohandas Gandhi led the Indian people in nonviolent protests in order to gain their freedom.

It was Mr. Gandhi who puzzled us most. He was educated in our schools. He has been to Britain. He was a lawyer and could have lived a life of comfort. Instead, he went on hunger strikes and spent much of his time in jail.

There was a knock at the door. Mr. Gandhi was announced. He entered. He was short, thin, bald, and toothless; he wore a simple Indian robe and sandals.

The governor-general blurted out, "Mr. Gandhi, what do you really want from us?" Before Gandhi could answer, the governor-general jumped out of his chair and said, "We British have brought law, order, sanitation, and industry to your country. We have given you our best people and our finest ideas. All of this has been done at great personal cost to the British people. Yet you are not grateful. You refuse to cooperate with us."

The governor-general had become red-faced. He pounded the desk. "For a hundred years, we British have done practically everything for you Indians!"

Gandhi shook his head sadly. He replied, "That, sir, is the supreme crime that you have committed against my people!"

Postscript

Gandhi believed that injustice was to be met with justice and violence with *nonviolence*. He called for nonviolent protests against the injustices of British rule. Protesters were asked to boycott offices, disrupt elections, refuse to pay taxes, and lie down across railroad tracks to prevent trains from moving. Protesters were instructed to protect themselves when confronted with violence, but to do nothing against those who were trying to hurt them. Using this tactic of *passive resistance,* Gandhi's followers often risked their lives protesting bad laws and immoral acts.

Gandhi urged his followers to spin and weave their own cloth rather than buy it from the British. The British retaliated by raising the tax on salt. Gandhi and his followers then marched 180 miles to the sea and picked up lumps of natural salt in defiance of the British law that decreed that only the British could process salt. Gandhi and many of his followers were arrested, but the protests continued. These acts of *civil disobedience* (the refusal to obey unjust laws) called worldwide attention to the plight of the Indian people and won them sympathy and support.

Gandhi was critical of some of the customs of his own people. He spoke out against the harsh treatment of Indian Untouchables and pledged to gain equality for them. He also attacked the Hindu caste system. Gandhi believed that intolerant and unjust ways would keep India a weak and divided country even if it managed to win its independence. In speaking out on these and other controversial issues, Gandhi made many enemies among his own people. He would pay a very high price for his vision of universal equality and justice.

QUESTIONS FOR REVIEW

1. Why did many Indians dislike the British?
2. Why were the British puzzled by Gandhi?
3. How did the Indian people under Gandhi's leadership show their opposition to British rule?
4. How did Gandhi advise his followers to deal with violence? What was the result?
5. Why did Gandhi make many enemies among the Indian people?

UNDERSTANDING THE STORY

A. Tell which item below makes each statement correct.

1. The caste system divided India by (*a*) age (*b*) skin color, jobs, and social class (*c*) political party.
2. The Indian people hoped that Gandhi would (*a*) free them from the British (*b*) make them wealthy (*c*) bring industry to India.
3. Indians refused to (*a*) pay taxes to the British (*b*) go to jail (*c*) give up their jobs.
4. Gandhi was a (*a*) doctor (*b*) merchant (*c*) lawyer.
5. Gandhi spent a good deal of time (*a*) in jail (*b*) going to dinner parties (*c*) making treaties with the British.
6. Gandhi wore (*a*) British clothing (*b*) silk robes (*c*) Indian clothing.
7. The British claimed that they brought all of these to India except (*a*) sanitation (*b*) the caste system (*c*) industry.
8. Gandhi accused the British of (*a*) not allowing Indians to help themselves (*b*) teaching Indians how to rule themselves (*c*) teaching Indians to be proud of their own customs.

B. Imagine that the United States has been taken over by a foreign power. How would Gandhi advise Americans to behave? Would you follow his advice? Explain.

ACTIVITIES AND INQUIRIES

1. Go to the library. Prepare a report on the life of Gandhi. Include Gandhi's plan for the Indian people after the British left India.
2. Pretend that you are a reporter. You are going to interview Gandhi. Write the questions that you would like to ask him. Answer these questions as you think Gandhi would have done.
3. You have been asked to interview the British governor-general of India. Write the questions that you would like him to answer. Answer these questions as you think he would have done.
4. Study the table on page 382. It tells you about living conditions in India a few years after the British left. Answer the questions that follow.

Living Standards in India, 1957

Earnings of average farmer	as low as 33 cents a day
Health	20 percent of the people suffered from diseases caused by malnutrition
Life span	26 years (average)
Infant mortality	50 percent of the children died before age one

Could a British person point to this chart and say that India would have been better off if the British had not left India? How would an Indian person answer this argument? Which argument do you think is the stronger of the two? Why?

11. The Final Sacrifice

Gandhi's weapon, passive resistance, was successful. In the 1930s he and his followers forced the British to grant the Indian people more self-rule. But Gandhi was not satisfied. He would settle for nothing less than complete self-rule.

When World War II broke out, the British asked for and received India's help. Two million Indians fought for the British. Indians worked in the new factories that were built to supply the war effort. A new, more powerful India was being born. This India would demand independence from England, and it would not take no for an answer.

But Britain was not India's only enemy. India was divided by the conflicts between its two major religious groups, the Hindus and Muslims. The Muslim minority feared living in a Hindu-controlled India. While the Hindus fought for independence, the Muslims looked for ways to separate themselves from the Hindus. The British stalled for time by playing one group against the other.

Finally, the British could delay no longer. After almost 100 years of control, they were forced to give up their brightest jewel. India was granted independence in 1947.

But what of the problems between the Hindus and Muslims? Was Gandhi able to find a way for these two groups to live in peace with each other? Our story may supply the answer.

New Delhi   1948

There was great shouting and noise as India's leaders debated the future of the country. Now that the British had left, Hindus and Muslims were turning against each other. Our beloved leader, Mohandas Gandhi, had spoken out in protest against acts of violence by Muslims and Hindus. He now prepared to speak before a gathering of Hindu and Muslim leaders in the Indian parliament. He stood up, and suddenly the room was quiet. Gandhi looked at his audience for a few moments. Then he spoke.

"I am here to remind everyone that I spent 25 years of my life in British jails because I believed in India. I did not ask our people to make sacrifices so that one day they would kill one another! Hindus and Muslims must learn to live together. Otherwise, India has no future."

There was silence. Gandhi sat down. He had risked the hatred of dangerous fanatics with this speech. But Gandhi had taken risks all his life. At last the meeting ended. Gandhi walked off by himself. He was deep in thought. His face was sad. He understood that the fight to bring the people of India together would be much harder than the fight to rid India of the British.

Suddenly, there was a sharp noise like an exploding firecracker. It was a gunshot. Everywhere there was confusion and panic. Delegates scattered. A tiny figure lay slumped on the ground. It was the beloved Gandhi, murdered by one of his own people!

Postscript

While achieving independence from Great Britain in 1947, India was partitioned (divided) into two countries, India and Pakistan, at the same time. (See map, page 384.) Hindu and Muslim leaders wanted their peo-

INDIAN SUBCONTINENT AND NEIGHBORING LANDS

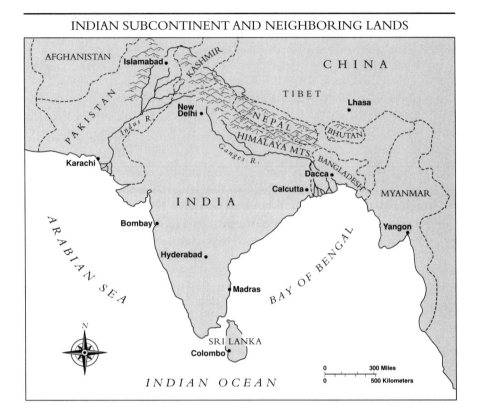

ple to live apart. Riots broke out soon after partition, and almost a million people lost their lives. The wounds have not yet healed. To this day, India and Pakistan are enemies.

Independence has not solved many of India's problems. Unemployment remains high, and many people live in poverty. Millions do not receive adequate health care and are sickly and undernourished. Over half of India's people are *illiterate* (can neither read nor write).

Violence continues to plague the Indian people and their leaders. India and Pakistan have fought wars over the status of disputed territories, including Kashmir and East Pakistan. The Sikh people of the Punjab, who are neither Hindu nor Muslim, have staged violent demonstrations in an attempt to win greater political independence from the Indian government. During one of these demonstrations, in 1984, government forces stormed the Golden Temple, the Sikhs' holiest shrine. The Sikhs retaliated several months later. Indira Gandhi, the Indian prime minister, was assassinated by her own Sikh bodyguards.

But in spite of these problems, India has made a number of advances. Jobs, education, political offices, and public buildings have been legally opened to India's millions of Untouchables. The government has removed a great many restrictions against women, and an increasing number are doctors and scientists and serve in the government. India has introduced modern technology into agriculture and industry. As a result, agricultural output has doubled since the 1960s. India also manufactures and exports iron, steel, and engineering products. The Indian government, a democracy, has remained stable throughout the years of economic and political turmoil. But in spite of the many advances, India continues to face severe economic and political challenges.

QUESTIONS FOR REVIEW

1. How was India divided by religious conflict?
2. Why was Mohandas Gandhi assassinated?
3. Why was India partitioned after it gained independence?
4. What problems does India continue to face?
5. What advances has India made since gaining independence?

UNDERSTANDING THE STORY

A. Write T for each statement that is true and O for each statement that is an opinion.

1. India should have solved all of its problems when the British left the country.
2. Hindus and Muslims turned against one another after the British left India.
3. The British should have left India in the 1930s.
4. Gandhi spent over 25 years of his life in British jails.
5. Gandhi was hated by many Indians.
6. Gandhi was shot by a person who loved India.
7. Gandhi's assassin (killer) was an Indian.

B. Some important leaders have been assassinated since Mohandas Gandhi was killed. They include John F. Kennedy, Robert Kennedy, Martin Luther King, Jr., and Indira Gandhi. Compare Mohandas Gandhi with one of them. Write what both had in common.

ACTIVITIES AND INQUIRIES

1. Pretend that you are writing a television film on the life and times of Mohandas Gandhi. Write an outline for your script.
2. Imagine that you are a reporter at Gandhi's funeral. Write the questions that you would ask the people who attend. Then write the answers that you would expect to get.
3. You are interviewing the English governor-general of India. Write what he or she would say about Gandhi's assassination.
4. Pretend that Gandhi is alive today. Write the things he might say about modern India.

12. The End of Imperialism

By the early 1990s, most of sub-Saharan Africa (south of the desert) was controlled by black Africans. But independence did not bring an end to Africa's problems. In our story, four United Nations delegates are having a drink in the delegates' lounge. They are from Britain, France, Belgium, and a new African nation.

See if this selection helps you to understand why modern-day Africa continues to face serious problems. Ask yourself whether the Europeans and the African can speak as equals. What changes had taken place in Africa by this time?

United Nations, New York   1993

BRITISH DELEGATE *(speaking to the African)*. Really, my friend, your speech today in the General Assembly was a lot of rot! Don't you think that it's a bit foolish to blame us for the problems that you yourselves can't seem to solve?

FRENCH DELEGATE *(also speaking to the African)*. Have you

forgotten that we always treated your people as equals? In our eyes, you were French. We need not apologize for anything!

AFRICAN DELEGATE. I see that my Belgian friend has nothing to say.

BELGIAN DELEGATE *(angrily)*. Oh, nonsense! We taught you a better way of life, and you kicked us out. You're just too dishonest to admit that you made a mistake. Admit it! You simply aren't ready to rule yourselves.

AFRICAN DELEGATE. So it comes down to that! "The poor, helpless, ignorant Africans can't manage without *bwana*" (the white boss). You laugh at us because we fight among ourselves, because we often suffer from poverty, disease, and bad leadership. But what of yourselves? How many times have you Europeans made war against one another? Have you solved your problem of poverty? Have you found a way to solve inflation? Are your leaders so very honest?

BRITISH DELEGATE. That's quite enough! You have a sharp tongue and a bright mind but a very poor memory. You forget that my country created your country's education system. Were it not for Europeans, your people would still be living as your ancestors did.

(At this, the French and Belgian delegates exchange smiles.)

AFRICAN DELEGATE. You Europeans still think of yourselves as the finest creatures on earth. For over a century, you pushed the people in Asia and Africa around. But today a new generation of Asians and Africans challenges you for the leadership of the world. Already you fear the developing technology of Asia. You worry about economic competition. You have led us into the twentieth century, but we will move into the twenty-first century under our own power! Now that you can no longer take what you need from us, it is you who begin to stumble!

BELGIAN DELEGATE. Sad to say, your recent history is not as encouraging as you would like to think. Based on your recent past, your future most likely is one of bad government, hunger, disease, ethnic strife, and civil war. One day, you will look back with longing and realize that we brought you your finest hour.

AFRICAN DELEGATE. No, it is for you to look back! Your greatness is already behind you. Ours is soon to begin! I bid you good day.

(The African walks quickly away from the other three.)

BRITISH DELEGATE. What gall!

FRENCH DELEGATE. You take the African delegate too seriously. Those statements show hopeless ignorance.

BELGIAN DELEGATE. Let us forget this bit of nonsense. I propose a toast. Let us drink to a bright future for our people everywhere.

(The British and French delegates are slow to pick up their glasses.)

Postscript

The nations that have struggled for and won their independence from imperial powers have continued to face enormous problems. These include a lack of trained workers, competition for power from rival ethnic groups, the reliance on a single crop or product for income, conflicts between traditional and modern values, the lack of confidence in the new governments, political instability, and wars between rival tribes, ethnic groups, and nation-states.

The newly independent nations have learned that education holds the key to the solution of many serious problems. Education provides a nation with its skilled workers and professionals. Education also helps to reduce or eliminate many of the crippling diseases that afflict vast numbers of people in Asia and Africa. Finally, education brings many people together and helps to prepare them for life in the modern world.

Once they became independent, these former colonies learned that cooperating with one another builds their economies. They have negotiated trade agreements, shared technological information, and maintained peace among themselves.

These new nations have also requested and received financial and technical help from the industrialized nations. Often they receive aid primarily because the industrialized nations need their resources or see them as politically important. The new nations are careful not to allow their industrialized trading partners to exert too much influence over them. They continue to do business with them while not getting involved with them politically.

AFRICA

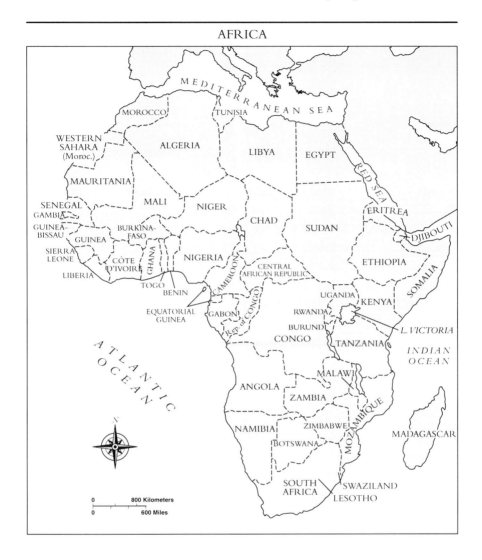

QUESTIONS FOR REVIEW

1. What arguments does the African delegate use to defend the newly independent nations?
2. What problems do the newly independent nations continue to face?
3. Why have many of these nations invested in education?
4. Why do many of these nations receive economic aid and other assistance from the industrialized nations?
5. What do the new nations try to avoid when dealing with the industrialized nations?

UNDERSTANDING THE STORY

A. With which of the statements would the African in the story agree?

1. Western leaders are not honest about Africa.
2. Westerners treated Africans as their equals.
3. The West taught Africans a better way of life.
4. The West has not solved its own problems. How can it expect Asia and Africa to be different?
5. We still suffer from poverty and disease.
6. African countries are just as powerful as European nations.
7. The West is afraid of the power of Asia and Africa.
8. One day Westerners will be called back to run Africa.

B. Assume that you are a visitor to the gallery of the United Nations General Assembly. You have heard the African, Belgian, French, and British delegates make speeches. Which of them impressed you most? Explain. Which of them impressed you least? Explain.

ACTIVITIES AND INQUIRIES

1. Go to the library. Prepare a report on an African nation. Include material on resources, population, climate, education, farm output, industrial production, exports, and gross domestic product. What is the nation's outlook for the future?
2. Imagine that you are the United States ambassador to the United Nations. The ambassador from an African nation speaks to you about United States aid. Prepare a list of questions you would ask the African. Write the answers that you would expect to receive.
3. Pretend that you are a reporter. Interview the Belgian representative to the United Nations. Ask about Belgium's treatment of the population in the Congo before the Congo gained independence. What will the Belgian say?
4. Assume that you are a leader in Congo today. Would you ever ask the Belgians to return and run your country? Explain.
5. Look at the map of present-day Africa on page 389 and answer the questions.
   a. A nation in Central Africa is (1) Algeria (2) Congo (3) South Africa.
   b. The nation that is between Zimbabwe and the Indian Ocean is (1) Zambia (2) Angola (3) Mozambique.

c. Angola has seaports on the (1) Atlantic Ocean (2) Mediterranean Sea (3) Indian Ocean.
d. Chad is south of (1) Libya (2) Congo (3) Gabon.
e. The Sudan is (1) south of Egypt (2) on the Mediterranean Sea (3) west of Chad.
f. Countries without seaports are (1) Zambia and Nigeria (2) Tanzania and Zimbabwe (3) Chad and Zambia.
g. Nations on the west coast of Africa are (1) Somalia and Tanzania (2) Algeria and Libya (3) Mauritania and Senegal.
h. Nations on the east coast of Africa are (1) Angola and South West Africa (2) Congo and Sudan (3) Kenya and Tanzania.

UNIT IX

World War I

As the world entered the twentieth century, it appeared to many people that the fruits of industrialization and scientific advances were to be spread throughout the world. More people in Europe, the United States, Asia, Africa, and the rest of the world were gaining opportunities for education and a more productive, healthier way of life. It appeared that the world was about to enter a golden age of peace and prosperity.

But the tensions that were building among the nations of Europe would explode into a great war involving Europe, the United States, and many other parts of the world. We follow the path of the war from the diplomatic maneuvers that preceded it to the peace treaty that ended it. Was the war really over? A decade later the question was still unanswered.

Europe. Our first story takes place at Versailles, France, in 1871. Two enemies, a German and a Frenchman, discussed the war their countries

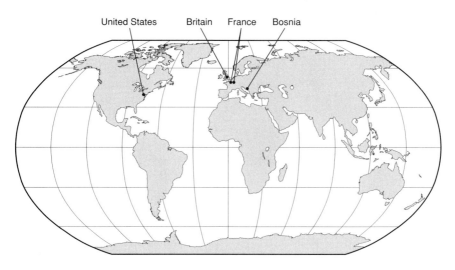

United States   Britain   France   Bosnia

had just fought against each other. The German, who represented the victorious country, believed that the war was over. The Frenchman, who represented the defeated country, thought otherwise. Neither man knew that the long-standing quarrel between their respective countries would cause a world war.

Our next story takes place in London, in 1907. Europe was splitting into two armed camps, and Britain would have to choose one to be its ally. Britain has been a rival of the countries in both camps. How should it choose between its enemies? The story provides an answer.

We now move to Sarajevo, Bosnia, in 1914. An assassin awaited his victims. Before the day was over, his actions would open the floodgates to a world war.

In our next story, we are in the trenches of Verdun, France, in 1916. A great battle was about to begin. We meet two soldiers. One had lost his taste for war, while the other was more determined than ever to do his duty. At the battle's end, both were on the winning side, yet both had lost.

United States. Now it is on to Washington, D.C., in 1917. Woodrow Wilson was reelected president on his promise to keep the United States out of the war in Europe. But much had happened to change Wilson's mind in the year since the election. Our story explains why Wilson had become determined to enter the war.

Next we go to Paris, in 1919, to the postwar peace conference. Wilson had a plan that he believed would put an end to all war. He asked the leaders of the victorious countries to put the interests of the world ahead of selfish national interests. The story tells us how they responded.

1. Prelude to War

As our first story opens, the Franco-Prussian War (1870–1871) has just ended. (See Unit VII, story 4.) Germany won and signed a peace treaty with France. Two diplomats, one French and one German, are discussing the treaty.

See if you can understand why many people think the Franco-Prussian War was really the first step that led to a world war in 1914.

Versailles   1871

"For the last time, Poincaré, why can't you listen to reason?"

"Schmidt, it is you Germans who are the unreasonable ones! You forced the war upon us. Now you push our faces in the mud and force us to sign this so-called peace treaty."

"Sir, I remind you that the French were the first to declare war. It was your Emperor Louis Napoleon, not our Prime Minister Otto von Bismarck, who swore to avenge his coun-

The Franco-Prussian War: Cavalry battle in 1871 between German (left) and French troops.

try's honor. Your government made a terrible mistake. Now the people of France must pay for it!"

"You make everything so simple, Schmidt. Even a lie sounds like the truth when it comes from your lips. We both know it was Germany that really wanted this war. We understand that it was Bismarck who tricked us into a war that we never even wanted. Louis Napoleon is a fool for having been tricked. But what can be said for a man like Bismarck? He unites his people with the blood of his neighbors!"

"Come, come, Poincaré. You are being carried away by your feelings. Be reasonable. You lost the war, and now you must pay. We Germans want nothing more than to live in peace with you from now on. Your wounds will soon heal. You will forget this war. Let us shake hands and look forward to the time when our countries will meet as friends."

"Never! Never will my people forget this insult! We will always remember how you Germans forced us to sign the treaty in the Hall of Mirrors of the palace of Versailles. We will remember the faces of your soldiers who occupied our country. We will hear the cries of our French sisters and brothers in Alsace and Lorraine, who have been stolen from us! They are being forced to live as Germans. We will remember! And one day we will present you with our bill!"

"Be careful, Poincaré. It is dangerous for a French person to speak this way to a German!"

"Schmidt, that is one more thing that I will remember!"

Postscript

The French and the Germans remained bitter enemies. Bismarck, the German prime minister, felt that France would go to war with his country only if it was helped by other nations. To stop this from happening, Bismarck worked hard to form alliances with Austria-Hungary and Italy. He sought an alliance with Russia, but this was difficult because Russia and Austria-Hungary were enemies. To get the Russians to agree never to join France in a war against Germany, Bismarck promised to lend Russia huge sums of money. But, in spite of Bismarck's efforts, the two countries went their separate ways.

QUESTIONS FOR REVIEW

1. Why were the French so angry with the Germans at the conclusion of the Franco-Prussian War?
2. According to Bismarck, under what circumstance would France go to war with Germany?
3. How did Bismarck try to prevent France from going to war with Germany?
4. How did Bismarck try to keep Russia from joining with France? Did he succeed?

UNDERSTANDING THE STORY

A. Decide who made or might have made the remarks that follow. Write S for each statement that Schmidt made or might have made and P for each statement that Poincaré made or might have made.

1. The Germans were unreasonable.
2. Louis Napoleon swore to avenge the honor of France.
3. France was forced to sign the peace treaty.
4. Bismarck tricked France into war.
5. France lost the war and now must pay for it.
6. France will never forget this insult.
7. Germany and France must look forward to meeting as friends.
8. Germany stole Alsace and Lorraine from France.

B. Imagine that you are the United States ambassador to France. Schmidt and Poincaré have presented their cases to you. Each tried to convince you that the other started the Franco-Prussian War. Write a report to the president of the United States. Outline the French and German viewpoints. Then add your own conclusions.

ACTIVITIES AND INQUIRIES

1. Use each of the following key terms in a sentence: Alsace-Lorraine diplomat   military occupation   treaty.
2. Imagine that you are a reporter. Your assignment is to interview Schmidt. Write the questions you would ask him about the Franco-Prussian War and the treaty ending the war. Now write the answers you would expect him to give.
3. Imagine that you are the same reporter. Your assignment is to interview Poincaré. Write the questions you would like to ask him about

the Franco-Prussian War and the treaty ending the war. Then write the answers you would expect him to give.

4. Go to the library. Prepare a report on either Germany or France in 1871. In your report, include the country's industries and its agricultural and military strength.

5. The caption of a cartoon is: "You stole Alsace and Lorraine from us!" Draw the cartoon. Who would agree with the cartoon, Schmidt or Poincaré? Do you agree with the cartoon?

2. The Power Balance

When Bismarck retired in 1890, Kaiser William II (the German emperor) refused to renew the treaty with Russia. The kaiser believed that Austria-Hungary was a more reliable ally than Russia, and by moving away from Russia, Germany would move closer to Austria-Hungary. In 1894, however, France and Russia signed a treaty to go to each other's aid if attacked by Germany. Bismarck's nightmare of a Germany surrounded by two enemies was beginning to come true. Europe was dividing into two armed camps, and Britain decided that it was time to join one of them.

In this story, two members of the British Parliament are privately debating Britain's future. See if you can predict which alliance the British will join. Why did they have to make a choice of alliances? How had Great Britain kept a balance of power in Europe?

London   1907

"Why should we join with any of them?" asked White. "I say let these foreigners threaten one another with war. Let's mind our own business!"

"White, as usual, you make no sense at all," said Brisbane. "Save your speeches for the people sitting in the gallery. Let us try to speak sensibly to each other."

"And what is the sensible thing for Britain to do, Brisbane?"

Brisbane thought for a moment. "There is no question. We must join one of the alliances."

"Why?" asked White. "Why can't we go on just as we have for the past hundred years? Why can't we wait for a war to begin before we decide which side to join? Why should we risk a war now? We have so little to gain by joining either side."

"Stop speaking like a fool!" answered Brisbane. "These alliances have made war more likely than ever. France, Germany, Russia, and Austria-Hungary are preparing for war. If a war starts, its flames will spread across the sea to us. We cannot avoid the war once it begins. But perhaps we can prevent a war by becoming a part of one of the alliances."

"And which side should we join?" asked White.

"That, sir, is a most difficult question," answered Brisbane. "We have been rivals of the French for a long time—especially in Africa and Asia. We are also rivals of the Russians in Asia. At the same time, the Germans talk about moving in on our African territories. They are building a navy that will soon be as powerful as ours. Truthfully, I don't like either side very much. But I do know that Britain must soon make a choice."

"And how can Britain choose between its enemies?" asked White.

"I suppose," answered Brisbane, "the way that Britain has always chosen."

"And what is that?"

"We have always joined with others against the most powerful country in Europe. This is how we have kept the balance of power on the continent."

"And which country is the most powerful in Europe today?" asked White.

"The country whose navy threatens our sea-lanes is the most powerful, White. *That* is the nation we must join against. Do I have to draw pictures for you? Or have I answered your question?"

"No, Brisbane. In answering my question you have just answered your own!"

Postscript

In 1907, France, Russia, and Britain joined together to form the Triple Entente. This group was opposed by the members of the Triple Alliance: Germany, Austria-Hungary, and Italy. For the next seven years, the members of both the Triple Alliance and the Triple Entente would risk war. Twice, Germany and France almost went to war because of arguments over Morocco. Once, Russia and Austria-Hungary threatened to go to war when Austria-Hungary took over Bosnia and Herzegovina. All of these incidents were serious and dangerous, yet somehow war was avoided. But Europe had become a tinderbox needing only a single match to set it aflame. The match was about to be struck.

QUESTIONS FOR REVIEW

1. What was Bismarck's nightmare, and why was it beginning to come true in the 1890s?
2. Why did Britain have a problem deciding which alliance to join?
3. How had Britain chosen its alliances in the 19th century?
4. What countries were members of the Triple Entente? What countries were members of the Triple Alliance?
5. How did war almost break out among members of the rival groups?

UNDERSTANDING THE STORY

A. Read the following passage about the Triple Entente. Then tell whether the statements that follow are true or false.

> Czar Nicholas II of Russia was not eager to ally Russia with democratic France. But in 1891 the French and Russian governments took the first steps toward friendship. By 1894 there was a miliary alliance between France and Russia. This alliance provided that France would help Russia if Germany attacked. Russia would help France if Germany attacked. The alliance between Russia and France would last as long as the Triple Alliance of Germany, Austria-Hungary, and Italy lasted.
>
> Britain was still not a member of any alliance. But the competition between Britain and Germany for world markets increased. The German navy also challenged the

British around the world. Britain saw that it could no longer stand alone and, in 1907, sided with France and Russia. The Triple Entente was born.

1. At first, the czar of Russia was not eager to form an alliance with France.
2. Germany was a member of the Triple Alliance.
3. An alliance between Russia and France protected both from an attack by the United States.
4. Britain entered into an alliance with Russia.
5. France would help Russia if Britain attacked.
6. Germany was happy to allow Britain to have as large a navy as it wished.
7. The alliance between Russia and France would last as long as the Triple Alliance.
8. Britain realized that it had to join an alliance.

B. Assume that most of the world is divided into two alliances. Also assume that the United States is not a member of either alliance. You are the top adviser of the president of the United States. What questions would you like answered before you talk to the president about the alliances? Would you advise the president to join an alliance? Explain. If your answer is yes, on what basis should the United States join? If your answer is no, what should the United States do in the event of war?

ACTIVITIES AND INQUIRIES

1. Look at the map of Europe in World War I, on page 404. Copy the map. Label the nations of the Triple Alliance. Then label the nations of the Triple Entente.
   a. What do you notice about the location of the Central Powers (the countries in the Triple Alliance)?
   b. What do you notice about the location of the Allies (the countries in the Triple Entente)?
   c. What are the advantages and disadvantages of these arrangements of countries to the nations of the other alliance?

2. Use each of the following key terms in a sentence: entente   rival   balance of power   alliance   armed camp.
3. Go to the library. Prepare a report on a war in which Great Britain

fought as a member of an alliance. Why did Great Britain join that alliance?

4. Prepare a poster on Britain and the Triple Entente. Should it read
    Britain Must Join the Alliance!
        or
    Britain Must Stay Out of the Alliance!
    Upon what did you base your decision?

3. An Assassin's Story

The incident that finally brought the nations of Europe to war involved a secret society and the actions of one of its members in the city of Sarajevo. The Austrian archduke was *assassinated* (murdered). World War I had begun.

See if you can learn why this one incident was explosive enough to lead to war. Why did Princip feel that it was his duty to kill the archduke?

Sarajevo   July 1, 1914

My name is Gavrilo Princip. I am a Bosnian Serb who dreams. I dream that some day all the Slavic people will be united under the flag of one country: Serbia.

I hate the rulers of Austria-Hungary. They do not like the Slavic people. They do not give us the same rights as the other peoples who live in their empire. It is my duty to wake up the Slavic people. They must revolt and join their brothers and sisters in building a greater Serbia!

For months I trained with members of a secret society called the Black Hand. We believed that only violence and terror would make our dream come true. My friends taught me how to use a pistol. I hoped to use this skill very soon.

"I could see the archduke and his wife. I reached for my gun, moved forward, and pointed at my enemy."

My friends and I were now ready for our most important mission. We knew that the Austrian archduke, Francis Ferdinand, and his wife were visiting Bosnia on June 28. They were not to leave the country alive! Our leaders told us that the archduke planned to make life easier for the Slavic people when he became emperor. We could not have this! If his reforms helped the Slavic people, they would never revolt. The archduke had to be stopped before he ruined our dreams of a greater Serbia!

The archduke and his wife were riding in an open car. One of our leaders had prepared a bomb. The car stopped at a bridge and the bomb was thrown. The crowd screamed as the bomb exploded. When the smoke cleared, I saw wounded people lying in the street. But the archduke and his wife were not hurt. I shivered to think that we had failed in our mission.

The driver turned the car past the corner where I was standing. It seemed too late for me to do anything. But wait! The car was slowly backing up. I could see the archduke and his

ALLIANCES IN WORLD WAR I

wife very clearly. They were sitting just a few yards in front of me. The car was moving very, very slowly. I reached for my gun, moved forward, and pointed it at my enemy. I shot once and hit the archduke in the neck. Then his wife covered him with her body. I shot her too! Long live the Slavic people! Long live Serbia!

Postscript

Archduke Francis Ferdinand and his wife were assassinated on June 28, 1914. One month later, Austria–Hungary declared war on Serbia.

Russia, Serbia's protector, alerted its troops and sent them to the borders of Germany and Austria-Hungary. Germany responded by declaring war on Russia.

Believing that the French would soon attack, Germany declared war on France. The British warned that they would enter the war if neutral Belgium was invaded by any of the nations at war. On August 4, 1914, Germany invaded Belgium. Britain then declared war on Germany. The two armed camps now tried to settle their differences on the battlefield.

The Triple Entente countries—France, Britain, and Russia—were joined by Italy and Japan. (Once a member of the Alliance powers, Italy joined the Entente powers after being promised Austrian territory by France and Britain.) The Entente powers were confronted by the Alliance powers, which now included Germany, Austria-Hungary, the Ottoman Empire (Turkey), and Bulgaria.

QUESTIONS FOR REVIEW

1. What was Gavrilo Princip's dream?
2. Explain how the following countries became involved in the war that erupted after the assassination of the Austrian archduke and his wife: Austria-Hungary, Russia, Germany, France, and Britain.
3. Which country left one treaty group to join the other? Why?
4. List the countries that fought on the side of the Triple Entente.
5. List the countries that fought on the side of the Triple Alliance.

UNDERSTANDING THE STORY

A. Tell which item makes each statement correct.

1. Germany and France almost went to war over (*a*) Morocco (*b*) Spain (*c*) Britain.
2. Princip hated those who ruled (*a*) Russia (*b*) France (*c*) Austria-Hungary.
3. The Black Hand believed in (*a*) the balance of power (*b*) violence and terror (*c*) passive resistance.
4. The Austrian archduke and his wife were visiting (*a*) Paris (*b*) Vienna (*c*) Sarajevo.
5. Princip shot the (*a*) French president (*b*) German kaiser (*c*) Austrian archduke and his wife.
6. A country that was not a member of the Triple Entente was (*a*) Italy (*b*) France (*c*) Russia.

7. Princip was (*a*) a member of the Russian underground (*b*) a member of the Black Hand (*c*) a special agent of the British Secret Service.

B. Imagine that the Black Hand never existed and Princip therefore had not killed the Austrian archduke and his wife. Would there still have been a world war? Explain. If you think there would have been a world war, how do you think it might have started?

ACTIVITIES AND INQUIRIES

1. Use each of the following key terms in a sentence: assassination Black Hand   Slavic   archduke   mission.
2. Imagine that you are a reporter at the trial of Gavrilo Princip. You are to visit him in his cell and interview him. Prepare the questions you want to ask. Answer the questions as you believe Princip would answer them.
3. Assume that your assignment is to defend Princip. Prepare his defense.
4. Assume that your job is to prosecute Princip. Prepare the case against him.
5. Go to the library. Prepare a report on Princip, the Black Hand, or Archduke Francis Ferdinand.

4. In the Trenches

When news of the war came, volunteers rushed to join the armed forces. Soldiers marched through the streets of their cities. Civilians cheered and threw flowers. Young and old alike marched off to the battlefields with a song on their lips. All were convinced that they would soon return victorious and covered with glory.

Let us see for ourselves what the soldiers of World War I experienced when they finally reached the battlefields. What does this story, set in Verdun, France (see map, page 404), tell you about the war? Why does Eric insist that he is not afraid?

Verdun 1916

Thousands of German soldiers were standing in their trenches waiting for the signal to attack. For several hours German artillery fire had been hitting the French positions. Now the shelling had stopped. Every German soldier knew that he would soon be given the order to leave his trench and try to capture the French strongholds.

Two soldiers with worried faces were talking. They nervously waited for the attack to begin.

"Hans, are you afraid?" asked Eric.

"Of course, I'm afraid. I'm not a fool or mad," answered Hans.

"Well, I'm not afraid," said Eric. "Anything, even death, is better than living like this!"

"Eric, don't talk like a fool!"

"Why shouldn't I? Aren't we all fools? Who but a fool would volunteer to spend two years living in mud and fighting with rats for scraps of bread?"

"Enough!" interrupted Hans. "Remember, you are a German soldier. You have taken an oath to protect the Fatherland. It is our duty to suffer, if suffering will bring peace to our country. Let us not complain like weak old people. Good soldiers must learn to hide their feelings."

"If only I could still believe these things," Eric answered sadly.

Suddenly the command "Charge!" was given. Hans and Eric picked up their weapons and pulled themselves over the trench wall. Now they somehow had to find their way across "no man's land," the area between the German and French trenches. Shells were exploding all around them. Suddenly, there was the smell of gas in the air. The soldiers stopped and quickly put on their gas masks. But some waited too long. Their lungs filled with the poison gas. They choked to death.

Hans and Eric approached the enemy trenches. There was barbed wire everywhere. The two men began to cut their way through. There was a burst of machine gun fire; rows of men fell in their tracks. Through all the noise and confusion, Hans heard one scream. It was Eric. The scream was the last sound

World War I trench warfare: German soldiers look out at the no-man's land separating them from their enemies.

he would ever make. Eric's arms and legs had been shot away. The rest of his body was caught on the barbed wire.

Hans stumbled forward and jumped into the enemy trench. He fired blindly, shooting at everything that moved. He saw a French soldier who was seriously wounded. The man looked at Hans, a plea for mercy in his eyes. Hans hesitated. There was a lump in his throat. He began to back away. Suddenly the madness of the moment gripped him once again. He ran his bayonet through the fallen soldier.

Later, when the battle was over, the German general congratulated his soldiers. "Men," he said, "I am proud of you. You have done your duty as soldiers of the Fatherland. Thanks to you, Germany is one step closer to peace!"

At these words, Hans began to cry.

Postscript

Fighting was intense on the Western Front in 1916. Trench warfare led to enormous losses on both sides. In the battle of Verdun, which lasted for five months, more than 900,000 French and German soldiers were killed. In spite of the heavy fighting, however, neither side was able to advance more than a few miles. The stalemate continued through 1916 and 1917.

The Germans met with much greater success on the Eastern Front, where they defeated the Russian army in battle after battle. Poorly trained and inadequately supplied, over a million Russian soldiers died, and the army was near collapse. In 1917 the Russian army was spared further bloodshed when a Communist revolution overthrew the Czarist government. The new government signed a humiliating treaty with Germany, which took Russia out of the war.

QUESTIONS FOR REVIEW

1. What were some of the weapons of war used during World War I?
2. What was the military result of the battle of Verdun?
3. Why was the Russian army near collapse?
4. Why was the Russian army spared further bloodshed after 1917?

UNDERSTANDING THE STORY

A. Study the table showing the military costs of World War I and complete the statements that follow.

Military Costs of World War I

Country	Total Armed Forces	Killed or Died	Wounded	Taken Prisoner
Austria–Hungary	7,800,000	1,200,000	3,620,000	2,200,000
British Empire	8,900,000	900,000	2,100,000	190,000
France	8,400,000	1,357,800	4,266,000	537,000
Germany	11,000,000	1,773,700	4,216,000	1,152,800
Japan	800,000	300	907	3
Russia	12,000,000	1,700,000	4,950,000	2,500,000
Serbia	707,000	45,000	133,000	153,000
United States	4,735,000	116,500	204,000	4,500

1. The country that had the largest number of soldiers killed was
   _____.

2. The country that had the smallest number of soldiers killed was
   _____.

3. The two countries that had the largest number of prisoners taken were _____ and _____.
4. The country that had the second smallest number of prisoners taken was _____.
5. The three countries that had more prisoners taken than soldiers killed were _____, _____, and _____.
6. The country that had the largest number of soldiers wounded was _____.
7. The country that had the smallest number of soldiers wounded was _____.

B. Imagine that the United States is involved in a war today to keep a free, democratic society from falling to an aggressor. Many Americans support this war, but just as many oppose it. Hans and Eric are American soldiers who are fighting in this war. You are a reporter and interview them. Who supports this war? Who opposes it? What reasons does each one give?

ACTIVITIES AND INQUIRIES

1. Go to the library. Write a report on a World War I battle.
2. Imagine that you are a soldier in a trench during World War I. Write a letter home. Tell what living in a trench is like.
3. Imagine that you are writing a script for a movie or television program about World War I. What would you call it? Write an outline for your script.
4. Hans broke down because he no longer believed in the things that he had once preached to Eric. Did you ever stop believing in something? Why? How did you feel?
5. A German soldier and a French soldier would probably have disagreed about many things. On what would they have agreed? Why?

5. Make War for Democracy

When World War I started in 1914, the United States said that it would not favor one side over the other. The United States was interested only in staying out of the war. In 1916 Woodrow Wilson was reelected president. He told the American people that thus far he had kept the country out of the war—and he meant to keep it out of the war. One year later, however, Wilson asked Congress to declare war against Germany.

In this story, Wilson is meeting with Representative Claude Kitchin of North Carolina. Kitchin is trying to convince Wilson not to send his war message to Congress. Why do you think that Wilson has changed his mind about the war? What are the main arguments that Kitchin uses?

Washington   March 1917

"And I tell you, Mr. President, that your message to Congress will cost thousands of American lives," argued Kitchin.

The two men had been discussing their differences for over an hour.

"Mr. Kitchin," said President Wilson, his eyes flashing, "may I remind you that I have done everything possible to keep the United States out of this mess? Congress demanded war when the Germans started their submarine attacks on American ships. But I asked for peaceful talks. I got the Germans to stop their attacks on our ships. No one wanted to keep America out of this war more than I. But now Germany has gone too far!"

"Perhaps it is the United States that has gone too far," answered Kitchin. "Why shouldn't Germany try to protect itself from us? Don't our ships deliver goods to Germany's enemies? Isn't it also true that Americans have loaned large amounts of money to Britain and France? I beg you to think of these things, Mr. President, before you ask Congress to declare war against Germany."

World War I submarine warfare: A German submarine sinks an unarmed British merchant ship. How did a neutral nation like the United States react to such acts of aggression?

"Mr. Kitchin, Americans have every right to sell their goods to any nation they wish. If private citizens want to lend money to foreign governments, that is not the business of this government. However, there is one thing that is the business of this government. The security of United States citizens everywhere must be guaranteed. By God, I'm not going to sit and do nothing while German submarines blow up our ships and kill our citizens!"

"Mr. President, it's still not too late. Stop our ships from carrying goods to Britain and France. United States business can survive without trade with these nations."

"Kitchin," answered the president a bit sadly, "I am no lover of war. In fact, I believe that our people will pay a monstrous price for getting into this war."

Kitchin interrupted. "Then stop it before it begins. Let us continue to live in peace. Mr. President, please don't send that war message to Congress."

"Can't you see, Kitchin," said Wilson quietly, "a new world is being born? We in the United States must help to shape it.

Can we really have peace at home when Europe is in this great crisis? The United States must help to make this world safe for democracy. We can enjoy peace when we join with free people everywhere. We must bring peace and safety to all nations."

Kitchin shook his head sadly. "Mr. President, you are a decent person. I know that you mean everything you say. But I'm convinced now that nothing I can say will stop you from sending that war message to Congress. I'm also afraid that, thanks to you, neither of us will ever again see a peaceful world."

Postscript

On April 2, 1917, President Wilson went before the Congress and asked for a declaration of war against Germany. On April 4 the Senate agreed with him by a vote of 82 to 6. On April 6 the vote in the House of Representatives was 373 to 50 in favor. A state of war existed between the United States and Germany.

QUESTIONS FOR REVIEW

1. What was the attitude in the United States toward the war in Europe when it began in 1914?
2. Why did President Woodrow Wilson change his mind about the war?
3. What did Representative Claude Kitchin suggest the United States do to avoid war with Germany?
4. What did Kitchin fear would happen if Congress declared war?
5. How did the United States Congress vote on President Wilson's call for a declaration of war against Germany?

UNDERSTANDING THE STORY

A. Write K for each statement that Kitchin made or might have made and W for each statement that Wilson made or might have made.

1. The president's war message will cost the lives of thousands of United States troops.

2. Germany has been warned to stop its submarine attacks against United States ships.
3. Germany should protect itself from the United States.
4. Germany has gone too far.
5. United States ships should not deliver goods to Germany's enemies.
6. United States firms have the right to sell their goods anywhere they choose.
7. The security of United States citizens everywhere must be guaranteed.
8. If the war message is sent, we will never again see a peaceful world.

B. Imagine that Wilson and Kitchin are candidates for the office of president of the United States today. Who would get your vote? Why?

ACTIVITIES AND INQUIRIES

1. Go to the library. Prepare a report on how the entry of the United States into World War I affected the outcome of the war.
2. Imagine that you are a reporter. Prepare the questions that you would like to ask President Wilson. Then answer the questions as he would have done.
3. Assume that you are the same reporter. Prepare the questions that you would ask Kitchin. Answer the questions as Kitchin would have done.
4. Study the following statements from the document called the Fourteen Points. This was a plan to end the war and keep the peace. Decide if they were written by Wilson or Kitchin. Explain.

> We entered the war because the rights of our people were ignored.
> We demand that the world be made fit and safe to live in.
> The pursuit of world peace is our program.

6. Winners Take All

In mid-1918, the German army's drive to Paris was stopped. Russia had been defeated, and Austria-Hungary had left the war. The British, French, and United States armies were preparing to sweep into German territory. Realizing that it was on the brink of defeat, Germany asked for an *armistice* (an end to the fighting). Now it was up to the leaders of the winning nations to draft a peace plan that would prevent war from breaking out again.

In this story, President Woodrow Wilson is meeting with leaders of the victorious European powers. They are talking about the peace conference that will soon take place.

See if you can guess how the winners treated the losers. Why was Wilson a hero in France? Why were there such great differences of opinion between Wilson and the other leaders?

Paris   1919

"Congratulations, Mr. Wilson," said Premier Georges Clemenceau of France. "How does it feel to be the most popular man in France?"

Wilson blushed. He was the first American president ever to visit Europe. He too was amazed by the way the French people had cheered him.

David Lloyd George, the British prime minister, looked up. "Yes, Wilson, I believe that the European people think of you as a shining knight. You are the one who will give back to them what this war has taken."

"And what do you suppose that is?" asked Wilson.

"I'll answer that," said Clemenceau. "My people want to make sure that Germany will never attack them again. They will be satisfied with nothing less than this security."

"And my people," added Lloyd George, "feel that someone must pay for the war. Germany started the war—shouldn't the Germans pay for it?"

Versailles peace conference, 1919: Leaders of the major powers (seated, from left) were Orlando of Italy; Lloyd George of Britain; Clemenceau of France; and Wilson of the United States.

"Gentlemen," said Wilson a bit sharply, "I didn't come to Europe to sign a peace treaty that will cripple Germany. We must deal justly with the Germans. Otherwise, there will be no lasting peace!"

"Treat them justly!" cried Clemenceau. "These people have invaded France twice in the last 50 years. They invaded Belgium, attacked passenger ships, and killed innocent civilians. They forced Russia to sign a harsh treaty. They would gladly have picked our bones clean if they had won. You ask for justice for these people?"

"Especially for these people," answered Wilson. "Gentlemen, these people believe in me. They asked that the shooting be stopped because they trusted me to see that they would be treated fairly."

"Nonsense, Wilson," boomed Lloyd George. "The Germans asked for a halt because they knew they were beaten. If we follow your advice, Germany will leave this conference the strongest country in Europe. Is that how you plan to build a lasting peace?"

The arguments continued for days. Wilson was no longer so sure of himself. He began to show signs of being tired and nervous. Slowly, he gave in on many of his ideas. Clemenceau and Lloyd George were too much for him. At last, the Treaty of Versailles was ready.

"Well, Wilson," said Clemenceau, "you may be proud of yourself. Thanks to you, we have agreed to a League of Nations. Never again will nations have to go to war to settle their differences. History will remember you as a good man who helped to make this war the last war. War is finished!"

Wilson thought for a moment. "I pray, sir, that your prediction will come true—not for my sake, but for the sake of people everywhere."

Postscript

The Treaty of Versailles forced Germany to give up some of its land in Europe and all of its colonies overseas. It had to pay a heavy fine to cover the costs of the war. The German army and navy were greatly reduced in size. The Germans protested, but they had no choice. They signed the treaty rather than risk starting the war again. New nations were carved out of the former territories of Austria-Hungary and the Ottoman Empire.

But the Versailles treaty also included a plan for creating an international organization called the League of Nations. Woodrow Wilson left Paris confident that the League would right all the wrongs of the treaty. He believed that the League would use its peacekeeping powers to prevent future wars. These powers included the promise that each member made to try to solve problems with other nations by discussion and negotiation rather than by war. If a member broke this promise and went to war, the other League members could act by refusing to trade with that country. If that action failed to discourage the member from continuing the war, the League could vote to use military force.

Wilson sent the Treaty of Versailles to the United States Senate for approval. Some senators feared that the League could involve the United States in a war even if Congress did not agree with the decision. Others wanted changes made in the treaty. Wilson, however, refused to make any changes, and the Senate refused to ratify it. Soon afterward, Wilson suffered a stroke from which he never recovered. He died a bitter man. His own people had turned their backs on his dream of world peace.

EUROPE AFTER WORLD WAR I

The Versailles peace conference, which Woodrow Wilson had hoped would bring "peace without victory," left many nations unhappy. Germany swore that it would regain the lands that the Versailles treaty had stripped away. Italy was unhappy with its share of Austrian territory and wanted more. Other nations also were unhappy, either because they had lost land or believed that they had received too little for being on the winning side.

We shall see the outcome of this discontent in Unit XI.

QUESTIONS FOR REVIEW

1. Why did Germany ask for an armistice?
2. How did Lloyd George of England and Clemenceau of France believe that the losers should be treated?
3. How did Wilson believe that the losers should be treated?

4. Why did Wilson believe that the League of Nations would right the wrongs of the Treaty of Versailles?
5. How did the United States Senate vote on the League? Why?

UNDERSTANDING THE STORY

A. Tell which statements Wilson would have agreed with.

1. Germany must be punished so that it will never make war again.
2. Germany should pay the full cost of the war.
3. The winning nations should not take advantage of Germany.
4. The Germans expect to be treated fairly.
5. Germany called for a halt in the war because it knew it was beaten.
6. The League of Nations will prevent future wars.
7. This war must be the war to end all wars.
8. The Treaty of Versailles was very fair to Germany.

B. Imagine that a war between the United States and another country has just ended. The war has been very ugly. Many people have been killed. The other country has called off the war. Now the United States must make up the peace treaty. How would Wilson have made up such a treaty? Would you approve of this treaty? Explain.

ACTIVITIES AND INQUIRIES

1. Imagine that you are present at the Paris peace conference. You are asked to draw up a treaty that will prevent future wars between the nations at the conference. Draw up your treaty. Explain why it will prevent wars.
2. Assume that you are a newspaper reporter. Which of the national leaders at the Paris conference would you want most to interview? Why? Write the questions that you would like to ask. Answer these questions as you think they would be answered.
3. Pretend that you are a reporter for a German newspaper. Write an article about what is happening at the peace conference. Write your opinion of the peace treaty that Germany is being forced to sign. Explain why you feel this way.
4. Go to the library. Prepare a list of Wilson's Fourteen Points. Then make a list of the terms of the actual peace treaty (the Treaty of Versailles). Underline the ideas that you think are good in Wilson's Fourteen Points. Underline the ideas that you think are good in the

Treaty of Versailles. Now put together the ideas you like in the Fourteen Points and the Treaty of Versailles. Add ideas of your own. Do you now have a treaty that will prevent future wars? Explain.

5. Assume that the peace conference is over. Germany has just signed the Treaty of Versailles. Draw a cartoon for a French newspaper showing how the French feel about the treaty. Next draw a cartoon for a German newspaper showing how the Germans feel about the treaty. Judging from the feelings in the cartoons, will the Treaty of Versailles end war between the French and German peoples?

6. Look at the maps of Europe in World War I, on page 404, and Europe after World War I, on page 418. Compare them. Notice the changes in the later map of Europe. Tell which item below makes each statement correct.

   a. A new country in eastern Europe in the 1920s was (1) Czechoslovakia (2) Germany (3) France.

   b. A new country in northern Europe in the 1920s was (1) Finland (2) Greece (3) Denmark.

   c. A country that lost territory in World War I was (1) Spain (2) France (3) Germany.

   d. A country that gained territory in World War I was (1) Germany (2) France (3) Austria–Hungary.

   e. A country divided into many other countries was (1) Great Britain (2) Austria–Hungary (3) Italy.

   f. A new country on the Baltic Sea in the 1920s was (1) Estonia (2) Sweden (3) Norway.

   g. A country in Europe that did not change in size as a result of World War I was (1) Austria (2) Germany (3) Switzerland.

   h. A country that lost territory to the new nation of Poland was (1) France (2) the Soviet Union (3) Bulgaria.

   i. Another Northern European country that did not exist before World War I was (1) Denmark (2) Lithuania (3) the Netherlands.

   j. A country north of Italy that was formerly part of an empire was (1) France (2) Switzerland (3) Austria.

UNIT X

Twentieth-Century Dictatorships

World War I caused much suffering for millions of people in many nations in Europe and the Middle East. Many people began to listen to politicians and radical speakers who sought total power in exchange for promises of food, clothing, jobs, and security. Some would later gain power and establish *totalitarian dictatorships*.

In a totalitarian dictatorship, all power is concentrated in the hands of one person. The government uses the army and the police to silence its opponents. People are arrested without charges and punished without

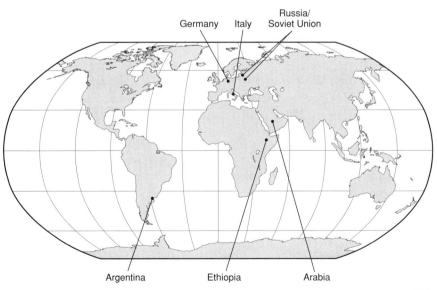

Germany　Italy　Russia/ Soviet Union

Argentina　Ethiopia　Arabia

trials. Newspapers, magazines, and the airwaves tell the people only what the government wants them to hear.

Europe. Our first story takes place in St. Petersburg, Russia, in 1905. There was much unhappiness in Russia. A large crowd had gathered outside the czar's palace in the hope that he would listen to their demands. But the czar's troops had readied a shocking reply.

Our next story takes place in Russia, a dozen years later. A revolution had forced the czar from power. The new government was weak. The man who had seized power believed that the people had to be taught to make decisions. His rival believed that the people had to be told what to do. One of these men would establish policies that shaped the destiny of the people for many years to come.

We next look at Moscow in 1938. A trial was about to take place. A man would confess to crimes he had not committed and would ask for punishment. How he was brought to confess is the subject of this story.

In Rome, Italy, in 1922, a man harbored a huge ambition: to become the dictator of the country. He used force, lies, threats, and promises. But when he called on the Italian people for their support, they refused to vote him the power he sought.

Our next story takes place in Munich, Germany, in 1920. A street corner speaker filled with hate had gathered a small group of listeners. Some disagreed with him. No one could know that the man would one day become Germany's most powerful person.

Next we find ourselves in Berlin, during the years 1933 and 1934. The street corner speaker had turned to the people for support, but they denied him the necessary votes. He had to find another way to make himself dictator of Germany.

Middle East. We move on to Cyprus, in 1925, where an Arab leader lived in exile. He had sacrificed much for his people but had earned much hatred for his efforts. Why this happened is answered in this story.

Africa. Now we visit Geneva, Switzerland, in 1936. An African leader stood before the League of Nations, and begged the League's delegates for aid. "What answer am I to take back to my people?" he asked. The story reveals the reply he received.

South America. Our final story takes place in Buenos Aires, Argentina, in 1952. We learn about a woman who helped her husband gain absolute power in their country. We also learn why they were worshiped by many people.

1. Russian Revolution—The Beginning

World War I brought sweeping changes to most of the countries of Europe. It had perhaps its greatest impact upon Russia. Russia on the eve of the war was a giant country, with a wide variety of natural resources. In spite of these natural gifts, however, Russia was one of the most backward countries in Europe. For over 300 years, it had been ruled by absolute monarchs—the czars. The great majority of the Russian people were poor and illiterate. They were surrounded by corrupt officials and secret police, and few dared to speak out against the government. Those who did were sent off to the icy wasteland called Siberia. They were usually not heard from again. For these reasons, Russia seemed to stand still as other nations moved forward.

In our story, a crowd has gathered outside the czar's palace. The Russian fleet had just been defeated by the Japanese. Workers are on strike, people are rioting, and revolution threatens. This crowd has come to make serious demands of the czar.

Ask yourself what the crowd wanted from the czar. How would he deal with the crowd?

St. Petersburg 1905

"We are just wasting our time," said Sonia, a young Russian. She had joined the crowd marching on the winter palace of the czar.

"You'll see," answered her friend Peter. "The czar is a good man. He'll listen to us."

"Do you really believe that your precious Czar Nicholas is so different from those who came before him? His ancestors made slaves of the Russian people, and Nicholas is no different."

"But Sonia," protested Peter, "the czar understands suffering. His own son dies a slow death from an incurable blood dis-

423

ease. Nicholas can only watch helplessly. He would give up his throne if it would save his son. If he has such love for his son, is he not capable of loving and protecting his own people? You'll see, Sonia; he'll help us."

"Peter, how can you be so stupid?" asked Sonia. "If the czar is such a good man, why are so many of us so poor? Whose fault is it that we break our backs at work and go home to miserable shacks? We watch our children go hungry while the czar and his friends live in palaces. They feed their dogs better than we feed our families!"

"It's not his fault," said Peter. "Things will be different for us after he hears what we have to say."

"He won't listen," said Sonia, her voice rising angrily. "He thinks of us as lowly dogs who should crawl on our bellies and beg to be petted. He will not listen to those who stand on their feet and make demands of him."

"Sonia, you have been influenced by your revolutionary friends," Peter replied. "They say these things about the czar without really knowing anything about him. I can only tell you that you and your friends are in for a surprise today."

"Most of my friends have already been surprised," said Sonia. "They were surprised in the middle of the night by the czar's secret police and taken away. No one knows where they are being held or if they will ever come back. This is the justice that your czar gives to those who stand up to him."

By this time, the crowd had arrived at the gates of the winter palace. Sonia and Peter pushed their way to the front lines. People holding banners and signs were calling out the czar's name. The crowd was respectful rather than angry. Men removed their hats and stood with bowed heads. Women and children stood at attention. Cries of "Little Father" were heard everywhere. It was clear that the crowd expected the czar to make an appearance soon.

Instead, the palace guard appeared. They marched up to the crowd and formed a human barricade. The officer in charge ordered the crowd to leave.

"For the last time," shouted the officer, "go now or else there will be trouble!"

Shots rang out. In less than a minute, the streets were red with blood.

"Not until we've seen the czar," answered many from the crowd.

The officer turned and signaled to the guard. The soldiers aimed their weapons at the crowd and awaited a signal.

A man shouted, "Will you fire upon unarmed men, women, and children? We come here in peace. Our only wish is that the czar will hear our pleas."

In answer, the officer signaled to the guard again. Shots rang out. In less than a minute, the streets were red with blood. Children shrieked as they saw their parents stagger and fall. People ran only to be cut down by swordsmen on horseback. Only a few escaped serious injury or death.

Hours later, people came to claim the dead. Peter, wounded and exhausted, wondered if he would have the strength to bury his friend.

Postscript

The strikes and riots of 1905–1906 did little to change the Russian government. Czar Nicholas continued to ignore cries for reform. Those who dared to criticize him openly were either imprisoned or forced to leave the country. Most Russians sighed and shrugged their shoulders. They quietly continued to live out their lives under the direction of the badly run and corrupt Russian government.

For the moment, World War I helped the Russian people to forget their problems. Eager to protect Russia from its enemies, the people rallied to the government's support. But defeats at the front and food shortages at home soon caused many Russians to complain bitterly about the czar and his government. Soldiers deserted the army, and crowds rioted in the cities. When an order to fire on the rioters was ignored, Czar Nicholas suddenly found himself helpless and abandoned. On March 15, 1917, Nicholas II gave up his throne.

QUESTIONS FOR REVIEW

1. Why was Russia one of the most backward countries in Europe?
2. How did Czar Nicholas react to the call for reforms?
3. How did the czar's troops deal with the people who gathered in the St. Petersburg square outside the winter palace in 1905?
4. How did World War I at first help the Russian government?
5. Why did World War I eventually lead to the downfall of the czar and his government?

UNDERSTANDING THE STORY

A. Decide who made or might have made the remarks that follow. Write S for each statement that Sonia made or might have made and P for each statement that Peter made or might have made.

1. Trying to see the czar is a waste of time.
2. Nicholas is no different from his ancestors.
3. The czar loves the people.
4. It is the czar's fault that many of our people are poor and cannot read or write.
5. The czar will help us after he hears what we have to say.
6. The czar uses the secret police to make us afraid of him.
7. The czar would give up his throne if it would save his son.
8. The czar thinks of us as dogs who should crawl and beg to be petted.

B. Imagine that the czar's palace guards had not been ordered to shoot the marchers. Instead, the czar agreed to meet with some of the people. What would Sonia have said to the czar? What would Peter have said to the czar?

ACTIVITIES AND INQUIRIES

1. Use each of the following key terms in a sentence: backward corrupt   protest   czar   illiterate   ancestor.
2. Peter has just buried his friend Sonia. He writes a letter about Sonia's death. Peter also tells his feelings about the czar. Write Peter's letter. Decide if Peter has changed his mind about the czar.
3. Pretend that the czar is on trial. You are Peter. Write down what you will say when you are called to the witness stand.
4. Imagine that you are a newspaper reporter. Your assignment is to interview the czar. Write the questions you would like to ask him. Answer the questions as you think the czar would.
5. Look at the illustration on page 425. Do you think it would have appeared in a Russian newspaper of the time? Explain.

2. Peace, Bread, and Land

As our story opens, the new Russian government is facing grave problems. The riots are worse than ever. Small, well-organized groups are trying to take over the government. The world war continues, and Russians suffer even greater losses at the hands of the Germans. The situation is desperate. Russia's very survival seems to be at stake.

Two men, both revolutionaries, are discussing their plans for Russia's future. Both agree that the czar and the nobility must be prevented from returning to power. They disagree on practically everything else. Both men will taste power. One will go on to change the course of Russian history. The other will live out his years in exile, lonely and forgotten.

See if you understand the reasons for the one man's success and the other man's failure.

Petrograd 1917

"And you call yourself a revolutionary," muttered Vladimir Ulyanov, better known as Lenin. He was talking to the government leader, Alexander Kerensky.

"Of course, I'm a revolutionary," answered Kerensky. "I am transferring the government from the czar to the people. I am saying good-bye to 300 years of misery and corruption. What else am I if not a revolutionary?"

"A fool," replied Lenin. "You are a fool who has come to believe in his own daydreams."

Kerensky reddened. "Stop talking down to me as if I were one of your schoolboy followers. While you make speeches on street corners, I am putting together a government that will give hope to Russians who love freedom. It will take time. Democracy moves slowly. But one day the people will understand what I have done for them. Then they will return the love I feel for them."

"Love you?" asked Lenin. "They hate you! Fool that you are, you don't even understand why."

Moscow: Lenin addresses a crowd after the successful Bolshevik revolution in Russia. Why did Lenin's party succeed while Kerensky's did not?

"Tell me why," said Kerensky.

"They hate you because you are a good man, and they understand only cruelty."

"I don't understand."

"Of course you don't, Kerensky. You don't understand that the people want to see this war over *now*. They want land and bread *now*. They don't care how they get these things. Our people are filled with hatred. They hate the rich, the educated, and the privileged. They hate all those who make them feel stupid, clumsy, and inferior. They will follow anyone shrewd enough to punish those they hate and strong enough to make them afraid."

"No, no!" objected Kerensky. "The Russian people aren't like that at all! They are brave people who will fight on until this war is over. They will get their land and their bread. But they know that these things take time. They understand that these things must be done properly. They must be done democratically. The people understand, and they will wait."

"Bah!" sneered Lenin. "You lead the Russian people but you don't understand them at all. Your picture of them is a lie!"

"But what of your picture of the Russian people?" interrupted Kerensky. "What an ugly picture you paint of them. I am beginning to think that you hate the Russian people!"

"I am above love and hate," sneered Lenin. "Russia is about to give birth to a great revolution. I am the doctor who will deliver this child. I will do anything—use any trick, sacrifice any person—to see the revolution live and grow strong!"

"You're mad!" cried Kerensky.

"Perhaps," answered Lenin. "Perhaps great visions come only to those of us who are a little mad. Maybe that's why we succeed where others fail!"

"Take care, Lenin," warned Kerensky. "You may become the thing you claim to hate the most!"

"And what is that?"

"The next Russian czar!"

Postscript

By August 1917, a small group of revolutionaries led by Lenin was able to seize power in Russia, a country of 150 million people. Lenin had organized his followers into *soviets*: groups of workers, soldiers, and landless farmers. To the soldiers, he promised peace. To the workers, he promised bread and the control of factories. To the landless peasants, he promised land that would be taken away from the wealthy landowners. The promises of "peace, bread, and land" won Lenin many new followers.

In the meantime, many Russians had lost confidence in the Kerensky government. Impatient with Kerensky's promise of a democratic government, they wanted immediate reforms similar to the promises Lenin was making and the Kerensky government was slow to deliver. Some of the old privileged group now called for a military dictatorship to hold the country together. The confusion offered Lenin the opportunity he needed to strike and take power. On November 7, 1917, Lenin's supporters, led by Leon Trotsky, took control of government buildings, arrested members of the Kerensky government, and declared a Soviet republic. Exhilarated by his success, Lenin now called for Communist revolutions throughout the world.

But the new government faced many problems. There were severe food shortages and breakdowns in the army, industry, railway transport, and commerce. Different national groups within Russia were threatening to break away and form their own countries. In desperation, the new government signed a humiliating peace treaty with Germany in 1918. Russia was forced to give up a great deal of land as the price for peace.

Fighting continued against the opponents of the Communist government. These included supporters of Kerensky's government as well as those who supported the czar. Upset with Russia's decision to leave the war and alarmed by Lenin's call for world revolution, France, Britain, and the United States sent armed forces to help these groups fight the Communists. But these groups were eventually defeated, and the foreign forces returned home.

Facing many problems that threatened to topple the new government, Lenin decided that it was necessary to establish a dictatorship. Armed with absolute powers, his government used violence to restore order. Government opponents were imprisoned and often tortured and killed. The czar and his family were also imprisoned and killed. To further stifle opposition, only one political group—the Communist Party—was permitted. The government also took control over major industries but allowed some small-scale industries and farms to be privately owned. In 1922, to unify the many different people who lived within the former Russian Empire, the government established the Union of Soviet Socialist Republics. Each republic represented a different area or nationality and was free to retain its own culture, but all republics followed the same constitution and were controlled by the Communist Party.

The Communists had ended the fighting with Germany, fought a civil war, defeated foreign invaders, and reorganized their government—all in just four years. But the Russian people had paid an enormous price for these accomplishments, and before long, the price would grow even higher.

QUESTIONS FOR REVIEW

1. Why was Lenin's small group of revolutionaries able to seize power?
2. What problems did the new government in Russia face?
3. Why did Lenin's government continue to face great problems?
4. How did the government deal with the world war?
5. What did the government do to restore order in Russia?

UNDERSTANDING THE STORY

A. Write T for each statement that is true, F for each statement that is false, and N for each statement that is not mentioned in the story.

1. The strikes of 1905–1906 did much to change things in Russia.
2. The Russian people wanted a democratic government.
3. Things continued just as before the strikes of 1905–1906.
4. World War I helped to force Nicholas II to give up his throne.
5. Conditions improved after Nicholas II gave up his throne.
6. The Russians continued to fight the war after Nicholas II gave up his throne.
7. Kerensky and Lenin had a great deal in common.
8. Lenin secretly wanted to be the next Russian czar.

B. Imagine that you are living in Russia in 1917. The czar has just given up the throne. Lenin and Kerensky are fighting for power. Which person would you follow? Why?

ACTIVITIES AND INQUIRIES

1. Use each of the following terms in a sentence: reform   soviet   exile   vision   inefficient   abandoned   sacrifice.
2. Prepare a report on the Russian Revolution of 1917.
3. Pretend that you are producing a television special. Both Lenin and Kerensky want to appear on your show. However, you can choose only one of them. Which one would you choose? Why?
4. Look at the illustration on page 429. Who is shown—Kerensky or Lenin? Explain. Draw a picture of the other man. Explain how the two pictures show the differences between Lenin and Kerensky.

3. Soviet Dictatorship in Action

Firmly in power, the Communists now tried to address their most serious problems. Could food production be increased? Could the Soviet Union be turned into a modern state? Could the revolution be protected from its enemies?

In 1924 another serious problem arose. Lenin suffered a stroke and died. Who would succeed him? Lenin had favored Leon Trotsky, who had led the Communists to victory. But another man stepped forward and claimed that he was Lenin's rightful successor. This man was Joseph Stalin. Under Lenin, he had served as the general secretary of the Soviet Union. Stalin used his position to gain control over the Communist Party. People were afraid to oppose him. Those who disagreed with him were condemned as traitors and imprisoned or murdered. Trotsky was forced to leave Russia and was later murdered while living in exile in Mexico. In 1929 Stalin was officially declared Lenin's successor.

Ask yourself what sort of man Stalin was. What plans did he have for the Soviet Union? Could Stalin turn the Soviet Union into a modern state? What price would the Russian people be asked to pay for Stalin's leadership and goals?

MOSCOW 1938

It was 3:00 A.M. Comrade Igor Kirofsky, a high-ranking Soviet official, was sound asleep. Suddenly, there was a loud knocking on the door.

"Who is it?" bellowed Kirofsky, as he tried to rub the sleep from his eyes.

"Open the door, comrade. It is the police."

Kirofsky angrily jumped from his bed and threw open the door. "How dare you come to my house at such an hour! Don't you know who I am? Whoever is responsible for this will pay dearly!"

433

Two men stepped inside the room. "Please, comrade," said one, "we have our orders. You are to get dressed and come with us immediately. All will be explained to you shortly."

Still muttering angry threats, Kirofsky dressed and left with the men. They soon arrived at a police station that was quite familiar to Kirofsky. He knew that spies and dangerous criminals were usually brought here for questioning. For the first time, he began to feel a little less sure of himself.

Kirofsky was ushered into a well-lighted waiting room. He was told that someone would soon speak with him. He was left by himself. An hour later, a man entered.

"Please come with me," said the man.

"What is this all about?" asked Kirofsky. He seemed far less angry than he had been earlier.

"Please come with me," repeated the man.

Kirofsky followed the man out of the waiting room and down a stairway leading to the basement. He was escorted to another room and asked to surrender his valuables. The door was locked behind him.

Deep in thought, Kirofsky did not notice that the room was a very unusual one. Later, after he had spent some time there, he discovered that the room had no windows. It had a single, glaring light, and it was soundproof. Each day a tray of food was pushed through a tiny compartment that could be opened only from the outside.

Minutes, hours, days, weeks, perhaps even months went by. Kirofsky lost all sense of time. Denied sound, books, and human contact, he retreated more and more into himself. Over and over, he silently asked himself the same question, "Why am I here?"

Slowly, Kirofsky became convinced that he was guilty of some monstrous crime. Why else would he be given this treatment?

He thought many times about Comrade Stalin. Kirofsky was confused. "Did I only think of him as a butcher, or did I call him that to his face?" he asked himself. "Did I tell Stalin I hated him for giving the order to execute the rich farmers and scatter their families? Did I accuse Stalin of murdering his closest friends and driving his wife to suicide? Did I criticize him

Over and over again, he asked himself the same question: "Why am I here?"

for enslaving the Russian people and forcing them to work in state factories and farms in exchange for scraps of bread? Did I plot to remove Stalin along with the others who have long since been arrested and executed? Did I think these things, or did I do them? I can't remember which. Does it really matter? Doesn't thinking these things or dreaming them make me as guilty as if I had done them anyway?"

Kirofsky had been secretly observed from the beginning. Sensing that at last the time was ripe, the official in charge of getting signed confessions ordered Kirofsky brought to his office.

Kirofsky was taken from the cell into the lighted corridor. His eyes hurt and his legs were weak. He needed help to walk to the official's office.

The official jumped up to greet Kirofsky. "Welcome, comrade," he said, and immediately offered him a cigarette. The official asked Kirofsky how he could make him more comfortable and help him in any other way.

"What a wonderful man!" Kirofsky thought. "I have plotted against the government, and am therefore guilty of treason of the highest order. Yet this man shows such concern for me. I must listen to him carefully and do what he says because he is a much better man than I."

"Comrade," the official said to Kirofsky, "you have been alone with your thoughts for a long time. I know that you are bursting to speak of them. Why don't you tell me what you have discovered about yourself. I am sure that you will soon feel better."

Kirofsky began to speak. At a signal from the official, a secretary began to write. The minutes ticked by and soon Kirofsky had confessed all his innermost thoughts.

"Comrade," the official said softly, "will you sign what you have just dictated and stand by these statements at your trial?"

"Of course I will!" answered Kirofsky. "A traitor like myself should be tried before the people. I have betrayed my country and I hate myself for it! I no longer care what happens to me. If I could ask for anything, it would be for an end to this life of mine!"

"Comrade," said the official, "the man you called a butcher is not without mercy. He will grant your last wish."

Postscript

Stalin held power in the Soviet Union for more than 25 years. During that time, the government added to its powers at the people's expense. The Soviet government controlled all the factories and farms. It set prices and wages and decided what was to be produced and how it was to be made. Unions and strikes were outlawed. People lived in fear because of the secret police, censorship, and the government's use of terror tactics. Millions of people who opposed the government were killed or sent to slave labor camps in Siberia.

After Stalin died in 1953, the terror he had brought about lived on. But even Stalin and the dictators who followed him could not crush the spirit of the Russian people and others who lived under their control. Many cried out for freedom, and the Soviet leaders began to listen. In 1956

Soviet premier Nikita Khrushchev denounced Stalin and the many crimes he had committed against the people while in office. Khrushchev promised greater freedom of speech and the press, the release of many prisoners from the slave labor camps, and an improvement in the low Soviet standard of living. These freedoms, limited as they were, whetted the appetites of the people and those who lived in the Soviet empire for more. A door had been opened, and no dictator would be able to force it fully shut again.

QUESTIONS FOR REVIEW

1. What were the major questions that the Communists had to address?
2. How did Stalin become Lenin's successor?
3. How did Stalin's government add to its powers at the expense of the people?
4. What promises did Khrushchev make to the people of the Soviet Union?
5. Why did Khrushchev make these promises? Did they satisfy the people who lived within the Soviet empire? Explain.

UNDERSTANDING THE STORY

A. Complete the sentences below.

1. Lenin promised _____, _____, and _____.
2. The Communists worried about how to _____ the country after the civil war was ended.
3. After Lenin's death, the brutal fight for power was won by _____.
4. Kirofsky was brought to a police station where _____ and dangerous _____ were usually taken.
5. Kirofsky was imprisoned in a room without _____.
6. Kirofsky became convinced that he was _____ of some monstrous crime.
7. Kirofsky thought that he had plotted to remove _____ from power.
8. Kirofsky _____ to many crimes against the state.

B. Although he was not beaten or physically harmed, Kirofsky signed a confession of guilt. Should the police in your community be allowed to use methods like those in the story to get confessions? Explain.

ACTIVITIES AND INQUIRIES

1. Use each of the following key terms in a sentence: Communist unite retreat official confess invade comrade plot treason.
2. Imagine that Kirofsky is on trial. You are to be his prosecutor. Prepare the case against him.
3. Pretend that you are to be Kirofsky's lawyer. Prepare the case in his defense.
4. Suppose that you are an American reporter at Kirofsky's trial. Write an article describing the trial. Tell if Kirofsky will be found innocent or guilty. Write your opinion of the verdict.
5. Look at the illustration on page 435. Describe the scene. Write your own title for the picture.

4. Benito Mussolini

Italy was on the winning side at the end of World War I. It entered the war on the side of Germany but in 1915 switched over to the side of Britain and France. Italy's leaders made the right choice, but the people had little about which to be happy. The Treaty of Versailles had not given them all the land they believed they deserved, and the war had been very costly. The Italian people were about to find out how costly.

The victorious Italian soldiers went home to a country that suffered from rising prices, low wages, high unemployment, and a scarcity of goods. In desperation, some workers took over factories in the hope that by managing the industries themselves they would change things for the better. But these takeovers were unsuccessful and led to greater confusion and even lower production. Most workers admitted their mistakes and agreed to return the factories to their owners. But the property owners had been frightened. From now on, they would throw their support and their money to those who promised to help them keep their property.

Out of the ashes of confusion would arise a man whose drive to power would not be stopped. His name was Benito Mussolini. Ask yourself how someone like Mussolini came to power. Should the factory owners have supported him? Did he have the answers to Italy's problems?

Rome   1922

You are Benito Mussolini, and you are about to become the most powerful person in Italy. You have worked hard to become somebody. You have been a teacher, a newspaperman, a soldier, and a political leader. Life for you has been hard but interesting.

You are no stranger to violence. You have seen men killed in battle, and you yourself were wounded in the war. As a young man, you got involved in several fights and once threatened a man with a knife. You are also outspoken, and you have spent time in jail because of this.

People are not sure what you stand for. You spoke out against the war when it first began. Later, you were thrown out of the Socialist party for speaking in favor of the war. You claim to be in favor of improving working conditions. Yet you have hired yourself out many times as a strikebreaker.

While others may be confused by your actions, you know exactly what you want: power! You will take any avenue that leads you through the corridors of power, up to the very top.

In the 1930s, Mussolini rearmed Italy and prepared for war.

You are clever enough to know that frightened and confused Italians respect strength and force. This is why you have organized a group that you call the Fascist party. You dress these men up in black shirts, and have them beat up your enemies. Sometimes your men get carried away and force castor oil down the throats of those who speak out against you. This always makes you laugh.

The Communist party has been very useful to you. Every time there is a strike or riot, you blame the Communists, and your men take to the streets and break workers' heads. The factory owners and landowners are grateful to you, and they see that a lot of money comes into your hands.

You have tried to take control of the government by legal means. The Italian people, for the most part, have not given you their support at the polls. You must find another way!

Now you have decided that the time is ripe to make your move. You will simply take over the government by force. The government is weak, and the king will do anything to keep his throne. He has already promised you his complete cooperation. Many in the government hate you, and they can stop you only if they stand together. You know that this will not happen!

You have sent 40,000 men to march on Rome to force the government to give in to you. But you take no chances—you wait safely in Milan. Should there be trouble, you are ready to make your escape to another country. But you have nothing to worry about. The march will go smoothly and will accomplish its purpose. The people will be impressed and the government will be frightened. You will be invited to go to Rome and take control of the government.

You can't possibly know it, but your worst days are in front of you. But you are now about to become the most powerful man in Italy, and today belongs to you!

Postscript

Riots, strikes, unemployment, high prices, and murder in the streets were all part of Italy when Mussolini assumed power. As dictator, he set to work to restore order to the country. Cities were cleaned up, crime was reduced, and more schools were built. Factories operated day and night, employing more workers. Electricity was brought to many rural areas, and even the trains were said to run on time.

But the critics of Mussolini's government complained that the Fascist secret police were everywhere. Those people who spoke out against the government were thrown into jail. Strikes were forbidden by law. The newspapers, the radio, and even the letters that people wrote were carefully watched by the government.

Mussolini's opponents claimed that the reason the factories operated day and night was to produce weapons so that Mussolini could prepare to fight another war, one he would help to start. Whatever benefits the Italian people were to receive from the Mussolini government would be purchased with their freedom and their blood.

QUESTIONS FOR REVIEW

1. Why were the Italian people unhappy with the Treaty of Versailles?
2. Why did Italy face serious problems at the conclusion of World War I?
3. How did Mussolini rise to power?
4. How did Mussolini try to restore order in Italy?
5. Why did many Italians reject the Mussolini government?

UNDERSTANDING THE STORY

A. Number the events below in the order in which they took place according to the story.

Mussolini was thrown out of the Socialist party.
World War I broke out.
Mussolini spoke out against World War I.
Mussolini's army marched on Rome.
Mussolini spoke out in favor of World War I.
Mussolini organized the Fascist party.
Mussolini took control of the Italian government.
Property owners supported Mussolini.

B. Imagine that Mussolini is in the United States. He wants to become the leader of the American people. Write a step-by-step plan telling how Mussolini would probably try to take power. Would this plan succeed? Explain.

ACTIVITIES AND INQUIRIES

1. Use each of the following key terms in a sentence: violence   strike-breaker   polls   Socialist   Fascist.
2. Go to the library. Prepare a report on how Mussolini rose to power.
3. Assume that Mussolini has just come to power. You are going to interview him. Write the questions that you would like to ask him. Now answer the questions as you think Mussolini would.
4. Imagine that you are an Italian newspaper reporter. Mussolini just became the most powerful person in Italy. Write an article about whether or not you think Mussolini will help the Italian people.
5. Imagine that you are working for Mussolini. He asks you to draw a poster. The poster is to tell people that Mussolini is going to solve Italy's problems. Draw the poster.

5. Poison in the Streets

Let us see what was happening in Germany now that World War I was over. Germany, a defeated country, faced many problems. It owed money to the countries that had defeated it. The people suffered from food shortages. Many factories were closing, and millions of people were out of work. Prices climbed higher from day to day.

All over Germany, people asked why this was happening. The speaker in our story believed that he had found the answer to this question, and, with it, the solution to Germany's problems. Let us now find out what this man has in mind.

Ask yourself why these things are happening in Germany. How does the street corner speaker in the city of Munich propose to solve these problems? Does he really have the answers?

Munich   1920

"The Jews—they are the ones who are to blame!" cried the street corner speaker. The crowd of onlookers began to grumble among themselves. Some nodded their heads, while others murmured angrily and walked away.

"We did not lose this war!" screamed the speaker. "We were stabbed in the back by Jewish traitors who made money while we shed German blood!"

"How much money is this arm worth?" yelled a one-armed man from the crowd. The crowd stood back as the man pushed his way toward the speaker.

"You have both your arms," angrily said the man facing the speaker. "I have donated one of my Jewish arms to the service of my country! You, sir, are a liar!"

At this moment, four men rushed the one-armed man and quickly moved him away from the crowd. Quietly and viciously, they beat and kicked him.

The speaker addressed the crowd once again. "You see how dangerous these Jews are? If you speak against them, they will do anything to stop you. I have seen this man before. He lost his arm in an accident. Now he wants you to believe that he lost it in the war. Don't feel pity for him. He is your enemy, and he is getting what he deserves. Today we punish him. One day soon we will deal with all of his race!"

"But," interrupted someone from the crowd, "even if we deal with the Jews, how will this help solve Germany's problems?"

"The Jews are not the only ones to be dealt with," answered the speaker, his eyes glistening. "We Germans are the master race. We were born to rule, not to serve! All inferiors—Jews, Gypsies, old people, cripples, the mentally retarded, and others of this kind—must be separated from us so that we can fulfill our destiny!"

"And what is our destiny?" cried a young man.

The speaker smiled. "Our destiny is to unite all German people everywhere in the world. Once we have done this, we must provide living space for our people. We must move to the east, take Russian lands, and make the Russians our slaves!"

"But that means another war!" yelled someone in the crowd.

"No," answered the speaker. "The West is afraid to fight. They know that they did not defeat us the first time. They will not

"How much money is this arm worth?"

want to meet us on the field of battle again. Besides, do they care what happens to a pack of Communist dogs?"

"Young man," cried an elderly Catholic priest, "I have listened to everything that you have said. I am shocked that only one person has spoken out against you!" The priest turned to the crowd and said, "How can you as Christians listen to these ugly things and remain silent? Have you no shame?"

At these words, many in the crowd turned red with embarrassment and lowered their heads. Some began to walk away.

The speaker's face now became red with anger. "You old fool! Don't you know that Jesus Christ was born and died a Jew? When Jesus said turn the other cheek, he meant for us to turn so that the Jews could slap us again. The Jews invented Christianity and gave it to us so that they could continue to control us through Christian teachings. For centuries, Christianity has been used by the weak to control the strong!"

The priest was silent for a moment. He said, "You are a bitter man—your mind is twisted and sick! As angry as the German people are today, they will never listen to you! You will soon crawl back into the sewer you came from, never to be heard from again!"

Having said this, the priest turned and walked away. Others looked around once or twice and slowly began to drift away. Soon, there were only a few people left.

One man, middle-aged, his suit a bit shiny and his collar frayed, walked up to the speaker. He said, "Never mind that old fool. You speak of things the way they really are. You have opened my eyes and I am grateful. I would like to know your name."

"My name," said the speaker, brushing his hair away from his eyes, "is Adolf Hitler."

Postscript

Adolf Hitler was an Austrian drifter who had failed at most of the things he had tried. He volunteered for military service in the German army and fought in World War I. After the war, Hitler determined that he would never again be a nobody. He decided to settle in Germany and enter politics.

Hitler joined a small party called the National Socialist German Workers' (Nazi) Party. He discovered within himself a talent for public speaking and organization and quickly rose to become head of the party. Soon, Hitler's party, the instrument of his own ideas, became one of the most powerful in Germany.

What did Hitler stand for? He wanted revenge for Germany's defeat in the world war and the harsh postwar treaties. He dreamed of a great German empire stretching from Europe deep into the Soviet Union. Hitler advocated replacing the democratically elected German government with a dictatorship, ruled by himself. The new government would help workers by controlling all businesses and the economy.

Hitler organized large public meetings (rallies) where he expressed his ideas. He used these rallies, parades, and violence to impress people with the power of the Nazi movement. He told the people what they wanted to hear, and he repeated, over and over, what he wanted them to believe. Those who spoke out against him were beaten up by his private army. He used violence to break up meetings held by rival political parties. Soon, this former nobody was known throughout Germany.

By 1923 Adolf Hitler felt that the time had come for him to make his first important move to take over all of Germany. He and his followers marched on Munich, the capital of the German state of Bavaria, hoping to take it over by force. After a violent clash with the police, Hitler was arrested and tried for treason.

Hitler was sentenced to five years in prison but served less than nine months. While in prison he set down his ideas in a book he entitled *Mein Kampf* (My Struggle). This work would one day become the best-selling book in Germany.

In *Mein Kampf*, Hitler repeated his major ideas. He called for Germans to renounce the Versailles Treaty by refusing to pay reparations and by rearming. Germany should take back all lands taken away from it in the war and should expand across Europe. To build a mighty German empire, it would be necessary to replace the current government with one party, one policy, and one leader to guide Germany's destiny.

Hitler maintained that Germany could accomplish all of its goals because it was a nation populated by a superior, or "master," race. But before the nation could embark on this program, it had to purify itself. It had to rid itself of all members of "inferior" races, since these races might inter-marry with the master race and weaken its bloodlines. Among the peoples Hitler earmarked as inferior were Jews, Slavs, and Gypsies. Seeking a scapegoat to blame for Germany's problems, Hitler called the Jews respon-sible for the loss of World War I, high unemployment, and the spread of communism both within and outside Germany. Hitler named the Jews the great enemies of Germany and Germans, encouraged anti-Semitic activities, and advocated the destruction of the Jewish people.

QUESTIONS FOR REVIEW

1. Why did Germany face serious problems after the world war?
2. How did Hitler explain why Germany lost the war?
3. According to Hitler, what was Germany's destiny?
4. What were Hitler's plans for the German government of the future?
5. How did Hitler become known throughout Germany?

UNDERSTANDING THE STORY

A. Read the selection and answer the question that follows.

> The German does not speak much. The people of other races talk a lot. They do not have anything important to say. The German chews his food with his mouth closed. Other races chew with a smacking noise like animals. Only the German race walks and stands fully upright. The German has a great mind. He has great courage. Other races walk like cows and ducks. They talk with their hands. The German is very clean. Other races live in dirt. The Germans have nothing in common with other races. The German has created all things fine and good. Germans are clearly better than all other races.

Do you agree with the statements in this reading selection? Why do you think the selection was written? Who might have written it?

B. Imagine that you hear a person making a speech in a local park. He or she is saying terrible things. The speaker blames one particular group for all the troubles of our country. The speaker asks that the crowd join together and throw those people out of the country. Would you stop to listen to this speaker? Explain. Should the speaker be permitted to make remarks of this kind? Explain.

ACTIVITIES AND INQUIRIES

1. Use each of the following key terms in a sentence: solution   twisted inferior   master race   destiny.

2. Look at the illustration on page 444. Describe what is happening. Write your own title for this picture.
3. Imagine that Hitler is on trial. He is charged with treason. Prepare the case against him.
4. Assume that you have been assigned to defend Hitler at his trial. Prepare the case in his defense.
5. Hitler's trial is over. Assume that you are a reporter assigned to interview Hitler in prison. Write the questions you would like to ask him. Now answer the questions.

6. The Fires of Evil

By 1928 good times had returned to Germany, and the breadlines had all but disappeared. The German people seemed pleased with their democratic-republican government. Few stopped to listen when the Communists and the Nazis held street corner rallies. The future for Germany and for world peace seemed very bright.

A national election was held in Germany in May 1928. The Nazi party, led by Hitler, received less than 3 percent of the votes and just 12 of the 491 seats in the *Reichstag* (legislature).

Prosperous times in Germany came to an end in the early 1930s, however. Germany was just one of the many countries to stagger under the impact of the worldwide economic depression that began in October 1929. But in spite of bad economic times, neither the Nazis nor the Communists could convince the German people to give them control of the government. In fact, no one German political party had a majority of the votes in the Reichstag.

Field Marshal Paul von Hindenburg, the president of the German Republic, faced the problem of how to create a governing coalition (majority) in the Reichstag. Without such a majority, laws could not be passed. He had to choose whether to join his Nationalist party with the Nazis or the Communists to achieve his majority. Hindenburg decided that it would be easier to control the Nazis than the Communists. He appointed Adolf Hitler the Chancellor (prime minister) of Germany.

Hitler gained this position in 1933. But he was still far from his goal of controlling the government. The Nazi party was still a minority, and Hitler could be dismissed any time the majority voted against him.

Had Hitler come this far only to be turned back before he could take control? Since President Hindenburg, the army generals, and the majority of elected representatives were against him, how could Hitler hope to achieve his ambitions? This story will describe his next move.

Berlin   1933–1934

"Fire! Fire!"

A crowd of frightened people watched in horror as the fire in the Reichstag building burned out of control. It was February 1933.

Angry shouts were heard everywhere. "It's the Communists!" "It's a Nazi trick!" "God help us all!"

The next day, a Dutch Communist was arrested and charged with the crime. He confessed on the spot. He did not mention that he had been hired by the Nazis to set the fire.

On the same day Hitler met with Hindenburg and waved a piece of paper at him. "You must sign this, Herr President," pleaded Hitler. "The German people need to be protected from the Communist terror. Granting me police powers will help to do the trick."

Hindenburg, old, tired, and forgetful, pretended to read the document. He nodded his head once or twice and signed.

Later Hitler met with his aides. "The old fool went for it," he said. "Now that the German people have lost their rights of freedom of speech and press, the Nazi party will win the next election. I'll see to it that the Communists are not allowed to hold rallies. In the meantime, we Nazis will say whatever we please about our enemies. We will convince people that there is a plot to destroy the government. The German people will be so frightened that they will trust only the Nazi party. You'll see—this time the German people will give me the majority!"

In March 1933, a general election was held. Over 90 percent of the German voters cast ballots. The Nazis won more votes than ever before, but they still fell short of winning a majority. Although Hitler was still disappointed by the results, he continued to make himself more powerful. By threatening, bullying, flattering, and promising, Hitler convinced a majority of government representatives to vote to change the constitution. All lawmaking powers were turned over to the chancellor—Hitler. Next, Hitler moved to break up all political parties except the Nazi party. Any who dared to start a new political party would face a stiff jail sentence.

Only two things now stood in the way of Hitler's becoming the dictator of Germany: President Hindenburg and the generals of the German army.

In 1934 the army chiefs met with Hitler and warned him about his storm troopers, who were his own private army. "You must put an end to this business," they demanded. "Your bullies beat up people; they steal and they arrest innocent people. Germany must have law and order. If you can't control these hoods, we will—even if we have to take the government away from you to do it!"

Hitler thought, "I need these men. One day they will help me to conquer Europe!" He decided to go along with them. "Gentlemen," he said, "I promise that I will take care of the problem. There will be only one army in Germany, and that will be the regular German army!"

Hitler moved against the storm troopers. He ordered the leaders of the storm troopers arrested or shot. Hitler's old political enemies were also rounded up and killed. In one June weekend, on Hitler's orders, over a thousand people were killed.

For these acts, Hitler was congratulated by army leaders and members of the government. He was cheered in the government hall when he announced, "I have saved Germany from those who would destroy it by revolution!" No one asked him to prove this charge.

In August 1934, President Hindenburg died. Hitler forced his cabinet to declare that the offices of president and chancellor were now combined into one. He would be called the *führer* (leader). He became the sole ruler of the German people as well as commander in chief of the armed forces.

One of his aides said to him, "Führer, you must be very happy. You are now one of the greats of history!"

Hitler stiffened. "Not yet," he replied. "After all, I have only conquered Germany." He paused. "So far, that is."

Postscript

Now that Hitler had become dictator of Germany, he began to follow through on the promises he had made in his speeches and in *Mein Kampf.*

In 1935 the Nazi government passed the Nuremberg Laws. These laws stripped German Jews of their citizenship and denied them basic rights. In 1938 violence broke out against Jews all over Germany. Jews were beaten, some were killed, their shops and homes were broken into, and their synagogues (houses of worship) were looted and burned. By then, 300,000 of Germany's 500,000 Jews had left the country.

Hitler leaves a rally in the 1930s. Huge public gatherings were used to promote Nazi doctrine to the German people.

After World War II began, Germany's remaining Jews and Jews from all over Europe were rounded up and shipped to concentration camps. There, most were either killed outright or worked and starved to death. Some 6 million European Jews died at the hands of the Nazis. This attempt by Hitler's government to exterminate the European Jews is called the *Holocaust*.

On other fronts, by violating the Treaty of Versailles, Hitler challenged the nations that had defeated Germany. He rearmed Germany and in 1935 sent troops to occupy the Rhineland, a German area on the border with France. In 1936 he intervened in the Spanish civil war on the Fascist side. In 1938 German troops invaded and conquered Austria.

The world's reaction to the Nazi government's treatment of the Jews and the violations of the Treaty of Versailles was the same. Nations grumbled and were very unhappy, but none did anything to stop Hitler. Many people believed that it was only a matter of time before Adolph Hitler would bring the world even closer to catastrophe.

QUESTIONS FOR REVIEW

1. Was the German national election in 1928 a triumph for Hitler and the Nazi party? Explain.
2. How was Hitler appointed chancellor of Germany?
3. How did Hitler become Germany's dictator?
4. How did Hitler's government rule at home?
5. How did Hitler's government act toward other European countries?

UNDERSTANDING THE STORY

A. Write T for each statement that is true, F for each statement that is false, and N for each statement that is not mentioned in the story.

1. The Nazi party won a majority in a free election.
2. A Nazi set fire to the Reichstag.
3. President Hindenburg became very fond of Hitler.
4. The Communists were blamed for the Reichstag fire.
5. Under Hitler, all political parties except the Nazis were forced to break up.
6. Hitler wanted the German people to keep their freedom.
7. The army chiefs warned Hitler to do something about his storm troopers.

8. Hitler had many of his storm troopers killed because he was afraid they would plot against him.

B. Imagine that the president of the United States wishes to become a dictator. What steps would he or she have to take? Could these steps succeed? Explain.

ACTIVITIES AND INQUIRIES

1. Use each of the following key terms in a sentence: minority party constitution cabinet Reichstag storm trooper *führer.*
2. Go to the library. Prepare a report on what life was like for the German people after Hitler became dictator.
3. Imagine that you are now living in a dictatorship. Look through your newspaper. Underline everything that a dictatorship would not allow to be published.
4. Imagine that you are a reporter. You have just interviewed a leader of the storm troopers. He was a close friend of Hitler's. He has told you much about Hitler. Write what this man told you about Hitler.
5. The Nazis believed that a woman's place was in the home. Married women should not work. Women should keep themselves attractive for their husbands, stay home, and raise children. Women should stay out of politics. Women should not hold important jobs. Only men were fit to hold important jobs. Write a report on the role of women in Nazi Germany. Did women stay home and raise children while men did all the important work? Did German women agree with the Nazis?

7. Hussein ibn Ali

For hundreds of years, as we saw in Unit V, the Ottoman Empire controlled the lands of Arabia and all who lived there. But by the end of the nineteenth century, the forces of nationalism that were sweeping through Europe had also reached the Arab world. A small group of Arab nationalists was determined to teach the Arab majority that they shared a common religion, culture, and language. The nationalists hoped that once the Arabs understood they were one people, they would join together and move toward the next step, independence from Ottoman rule.

Hussein ibn Ali (1854–1931) was the person who would help lead the Arab people to this next step. Here, he tells his story.

Cyprus   1925

My name is Hussein ibn Ali. I trace my ancestry back to the Prophet Muhammad through Ali and Fatima's older son, Hassan. I had a dream: One day my Arab brothers and sisters would overthrow their Turkish masters and live in freedom under an Arab government.

Before the outbreak of World War I, in 1914, I was the amir of Mecca. But neither I nor the Arabic people were free. We were controlled by the despots who ruled Turkey. These

Hussein ibn Ali led the Arab revolt against the Turks during World War I. Here he is seen in 1924, in the city of Amman.

Turkish rulers distrusted me. They believed that at heart I was an Arab nationalist. They suspected I dreamed that one day all the Arab people would have a government of their own.

In 1914, as war clouds began to gather in Europe, I engaged in secret talks with the British. The British were concerned that, if war did break out, Turkey would join with Britain's enemy, Germany. The British asked me if I would rally the separate Arab tribes and make war on Turkey in the event that Turkey joined with Germany. The British assured me that they would support my troops with guns and money. I asked them for something more. I asked that, in exchange for my cooperation, the British would guarantee the independence of the Arab people from Turkey and any other country or countries. The British hinted that this could be arranged.

The war began, and Turkey did join with Germany against Britain and its allies. True to my word, I began to rally the Arab people, using the British promise that they would treat us fairly and support our independence if we helped them defeat the Turks. Many Arab tribes agreed to join the fight.

The Arab people began their war for independence by firing upon the Turkish troops who were garrisoned in the holy city of Mecca. The Turks surrendered the city three weeks later. Other victories followed in rapid order. We defeated the Turks at Qunfudah, Jiddah, Rabigh, Yenbo, and Aqaba. After our victory at Aqaba, the British recognized that we could be a fighting force of real value. They supplied us with all the guns and money we needed to defeat the Turks and drive them from our lands.

 Now we prepared for our greatest effort, to drive the Turks from Damascus, Syria. We would have to outrace the European armies that were headed in the same direction, and then we would have to defeat a large Turkish army.

But we were not to be outdone. We won the race, and we won the battle. We had the great pleasure of driving the Turks from Damascus in 1918. Our army, a mixture of Arab soldiers who had deserted from the Turkish army and tribal people who were totally untrained in the methods of modern warfare, fought a modern army and won a glorious victory. Four weeks after the Turks' surrender at Damascus, Turkish armies everywhere laid down their weapons and surrendered.

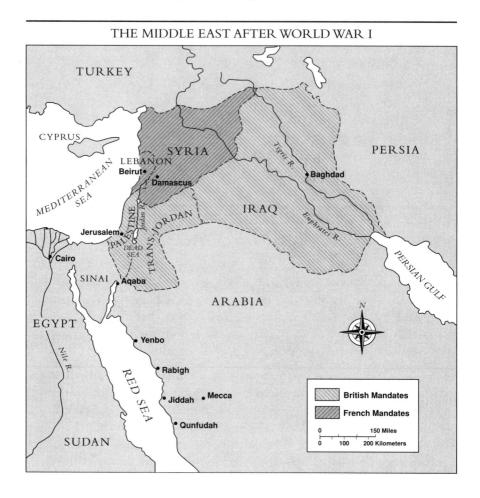

THE MIDDLE EAST AFTER WORLD WAR I

My Arab brothers and sisters and I were elated. Independence at last! Alas, our joy was short-lived. The British, who had promised to support our independence, instead bargained away our lands to other European powers in the postwar treaties. Instead of independence, we were about to exchange our Turkish rulers for new ones.

The British offered to keep me in power in my Mecca stronghold only if I would agree to recognize their right to control the lands that belonged to the Arab people (the Fertile Crescent—Iraq, Syria, and Palestine). I refused to settle for anything less than complete independence for the Arab people.

I had made many enemies among the Arab people for having negotiated with the British, and soon my enemies took the field of battle against me. I had to leave my beloved country and move here to Cyprus.

My name is Hussein ibn Ali. I fought for the freedom and independence of my people. For one glorious moment my people had tasted victory. We had driven out our enemy. Perhaps the Arab people will remember that moment and it will bring them together once again.

Postscript

Although Hussein was forced to leave Mecca, he had seen his son Abdullah become the amir of Trans-Jordan and his son Faisal become the king of Iraq. Hussein's dream that one day the Arab people would live in freedom under Arab governments came true in the following decades. Egypt became independent in 1922, Iraq in 1932, Lebanon in 1943, and Syria and Trans-Jordan in 1946.

QUESTIONS FOR REVIEW

1. What did Arab nationalists hope to accomplish during the world war?
2. Why did Hussein ibn Ali agree to help the British?
3. Why was Hussein ibn Ali so proud of the Arab victory at Damascus?
4. How did the British disappoint Hussein ibn Ali and his followers?
5. What happened to Hussein ibn Ali's dream that one day the Arab people would live in freedom under Arab governments?

UNDERSTANDING THE STORY

A. Write T for each statement that is true and O for each statement that is an opinion or a point of view.

1. The Arab nationalists were very effective in their efforts to teach the Arab majority that they shared a common heritage.
2. Hussein ibn Ali claimed that he could trace his ancestry back to the Prophet Muhammad.

3. The Turkish rulers distrusted Hussein ibn Ali.
4. The British sincerely wanted the Arab people to gain their independence from Turkey.
5. Turkey joined with Germany against Britain and its allies.
6. Turkey surrendered the city of Damascus after being attacked by Arab troops.
7. The Arabs fought against a modern Turkish army and won glorious victories.
8. Some Arabs hated Hussein ibn Ali because they were jealous of him.

B. Imagine that Hussein ibn Ali is visiting a present-day country where a civil war is raging. What advice might he have for preventing a future civil war in that country?

ACTIVITIES AND INQUIRIES

1. Look at the map of the Middle East after World War I on page 456. Locate each of the following on the map: Mecca, Jiddah, Rabigh, Qunfudah, Yenbo, Aqaba, and Damascus.
2. Imagine that you are interviewing Hussein ibn Ali. You ask him if he thinks that he has failed the Arab people. Write his answer and the reasons he gives.
3. Hussein ibn Ali sends a letter to the editor of a leading British newspaper. He writes about his feelings toward the British government. Write the letter you think he would have written.
4. Imagine that Hussein ibn Ali is placed on trial by the Arab people. List the crimes with which he is charged.
5. You are Hussein ibn Ali's attorney. Outline your defense for his case.
6. You are the judge at the trial. What is your verdict? Explain how you reached your decision.

8. "What Answer Am I to Take Back to My People?"

By the early 1930s, Ethiopia was only one of two African countries that had not come under European control. (Liberia had always been independent.) But this was about to change. Benito Mussolini, Italy's dictator, wanted to expand his country's territories in East Africa and win military glory. He used an argument over a border to force a quarrel with Ethiopia.

Mussolini believed that his army would win an easy victory mainly because the Ethiopian army lacked modern weapons and Western-style military training. Italy prepared for war by building up its forces in Italian Somaliland to 250,000 troops. In October 1935 armed with a modern air force and tanks, Italy invaded Ethiopia.

In desperation, Ethiopia turned to the League of Nations for help. Haile Selassie (1892–1975), the emperor of Ethiopia since 1930, called upon the League for protection from Italian aggression. Many League members sympathized with Ethiopia. Some agreed to suspend trade with Italy until it agreed to withdraw from Ethiopia. But most League members wanted to avoid an all-out war and were afraid to provoke a fight. They continued to trade with Italy.

Our story takes place in 1936. Haile Selassie has fled Ethiopia and is in Geneva, Switzerland, where he is addressing the General Assembly of the League of Nations. The emperor's address to the League is interspersed with flashbacks that describe what had been happening in Ethiopia during the seven months of the invasion. Here is the story.

Geneva   June 30, 1936

Haile Selassie addressed the League of Nations:

"On behalf of the Ethiopian people, . . . I renew my protest against the violations of treaties, of which the Ethiopian people have been the victims."

459

An Ethiopian chief described what happened during one of the attacks:

> We saw several Italian airplanes. The enemy
> dropped strange containers that burst open almost
> as soon as they hit the ground, releasing streams of
> colorless liquid. A hundred of my men were
> splashed by this fluid. Soon they began to scream at
> the top of their lungs. Blisters broke out on their
> feet, hands, and faces. Some rushed to the river and
> took great gulps of water to cool their fevered lips.
> But soon they fell and writhed in agonies that
> lasted for hours before they died. My chiefs sur-
> rounded me and asked what they should do. But I
> was completely stunned. I did not know what to
> tell them, or how to fight this terrible rain that
> burned and killed.

Haile Selassie continued to address the League of Nations: "I declare before the world that the emperor, the government, and the people of Ethiopia will not bow before force."

> The Ethiopians caught the Italian army in a moun-
> tain pass and managed to disable some of its tanks
> by tearing off the treads. The tanks might have
> been animals. Men in flimsy cotton *shammas*
> attacked the steel monsters with their bare hands.

This is a description of how the Ethiopian army behaved in battle:

> Wave upon wave of brilliantly clad tribesmen
> attacked the Fascist lines. They kept advancing even
> as the machine gun bullets cut through their ranks.
> Soon the dead were piled up so high in front of the
> Fascist lines that the machine gunners had to raise
> the muzzles of their weapons to fire over the dead
> and into the next wave of Ethiopians. A few
> Ethiopians broke through the first Fascist lines, but
> then bayonets and hand grenades did their deadly
> work.

Haile Selassie wanted to press on with the resistance to the attack, but his generals had had enough. The emperor was

At Geneva, in 1935, Haile Selassie asked the League of Nations to condemn and stop the Italian invasion of Ethiopia. Was he successful?

forced to order a retreat. He was prepared to continue to fight from the mountains, but his advisers begged him to leave Ethiopia, go directly to the League headquarters, and make one final appeal. Haile Selassie hated to leave his soldiers, but he could not deny this last attempt to save his people from the Fascist army.

Haile Selassie concluded his address to the League of Nations: "I ask the nations that have promised to help the Ethiopian people resist the aggressor: What are they willing to do for Ethiopia? What answer am I to take back to my people?"

Postscript

By their lack of response to his plea for help, the League members gave Haile Selassie his answer. They looked the other way as Italy proceeded to annex Ethiopia. Even as he was addressing the assembly, the Fascist army was entering the capital city of Addis Ababa. The Fascists had won the war and conquered the country.

Five years later, however, British and French armies joined with a force of Ethiopian patriots and troops from Nigeria, Ghana, Sierra Leone, the Congo, and Equatorial Africa. By May 1941, Addis Ababa had been retaken and the Fascists driven out. Haile Selassie sat on his throne once more. He reigned for 33 more years.

QUESTIONS FOR REVIEW

1. Why did Mussolini force a quarrel with Ethiopia?
2. How did Emperor Haile Selassie try to get help for Ethiopia?
3. How did the Ethiopian army try to fight the modern Italian army?
4. How did the League members respond to Haile Selassie's request for help? Why?
5. How did Haile Selassie regain his throne?

UNDERSTANDING THE STORY

A. Tell which statements are true according to the story.

1. Ethiopia accepted Italian annexation without a fight.
2. Mussolini wanted to expand Italian territories in East Africa.
3. Many League members made promises to help Ethiopia.
4. Mussolini was sorry he had invaded Ethiopia.
5. The Ethiopian troops fought bravely but lacked modern weapons.
6. Most League members were afraid to provoke Italy.
7. The League took no action as Italy proceeded to annex Ethiopia.
8. Forced to flee the country, Haile Selassie never again ruled Ethiopia.

B. Imagine that a weak country is suddenly attacked by a strong one, which wants to take it over. Is there someplace where that weak country can turn for help? Would that country get help? Explain your answer.

ACTIVITIES AND INQUIRIES

1. Imagine that you interview Mussolini. What reasons does he give for his country's invasion of Ethiopia?
2. Now you interview Haile Selassie. You read him what Mussolini said about Italy's invasion of Ethiopia. How does Haile Selassie respond?
3. You are a war correspondent for a major newspaper. You are assigned to cover a battle that is raging in Ethiopia. Describe what you see.

4. Haile Selassie asks you to help him write a speech that he will deliver before the delegates to the League of Nations. Write that speech.
5. You interview a delegate to the League who is sympathetic to Ethiopia but will not stand up to Mussolini. How does the delegate explain this position to you? What is your opinion of the delegate's position? Why?

9. Juan and Eva Perón

Like most other Latin American nations, Argentina was born in revolution and had been led by a succession of powerful leaders. These dictators were strong men, who usually gained the support of the military and then took power by force. Thus, no matter what his background, a bright and ambitious young man could join the army, rise through the ranks, and use his military career to bring him power and wealth.

If she hoped to better herself socially and economically, a young woman, especially one born in poverty, had a more difficult time. She could either marry a wealthy person or enter one of the few professions open to women.

Juan and Eva Perón were both ambitious and eager to make their mark on the country of their birth. Here is their story.

Buenos Aires   1952

You are Juan Perón, and you admire power. You dreamed that one day you would taste the power you admired in others who ruled their countries by force.

As a youth you were sent to military school and studied under German instructors. You learned your lessons well. You decided that a career in the army would give you that which you craved most: power. You entered the army and rose so rapidly that you were a captain by the time you were 29 years old.

In 1930 you joined with others in the military to overthrow the Argentine president and replace him with one the military could control. You were rewarded by being appointed military attaché to Italy. You saw how Italy's dictator, Benito Mussolini, ruled over his people, and you were greatly impressed. You wondered if, one day, you might rule the people of Argentina in the same way.

Returning to Argentina in 1943, you saw that many people were unhappy with the corrupt and inefficient rule of the government. Now a colonel, you decided that the time was ripe for you to make a bid for power. You gathered around you a group of dissatisfied young army officers, and together you overthrew the government and took control of the nation.

But you really wanted to rule Argentina all by yourself. You began to plot with influential, rich, and powerful Argentine Fascists to make yourself the Mussolini of Argentina. Appointed to the post of Secretary of Labor and Social Welfare, you made many promises to the working poor. You told them that their enemies were your enemies. The people cheered you, and you decided that it was time to make your move to seize power all by yourself. To prepare for this move, you appointed yourself vice president and war minister. But the other ruling military officers now knew what you wanted to do, and they had you arrested.

Imprisoned in 1945, you desperately needed someone to rally the poor to your side. That someone would be your future wife, Eva.

You are Maria Eva Duarte Perón, called Evita. A child of poverty, you dreamed that one day you would be rich and famous and that people everywhere would look up to you.

You found employment with a radio station and worked very hard to turn yourself into a popular radio actress. Along the way you met and fell in love with a military man who secretly hoped to become the dictator of Argentina, Juan Perón.

Juan Perón needed you. He needed you to help rally the poor to free him from prison. And you needed Juan Perón to help

Eva and Juan Perón during their years of popularity in Argentina. What happened to weaken and finally destroy Juan Perón's power?

make all your dreams come true. Your dream and his dream came together and gave you the spirit and energy that you needed for the job you had to do.

You went to work. You appealed to the poor, the "shirtless ones," and told them that their champion needed them. You called on them to gather and demonstrate in protest, and hundreds of thousands of people answered your call. The demonstration worked. Perón was released from jail. Soon after, he was elected to the presidency by a large majority. He had learned how valuable you could be to him, and he wanted you by his side, always. When he proposed marriage, you accepted.

Perón made promise after promise to the poor, the labor unions, and the industrialists. He became so powerful that he was able to appoint himself the dictator of all of Argentina. And now he had a job for you. He asked you to take control of his programs to benefit the poor.

You did your job well. You raised wages, shortened working hours, provided holidays with pay, established minimum wages and the unions' right to collective bargaining, and built housing projects for the workers. You also distributed gifts and favors to the poor and needy. Everything you did for the workers and the poor convinced them that you cared about them. In return, they worshiped you.

Perón was also busy. He helped to build factories, took over or bought out many industries that were controlled by foreigners, and spent a great deal of money on public works. His program to modernize the country was successful but extremely expensive. Argentina was on the verge of going bankrupt.

People began to tell stories about Perón. It was said that he took graft and had stolen a fortune. They claimed that he had spent Argentina into bankruptcy and had neglected agriculture, causing a 50 percent drop in wheat and beef exports. Those who spoke out against Perón were jailed. Newspapers that criticized him were shut down. And what did the "shirtless ones" say when they heard these accusations? They answered that it was the rich who said these things. Even if everything the critics said were true, only Juan and Evita truly cared about the poor and the starving.

But soon another enemy made its appearance, one that you could not defeat—cancer, the dreaded illness. An operation was performed, and 20,000 people waited silently on the streets outside the hospital for news of your condition. But you grew worse, and you knew that you had little time left.

Your last thoughts were of the people who loved and followed you. In your will, which would be read to the people after your death, you wrote:

"I was born of the people and suffered with them. I have the body and the soul and the blood of the people. I can do nothing other than surrender myself to my people."

Postscript

Deprived of Eva's support, Perón found himself in great trouble. In 1955 his enemies joined forces, and the military drove him from power. Perón fled to Spain.

But the poor did not forget Perón. In 1973, 18 years after he had fled the country, they brought him back to power. Perón died the next year, and he was succeeded by his third wife, Isabel. She was ousted by the military two years later.

In the 1990s, the government of Argentina has sworn to build a democracy in a country that has been ruled by dictatorships and military governments. The government promises to punish those in the military who have abused the rights of others, cut military spending, and rebuild Argentina's economy.

Juan Perón had insisted that the government should own, control, and regulate just about everything in the country. But under this policy, Argentina became a riches-to-rags story. While other nations advanced, Argentina stood still. It fell into a slump that lasted for decades.

Today, in the 1990s, the picture is much rosier. The government has placed most major state-owned businesses and utilities into private hands. The rules and regulations that controlled everything in the economy have been eliminated. Exports have increased and the budget is balanced. Argentina may once again turn out to be one of the most prosperous countries in South America.

QUESTIONS FOR REVIEW

1. Why were many bright and ambitious young Argentinians drawn to the military?
2. How did Juan Perón become Argentina's dictator?
3. How did Eva Perón play a key role in Juan Perón's rise to power?
4. Why did many people look up to Eva Perón?
5. Why was the Perón government criticized? Why did its policies help to bankrupt the country?

UNDERSTANDING THE STORY

A. Complete each of the following sentences.

1. Juan and Eva Perón were both _____ and eager to make their mark on the country of their birth.
2. Juan Perón joined the army in order to gain _____.
3. Juan Perón learned a great deal from a dictator named _____ _____.
4. Juan Perón gathered a group of officers together, and they _____ the government and _____ _____ of the nation.
5. Born in poverty, Eva Duarte dreamed that one day she would be _____ and_____.

6. Eva Duarte organized a huge —————————— in order to help her free Juan Perón from prison.

7. The workers and the poor —————————— Eva Perón because they believed that she —————————— about them.

8. When those who supported Perón heard accusations against their leader, they said that it was the —————————— who said these things. Only Juan and Eva Perón cared about the —————————— and ——————————.

B. Friends tell you that the only way to end poverty in this country is to give total power to one person who will be able to govern without interference. Do you agree? Explain your answer.

ACTIVITIES AND INQUIRIES

1. Look through your newspaper and decide which articles would not have been printed if our country were under the control of a dictator like Juan Perón.

2. You are doing research for an article about Juan and Eva Perón. You interview people who supported the Peróns. How do they explain why they supported the Peróns?

3. Now you interview people who opposed the Peróns. How do they explain why they opposed the Peróns?

4. You interview Juan Perón. You ask him how he gained power and how he used this power. Write his answers to your questions.

5. You interview Eva Perón. You ask her how she got the people of Argentina to worship her. Write what she tells you in this interview.

UNIT XI

World War II and Its Aftermath

Although many efforts were made to keep the peace after World War I ended in 1918, a second, even more terrible, war broke out in 1939. This war involved all parts of the world and brought great changes everywhere. After this world war ended in 1945, several areas endured long and harsh fighting.

Asia. We begin in China in 1931. A dictatorship was about to challenge the League of Nations by committing an act of aggression against another country. The stakes were much higher than anyone knew. If the League failed to act, it might help to make a larger war possible.

Europe. We move to Germany in 1938. A dictator wanted to seize

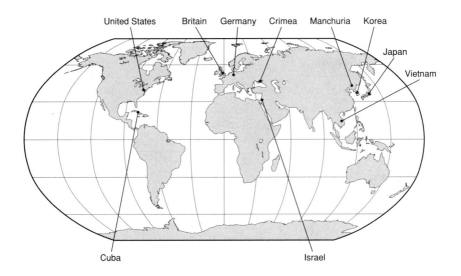

part of a free and independent country. The democracies had sworn to protect this country, and now they were going to be put to the test. What happened next was crucial to whether there would be peace or war.

Asia. Our next setting is Tokyo, Japan, in 1941. Much of the world already was at war. One powerful nation, the United States, had managed to stay out of the war and hoped to remain neutral. But the United States was in for a great shock, as our story tells.

Europe. In the early 1940's, Great Britain fought alone in its battle against Germany and held the attackers off. How did the British manage to do this? Our story helps to answer this question.

We travel to Munich, Germany, in 1944. The war was still raging, even as another war was being fought, a war against innocent civilians. The Nazi regime was doing its best to cover up the crimes it had committed against these people. Our story exposes these horrors for all to see.

Asia. Next, we return to Tokyo. The United States had developed the world's most devastating weapon of destruction, the atomic bomb, and used it twice in 1945 against Japanese civilians. Our story tells us the result.

Europe. We move to Yalta, in the Soviet Union, in 1945. A conference was taking place between the leaders of the United States, Britain, and the Soviet Union. The outcome of this meeting would help to determine what the world would be like after the war was over.

Our next story details the costs of two world wars. It also tells what the nations involved could have purchased with this money if they had chosen peace instead of war.

Middle East. We now travel to the Middle East in 1948. A new country was struggling to be born, but there were those who wished to destroy the infant nation. Our story tells us why.

Asia. We next find ourselves in Korea in 1950. Once again, a dictatorship had decided to commit an act of aggression with the expectation that the democracies would do nothing. Our story tells us how the United States responded.

We move to Vietnam, in Southeast Asia, in 1944. Our story helps to explain how the lessons learned in one war may be used successfully years later in another war.

The final story in this unit takes place in Moscow, Washington, and aboard a ship in the Caribbean Sea. The year is 1962. An international crisis might have led to war between the world's two superpowers.

1. The Test

World War I had been a nightmare. People all over the world prayed that war would never take place again. The leaders of the world tried hard to achieve this. Conferences were called and peace treaties were signed. By 1928 it looked as if the chances for a lasting world peace were very good indeed. Armed with the League of Nations, world trade agreements, and the Kellogg-Briand Pact—signed by League members—outlawing war, the peacemakers looked forward to a rosy future.

By 1930, however, the picture had changed completely. A worldwide economic depression made desperate people look for any solution to their problems. Many democratic governments fell, and dictatorships took their place. The dictators made promises to their frightened and hungry people. They promised jobs and prosperity. They promised to win back the lands lost in the "Great War" (World War I). These promises would be kept in blood. When the time came for the dictatorships to make their move, would the democracies stand up to them? What would happen if the democracies failed to stand up to them?

As the newspaper headlines below tell us, a military dictatorship was about to put the democratic nations to the test.

September 18, 1931: Bomb explodes in Mukden, China, damaging Japanese railway. Japanese blame Chinese. Japanese troops invade Manchuria.

September 19: Chinese say Japanese lie, accuse them of blowing up own railway. Claim Japanese are looking for an excuse to take over Manchuria.

September 21: Reporter says that Japanese refuse to talk about Mukden bombing. Damage so slight that trains continued to run on schedule after blast.

September 25: League of Nations upset by Japanese invasion. Action promised soon. League commission will make full investigation.

A 1930s cartoon dramatizes Japanese military violations of the postwar peace treaties.

October 5: United States says Japanese may have broken peace treaties. Statement of United States policy expected.

November 3: Chinese refuse to buy Japanese goods. Will not trade with Japanese as long as they occupy Manchuria.

January 7, 1932: United States sides with China. Says Japan should pull troops out of Manchuria. Secretary of State Stimson says that the United States will not recognize Japanese gains in Manchuria.

January 9: League members applaud United States policy statement. Many hope that League actions will force Japanese to leave Manchuria.

February 18: Japanese rename Manchuria "Manchukuo." Say that people in the area demand rule by Japanese. China complains to League.

May 12: Japanese Premier Inukai calls for peaceful settlement of China-Japan problems. Japanese military angry at speech.

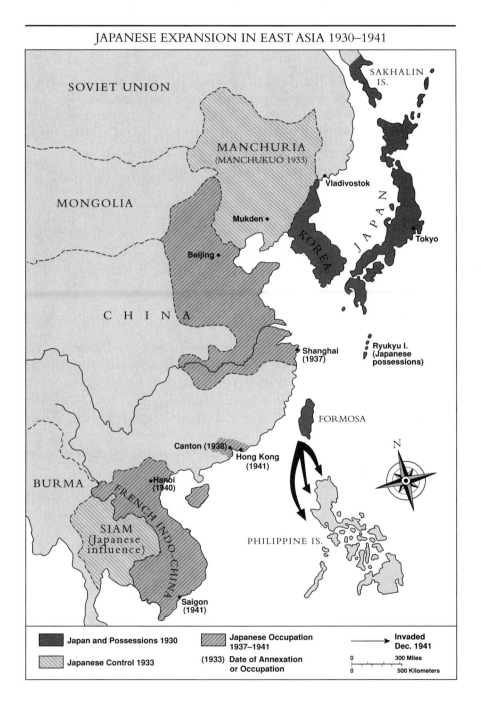

JAPANESE EXPANSION IN EAST ASIA 1930–1941

SOVIET UNION

SAKHALIN IS.

MANCHURIA
(MANCHUKUO 1933)

Vladivostok

MONGOLIA

J A P A N

Mukden •

K O R E A

Tokyo

Beijing •

C H I N A

Shanghai
(1937)

Ryukyu I.
(Japanese
possessions)

FORMOSA

Canton (1938) •

Hong Kong
(1941)

N

BURMA

• Hanoi
(1940)

FRENCH INDO-CHINA

SIAM
(Japanese
influence)

PHILIPPINE IS.

Saigon
(1941)

Japan and Possessions 1930

Japanese Control 1933

Japanese Occupation
1937–1941

(1933) Date of Annexation
or Occupation

Invaded
Dec. 1941

0   300 Miles

0   500 Kilometers

May 15: Inukai assassinated! Plot by Japanese military suspected.

October 2: Lytton Commission reports to League. Japan accused of aggression in Manchuria. League will seek Japanese agreement to peaceful solution.

February 24, 1933: League approves Lytton Report, refuses recognition of Japanese gains in Manchuria. Japan warned about military activity. Stronger actions may follow.

May 27: Japan resigns from League! Warns League not to interfere. League expected to vote trade blockade of Japan.

July 8: China charges League's failure to act on trade blockade has placed Manchuria in Japanese hands.

Postscript

Two delegates to the League of Nations, who had watched the Japanese-Chinese incident from the beginning, shared some thoughts over lunch.

"Well," said the first, "the League has really made a mess of things by its 'no-action' policy on the Japanese problem. Imagine the message we have given to those people in the world who love peace!"

"Worse yet," said the second. "Imagine the message we have given to those in this world who love war!"

QUESTIONS FOR REVIEW

1. How did the world's leaders try to prevent another world war?
2. Why did the prospects for world peace become much dimmer by the year 1930?
3. How did the Japanese government try to challenge the League of Nations?
4. How did the League of Nations respond to Japan's challenge?
5. Why did the League's response to the Japanese actions pose a threat to world peace?

UNDERSTANDING THE STORY

A. Write T for each statement that is true and F for each statement that is false.

   1. In 1928 chances for lasting peace were good.
   2. Dictatorships replaced a number of democratic governments in the 1930s.
   3. Manchurian troops invaded Japan in 1931.
   4. The Chinese said the Japanese were looking for an excuse to invade Manchuria.
   5. Dictators made promises to hungry people.
   6. United States Secretary of State Stimson approved of Japan's invasion of Manchuria.
   7. Japan changed the name of Manchuria to "Mongolia."
   8. The League of Nations refused to approve Japan's gains in Manchuria.

B. Imagine that you are a member of the Lytton Commission. You have been appointed by the League of Nations to look into Japan's invasion of Manchuria. What would you write in your report about Japan's actions? What actions do you think the League of Nations should take?

ACTIVITIES AND INQUIRIES

   1. Use each of the following key terms in a sentence: outlaw   invasion   crisis   dictatorship   Manchuria   Kellogg–Briand Pact.
   2. Study the map of Japanese expansion in Asia from 1930 to 1941 on page 473. Tell which item makes each statement correct.
       a. An area in Japan's possession in 1930 was (1) Korea (2) Manchuria (3) Mongolia.
       b. A country in Asia that does not touch Manchuria is (1) Japan (2) Korea (3) the Soviet Union.
       c. A Chinese coastal city is (1) Shanghai (2) Canton (3) Hong Kong.
       d. North of Manchuria is (1) Outer Mongolia (2) the Soviet Union (3) Korea.
       e. South of Beijing is (1) Manchuria (2) Outer Mongolia (3) Hong Kong.
       f. A city in Indo-China that was occupied by Japan was (1) Saigon (2) Hong Kong (3) Canton.

3. Imagine that you are a reporter at the League of Nations. You are assigned to interview the Japanese representatives. Write the questions you would like to ask them. Then write the answers you think they would give.

4. You are the same reporter. Now interview the Chinese representatives. Write the questions you would like to ask them. Answer the questions as you think they would.

5. The caption of a cartoon about Japan and the invasion of Manchuria is: "How dare you keep us out of your territory!" Who do you think said this? Explain. Were they right to say this? Explain. Draw the cartoon.

2. Meeting in Munich

The failure of the League of Nations to act against Japanese aggression in China gave other dictatorships the signal they were waiting for. In 1935 Italy attacked Ethiopia and took it over. (See Unit X, story 8.) Encouraged by the League's failure to act, Adolf Hitler in 1935 began openly to rearm Germany, even though rearmament was forbidden by the Treaty of Versailles.

When civil war broke out in Spain in 1936, Germany, Italy, and the Soviet Union interfered in spite of the League's warnings. Once again, countries were able to ignore the League and get away with it. The war in Spain also brought Germany and Italy closer. In 1936 they formed a military alliance and became known as the *Axis powers*. Japan later joined the Axis.

Hitler realized that he could win territories by bluffing the frightened League members. He was almost sure that war would not be declared against him until it was too late.

Hitler claimed that Austria and Germany should be united because many Germans lived in Austria. This too was forbidden by the Treaty of Versailles, but the bluff was successful. Austria and Germany were united, even though this was against the wishes of most Austrians.

Hitler next cast his eyes upon the country that was to be his key to the gates of Eastern Europe. This country, Czechoslovakia, was well armed, and it was protected by both France and Britain. Hitler insisted that the Sudetenland, the western part of Czechoslovakia, should be part of Germany. Many German people lived in this area. Britain, France, and Czechoslovakia prepared to go to war rather than let this happen.

As our story opens, a four-power conference—of Germany, Britain, France, and Italy—has been called in a final effort to prevent all-out war. Ask yourself what Hitler will demand at the conference. What will the others want in return? Who will get the better deal?

Munich   September 1938

"No! No!" cried Neville Chamberlain, the prime minister of England. "We have gone over this before, Herr Hitler, and you know our position. We will not let you occupy the Sudetenland starting on October 1."

Having said this, Chamberlain turned to Premier Edward Daladier of France and shook his head slowly. Daladier nodded in return. Daladier knew that Chamberlain was doing his best to prevent a war from breaking out but that Hitler's demands were impossible to meet.

Hitler now prepared to answer Chamberlain. He was furious that Chamberlain refused to give in to him, and once more tried to explain his position.

"Gentlemen," he said, speaking to both Chamberlain and Daladier, "you understand that most of the people who live in the Sudetenland are Germans. You also understand that these Germans have never cut their ties to the Fatherland. Finally you understand that my people, the Germans of the Sudetenland, are surrounded by unfriendly races. They are in great personal danger—"

"Hear! Hear!" interrupted Chamberlain.

"Let me finish!" Hitler thundered. "You must understand why it is so important for me to send troops to protect my people."

"Herr Hitler," said Chamberlain, in what he hoped was a steady voice, "Czechoslovakia is an independent country."

"Nonsense!" Hitler said. "It is a creation of that idiotic Treaty of Versailles!"

"As I was saying," continued Chamberlain, "an independent country does not welcome foreign troops on its soil. As for Britain and France," said Chamberlain, nodding to Daladier, "we are agreed that we will do what we must to stop the occupation of Czechoslovakia by Germany, or any other power for that matter."

Mussolini, who had been quiet, now chose this moment to speak. "Gentlemen," he said to the three men, "we are here to keep the peace, not to make a war. Let us be reasonable. Let each side give a little bit."

"What do you suggest?" asked Daladier.

"Suppose we do this," answered Mussolini. "Let Germany transfer to itself any Czech territory in which 50 percent or more of the people are German. And, to satisfy the Czechs, you, Chamberlain, and you, Daladier, will personally guarantee the safety of the remaining Czech territories."

At this, Daladier whispered to Chamberlain, "Czechoslovakia will never accept this."

Chamberlain whispered back, "The Czechs won't like this, but what choice do they have? Without our protection, Czechoslovakia cannot exist for a moment, and the Czechs know it! They will do anything we suggest."

"I tell you what," Hitler said. He had carefully watched the exchange between Chamberlain and Daladier, and cleverly guessed that they were close to giving in to him. "I won't move into the Sudetenland until October 1. I'll take over one district at a time over a ten-day period. And, if you like, you can have an international commission stand watch over Czechoslovakia's new borders. Is that reasonable enough?"

"That sounds reasonable," said Chamberlain. "But how do we know that you will not move against the rest of Czechoslovakia?"

"Mr. Chamberlain," answered Hitler, "it is no secret that I am a racist. We Germans want no Czechs. Besides, I am ready to give my word that Germany wants no more territory in Europe. My word must count for something!"

"To an English person," said Chamberlain, "one's word counts for everything!"

Postscript

When Neville Chamberlain returned home, he was greeted by cheering crowds at the London airport. He said that he had returned from Germany "bringing peace with honor." He finished: "I believe it is peace for our time."

AXIS EXPANSION IN EUROPE AND AFRICA 1935—1939

Prague, 1939: After earlier promises of peace, German troops invaded and occupied Czechoslovakia.

On October 1, 1938, however, the German army crossed the Czech frontier and occupied the Sudetenland. By March 1939, Hitler had decided to move on. No longer would he cry that for their protection Germans living in foreign countries had to be reunited with the "Fatherland." The new cry would be the need for "living space" for the German people.

On March 14, 1939, Hitler met with President Hacha of Czechoslovakia and gave him one hour to sign his country over to Germany. Threatened and bullied, Hacha gave in. The next morning, German troops seized what was left of Czechoslovakia.

QUESTIONS FOR REVIEW

1. How did Italy and Germany react after the League failed to take action against the Japanese?
2. What was Hitler's strategy for winning territories?
3. Was Hitler's strategy successful? Explain.
4. Why did Hitler want to move against Czechoslovakia?
5. How did Britain and France deal with Hitler concerning the question of Czechoslovakia? Did Hitler keep his word? Explain.

UNDERSTANDING THE STORY

A. Tell which statements Chamberlain would have agreed with.

1. Czechoslovakia must remain an independent country.
2. A free country does not want foreign soldiers on its soil.
3. Czechoslovakia is the creation of the Treaty of Versailles.
4. Do anything you want, but don't invade Britain.
5. Without our protection, Czechoslovakia cannot exist.
6. We will defend Czechoslovakia to the last soldier.
7. Hitler is a liar! This means war!
8. I believe it is peace for our time.

B. The word "appease" means to calm or soothe, to satisfy someone's wants or needs. Have you ever tried to appease someone? Describe the situation. What was the result? Was Chamberlain right when he tried to appease Hitler? Explain. What else might Chamberlain have tried to do?

ACTIVITIES AND INQUIRIES

1. Study the map of German and Italian expansion before World War II, on page 479. Then complete the sentences.
   a. A member of the Axis powers was (1) France (2) Italy (3) Belgium.
   b. A country controlled by the Axis was (1) Czechoslovakia (2) the Netherlands (3) Yugoslavia.
   c. A country north of Germany is (1) Denmark (2) Austria (3) Albania.
   d. The Sudetenland was part of (1) Yugoslavia (2) Albania (3) Czechoslovakia.
   e. Munich is a city in (1) France (2) Germany (3) Italy.
   f. The Rhineland is located between (1) Poland, Germany, and Czechoslovakia (2) Germany, Switzerland, and Austria (3) Germany, France, and Belgium.
   g. Poland is located between (1) Germany and the Soviet Union (2) France and Germany (3) Germany and Czechoslovakia.

2. Use each of the following key terms in a sentence: racist   aggression independent   honor   Axis   international.
3. Go to the library. Prepare a report on Hitler, Mussolini, Daladier, or Chamberlain.

4. Imagine that you are a reporter assigned to interview either Hitler or Mussolini. Write the questions that you would like to ask him. Now answer your questions as he would.

5. You are the same reporter. Your assignment is to interview Daladier or Chamberlain. Write the questions you would ask. Then answer the questions.

3. A Fateful Decision

Shocked by the German takeover of Czechoslovakia, Britain and France were jolted again when Italy moved into Albania in April 1939. Now they knew that they could not bargain with the dictators. Both countries began to arm themselves. Both agreed that the next move by the dictators against an independent country would have to be met with force.

On August 23, 1939, Germany and the Soviet Union signed a treaty that cleared the way for Germany's next move. It was not long in coming. On September 1, Germany invaded Poland. Fifty hours later, on September 3, Britain declared war on Germany. Europe was plunged into the second world war in less than 25 years.

To the horror of the free world, the dictatorships—Germany, Italy, and Japan—made fantastic gains. In Europe, Poland, Estonia, Latvia, Lithuania, Denmark, Norway, Holland, Belgium, Luxembourg, France, Bulgaria, and Yugoslavia fell. In Asia, Hong Kong, Thailand, Indonesia, and parts of China all fell to the dictatorships.

Europeans now took the Japanese seriously. They did their best to stop Japan from taking over other territories in Asia. With the outbreak of World War II, the Europeans prepared to fight with one another. They could no longer keep a watchful eye over their colonies in the Far East. This was the chance that the Japanese had been waiting for. They began to move their troops into East Asia.

One nation not yet involved in the world war seemed to stand in the way of Japanese ambitions. This nation was the United States. As our story unfolds, the Japanese Imperial High Command reaches a fateful decision.

Ask yourself why the Japanese were interested in the West's colonies in Asia. Why did the United States seem to stand in Japan's way?

Tokyo   November 1941

The setting is the headquarters of the Japanese Imperial High Command in Tokyo.

"Gentlemen, let us come to order," said Prime Minister Tojo. "The United States says it will not recognize our territorial gains in China. We must now decide how to deal with the United States."

There was a sharp outcry from the admirals and generals. All agreed that something had to be done.

The prime minister continued. "We all know that Japan is the most advanced nation in Asia. Therefore, the people of Asia look to us for leadership and protection. Now that the Western imperialists are fighting a war to the death among themselves, we have our chance to rid all Asia of those vultures! I say let us strike fear in the American heart and send it back to the other side of the sea where it belongs!"

At this, the military officers in the room leaped to their feet and shouted their approval. Only one man—Admiral Yamamoto—remained seated. It was obvious that he did not entirely share Tojo's opinions.

Admiral Yamamoto spoke. "Gentlemen, we enjoy a profitable friendship with the United States. It supplies us with oil, scrap iron, and many other valuable materials. We need these things, and the United States needs our business. We all know that the Americans still suffer from an economic depression. I do not think that they can afford to stop trading with us. Americans are reasonable people. I do not think that they are looking for trouble. Let our ambassadors, and not our guns, convince the Americans to mind their own business. Remember, gentlemen, war is costly. The United States may not be as weak and foolish as it appears."

The men spoke excitedly to one another. While they did not cheer the admiral, they were impressed by what he had said. Suddenly, an official rushed into the room and gave a message to the prime minister. The room was hushed as Tojo read the message.

Tojo looked up with flashing eyes. He said, "My brothers, the United States has just turned down every one of our demands.

The message says that, if we wish to continue to trade, we must give up the parts of Asia that we now protect. They order us about as if we were mindless children! We have taught the Chinese to respect us. Now I say that it is time to let the Americans feel our sting! Let us invade their bases in Hawaii!"

The officers stood once more and flooded the room with cries of agreement. This time, not a single officer remained seated.

Postscript

On December 7, 1941, Japanese warplanes attacked the U.S. naval base at Pearl Harbor in Hawaii. The attack sank or damaged 18 United States ships, destroyed 188 planes, and was responsible for the loss of over 2,500 lives. The Japanese air force also attacked other United States bases in the Pacific as well as British holdings in Malaysia and Hong Kong. On December 8, the United States and Britain responded by declaring war against Japan. A few days later, the other Axis powers, Germany and Italy, declared war on the United States.

Pearl Harbor, December 1941: Japan's surprise attack on the Navy base in Hawaii brought the United States into World War II.

QUESTIONS FOR REVIEW

1. What lesson did Britain and France learn as a result of German and Italian aggression?
2. How did World War II begin?
3. Which side seemed at first to be winning the war? Explain.
4. How did the United States become involved in World War II?
5. Why did the Japanese bomb Pearl Harbor?

UNDERSTANDING THE STORY

A. Write T for each statement that is true and O for each statement that is an opinion or that is not found in the story.

1. European nations were afraid to stop Japan from moving into East Asia.
2. The Japanese military believed that the United States stood in its way.
3. The people of Asia looked to Japan for leadership and protection.
4. Japan would easily frighten the United States.
5. Japan was the most advanced country in Asia.
6. The United States supplied Japan with valuable materials.
7. The United States needed to continue trading with Japan.
8. The United States could be convinced to mind its own business.
9. Japan and the United States disagreed about many things.

B. The year is 1941. Imagine that you are an adviser to the president of the United States. You are asked how to deal with the Japanese threat of war. What advice would you give the president?

ACTIVITIES AND INQUIRIES

1. Imagine that you are a reporter interviewing Prime Minister Tojo of Japan. Write the questions that you would ask him. Answer the questions as he might have done.
2. Now imagine that you are a reporter interviewing Admiral Yamamoto. Write the questions that you would ask him. Answer the questions as he might have done.
3. Go to the library. Prepare a report on the Japanese attack on Pearl Harbor. Was the United States government really surprised that the attack took place?

4. Imagine that you are a Japanese person living in the United States before World War II. Write a letter to relatives in Japan. Tell them what life is like for you in the United States.

5. Draw a cartoon that shows at least one reason why Japan decided to go to war with the United States. Do you think that the Japanese military had good reasons for attacking the United States? Explain.

4. The Finest Hour

The future looked very gloomy for the democracies. The dictatorships—Germany, Italy, and Japan—were on the move. They won battle after battle. It looked as if nothing could stop the dictatorships from gaining control over the entire world.

What, then, turned the tide in favor of the unconquered countries? Perhaps more than anything else, it was the human spirit, which refused to surrender in the face of almost impossible odds.

London 1950

You are Winston Churchill, and you have been loved and hated since you were a small boy.

You have been a soldier, journalist, historian, politician, public speaker, and head of state. Yours has been a most exciting life.

You were put in charge of the British navy at the beginning of World War I. You spoke bluntly, stepped on many toes, and made many enemies. You had many original ideas for fighting this war. But they were too far ahead of their time, and most were ignored. Stubborn as always, you fought for your ideas, and finally got to put a few into action. These failed miserably and, ten months after the outbreak of World War I, you were fired from your job as head of the navy.

You told your friends that you were finished. You were convinced that you would never again play an important role in the shaping of your country's history. You retired for a while to your country home, but it was not long before you returned to public life. You were elected to Parliament.

You watched carefully as Adolf Hitler built up Germany's armed forces. Yours was one of the few voices raised in protest against Hitler's actions. From the first, you called for Britain to stop Germany before it was too late. As usual, you were ignored.

You begged your fellow Britons to arm themselves after Germany moved into the Rhineland. For your troubles, you were labeled a warmonger.

In September 1939, a year after Chamberlain handed Czechoslovakia over to Hitler, Germany invaded Poland. World War II had begun! Now people had to admit that perhaps you had been right all along. You were asked to head the navy again, and you were happy for the chance. Unknown to you, you would soon be asked to fill a much more important job.

In 1940, after the fall of France, Belgium, and the Netherlands, Chamberlain stepped down, and you were asked to lead the government. You did so gladly. You told the British people that you had nothing to offer them but "blood, toil, tears, and sweat." They understood, and they loved you for telling them the truth.

After the fall of France, Britain was forced to fight alone. You faced your people and gave them the courage and determination that they needed. When it seemed that Germany was about to invade your country, you told the people: "We shall defend our island, whatever the cost may be, we shall fight on the beaches, we shall fight on the landing grounds, we shall fight in the fields and in the streets, we shall fight in the hills; we shall never surrender."

The British people believed you.

Britain was bombed and battered. After each attack, the people dug themselves out and were even more determined to fight back. You went into the streets, picked up a shovel, and dug out with the rest. The people knew that you were willing to put up with anything to bring the country through. They caught fire from your spirit!

Winston Churchill inspects the ruins of medieval Coventry cathedral, destroyed by German bombs.

Britain's magnificent stand held off the Germans. It gave Britain's Allies, the Soviet Union and the United States, time to prepare themselves to fight on your side. No one hated the Soviet dictatorship more than you, but you were willing to pay any price to defeat the Axis powers.

By 1943 the tide had turned in the Allies' favor. The Germans, Italians, and Japanese were being beaten back. It was now just a matter of time. The war lasted until September 2, 1945. You lived to see Germany, Italy, and Japan go down to total defeat. You took no small satisfaction at the deaths of your enemies Mussolini and Hitler. But you were saddened at the death of one of your closest wartime friends, United States President Franklin Delano Roosevelt.

Two months after this great victory, British voters turned your party out of office. You were shocked. Perhaps you never understood that the people wanted to forget the wartime nightmare, and you and your government were a constant reminder of it. Perhaps, too, this was the people's way of saying that a democracy does not reward a great hero with a lifetime key to the powers of government.

You soon got over your disappointment. It wasn't long before you were your old self, making speeches and writing books. You would be brought back to power one more time, but your greatest years were behind you.

You once told the British people that, if the British Empire lasted for a thousand years, people would look back at Britain's stand in 1940 and say, "This was their finest hour."

You are Winston Churchill, and you have been loved and hated since you've been a small boy. But when others stood ready to snuff out your island, you rose magnificently to defend it.

This was *your* finest hour.

Postscript

The British people defended their island at a very high cost. British military casualties included over 300,000 military casualties. In addition, nearly 100,000 British civilians were killed, and enemy bombs damaged or destroyed almost 4 million homes.

QUESTIONS FOR REVIEW

1. Why did Winston Churchill make many enemies?
2. How did Churchill feel about Hitler?
3. How did Churchill become the British prime minister? What promises did he make to the British people?
4. Describe the way the British fought off the Germans.
5. What price did the British people pay in defending their island?

UNDERSTANDING THE STORY

A. Write T for each statement that is true, F for each statement that is false, and O for each statement that is an opinion.

1. Britain refused to arm itself until the war began.
2. A democracy is always stronger than a dictatorship.
3. In the first years of World War II, the democracies were very successful.
4. Winston Churchill was the greatest politician the world has ever known.
5. Churchill had been a soldier and historian.
6. Churchill replaced Chamberlain as prime minister of Britain.
7. The Nazis' bombing of Britain stopped as soon as Churchill became prime minister.

B. Suppose that the British people had not chosen Winston Churchill to lead them during World War II. Instead, Neville Chamberlain remained the prime minister. Do you think that the outcome of the war might have been different? Explain.

ACTIVITIES AND INQUIRIES

1. Go to the library. Prepare a report on life in Britain during World War II.
2. Imagine that you are a reporter. Your assignment is to interview Hitler. You ask Hitler what he thinks of Winston Churchill. Write what you think Hitler would say about Churchill.
3. You are the same reporter. You have been interviewing Mussolini. You asked him what he thought about Churchill. Write down what Mussolini would say about Churchill.
4. Go to the library. Prepare a report on the activities of women during World War II.
5. Use each of the following key terms in a sentence: journalist politician   head of state.

5. Victims

While World War II was raging on the battlefields, in the air, and on the seas, another war was being fought behind the lines. The victims of this war were innocent men, women, and children. Ask yourself why Hitler made victims of innocent people.

Munich 1944

They say that my mind is gone. Yet I have never seen things so clearly. For the first time I am beginning to understand everything. That is what makes them afraid of me.

They don't know me anymore, those friends of mine in the SS. They want to remember only the man who, like them, cheered when Hitler spoke of the need to rid Germany of the Jews and other "undesirables."

At first we storm troopers believed that all Hitler wanted us to do was to break a few shop windows and beat up some people. It seemed like a good idea at the time. We didn't like these people. Hitler told us that they were the cause of all of Germany's problems. We believed everything Hitler said.

We frightened many into leaving Germany. Many Germans agreed with us. Most of those who did not agree were too afraid to speak out. We were teaching the German people how to obey their masters.

But our taste for violence grew. We were no longer satisfied with just clubbing people in the streets. We began to round them up. We made them dig their own graves. We forced them to undress and then we shot them down.

I was a storm trooper doing my job. Jews, Gypsies, Christians—they were all the same to me. They were the enemies and had to be dealt with harshly. In the concentration camps, gas chambers and giant furnaces were built so that thousands could be killed each day. Our doctors experimented with these people. Babies were drowned in vats of cold water. Young girls were used as prostitutes for German soldiers. Many others were worked, starved, and beaten to death. Hitler was not a cruel man. These people deserved what they were getting.

But then Sister Catherine changed everything for me.

I first saw her on the campgrounds two months ago. "What are you, a nun, doing in this camp?" I asked. She stared at me and said nothing.

"Don't you remember me? I'm Albert Bauer. I was a student of yours many years ago." Again she stared and seemed to recognize me. But she quickly turned her face away.

I tried to find out from the others why she had been sent here. No one could tell me anything. I had to know. Perhaps it was all a mistake. I looked up her records. It was no mistake. Sister Catherine had been caught hiding Jewish families. For this she would have to die.

I sent for her. I asked, "Why, Sister Catherine? Why did you hide these people? You are not Jewish."

She said nothing.

Again I asked, "Why did you do it?"

She looked at me and asked quietly, "Why do you murder people, Albert?"

I answered, "I do Hitler's work. I follow orders. These people must be destroyed."

"I do the Lord's work," answered Sister Catherine. " All human life is sacred."

I ordered that she be taken back to her quarters.

Weeks passed. I did not see Sister Catherine. But I thought about her all the time. I had to admire her. She was a brave woman. She had risked her life to protect the lives of others. But why did she try to help Jews? And where did she get her strength?

Yesterday I saw her again. She was being marched along with the others to the gas chamber. I walked alongside of her. "Please," I asked, "why did you let this happen to you?"

Silence.

The march ended and people were lined up for entry into the

The Holocaust: Survivors of the German death camp Nordhausen, in 1945. The Nazis murdered over six million Jewish people in such camps.

chamber. I began to feel uneasy. My stomach was churning. A lump came to my throat. Now her turn came. She crossed herself and said a silent prayer. Then she took the hand of a child and walked toward the chamber. Just before she entered, she turned and looked at me.

"You see, Albert, Hitler makes victims of us all."

I stood there with my mouth open and watched her disappear into the chamber. I knew what would happen next. The doors would be locked and the gas would be turned on. All inside would die. I had watched this scene many times. It had meant nothing to me. I had always believed that dangerous animals were being put to sleep. But there was at least one human being in that chamber now. And perhaps—perhaps—there were more.

Suddenly my head cleared. I now saw things as they really were. I fell to my knees and begged forgiveness for my sins. My companions looked at me with horror. They grabbed me and took me to my room.

Today I am being taken to a hospital for the mentally ill. The doctors say that I have suffered a nervous breakdown. What they don't understand is that the German people have all suffered a nervous breakdown. All Germany is an asylum.

Sister Catherine was right. We are all Hitler's victims.

Postscript

Hitler's dream of making Germany the greatest nation in the history of the world would soon come to an end. His armies had been driven out of Africa, Western Europe, and the Soviet Union, and the Allies were now closing in on him.

By early 1945, Italy had been taken by the Allies, and Japan was close to losing the war in Asia. Hitler told the people around him that he hoped for a turnaround in Germany's efforts. Secretly, he believed that all was lost. He gave orders that in the event of his death, his body was to be soaked in gasoline and burned to ashes. He did not want his body hung and placed on exhibit, as was the body of his former ally Mussolini.

The Soviet army moved closer to Hitler's headquarters in the German capital city of Berlin. On April 30, 1945, he was told that the Soviet army would enter the city in a matter of hours. Adolf Hitler pointed a pistol at himself and pulled the trigger.

QUESTIONS FOR REVIEW

1. How did Hitler's followers try to force certain groups of people to leave Germany? Why did they want these people to leave?
2. How were people dealt with in the concentration camps?
3. What had Sister Catherine done to be condemned to die?
4. Why did Albert Bauer suffer a nervous breakdown?
5. How did Hitler die? Explain.

UNDERSTANDING THE STORY

A. Write T for each statement that is true and F for each statement that is false.

1. Albert Bauer was a soldier on the Eastern European front.
2. Adolf Hitler plunged Germany into World War II.

3. Sister Catherine at first refused to talk to Albert Bauer.
4. The victims of Hitler's war behind the lines were often innocent people.
5. Albert Bauer could not understand why Sister Catherine was in a concentration camp.
6. The last time Albert Bauer saw Sister Catherine she was being released from the concentration camp.
7. Adolf Hitler said that the Austrians and the French were the cause of Germany's troubles.
8. Sister Catherine helped Albert Bauer understand what had happened to the German people.

B. When World War II ended, the Allies brought Nazi leaders to trial in Nuremburg, Germany. They were accused and found guilty of wartime atrocities and crimes against humanity. Imagine that you are one of the judges at these trials. What sentence would you pass on the war criminals?

ACTIVITIES AND INQUIRIES

1. Go to the library. Prepare a report on life in the German concentration camps.
2. Imagine that you were the last person to speak to Sister Catherine. She told you how she felt and why she was going to the death chamber. Write the things she told you.
3. The commandant of a concentration camp is on trial. Prepare the case against him.
4. Assume that the camp commandant is defending himself. Write the things he will say in his own defense.
5. Imagine that you are interviewing a person who was imprisoned in a concentration camp. Write the questions you would like to ask this person. Answer the questions as you think this person would.

6. A Survivor's Story

After the Japanese shocked the United States with their surprise attack on Pearl Harbor, a long, ugly series of battles between the two followed. The Japanese suffered terrible defeats. By 1945 they were preparing to defend their homeland against a United States invasion.

Ask yourself why the Japanese found it impossible to conquer the United States. Why did the United States use the atomic bomb?

Tokyo 1950

I am a Japanese woman. I have been in a hospital for five years, since I was 16. I am here because something terrible happened to me and my people.

Five years ago I was a schoolgirl. I lived with my parents in the city of Hiroshima. Japan was at war with the United States. We were told we were fighting for our national honor. My teacher would point to a map of the world and show us how small our country was compared to the United States. This made me feel proud. We Japanese would not let anyone back us down.

All the boys in my class were afraid that the war would end before they had a chance to fight. They were such fools! I hated the war! It had taken the lives of my two brothers. My father told me to be proud of my brothers. He said that both had died fighting bravely for our divine emperor. They had been rewarded with eternal life in heaven. My father told me not to cry for them. But I heard him cry late at night when he thought I was asleep.

We knew that the Americans were near Hiroshima because their planes flew over and dropped leaflets. These leaflets warned us to leave the city. They said that a terrible weapon would soon be used against us. This frightened many people. But our leaders said it was just another American trick. We were reminded to have faith in the emperor. We had to work hard so that we could win the war. I wanted to believe this with all my heart and soul. But I could not help feeling afraid.

496

Hiroshima, 1945: Japanese soldiers took refuge in the ruins of the railway station after the atomic bomb destroyed most of the city.

Then it happened. I was miles away from Hiroshima visiting with relatives. I heard a terrible noise. Then I saw fire and smoke. My heart sank. I could see that Hiroshima was in flames. My family was trapped. I tried to run back to my city, but my aunt held me. She begged me to wait. We both held on to each other and cried.

Later, when the fires had died down, I rushed back to Hiroshima to find my family. As I got closer to the city, I began to smell burning flesh. People with parts of their faces ripped away rushed past me. Others had burns all over their faces and bodies. My city had become a furnace.

I ran to where we had lived. But there was nothing where my home had been. I sank to my knees and cried. I would never see my family again.

I wandered around for days. Finally, I was picked up by a medical team and brought to this hospital. The doctors told me that I had suffered from exposure to radiation. I was given many treatments. I lost a great deal of weight and was in intense pain. And I was not alone. Hundreds were in this hospital suffering from the same sickness. Many have already passed into the next world.

The doctors still try to cheer me up. They tell me that one day I will be well again. I know better. I am growing weaker. I am being fed through my veins. But my nightmare is almost over. Soon I will be with my family.

Independence, Mo. 1965

United States President Harry Truman was interviewed many times about his decision to drop the atomic bomb. Here are the highlights from one of these interviews.

"Mr. President," said the writer, "didn't you give it a lot of thought?"

"We were about to invade Japan. Perhaps a million American soldiers would be killed or wounded. The Japanese would suffer as much or more. The nightmare had to be ended. The bomb took care of all that."

"Mr. President, you say you wanted to save lives by using the atom bomb. Yet a lot of people lost their lives because of the bomb. If you could make that decision again, would you make it the same way?"

President Truman thought for a moment. "Yes. Perhaps because of what has happened in Japan, no one will ever again use this bomb against human beings."

Postscript

An atomic bomb was dropped on Hiroshima on August 6, 1945. Three days later, a second atomic bomb was dropped on Nagasaki. The Japanese surrendered. Together, the two bombs killed over 120,000 people. About the same number of people were seriously injured.

Japan today is at peace with the world and has a democratic government. It is also one of the wealthiest nations in the world.

The Japanese have kept part of the city of Hiroshima as it was after the atomic attack. To this day, Japan will not stockpile nuclear weapons of any kind.

QUESTIONS FOR REVIEW

1. How did the Japanese know that the Americans were near Hiroshima?
2. Describe the damage done as a result of dropping the atomic bomb on Hiroshima.
3. Why were the Japanese people affected for many years after two atomic bombs were dropped on their country in 1945?
4. Why did President Harry Truman decide to use the atomic bomb against Japan?
5. How did Truman later defend his decision to drop the bomb? Do you agree with him? Explain.

UNDERSTANDING THE STORY

A. Tell which statements show how the atomic bomb affected Japan.

1. The atomic bomb caused the war between Japan and the United States.
2. The bomb caused the deaths of the two brothers of the woman in the story.
3. The bomb helped bring the war to an end.
4. The bomb caused great suffering for the Japanese people.
5. Two cities, Hiroshima and Nagasaki, were practically destroyed by atomic bombs.
6. The bombings made the Japanese even more determined to win the war.
7. As a result of the dropping of the atomic bomb, the war continued for two more years.
8. The Japanese people have never forgotten the bombing of the two cities.

B. Imagine that President Truman has not yet decided whether to use the atom bomb against the Japanese. He asks your advice. Give your reply and explain your reasons.

ACTIVITIES AND INQUIRIES

1. Study the table below and answer the questions that follow.

Destruction Caused by United States Bombing of Tokyo, March 9, 1945

Homes destroyed	250,000
Persons made homeless	1 million
Persons killed	85,000

This bombing raid on Tokyo did more damage than the atomic bomb that was dropped on Hiroshima five months later. Why then did the Japanese surrender after the United States had dropped just two atomic bombs? How would President Truman use this table to back up his decision to use the atomic bomb?

2. Imagine that President Truman is on trial for using the atomic bomb against the Japanese people. Prepare the case against President Truman. Go to the library. Prepare a report on the bombing of Hiroshima or Nagasaki. Use this report as part of your evidence against President Truman.

3. Prepare the case in favor of President Truman. Go to the library. Prepare a report on the American invasions of Japan's islands in the Pacific Ocean. Use the casualty figures (numbers of dead and wounded) as evidence to support President Truman's decision to use the bomb.

4. You are a member of the jury hearing the case against Truman. Vote "guilty" or "not guilty." Explain the reasons for your vote.

5. Pretend that you are a Japanese reporter covering the trial for your country. What questions would you like to ask President Truman? How would he answer these questions? Are you satisfied with his answers? Explain.

7. Meeting at Yalta

When World War I ended, the winners met and signed the Treaty of Versailles. This treaty shaped world history for the next 20 years. Now, as World War II drew to a close, the probable winners decided to meet to discuss treatment of the losers. They also wanted to prevent future wars. Once again, an agreement was reached that would shape world history for years to come.

The three most important world leaders—Franklin Roosevelt of the United States, Winston Churchill of Great Britain, and Joseph Stalin of the Soviet Union—met to talk over some very important problems. All three had at least one thing in common: They wished to see the downfall of Hitler. Beyond that, however, there were problems that seriously divided the three leaders.

Could Britain and the United States trust the Soviet Union? Could the Soviet Union trust Britain and the United States? Would the Soviet Union agree to join the fight against Japan once Germany was defeated? And, perhaps most important of all, would the Soviet Union permit free elections in the East European countries it had recaptured from the Germans and now occupied (for example, Poland)?

Ask yourself why Roosevelt, Churchill, and Stalin had trouble coming to an agreement. How did they try to prevent future wars? Did the Yalta conference bring lasting peace?

Yalta (the Crimea) February 1945

As the conference opened, Churchill said to Roosevelt, "We could not have found a worse place than Yalta for a meeting if we had spent ten years looking!"

"You know that Stalin refused to meet anywhere but in Soviet territory," Roosevelt replied. "Besides, now that we have given in to him on this point, perhaps he will give in to us on others."

Churchill shook his head.

Stalin now cleared his throat and nodded to President Roosevelt. The conference began. "Mr. President," Stalin said through his interpreter, "would you like to make some remarks to open the conference?"

At Yalta, in 1945, Churchill, Roosevelt, and Stalin met to discuss the fate of postwar Europe.

Roosevelt, a charming man and a great speaker, thanked Stalin. "My friends," said Roosevelt, "let us work together in a spirit of friendship and cooperation so that all people will know that the powerful nations are of one mind."

At this, Churchill, Stalin, and the staff members of the three men burst into applause.

Now Stalin spoke. "Gentlemen, as long as we three live, none of us will allow our countries to make war on other nations. But, after all, none of us may be alive in a few years. A new generation may come that will not know the lessons that we have learned. We must try to build a lasting peace. We must remember that the greatest danger for the future is the chance that our countries will one day turn on one another."

"I agree completely!" said Churchill, speaking directly to Stalin. "It is good that you speak this way. Now perhaps we can settle this Polish business."

Stalin frowned. Churchill had touched upon the most difficult question of the conference: how to deal with Poland.

The three men knew Poland's history only too well. Granted independence after World War I, Poland was attacked first by Germany and then by the Soviet Union at the start of World War II. The Poles fought hard, but when it became clear that they were doomed to defeat, Polish officials escaped to London. There they formed a government in exile. This government was immediately recognized by Britain and the United States.

In the meantime, in 1941, Germany attacked the Soviet Union, and Soviet troops were driven out of Poland. A group of Polish Communist leaders formed an underground movement. They continued to fight the Germans.

Now that the war was coming to an end, an important question was to be answered: Which group should govern Poland? Should it be the one in London, recognized by the British and the Americans? Or should it be the one in Poland, recognized by the Soviet Union?

Churchill now continued, determined to make his point. "Gentlemen, Britain can be happy only with a plan that will leave Poland a free and independent state. Poland must be the ruler of its own house. I say that we should agree on a temporary government now and call for free elections in the near future. Let the Polish people decide which government will represent them. Let us all agree to recognize that government. If we can agree on this, we will leave this table knowing that we have brought the world one step closer to lasting peace!"

"Not so fast!" said Stalin. "I hope you gentlemen haven't forgotten that twice in the past 30 years the Soviet Union has been invaded through Poland. We must look very carefully before we decide to recognize any Polish government! Besides, there already is a government of Poland. The Polish people support the Lublin government. They need no other government."

Roosevelt looked tired and upset. He had come to the conference to make sure that the Soviet Union would continue to cooperate to bring the war to an end. The Polish question could wreck everything.

"Aren't you forgetting the Polish government in London?" asked Roosevelt. "Britain and the United States believe that the London government represents the Polish people."

Stalin replied quickly. "Nonsense! The Lublin government remained in Poland. It did not abandon the Polish people in their hour of need. *Your* Polish government is in London, over a thousand kilometers away from the Polish people. What do the Poles in London know of the needs and dreams of the people in Poland? Why aren't they in Poland now?"

Roosevelt seemed worn out by the argument. He said, "We will accept the Lublin government. But it should be reorganized to include Polish leaders from Poland and London."

"I agree," said Churchill. "However, I must insist that elections be held in Poland as quickly as possible. And these elections must be absolutely free. There must be no interference with the voting of the Polish people."

"I accept," said Stalin. "The Lublin government will be enlarged. I have nothing to fear from free elections. I agree to hold them within a month or two. The Polish people will choose the government that has fought not from London, but from within Poland itself."

Both Roosevelt and Churchill brightened at these words. Perhaps the conference was going to be successful after all.

"One more thing, Premier Stalin," said Roosevelt. "You have read my Declaration on Liberated Europe. You know that it calls for the right of all peoples to choose through free elections the form of government under which they will live. Will you put your signature to my declaration?"

Stalin hesitated for a moment. "Mr. President, I approve of your declaration, and I will sign it!"

This, for Roosevelt, may have been his greatest personal triumph.

Later, Roosevelt met privately with Churchill. "Didn't I tell you that we could get Stalin to give in to us?" asked Roosevelt.

"Mr. President," said Churchill, "it seems to me that you have worked a miracle! Stalin has signed your declaration. He has promised free elections in Poland and other countries in

Eastern Europe. He has also agreed to enter the war against Japan, as well as to support Chiang Kai-shek. He has even agreed to take part in our plan for an international peacekeeping organization called the United Nations. One thing bothers me, though."

"What is that?" asked Roosevelt, a bit annoyed that Churchill was not as elated as he.

"I keep remembering an old saying: 'You have to buy a horse twice when dealing with a Russian!'"

Postscript

President Roosevelt was convinced that he could talk Stalin into continued cooperation with the West. But Roosevelt died later in 1945.

In April 1945, delegates from 50 nations, including the Soviet Union,

EUROPE AFTER WORLD WAR II: THE COLD WAR

met in San Francisco and adopted the charter of the United Nations. The charter calls upon all members to bring their disputes with others to the United Nations for peaceful settlement. The members of the UN also agreed to work together to eliminate world poverty, hunger, disease, and illiteracy.

In spite of the agreement at Yalta, free elections to reorganize the government of Poland were not held. An election in 1947 was strictly controlled by Soviet authorities. Only candidates of Soviet choosing were permitted to seek office. Poland became a Communist state.

Winston Churchill, in a speech in the United States, declared that an "iron curtain" was falling across Europe. Ignoring Roosevelt's declaration, the Soviet Union was turning the nations of Eastern Europe into Communist satellites (dictatorships).

QUESTIONS FOR REVIEW

1. What were the problems that divided Roosevelt, Churchill, and Stalin when they met at Yalta?
2. Why was the question of how to deal with Poland one of the most difficult ones of the conference?
3. What was Churchill's plan for Poland?
4. What was Stalin's plan for Poland?
5. What was agreed upon at the Yalta conference? Did Stalin keep to the agreement? Explain.

UNDERSTANDING THE STORY

A. Tell who made or might have made the statements that follow. Write C for each statement that Churchill made or might have made, R for each statement that Roosevelt made or might have made, and S for each statement that Stalin made or might have made.

1. Britain wants a free, independent Poland.
2. Twice in the last 30 years we have been invaded through Poland.
3. Let the Polish people decide who will represent them.
4. I have nothing to fear from free elections in Poland.
5. Will you sign my Declaration on Liberated Europe?
6. The Soviet Union will enter the war against Japan.
7. We could not have found a worse place to meet than Yalta.
8. You have to buy a horse twice when dealing with a Russian.
9. Let us work together in a spirit of friendship and cooperation.

B. The leaders of major nations meet with other heads of state from time to time. These meetings are often called "summit conferences." Assume that you are an adviser to the president of the United States today. Which heads of state would you recommend that the president meet in a summit conference? Why? What topics should the president and the other leaders discuss?

ACTIVITIES AND INQUIRIES

1. Use each of the following key terms in a sentence: declaration downfall free election liberated generation iron curtain interpreter.
2. Imagine that you are a reporter at the Yalta conference. You ask Churchill how the conference is going. Write down what you think he would say to you.
3. You then ask Roosevelt how things are going at the conference. Write down his answer.
4. Finally you speak to Stalin and ask him about the conference. What would he tell you?
5. The caption of a cartoon is: "You have to buy a horse twice when dealing with a Russian!" Why did Churchill say this? How would Stalin complete this sentence: "When you deal with the British, you have to ————"? How would Roosevelt answer Churchill? How would Roosevelt answer Stalin?

8. The Costs of War

World War I took, all told, 10 million lives. The war's dollar cost was put at $400 billion (in 1920 dollars).

In 1920 a well-off American family had a home worth $2,500 and furniture worth about $1,000. The home was on five acres of land worth $100 an acre. In 1920 the money that had been spent on World War I could have bought land and built and furnished a home for every family in the United States and ten other countries that fought in the war.

Allied bombing raids during the war left many German cities in ruins. Can we truly estimate what wars cost in human terms?

In addition, a $5 million library and a $10 million university could have been built in every large city in these 11 countries. And, from what was left, enough money could have been set aside to pay yearly salaries of $1,000 to 125,000 teachers and 125,000 nurses.

But, you ask, how does this apply today? How do you build and furnish a house so cheaply? How can you build so many libraries and schools and pay such low salaries?

You are right, of course. But if you multiply all of the 1920 dollar figures by ten, the costs of salaries, homes, libraries, and schools are a little more realistic for the year 1945.

Now multiply the dollar costs of World War I—$400 billion—by ten. Change the number killed to 53 million persons. Now you have the human and dollar costs of World War II.

Can we afford a third world war?

QUESTIONS FOR REVIEW

1. How much did World War I cost in lives and dollars?
2. How much did World War II cost in lives and dollars?
3. What could have been done with the money that was spent on both world wars?
4. What lessons should we learn from this selection?

UNDERSTANDING THE STORY

A. Study the table of lives lost in World War II. Tell which item makes each statement correct.

Lives Lost in World War II — Military and Civilian Casualties

Country	Military Casualties	Civilian Casualties
China	2.2 million	22 million
Germany	3.5 million	780,000
Japan	1.2 million	672,000
Poland	5.8 million[*]	
Soviet Union	7.5 million	7 million
Great Britain and Northern Ireland	329,000	92,000
United States	405,000	6,000
Yugoslavia	305,000	1.2 million

[*] Separate figures for civilians and military are not available.

1. The country that suffered the largest number of civilians killed was (a) China (b) Yugoslavia (c) the Soviet Union.
2. The country that suffered the largest number of combatants killed was (a) the United States (b) the Soviet Union (c) Germany.
3. The total number of Soviet civilians killed was (a) more than three times that of China (b) greater than that of all nations combined, with the exception of China (c) greater than the number of Soviet combatants killed.

4. The country that suffered the smallest number of civilians killed was (a) Britain (b) Japan (c) the United States.
5. The country that suffered the smallest number of combatants killed was (a) Britain (b) the United States (c) Yugoslavia.
6. A country that lost more civilians than combatants was (a) the Soviet Union (b) Germany (c) China.
7. Two countries whose combat losses were about the same were (a) Britain and Yugoslavia (b) China and Japan (c) Germany and China.
8. Another country that lost more civilians than combatants was (a) Yugoslavia (b) the United States (c) Britain.
9. The three countries that lost the largest total number of civilians plus combatants were (a) the Soviet Union, China, Poland (b) Germany, China, Britain (c) the Soviet Union, China, Germany.
10. The three countries that lost the smallest total number of civilians plus combatants were (a) the United States, Britain, the Soviet Union (b) Yugoslavia, the United States, Britain (c) Germany, Japan, Britain.

B. Assume that you are one of a group of experts. You are discussing the question "Can the world afford another world war?" What position would you take? Explain. What one fact would you use from the reading to prove that the world cannot afford a third world war?

ACTIVITIES AND INQUIRIES

1. Imagine that you are an infantry soldier in battle during World War II. In a diary describe your experiences in one day of the war.
2. Pretend that you are a reporter during World War II. Your assignment is to interview Allied soldiers returning from battle. Write the questions you would like to ask the soldiers. Then answer the questions as you think they would.
3. As a reporter during World War II you also have the chance to speak to Axis soldiers returning from battle. Write the questions you would like to ask these soldiers. What answers would they give to your questions. How different would the answers of the Allied soldiers and the Axis soldiers be? Explain.

9. The Middle East: The Birth of Israel

For centuries, the Jewish people had longed to return to the land that had belonged to them in the time of David and Solomon. (See Unit II, story 7.) In the twentieth century, Jewish settlements had been established in this land, now called Palestine, and the settlers had worked hard to turn a barren desert into a land of milk and honey. During World War I, the British, who controlled the country, had received help from the Jewish settlers. The British issued a promise that they would favor the establishment of a Jewish homeland in Palestine at the war's end. This promise was called the Balfour Declaration (1917).

But the Palestinian Arabs and those who lived in neighboring lands were opposed to a Jewish homeland in their midst. They did not want to give up any land and vowed to do everything possible to prevent the creation of a Jewish homeland.

Those who considered moving to Palestine were warned that life there would be difficult and dangerous. They would need courage and determination to survive the challenges that awaited them. A number of people accepted these challenges, and Golda Meir was one of them. Here is her story.

Tel Aviv   1948

My name is Golda Meir, and my dream is that one day my people will live in peace in a land of their own.

I was born in the Ukrainian city of Kiev, in the Russian Empire. One of my first memories was of my father nailing boards over our front door because we believed that the Jewish community was about to be attacked by troublemakers. These troublemakers were encouraged by the Russian government. They would enter a Jewish community and riot, steal, break windows, and hurt and kill people while the police stood by and did nothing. The memory of such times added to my conviction that the Jews of the world would only find peace when they found a land of their own.

My family moved to America when I was eight. I spent many happy years there. I loved my adopted country, and I learned much about freedom there. But I knew I had important work to do elsewhere. My life's task would be to help build a Jewish homeland.

I was 23 years old when I left the United States with my husband and emigrated to Palestine. Our life was difficult, but I loved the land and the people. At first, we lived on a *kibbutz* (a communelike farm), where my job was to take care of the chickens. I also helped to raise crops and defend the kibbutz. I always remember the three years I spent there as one of the happiest periods in my life.

I moved to the city of Tel Aviv and became active in politics. By this time, Adolf Hitler had risen to power in Germany and had introduced his anti-Jewish laws. The Jews in Germany were desperate to emigrate, but other countries were reluctant to take them. I attended an international conference where representatives of many countries said that, while they were sorry for the Jews of Germany, their countries had no room for them. I stood up and promised that if other nations would not help, we settlers in Palestine would take in the German Jews and share the little we had with them.

But my promise was not fulfilled. The British, who ruled Palestine, decided that the Arabs would feel threatened if many more Jews moved to Palestine. In 1939 they issued a white paper (diplomatic report) stating that the number of Jewish immigrants to Palestine would be limited to 75,000 over the next five years, and then all Jewish immigration would stop. There were 10 million Jews in Europe, and most were in danger of losing their lives! (The British white paper amounted to a death sentence to these people.)

The next five years were horrible. Six million Jews were murdered by the Nazis, and no one could do anything to stop the killings. The British policy forced us to sit here helpless at a time when we were convinced we could have saved hundreds of thousands of lives. I realized that we Jews could depend only on ourselves for survival. More than ever, I dedicated myself to building a homeland for the Jewish survivors of the Holocaust and for Jews anywhere who were in need.

The years right after World War II were marked by violence.

Golda Meir was a leader in the successful movement to establish the state of Israel as a homeland for the Jewish people.

We fought the Arabs, who wanted to chase us from the land, and the British, who had once promised us a homeland and now appeared to have changed their minds. A United Nations Special Committee on Palestine visited the country and learned firsthand what was going on. After considering all the facts, this committee decided that it would recommend the establishment of a Jewish state.

In 1947 the United Nations voted for the establishment of a Jewish state. Our Arab neighbors refused to accept this decision. We knew that we would soon be attacked. We needed arms and money in order to fight back. I was sent to the United States to raise money and was told not to expect too much aid. But the American people warmed to my message and contributed over $50 million to our cause.

I met with King Abdullah of Trans-Jordan and asked him not to join in an attack against my people. The king was sympathetic but told me that he would lose face if he did not join with the other Arab leaders. He suggested that my people should not hurry the proclamation of a state. I answered that my people had been waiting for 2,000 years. Is that hurrying?

On May 14, 1948, I was one of the 25 signers of Israel's declaration of independence. When I had studied American history as a schoolgirl and read about those who signed the United States Declaration of Independence, I couldn't imagine these were real people doing something they cared about a great deal. Yet there I was signing a declaration of independence for my beloved land.

My name is Golda Meir, and my dream is that one day my people will live in peace in a land of their own. Miraculously, we have found a land of our own. Peace still escapes us, so we have been obliged to become good soldiers.

Postscript

In 1969 Golda Meir became the prime minister of Israel. She faced many crises, the most difficult of which was the war with Egypt and Syria in 1973. Of the soldiers who died in the war she said, "Every single death is a tragedy. We don't like to make war, even when we win."

The war exhausted her and she left office in 1974. She died four years later. Golda Meir was 80 years old and had suffered from leukemia for 12 years.

QUESTIONS FOR REVIEW

1. What promise did the British make to the Jewish settlers in Palestine who helped them during World War I?
2. Why did the British fail to fulfill their promise?
3. Why did many Jews look upon the British "white paper" as a death sentence?
4. How was the Jewish state of Israel established?
5. What problems did the new state of Israel face?

UNDERSTANDING THE STORY

A. Tell which statements Golda Meir made or might have made.

1. The Jews of the world will find peace if they remain in the lands where they were born.

2. My life's work was to help build a Jewish homeland.
3. One of the happiest periods of my life was when I lived on a kibbutz in Palestine.
4. We Jews knew we could depend only on ourselves for survival.
5. We offered to take in the German Jews and share what little we had with them.
6. We were convinced that we could have saved hundreds of thousands of lives during World War II.
7. I was in no hurry to see the state of Israel proclaimed.
8. We don't like to fight a war, not even when we win.

B. Imagine that you are a member of the United Nations Special Committee on Palestine in 1947. You have just returned from a visit to Palestine, and now you must make your recommendation. Would you recommend the creation of the state of Israel? Explain.

ACTIVITIES AND INQUIRIES

1. Imagine that you are interviewing Golda Meir. You ask her if she believes that the creation of the state of Israel was a miracle. How does she answer?
2. Imagine that the state of Israel has just been established, and you have decided to move there. Describe the life you will lead in this new country.
3. You interview an Arab leader. You ask him why he is opposed to the establishment of a Jewish state. What does he tell you?
4. Imagine that you are an Israeli citizen. You have accompanied Golda Meir on her trip to the United States to raise money for Israel. How would you try to convince Americans to donate money to your country?
5. Draw a cartoon that will help to convince Americans and others around the world to support Israel.

10. When Worlds Collide: The War in Korea

Even after Japan's defeat in World War II, East Asia remained a region of great tension. United States armed forces occupied the major Japanese islands. The Soviet Union occupied other northern Japanese islands. Both Soviet and United States forces occupied Japan's former colony of Korea.

Korea was divided into two zones, north and south, at the 38th parallel. The United States pushed for and won approval for elections to be held under United Nations supervision. In 1948 elections in the United States zone resulted in the creation of an independent government for South Korea. A rival Communist-run government was quickly set up in North Korea.

Both governments claimed to represent all the Korean people. Both threatened to reunify the country by force, if necessary. The United States and the Soviet Union pulled their troops out of Korea, but the area remained tense.

On the morning of June 25, 1950, North Korean troops poured across the 38th parallel into South Korea. It seemed likely that the North Koreans would overrun all of South Korea in a short time and unify the country under a Communist government.

United States leaders had discussed whether they should support South Korea in case of war. In public statements the United States had indicated that it would not do so. It did not wish to send troops to fight another war so soon after the end of World War II. Would the United States now change its mind? Here are the headlines and the stories behind them, which tell us the rest of the story.

June 25, 1950

NORTH KOREA INVADES SOUTH; COMMUNISTS ADVANCE RAPIDLY

That afternoon, in New York City, the United Nations Security Council passed a resolution ordering a cease-fire. It accused North Korea of starting the war and ordered it to withdraw its forces from South Korea.

516

In Washington, President Harry Truman met with his advisers and decided that it was necessary to stop this invasion of South Korea. Truman thought that the United States was being tested to see if it would allow independent nations to be taken over by armed invasion. He believed that if the United States permitted the invasion of South Korea to go unchecked, the country would be tested again and again until it would have no choice but to face another world war.

June 27, 1950

TRUMAN COMMITS U.S. FORCES IN KOREA

President Truman ordered United States air and sea forces into action in South Korea. On June 30, after North Korea had captured the South Korean capital of Seoul, Truman sent in United States ground troops with the approval of the United Nations.

The Korean War: In 1950 U.S. troops recaptured the South Korean capital city of Seoul from the North Koreans.

In July the UN went further. It asked the nations that were sending troops to Korea to place them under the command of the United States. In time, some 17 nations would fight the North Koreans under the command of the United States but under the flag of the UN. Americans and South Koreans would make up nine-tenths of the total force.

September 15, 1950

UN MAKES DARING LANDING AT INCHON

The UN troops landed at Inchon near Seoul. Sweeping eastward, they threatened the North Korean line of support. North Korean troops began to retreat, and by the end of September they were crossing the border, the 38th parallel, back into North Korea.

October 1, 1950

SOUTH KOREAN TROOPS CROSS AT 38TH PARALLEL

On October 7, United States ground troops entered North Korea for the first time. The goal seemed to be a quick drive to unify Korea under a non-Communist government.

Truman grew concerned as United States troops pushed north. North Korea borders on both China and the Soviet Union, and the president worried that having United States troops on their borders would bring both countries into the war. He warned U.S. General Douglas MacArthur, the commander of the UN forces, to make sure that no United States troops got any closer than 40 miles from the Soviet and Chinese borders. Only the South Korean troops were to be used to secure this border territory.

October 26, 1950

UN FORCES REACH YALU RIVER

North Korea's capital, Pyongyang, fell to UN troops on October 20. By October 26, the first UN troops had reached

THE KOREAN WAR 1950–1953

the Yalu River, the border between China and North Korea. Other UN forces were approaching a major complex of dams on the Yalu—dams that provided hydroelectric power for North Korea, China, and the Soviet Union. A few thousand Chinese troops had moved into North Korea to protect these dams. Against orders, MacArthur sent United States troops into the border regions. MacArthur was highly critical of the way Truman wanted the war fought. Eventually, Truman would replace him with another commander.

November 26, 1950

MASSIVE CHINESE ATTACK ACROSS YALU RIVER

A force of some 300,000 Chinese troops smashed south across the Yalu River. The surprised UN troops began a retreat that would take them back into South Korea by Christmas. Seoul fell but was recaptured by mid-March 1951. This brought the front lines once again near the 38th parallel, where the war had begun. The United States and its allies, under UN leadership, were ready to enter into negotiations to bring the war to an end.

Peace talks began in July 1951, but the war did not end. While the two sides argued back and forth for months, their troops kept on fighting.

President Truman did not run for reelection in 1952. The winning candidate was General Dwight D. Eisenhower, leader of the Allies' European forces in World War II. During the campaign, he promised to "go to Korea" and bring the war to an early end. Eisenhower did visit Korea, and his administration continued the peace talks.

July 27, 1953

TRUCE ENDS KOREAN FIGHTING; 38TH PARALLEL IS TRUCE LINE

In July 1953, an agreement between the UN and North Korea was reached, and the fighting stopped. But this was only an armistice (a truce), not a peace treaty. Korea remained divided at the 38th parallel. Hostile armies continued to face each other across a narrow strip of territory known as the demilitarized zone (a neutral area in which no warfare could be waged).

Postscript

The Korean War cost the United States some 54,000 dead and 103,000 wounded. Total UN casualties reached some 400,000 dead or wounded. South Korea suffered close to a million civilian casualties, with several million made homeless. Nearly 1 1/2 million North Korean and Chinese soldiers were dead or wounded. Much of Korea lay in ruins.

Four decades later, Korea remains a divided country. North Korea is controlled by the Korean Communist Party and is ruled by a dictatorship. The government owns and operates the major industries and farms.

In 1960 an elected South Korean government was overthrown by a military group. The next year another elected leader was overthrown by the military. The country was ruled by the military until 1993, when a civilian government was elected to office.

Many South Korean industries and farms are privately owned and operated, and the economy has grown rapidly since the 1970s. North Korea is richer in natural resources, but South Korea has made far greater gains than the north in industrial development and agricultural output.

QUESTIONS FOR REVIEW

1. Why did East Asia remain an area of great tension even after Japan's defeat in World War II?
2. Why did North Korea go to war against South Korea?
3. Why did the United States become involved in the Korean War?
4. Why did U.S. President Harry Truman relieve General Douglas MacArthur of his duties as the commander of the United Nations forces?
5. How did the Korean War end? What has happened to North Korea and South Korea since the war's end?

UNDERSTANDING THE STORY

A. Tell which statements describe President Truman's views or policies about the Korean War.

1. The United States was being tested by the invasion of South Korea.
2. We must stamp out the Communist government in North Korea.
3. United Nations forces should push as far into North Korea as is necessary to win the war.
4. I will support whatever decision General MacArthur makes about the conduct of the war.
5. I will do everything possible to win this war, even if it means war with the Soviet Union.
6. United Nations forces should not get any closer than 40 miles from the Soviet and Chinese borders.

7. It is my job to make United States foreign policy.
8. I am sorry that I ever gave the order to get the United States involved in this war.

B. Imagine that you are the president of the United States. The country is at war, and one of your generals tells you that the conduct of the war should be left to the generals. What is your answer?

ACTIVITIES AND INQUIRIES

1. Study the map of Korea on page 519. Then choose the term or phrase that best completes each statement.
   a. The Yalu River is a northern boundary of (1) China (2) North Korea (3) the Soviet Union.
   b. The body of water west of Korea is the (1) Sea of Japan (2) Pacific Ocean (3) Yellow Sea.
   c. The distance from Pyongyang to Seoul is about (1) 120 kilometers (2) 375 kilometers (3) 250 kilometers.
   d. The distance from Pusan to the Yalu River is about (1) 900 kilometers (2) 240 kilometers (3) 500 kilometers.
   e. The label 38° on the map refers to (1) the number of miles from Korea to Japan (2) a geographical boundary separating North Korea from South Korea at the 38th parallel (3) the average temperature in Fahrenheit in South Korea during the month of January.

2. Reread the stories about President Harry Truman in this unit. Prepare a report card for Truman. Grade him in the following areas and justify each grade: (*a*) leadership   (*b*) point of view   (*c*) accomplishments while president   (*d*) maturity.

3. Imagine that you are a reporter and are interviewing President Truman. What questions would you ask him about his role in the Korean War? How might he answer your questions? With what do you agree? With what do you disagree? Explain.

11. The Lesson

Our story begins in 1944. The tide of war is turning against the Japanese. But in French Indo-China, in the area now called Vietnam, Japan is still in control.

The first half of this story takes place in a small jungle camp near the Vietnam-China border. A United States special forces team has joined a band of Vietnamese guerrillas. The United States soldiers are teaching the Vietnamese how a small group can fight a large army. The Vietnamese are using this training to drive the Japanese from their country.

In our story, United States Colonel David Johnson is talking to Ho Chi Minh, the leader of the Vietnamese Communists. Each man likes and respects the other. The second half of the story tells what happened to Vietnam in the three decades after the meeting of Ho and Johnson.

Vietnam 1944

"You Americans are different," said Ho Chi Minh.

"How do you mean that?" David Johnson asked.

"I mean that you are not like the French."

"And what makes us different from French people?"

"Your history is like ours," Ho replied. "You fought the English for your independence. We will soon fight the French for our independence. Our peoples have much in common. You are teaching us how to destroy our enemies, and we are grateful."

Johnson was pleased. "Ho, you and your soldiers are good students. You learn quickly. The Japanese have better weapons and more troops. Yet each time you fight them, you hurt them more than they hurt you. Your enemies will have to think twice before they make war against you!"

Ho Chi Minh (1890–1969) led the Vietnamese Communists' fight against Western colonial powers.

"David, I hope that when this war is over you will bring back a message to your people," Ho said. "Tell them that we Vietnamese want only to get back our own country. Tell them that we will fight anyone—the Japanese, the French—who stands in our way! And tell them this, please. I hope that the United States and Vietnam can be good friends."

"You know a great deal about the history of my country," David said to Ho. "But I know nothing of your country's history. What can you tell me?"

Ho answered, "My country's history is a very proud one. My people have suffered at the hands of foreigners through the ages. The Chinese ruled us for over 1,000 years. We fought more than ten wars with them. At last we chased the Chinese from the country. Today, the Japanese and the French are our enemies. Tomorrow, others may try to rule us. No matter. We are a stubborn people. We have learned how to suffer and wait. We are in no hurry. The longer we wait, the greater will be our enemies' defeat!"

Vietnam 1945–1976

In 1945, at the end of World War II, Ho asked the United States government to help him stop the French from regaining control of Vietnam. The United States government did not trust Ho, however, because he was a Communist. Instead, the United States decided to help the French.

The French were armed with heavy weapons. They had a well-trained army and air force. The United States sent more guns and money. Ho's army was a small band armed with light weapons. Ho would not admit defeat. His army lived and worked alongside the people of Vietnam. The soldiers used hit-and-run tactics. They ran from the French in the morning and attacked them the same afternoon. The French suffered defeat after defeat. At last, in 1954, the French gave up. They left Vietnam. Vietnam was divided into two parts: the North had a Communist government in Hanoi, and the South had a non-Communist government in Saigon.

Slowly, the United States began to take the place of the French in Vietnam. At first, Americans helped only to train and supply the South Vietnamese army. Then, United States soldiers were sent as military advisers to the South Vietnamese. By 1964 United States planes were dropping bombs on North Vietnam. Less than a year later, United States troops were in battle. Both sides suffered heavy losses. North Vietnam fought for control of the entire country. The United States fought to keep the Communists from gaining control over more people. The United States also fought to help the South Vietnamese choose their own way of life.

The war became uglier. Communist troops tortured and killed both soldiers and civilians. Vietnamese peasants were afraid not to help the Communists. People who didn't help the Communists had their throats slit as examples to others. Life became very cheap in Vietnam.

The ugliness of the war also touched the United States soldiers. Reports from the battlefield told of United States soldiers who shot up entire villages because they believed that the enemy was everywhere. People in the United States learned of atrocities in Vietnam. Who was to blame? There was a public outcry against the war. Demands for peace were everywhere.

In 1973, the United States signed a peace treaty with North Vietnam. The north agreed to end the fighting if the United States troops would go home. The United States had trained the army of the south very carefully. It had supplied the south with many weapons and was ready to keep on doing so. South Vietnam could now take care of itself.

The cease-fire did not end the war in Vietnam. Fighting went on between the armies of the north and the south. The United States watched from the sidelines. The soldiers of North Vietnam won province after province, city after city. On April 28, 1975, South Vietnam surrendered to North Vietnam. Saigon, the former capital city of the south, was renamed "Ho Chi Minh City." Another long war had come to an end.

Postscript

In 1976 North and South Vietnam were unified into one nation, under the control of the North, called the Socialist Republic of Vietnam. The capital is the North Vietnamese city of Hanoi.

North Vietnam immediately began to regulate the currency, goods, and businesses of the entire country. People were required to exchange South Vietnamese money for a new national currency. Many goods were rationed, and strict controls were placed on all privately owned businesses.

Education was also regulated. Textbooks were revised, and teachers were retrained by North Vietnamese advisers. Only people whose parents were workers or small farmers were allowed to attend universities. All students were expected to spend part of their time working on farms or doing some form of manual labor.

The new government faced severe problems. Floods caused great crop damage and led to food shortages. The government was forced to import rice. Hundreds of thousands of people fled the country in search of a better life elsewhere. Those who left by sea were called "boat people." A great number of these refugees died at sea. Those who reached other countries often spent months in refugee camps before obtaining permission to resettle. The United States admitted over 600,000 Vietnamese refugees from the 1970s to the early 1990s.

The government of Vietnam has sought to establish diplomatic relations with its former enemy, the United States. Vietnam has also asked for monetary and technological assistance as well as an opportunity to trade with the United States. Vietnam cooperated in the search for several thou-

EAST ASIA

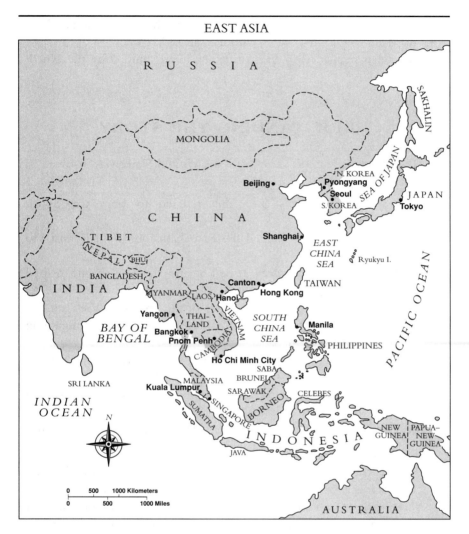

sand American soldiers who were listed as missing in action and remained unaccounted for. In 1994 the United States lifted its 19-year ban on trade with Vietnam.

QUESTIONS FOR REVIEW

1. Briefly describe Vietnam's history up to World War II.
2. How did the United States try to help the Vietnamese during World War II? Why?

3. How did the United States get involved in the war in Vietnam?
4. Why did the United States withdraw from Vietnam?
5. What has happened to Vietnam since it was unified by the North Vietnamese?

UNDERSTANDING THE STORY

A. Tell which statements show how the United States was involved in Vietnam.

1. The United States army never tried to train the South Vietnamese army.
2. The United States helped the French in their fight against Ho Chi Minh.
3. Later, the United States turned against the French and helped Ho Chi Minh.
4. The United States took the place of the French in Vietnam.
5. The United States fought to keep the Communists from gaining control in Vietnam.
6. The United States was involved in an ugly, brutal war in Vietnam.
7. The United States government supplied the South Vietnamese army with many weapons.
8. After the United States forces left, the North and South Vietnamese became great friends.

B. Assume that you are an adviser to the president of the United States. The year is 1950. The president tells you that the United States has three choices in Vietnam: help the French, help Ho Chi Minh, or remain neutral and stay out of Vietnam. What would you recommend to the president? Explain.

ACTIVITIES AND INQUIRIES

1. Use each of the following key terms in a sentence: special forces combat   hit-and-run tactics   ambush   cease-fire.
2. Go to the library. Prepare a report on the activities of either France or the United States in Vietnam.
3. Imagine that you are Colonel David Johnson. You are speaking to Ho Chi Minh. Ho tells you that the United States and Vietnam can be friends. But he adds that his people will fight any group that

stands in the way of independence for Vietnam. What would you tell Ho Chi Minh? How do you think Ho would answer your remarks?

4. The caption of a cartoon is: "We are a stubborn people. We have learned to suffer and wait." Who is the speaker? What does the speaker mean by "suffer and wait"? Is it possible to win freedom by suffering and waiting? Draw the cartoon.

5. Study the map of East Asia today on page 527. Tell which item makes each statement correct.

   a. The capital of Vietnam is (1) Hanoi (2) Ho Chi Minh City (3) Bangkok.

   b. The country north of Vietnam is (1) Malaysia (2) Indonesia (3) China.

   c. The country situated between northern Vietnam and Thailand is (1) Nepal (2) Laos (3) Cambodia.

   d. The country situated between southern Vietnam and Thailand is (1) Myanmar (2) Laos (3) Cambodia.

12. The Cuban Missile Crisis: High Noon in the Caribbean

The two decades following the end of World War II in 1945 were difficult ones. Riots, revolutions, civil wars, and wars between nations occurred all over the world. The world's two superpowers, the United States and the Soviet Union, were engaged in a "cold war." They supported different sides in battle—sometimes just with arms, sometimes with soldiers and arms. But they were careful not to confront each other in an all-out "hot" war.

The United States stood by while the Soviet Union took over Czechoslovakia in 1948, put down a riot in Poland and a revolution in

Hungary in 1956, and built a wall between East Berlin and West Berlin in 1961. The United States even sided with the Soviet Union in 1956 in the Middle East. At that time, Egyptian President Nasser took control of the Suez Canal. Israel, Britain, and France retaliated by invading Egypt. The Soviets threatened war if those countries did not pull back at once. The United States also opposed the invasion because it feared that the attack might lead to a world conflict. The United Nations, backed by both the United States and the Soviet Union, intervened and forced the attackers to withdraw. UN forces were also sent to keep peace on the border between Israel and Egypt.

The Soviet Union watched as the United States sent guns to Greece in 1947 to help put down a Communist threat. It stood by as the United States rearmed Western Europe in 1949 by forming the North Atlantic Treaty Organization (NATO). The Soviet Union did not send troops to Korea in 1950 or to Vietnam in 1962, even though the United States was sending both arms and troops to those places.

Both nations fought with speeches, threats, aid to other nations, and in the United Nations. But neither used direct force against the other.

This seemed about to change in 1962 as the two superpowers prepared to engage in life-or-death struggle over Cuba. Only 90 miles off the coast of Florida, Cuba had been the scene of a bloody revolution. Fidel Castro and his guerrilla forces fought for three years (1956–1958) to overthrow the dictatorship of Fulgencio Batista. Once in power in 1959, Castro established a Communist dictatorship and allied himself with the Soviet Union.

In 1961 the United States backed a Cuban force that tried to invade Cuba. The invasion failed, and the Cuban government turned to the Soviet Union for help against possible United States-backed invasions. The Soviet Union responded by agreeing to build and stock missile bases in Cuba.

In our story, we examine the incident that nearly brought the two superpowers to all-out war.

Moscow   April 1962

"Impossible! The United States will never stand for it!" cried Alexei Adjhubai. He was speaking to his father-in-law, Nikita Khrushchev, premier of the Soviet Union.

"Don't be a fool!" replied Khrushchev. "They will never know the truth until it is too late. We will fool them into thinking that we are building bases in Cuba for short-range ground-to-air missiles. Instead, we will build bases for missiles that can hit the United States. These bases will be so well disguised that United States planes won't be able to spot them. Besides, this is their election time. President Kennedy will be too busy making speeches to give this his full attention."

Beginning in late June, several ships per week left the Soviet Union carrying missile parts, fuel, and technicians to Cuba.

Washington   October 1962

"Mr. President," said MacGeorge Bundy, the special assistant on national security, "the Cuban photos prove it! The Soviets are building ground-to-ground missile bases!"

"Are we certain?" asked President John F. Kennedy.

"Absolutely!"

The president bit his lip in anger. "Only yesterday Khrushchev said that we should all join hands and keep the peace. And all this time he has been playing nuclear war games!"

"Well, then, God help him!" interrupted Bundy.

"God help us all!" said the president.

Washington   October 17, 1962

Soviet Foreign Minister Andrei Gromyko had just been shown into President Kennedy's office. He was concerned by rumors that Kennedy knew something about the Soviet missile buildup in Cuba. He was there to find out as much as he could.

"Mr. President," said Gromyko, "let me come directly to the point. My government would be most happy if you Americans would make peace with Cuba instead of always threatening it."

"Your government," said Kennedy, "asks that we make peace with Cuba while at the same time it prepares Cuba for war!"

"Not so!" protested Gromyko. "We are shipping only farm tools and some small defensive weapons to the Cubans. Speaking for Mr. Khrushchev, I pledge that the Soviet Union will never ship ground-to-ground missiles or any other offensive weapons to Cuba."

CENTRAL AMERICA AND THE CARIBBEAN

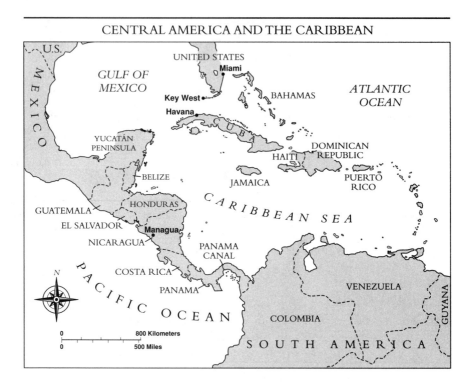

President Kennedy gripped the edge of his desk. He looked at Gromyko and said firmly, "I must warn you that the United States will never allow offensive weapons in Cuba. We will take any step—I repeat, any step—necessary to rid Cuba of them!"

Washington   October 19

"Well, Bob," said President Kennedy to his secretary of defense, Robert McNamara, "give me the bad news."

"Mr. President," replied McNamara, "an invasion of Cuba will need 250,000 soldiers and 2,000 air strikes. At least 25,000 of our people will die in battle."

"Why can't we just hit the bases with a surprise air attack?" asked Kennedy.

"An air attack may not destroy all of the missile sites and missiles in Cuba," McNamara replied.

"Then unless the Soviets bend, we have no choice," said Kennedy.

"We have no choice, Mr. President."

Washington   October 22

"In here, sir," said the presidential assistant to Soviet ambassador Dobrynin, as he ushered him into the president's office.

"Mr. President," said Dobrynin with a wide smile, "what a great pleasure to see you again. How may I serve you?"

"Mr. Dobrynin," Kennedy said crisply, "please read this."

"May I ask what I am reading?" asked Dobrynin, still smiling.

"It is a speech I am going to make to the American people in exactly one hour."

Dobrynin began to read. Slowly the smile faded from his face. He opened his mouth to speak but Kennedy continued.

"Mr. Dobrynin, we are done with lies in this office. Tell Premier Khrushchev that the American people have warned that they will never allow missile bases and missiles in Cuba. Now they are ready to make good their warning!"

Unsmiling, Dobrynin replied, "I will deliver your message to Premier Khrushchev."

Caribbean Sea, aboard a U.S. destroyer   October 24

"Sir, they keep coming!" said Navy Lieutenant Hodges to Captain Ford. Hodges' voice was strained.

"Do you see anything else on the radarscope?" asked Ford.

"Only what I saw before, sir. Two Soviet ships are moving rapidly toward our position, and 30 more are following behind them!"

"How much longer will it be before they get here?"

"The two ships should be here in about 25 minutes, sir."

The two men exchanged glances. Despite the air-cooled room, drops of perspiration formed on the lieutenant's brow.

"Sir," said Hodges, his voice rising, "something is happening! A Soviet submarine in moving into position between the two ships!"

"Quick," said Captain Ford to his communications officer, "wire the White House. Tell them that we are standing by for instructions!"

Moments later, a message was received from the White House.

"What are our instructions, sir?" asked Hodges.

Captain Ford, in a serious tone, said, "Our instructions are to do whatever is necessary to stop those ships!"

The minutes ticked by. The Soviet ships drew closer. The entire crew waited, each man a heartbeat away from disaster.

"Captain!" shouted Lieutenant Hodges, "the Soviet ships have stopped! They have stopped dead in the water! Some are even beginning to turn around and head back!"

The captain bowed his head and whispered, "Thank God!"

Postscript

In a message to President Kennedy, Premier Khrushchev offered to remove the missiles in Cuba in exchange for a United States promise not to invade Cuba. Kennedy agreed. On October 28, Khrushchev announced that the Soviet missiles would be withdrawn. The crisis was over.

Over the years, the United States and Cuba supported rival groups in Latin America and Africa. The United States helped nations in need in Latin America, often to keep them out of the Cuban camp. The United States and Cuba did not have diplomatic relations, nor did they trade with each other. Cuba depended on the Soviet Union for its weapons, technology, and much of its food supply.

In the 1990s, the United States and Cuba continue to have little diplomatic contact. The economic collapse of the Soviet Union in the late 1980s cut off much of the food, machinery, and technology that the Cuban people needed. Observers wondered whether Cuba was headed for economic and political collapse.

QUESTIONS FOR REVIEW

1. Describe a world crisis since the end of World War II in which the United States and the Soviet Union supported different sides.
2. Why did the United States side with the Soviet Union over the British-French-Israeli invasion of Egypt?
3. How did the United States and the Soviet Union avoid going to war with each other?
4. Why did the Cuban missile crisis pose such a great threat to world peace?
5. How was an all-out war between the United States and the Soviet Union over Cuba narrowly avoided?

UNDERSTANDING THE STORY

A. Write T for each statement that is true and O for each statement that is an opinion.

1. The United States and the Soviet Union did not want to go to war with each other.
2. The United States and the Soviet Union backed opposing sides in various wars around the world.
3. The Soviet Union set up missile bases in Cuba.
4. The Soviets should not have sent missiles to Cuba.
5. The United States avoided making threats of war over the Cuban missiles.
6. When faced with U.S. naval power, the Soviet ships came to a halt and began to turn back.
7. The United States and Cuba will never have full diplomatic contact.

B. Imagine that you are an adviser to Premier Khrushchev in 1962. Khrushchev asks you whether the Soviet Union should build missile bases in Cuba. He also asks what the United States might do if the bases were built. What advice would you give Khrushchev? Explain.

ACTIVITIES AND INQUIRIES

1. Imagine that you are a reporter. You are assigned to interview President Kennedy in Washington, D.C., in October 1962. Write the questions that you would like to ask him about the Cuban missile crisis. Answer the questions as you think he would have done.

2. As a reporter, you are now assigned to interview Khrushchev in Moscow in October 1962. Write the questions you would ask him about the Cuban missile crisis. Answer the questions as you think he would have done.

3. Study the map of Central America and the Caribbean on page 532. and answer the following questions.
   a. The distance from Havana, Cuba, to Key West is about (1) 125 miles (2) 250 miles (3) 375 miles.
   b. The distance from Havana to the Panama Canal is about (1) 200 kilometers (2) 1,600 kilometers (3) 600 kilometers.
   c. Cuba is west of (1) Mexico (2) Haiti (3) Jamaica.
   d. An island to the south of Cuba is (1) Puerto Rico (2) the Dominican Republic (3) Jamaica.
   e. Study the map once again. Why was the United States so concerned that Soviet missiles were placed in Cuba?

4. Suppose that your class is going to hold a debate between the Soviet and United States delegates to the United Nations in 1962. The topic is the Cuban missile crisis. Prepare the case for the United States.

5. Now prepare the case for the Soviet side of the Cuban missile crisis. Hold the debate and have the class decide the winner.

UNIT XII

The Present Day

The world continued to change at a rapid pace in the 1990s. People altered the ways they were governed and changed their ways of life. Many old rivalries were set aside as people sought to attain greater freedoms and a better way of life. But just as soon as old problems were solved, new ones arose to take their place. The world continued to face dangerous and complex challenges.

Europe. In our first story, we read about events that most people believed would never happen: the collapse of Soviet communism and the breakup of the Soviet Union. The four-and-a-half-decade cold war between Russia and the United States was over, and a new era of peace between the two superpowers had begun. Yet new problems had appeared

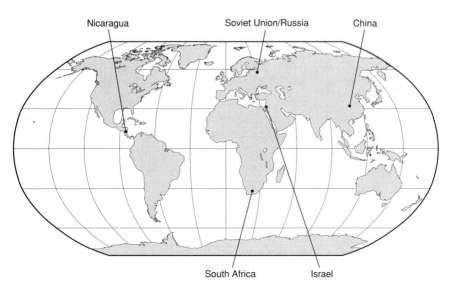

Nicaragua · Soviet Union/Russia · China · South Africa · Israel

which, in their own way, were just as complex as those presented by the cold war.

Africa. Our second story focuses once more on the fight for freedom in South Africa. We follow the long and often painful struggle of a black leader who was determined to free his people from oppression.

Asia. Our third story takes place in Beijing, China. A group of students called out for political freedom, and their call was heard around the world. Their government had also been listening, and it had a terrifying reply for those who rebelled against its authority.

Latin America. The fourth story focuses on the troubles in the Latin American country of Nicaragua. A courageous woman, whose family opposed tyranny, became her country's president. In spite of her love for her country and her concern for her people, she found herself with many problems.

Middle East. The next story looks at the Middle East, where as the story shows, two rival groups were beginning to believe that they were both engaged in a conflict that neither could win. Many of their followers continued to believe in the struggle, and each side distrusted the other. Could they find the courage to take the steps toward peace?

United States. In our final story, a scientist warns of the devastated world of the future if humanity continues to abuse and neglect the environment. Progress is sometimes purchased at a very high price. The price for the way we are living may be a higher one than we or our descendants can afford to pay.

1. The Last Soviet "Czar"

From the end of World War II in 1945 to the early 1980s, the Soviet Union continued to keep pace with the United States as one of the world's great military superpowers. But in the 1980s the Soviet Union found that this competition with the United States came at a very high price, one it would soon be unable to afford.

The emphasis on military supplies and equipment caused critical shortages in clothing, food, and household goods for the people at home. Crop failures added to the problem, and people began to grumble and complain.

In 1979 the Soviet Union invaded Afghanistan in order to help protect the Communist government from rebel troops. But the Soviet troops were never able to put down the rebellion completely, and the fighting lasted for years. This adventure proved to be very costly to the Soviet Union as it caused a serious morale problem among the troops and created even greater shortages at home.

Premier Nikita Khrushchev (see Unit XI, story 12) had been replaced by a series of hard-line Stalinist dictators. When the last of these men died, the Soviet Politburo (government leaders) decided to replace him with a much younger person, Mikhail Gorbachev.

Unlike his predecessors, Gorbachev had neither fought in World War II nor risen to power during the repressive Stalin era. Shaped by different forces, he called for economic, social, and political changes, and he promised to speak openly and honestly about the nation's problems. He also promised to continue the policies of his predecessors. Many wondered if he would and could keep his word.

Here is his story.

Moscow   December 1991

Mikhail Gorbachev stared at the paper in front of him. He had worked on this document for a number of days, searching for the right words. The document was his letter of resignation as president of the Soviet Union.

Moscow, 1991: Mikhail Gorbachev signs his resignation and announces the end of the Soviet Union.

He had been a man with a mission. Even as far back as his days as a law student in Moscow, he had known that his country was in deep trouble. To him, communism stood for jobs and food for everyone. It meant a place for everyone in a society where all were regarded and treated as equals. He knew that the Soviet people and those of other countries who were forced to live under the Communist banner had a very different picture. He vowed that, if ever the chance came his way, he would do all in his power to bring his brand of communism to the people.

Gorbachev became a member of the Communist Party in 1952 and spent more than 30 years working hard to make his way to the top. In 1985 he was appointed general secretary, or leader, of the Communist Party and was thus the most powerful person in the Soviet Union.

Gorbachev learned, much to his dismay, that conditions in the Soviet Union were even worse than he had believed. The country was on the brink of disaster. The economy was failing miserably and showed signs of getting worse. The country was on the verge of bankruptcy. No longer could it afford to keep up the expensive arms race with the United States. Nor could the Soviet Union send troops to other parts of the world to support Communist regimes that were in trouble. It could not even afford to assist the allies that depended on Soviet aid.

"What am I to do?" Gorbachev asked himself. He could choose to do as others before him had done—ignore the problems and hope that somehow things would improve. He could even make a few changes in the economy over a long period of time and risk little for himself. But he knew that unless sweeping changes were made, the country was doomed.

Gorbachev went to work. He called for political openness (*glasnost*) and economic and social reform (*perestroika*). He also decided to tighten discipline within the Soviet Union by raising the price of alcohol as a way of discouraging excessive drinking. He spoke out against absenteeism from work and denounced crime. He called for people to work harder and produce more. Many people responded to his call for openness by speaking out against him and his policies. Many also continued to drink heavily. Crime increased, absenteeism continued, and consumer lines became longer as goods grew scarcer. People became angrier and more outspoken.

Gorbachev's policies away from home were far more successful. He withdrew Soviet forces from trouble spots around the world. He also signed agreements with the United States that resulted in both sides reducing their weapons stockpiles. His policies were so highly regarded that he was awarded the Nobel Peace Prize in 1990.

But conditions in the Soviet Union grew worse. And now there was a new threat. The people of Eastern Europe had also been influenced by Gorbachev's call for openness. They had become so outspoken that they were threatening to overthrow the Communist leadership and declare their independence from the Soviet Union. Gorbachev had a choice. He could either use force against these people or he could let them go their own way. He decided that he had neither the armed forces nor the will to suppress these people and their movements. Instead, he watched helplessly as the three Baltic republics (Estonia, Latvia, and Lithuania), Czechoslovakia, East Germany, Poland, Romania, and the other countries in Eastern Europe began to move out of the Soviet orbit.

The political reforms Gorbachev had promised to the Soviet people were slow in arriving. He decided that what was needed were lawmakers who were chosen by the people instead of the Communist Party bosses. Over the objection of many in the party, he pushed through a plan to give voters a choice of candidates in local elections. In 1990, in the first free elections in the Soviet Union since 1917, the people voted many party officials out of office. Sensing that this was what the people wanted, Gorbachev declared that the Communist Party's political monopoly was ended. He opened all political offices everywhere in the Soviet Union to free elections. In the elections that followed, those lawmakers who opposed this new democracy went down to humiliating defeat.

The economy continued to decline, however, and new reforms were called for. Gorbachev's advisers told him that the only way to save the Soviet Union was to scrap the Communist system. This he could not do. Angered by the lack of action on the part of the central government and having tasted real freedom, the people of the Soviet republics began to demand their independence. Gorbachev's advisers demanded that he use force to stop the move for independence, and at first he agreed. But when Soviet army forces clashed with the people in Lithuania and killed a dozen people, he had had enough. He would no longer consent to unleash Soviet troops against the people. Republic after republic proclaimed its right to declare independence.

Others in the Communist Party had also had enough. In 1991 a small group of military and political leaders attempted to oust Gorbachev by force. They kidnapped him, placed him under house arrest, and tried to take power. But they were stopped by the Soviet people. The people had tasted the right to speak out, and they were not about to surrender to a new dictatorship which would deny them that right. The group's leaders were punished, and Gorbachev was temporarily restored to power.

But the cries for independence and freedom continued to be heard. Gorbachev watched as the people began to turn to others for leadership. They looked to people like Boris Yeltsin, the president of the Russian republic, whose goal was to bring the Soviet Union to an end and replace it with an association of

EUROPE AND NEIGHBORING MEMBERS OF THE
COMMONWEALTH OF INDEPENDENT STATES

independent republics. It became apparent to Gorbachev that a
new government was being born, and it had little need of
him.

Gorbachev stared again at the document that announced his
resignation. He had taken office with the hope that he would
save the Soviet system, but instead had introduced policies that
had helped to destroy it. But he had also helped to free millions of people from a system that no longer worked, and he
had, he hoped, brought the world closer to peace.

On December 25, 1991, nearly six years after he had succeeded to power, Mikhail Gorbachev announced his resignation. What followed was the end of the Communist Party's
seven-decade-long domination, and the end of the Soviet
Union.

Most of the former Soviet republics formed a loose political
organization called the Commonwealth of Independent States.

Postscript

The Yeltsin-led Russian government moved to make drastic economic changes. Price controls and subsidies on most goods and services were eliminated. Almost immediately, the prices of many goods began to soar beyond the ability of many people to pay. The government tried to help by raising the minimum wage, but many people, especially those on small, fixed incomes, found they had to make do with far less than before.

Some officials called for the government to slow down and even cut back on its reforms. Others demanded even more drastic reforms. In the background were blocs of hard-line Communists and right-wingers who opposed democracy and capitalism and called for a return to the Communist system.

In September 1993, Yeltsin announced that he was disbanding the Russian parliament and called for new elections. The hard-line lawmakers in the parliament immediately voted to impeach Yeltsin and remained in the building. When their supporters built barricades around the building, violent clashes with the police followed.

In early October, the violence grew. Rock-throwing anti-Yeltsin demonstrators continued to fight with the police. Troops were called in. Thousands of heavily armed demonstrators now thronged the streets and began an assault on government offices and a television station. Yeltsin announced that the attempted coup would be crushed in the shortest possible time. Government troops soon regained control of the situation. Tanks and helicopters fired upon the parliament building. As fires burned throughout the building, hundreds of people poured out and were immediately arrested. By the end of the day, the anti-Yeltsin leaders were under arrest. For the moment, the uprising was silenced.

In the December 1993 elections, the Russian people ratified a new constitution guaranteeing many personal freedoms, but they also elected many reactionary, anti-Yeltsin delegates to the parliament. In December 1994 the government denounced the republic of Chechen's declaration of independence from the Russian Federation. The Russian army was ordered to seize control of Grozny, the Chechen capital, and disarm the rebellion. Thousands of Chechens were killed, the capital was destroyed, and the rebellion was brutally suppressed. There was international condemnation of Russia's actions. Observers wondered whether Boris Yeltsin had surrendered control to the military hard-liners in his government.

But even worse was yet to come. This time, it was the Russian people who suffered. Yeltsin's government teetered on the edge of collapse for several years. It was unable to collect taxes, set up a sound banking system, pay government workers their salaries, or keep the Russian currency (the ruble) from losing value. The economy was kept afloat only by large loans from rich nations and international organizations. Finally, in summer 1998, after the ruble had lost nearly three-quarters of its value, most of Yeltsin's cabinet ministers were fired or resigned.

Yeltsin nominated Foreign Minister Yevgeny Primakov as the new Prime Minister, and he was approved by the Parliament. Primakov was to manage Russia's affairs until the next election. Russians continued to suffer, as personal incomes declined and crime increased. Solutions to Russia's problems seemed very far away.

QUESTIONS FOR REVIEW

1. Why did the Soviet Union in the 1980s find it increasingly difficult to continue competing with the United States?
2. Why was Mikhail Gorbachev forced to resign as president of the Soviet Union?
3. What economic changes did Boris Yeltsin's government make? What were the effects of these changes?
4. Why did Yeltsin and the parliamentary hard-liners clash in 1993? What was the result of this clash?
5. What problems remained to be resolved in the former Soviet Union?

UNDERSTANDING THE STORY

A. Write T for each statement that is true and F for each statement that is false.

1. The Soviet invasion of Afghanistan proved to be very costly for the Soviet Union.
2. Gorbachev hated what communism stood for.
3. When he took office, Gorbachev learned that conditions in the Soviet Union were even worse than he had believed.
4. Gorbachev decided not to make any changes.
5. Many people responded to Gorbachev's call for openness by speaking out against his policies.
6. Gorbachev allowed the first free elections in the Soviet Union since 1917.
7. Economic conditions improved after free elections were held.
8. Gorbachev survived an attempted military coup only to resign from office.

B. Imagine that Gorbachev is about to come to power. He tells you of his plans for the Soviet Union and asks for your advice. What advice would you give to him?

ACTIVITIES AND INQUIRIES

1. Imagine that a press conference has just been called. Gorbachev, Yeltsin, and a representative of the parliamentary hard-liners are seated on the panel. What questions would you ask of Gorbachev? How would he answer your questions?
2. What questions would you ask of Yeltsin? How would he answer your questions?
3. What questions would you ask of the hard-liner? How would this person answer your questions?

2. Free at Last

In the 1970s, the South African government adopted a new constitution that included separate parliaments for people of mixed ancestry and for Asians. Interracial marriage was legalized. The hated pass laws were abolished. Urban blacks were finally granted citizenship in their own country, but they still did not have the right to vote. They protested that these measures fell far short of granting them full political equality. Educational and economic opportunities for blacks remained far inferior to those that whites enjoyed.

South African racial policies came under a great deal of world criticism. In the 1980s, many countries, including the United States, passed laws prohibiting investment in and trade with South Africa until it made changes. These boycotts hurt the South African economy and helped to convince the government that change was necessary.

The decades-long struggle of black South Africans caught the attention of the world in the 1970s and 1980s. Nelson Mandela embodies the spirit of the black South Africans who fought so long for their freedom. Here is Mandela's story.

Johannesburg 1994

The man who had just been sworn in as the tenth president of South Africa since its union in 1910 addressed the large crowd of blacks, whites, and Asians:

"Never, never, and never again shall it be that this beautiful land will again experience the oppression of one by another," he said.

"We can loudly proclaim from the rooftops: free at last!"

As the crowd roared its approval, Nelson Mandela's thoughts were of the long, tortuous journey that had led him to this day's triumph. He had always believed that he was born to lead others. The son of a South African chief, his royal blood entitled him to become a chief by inheritance. Instead, he chose to attend the university—a black one—so that he could determine his own future. He studied law, passed the bar examination, and became a lawyer.

Mandela knew he was not a free man so long as his country practiced racial laws that discriminated against him and all black South Africans. To protest the government's policy of *apartheid*, which kept blacks separate from whites, he joined the African National Congress (ANC).

The ANC had been formed to help black South Africans win important rights and freedoms. Mandela helped to write its freedom charter, which called for a democratic state with equal rights for all races. Threatened by this charter, the South African government in 1956 had Mandela and other ANC members arrested and charged with high treason. The trial lasted for five years, but the government could not prove its case. Mandela and the others were cleared of all charges.

In 1960 the police fired on a peaceful protest demonstration and killed over 50 unarmed black protesters. A nationwide black protest followed, and the government banned the ANC. Many of its leaders fled the country, but Mandela chose to stay and continued to lead the struggle. He had always believed in nonviolence, but the violence of the government forced him to change his mind. He would now fight force with force in the struggle for freedom.

In 1962 Mandela was arrested. He was charged with leaving

the country without a passport and inciting people to strike against the government. At his trial he admitted that some of the charges against him were true, since all lawful means of protest had been closed to him and his people. Mandela called himself an African patriot who wanted a just share in the whole of South Africa for his people. He had dedicated himself to this struggle by the African people. He had fought against both white and black domination. He envisioned a democratic and free society in which all persons lived together in harmony and with equal opportunities. If need be, he was prepared to die for this vision.

The government listened carefully to what Mandela had to say. In 1964 he was sentenced to life imprisonment. Mandela never lost his dignity during the long years in prison. People never forgot him. Many prominent people around the world called for his release. Twice, the South African government offered to release Mandela. He answered, "What freedom am I being offered while the organization of my people remains banned? . . . When I may be arrested on a pass offense? . . . When I must ask permission to live in an urban area? . . . When my very South African citizenship is not respected? Only free men can negotiate. Prisoners cannot enter into contracts."

The voices clamoring for Mandela's freedom grew louder. Many white South Africans opposed the government's policies. South Africa was hurt by the economic boycotts of other nations. Finally, in 1990, 27 years after he had been imprisoned, the government decided to free him without conditions.

Mandela continued the struggle for freedom with the government of South Africa and its leader, Frederik W. de Klerk. He forced the government to negotiate with him and other black African leaders. In 1993 the government finally agreed to hold free elections. For the first time, blacks would vote for members of the South African Parliament in 1994.

The Swedish Academy announced in 1993 that Mandela and de Klerk, the former enemies who worked together to dismantle apartheid and lead their country to its first all-race elections, had been awarded the Nobel Peace Prize.

There was opposition from both whites and blacks to free elections, but this did not stop the millions of people, blacks and whites, who were determined to vote. When all the votes

South Africa, 1994: Nelson Mandela celebrates his victory in the first national elections in which black South Africans were able to vote.

were finally counted, the African National Congress had won 63 percent of the votes.

Mandela in May 1994 pledged to liberate all the black people of South Africa from the continuing bondage of poverty, deprivation, suffering, and discrimination. "Let there be justice for all! Let there be peace for all! Let each know that for each the body, the mind, and the soul have been freed to fulfill themselves! Let freedom reign! God bless Africa!"

Postscript

Black-ruled South Africa faced very difficult problems. The damage done by years of racism and oppression would take a long time to repair. Unemployment, illiteracy, and violence had to be dealt with. But the new government, led by Nelson Mandela, had an opportunity to turn a former racist society into one where people of all races could live and work together in harmony.

South Africa has many valuable natural resources, such as gold and other metals. It also has great human resources. Perhaps the most important one is Nelson Mandela.

QUESTIONS FOR REVIEW

1. Why was Nelson Mandela imprisoned?
2. Why was Mandela finally released?
3. What convinced the South African government to change some of its policies?
4. What occurred in South Africa after Mandela was released?
5. What was Mandela's vision for the future of South Africa?

UNDERSTANDING THE STORY

A. Tell which statements Nelson Mandela would agree with.

1. Blacks were totally satisfied when the government adopted a new constitution in the 1970s.
2. It was most important to protest the policy of apartheid.
3. A person should do everything within his or her power in the struggle for freedom.
4. The struggle against poverty, inequality, and discrimination is finally over.
5. People should continue to fight for freedom no matter how high the cost may be.
6. No ideals are worth going to prison for.
7. When negotiating, it is important to be able to compromise.
8. Economic boycotts helped us win the struggle in South Africa.

B. Imagine that you are asked how it was possible that Nelson Mandela, who once advocated the use of force and spent 27 years in prison, was awarded the Nobel Peace Prize. How would you answer this question?

ACTIVITIES AND INQUIRIES

1. Imagine that you are interviewing Nelson Mandela in prison. You ask him why he is there and why he has refused an offer to be released. How does he answer your questions?

2. Now you interview Frederik de Klerk. You ask him why he agreed to free Mandela and to negotiate with him. How does he answer you?

3. You interview a white person in South Africa after the election of Nelson Mandela as president in 1994. What questions will you ask, and how will this person answer your questions?

4. You interview a member of the ANC after the 1994 election. What questions will you ask, and how will this person answer your questions?

5. Imagine that you can see into the future. Describe what South Africa will be like in the next few years.

3. China: The Quest for Democracy

The Communist government has made great strides forward since taking control of the vast Chinese mainland in 1949. China has established diplomatic and economic ties with the United States and has been admitted to the United Nations. At home, China has permitted its people a limited amount of economic freedom by allowing them to operate some businesses of their own. China has even reached out to the West for some of its technology and management methods.

But political freedom, the right to speak freely and to criticize their government, is still denied to the Chinese people. In the 1950s, Chinese Communist Party Chairman Mao Zedong called on people to criticize the government and then had them arrested for doing so. From time to time, individuals have spoken out against the government only to be imprisoned or forced into exile.

In our story, Wei, a male student, and Dai, a female student, are part of a student protest movement that is determined to bring greater freedom to the Chinese people. Let us find out more about these two students and the democracy movement that they represent.

Beijing   June 2, 1989

"Dai, I believe that we have delivered our message to the government. Now it's time for all of us to go back to our schools and jobs," said Wei.

Dai shook her head. "I disagree," she said. "If we leave Beijing now, the government will think that we are weak and will disregard all we have done."

"How can our government leaders ignore what has happened?" asked Wei. "Thousands of students from all over China have marched in the streets of Beijing, demanding the right to speak out freely. We have been seen and heard around the world. Television stations everywhere have shown us marching and demonstrating. Newspapers everywhere have written about how the workers have joined with us, and that many others also seem to stand with us.

"Even the soldiers sent by the government have been unable to get us to move," he continued. "We have pleaded with the soldiers and tank crews to join us. While they decline to do so, they also refuse to turn their guns on us. No matter how hard our government leaders try to ignore what has happened here, we and the world will never allow them to do so."

"Then why are you so eager to give up the fight and go back to school?" asked Dai.

"Because it is both unhealthy and dangerous for us to remain here," said Wei. "Thousands of us are now packed into Tiananmen Square. Surrounded by filth and garbage, we may all become seriously ill. Even if this doesn't happen, the government may soon take violent action. Many people may die needlessly. I say that we should all return to our schools and jobs and continue to petition the government to meet with us and discuss our grievances."

Dai shook her head once more. "The government is frightened and confused by our refusal to leave the square. Our demonstrations have embarrassed the leaders, and I believe they are ready to give in to us. This is not the time for us to remove the pressure. We finally have an opportunity to give the Chinese people the most precious gift of all: democracy. If we leave now, we may not get another chance."

China, 1989: Beijing protesters demand an end to absolute rule by the Communist party. How did the government respond to their demands?

Wei nodded. "I respect what you have to say, and I wish you and the others well. As for me, I'm going back to my school today."

Dai and Wei embraced each other and said farewell. Many like Wei left Tiananmen Square and went back to their schools. Thousands of others like Dai stayed and continued to protest and make demands on the government. Two days later, on June 4, the government gave its answer. It ordered the army to clear away the demonstrators. Tanks and armored trucks rolled into Tiananmen Square and ran over people who stood in their way. Troops shot people in the streets. Hundreds were killed, and many more were wounded. Later, thousands of workers and students were arrested. The protesters were hunted down. Some escaped to freedom and exile in the West; others not so fortunate went to prison in China. The Chinese students and workers had demanded democracy, and the government had given its answer.

Postscript

The Chinese government blamed the Tiananmen Square protest on "hooligans" who, it said, were trying to disrupt society, and it praised the soldiers for defending their country.

The number killed was estimated at from 700 to several thousand persons. As many as 10,000 students and workers were arrested. Of these, 31 were tried and executed. Those in the government whose policies or sentiments were believed responsible for fueling the protests were dismissed from office. The hard-line Communist leaders remained in power.

The government continued to portray itself as advocating sweeping reforms in China. But the changes it called for were economic, not political, ones. The young people of China had raised their voices to demand the right to speak out freely. Would the government's use of force be enough to silence them? People around the world wondered and waited to see what would happen next.

QUESTIONS FOR REVIEW

1. What advances has the Chinese government made since 1949?
2. Why do many Chinese people still have complaints against the government?
3. Why did students stage a protest in Beijing's Tiananmen Square in 1989?
4. How did the government respond to this protest?
5. How did the government try to explain the protest and its response?

UNDERSTANDING THE STORY

A. Decide who might have made the remarks that follow. Write P for each statement a protester might have made and G for each statement a government official might have made.

1. All citizens have the right to criticize the government openly.
2. People should trust the government to make the right choices for them.
3. Elected officials are always wiser than the people they serve.
4. Student demonstrators should leave the square and go back to school before they get hurt.
5. This is not the time for us to remove the pressure on the leaders.

6. Demonstrations are dangerous acts and must be put down with force.
7. Hooligans were responsible for the violence that took place in Tiananmen Square.
8. Democracy is the most precious gift we can give to the Chinese people.

B. Imagine that you are with the protesters in Tiananmen Square in 1989. Describe what you see.

ACTIVITIES AND INQUIRIES

1. Imagine that you are a lawyer at the trial of the student leaders of the Tiananmen Square protest. Prepare the government's case against them.
2. Now prepare the case for the student leaders' defense.
3. Write a newspaper article describing the outcome—the verdict and sentences, if any—of the trial.
4. Bring a newspaper to class. Put an asterisk (★) next to every headline that the Chinese Communist government would not allow in a newspaper.
5. Draw a cartoon showing either the protest in Tiananmen Square or the trial of the protesters.

4. Nicaragua: Violeta Barrios de Chamorro

For a period of 42 years (1937–1979), the people of the Central American country Nicaragua were ruled by a dictatorship that was controlled by the Somoza family. In 1979, this government was overthrown by a group that called itself the Sandinistas in honor of a Nicaraguan rebel leader, General Augusto Sandino.

The Sandinistas set out to bring important reforms to Nicaragua. They promised to fight illiteracy and disease. They aimed to help people escape poverty by giving them land of their own. They also promised to allow the basic freedoms—speech, assembly, and petition—and to hold free elections in the near future.

But as time passed, the Sandinistas became more and more determined to run the country their own way, and many of their early promises were forgotten. The people and the press were denied the freedom to speak out against the government, and free elections were delayed for nearly five years. The Sandinistas moved closer to Communist governments and parties in other countries and began to support a revolution in El Salvador.

Many courageous people in Nicaragua stood up to the Sandinistas. Our story is about one of them.

Managua   1990

Your name is Violeta Barrios de Chamorro, and, more than anything, you want your people to live in freedom.

You were the wife of the editor of your country's leading newspaper, *La Prensa* (The Press). The Somoza regime controlled the government, and it was feared by most Nicaraguans. This government was a dictatorship. It warned people like your husband not to criticize it or else there would be grave consequences. In spite of these warnings, your husband, Pedro Joaquín Chamorro Cardenal, stood up to the government and continued to criticize it in the newspaper. For this he was imprisoned and eventually forced to leave the country. But your husband was a courageous man who dreamed of the day when his country would be ruled by a just and democratic government. He returned to Nicaragua to continue the fight against the Somoza regime. This time he went too far. In 1978 he was assassinated by agents of the government.

But others in Nicaragua had joined in a movement to overthrow the Somoza government by force. This movement was called the Sandinistas National Liberation Front. In 1979, after much fighting and destruction, the Sandinistas triumphed. They proclaimed that, to bring justice and order to the country, they would appoint a five-person group to govern the country. In honor of your late husband, you were asked to be one of the five members. You accepted.

But it wasn't long before you learned disturbing things about this new government. The real government was not the group to which you belonged, but a nine-member group that few people knew anything about. This latter group actually made all the important political and economic decisions. In 1980, you quit your post rather than stay and be used as a puppet.

The Sandinistas were led by Daniel Ortega, who was elected president in 1984. They seemed to care for the people, but they also supported revolutions in other parts of Latin America. The Sandinista government served notice that it was in sympathy with the aims and goals of Communist governments around the world, and it began receiving aid from the Soviet Union and some of its allies.

You saw that the Nicaraguan government was becoming more and more like a dictatorship. You decided to do what your husband had done. You would publish *La Prensa* and tell the truth about the government no matter what the cost. The government hated what you printed, but at first did not close down the newspaper. It feared that world criticism would compare it to the Somoza government. You were unharmed, for the same reason. Only later, when conditions worsened in Nicaragua and the government refused to allow any criticism or free speech, were you forced to shut down your paper.

It wasn't long before the country was once again torn apart by war. The government was accused of violating the rights of the Miskito Indians and other ethnic minorities in order to bring them under its control. The government also sent arms and soldiers to aid the rebels in El Salvador. A group of Nicaraguan rebels known as the *contras,* who were supported by the United States government, took to the hills. They began to attack government forces very much the way the Sandinistas had done to the Somoza regime. The living conditions of the people grew much worse, and many wondered if they would ever see an end to poverty and suffering.

But in the late 1980s a startling new development was to have an impact on the country. Communist governments throughout the world were beginning to fall. They could no longer send economic aid to the Sandinista government. Even the Soviet

Managua, 1990: Violeta Chamorro greets a crowd after winning the election for president of Nicaragua.

Union announced that it could no longer be counted on for support. The Sandinistas realized that if they were to continue in power, they would have to try to win back the support of the people.

The government decided to allow the people some freedoms. You were allowed to resume publishing your newspaper. As before, the paper criticized the government severely. Others spoke out against the government and demanded fair and free elections in 1990. President Ortega agreed and announced that he would be the Sandinistas' candidate. You were chosen to run against him.

The Sandinistas were determined to win. They gave government workers time off and transportation to attend political rallies. By comparison, your rallies were poorly attended, and the polls reported that you were running far behind.

At last, the election was held. When the results were announced, the nation was astonished. You had won the election by a large margin! Political observers said that you had won because people feared that Nicaragua would continue to be a poor and neglected country as long as the Sandinistas remained in power. You thought differently.

You told the people, "We have shown the world that we Nicaraguans want to live in a democracy, we want to live in peace, and above all that, we want to live in freedom!"

Postscript

Violeta Chamorro's government was criticized for not moving quickly enough to solve many of Nicaragua's grave problems. In an effort to heal the wounds caused by ten years of civil war, President Chamorro had appointed several Sandinista followers to key government posts. She also allowed Humberto Ortega, the brother of former Sandinista president Daniel Ortega, to remain in control of the armed forces. There were reports of human rights abuses by the military, and many people called for President Chamorro to remove Ortega from office.

Chamorro was also criticized by Nicaraguan business groups, which accused the government of not acting quickly enough to introduce economic reforms. The Sandinistas' followers also worried that the Chamorro government would undo many of their reforms.

Chamorro answered her critics by pointing to the political freedoms that she had brought to the Nicaraguans and the war she helped bring to an end. But when she left office in 1997, vast problems still remained. The new president, Arnoldo Alemán, pledged to create half a million new jobs and to set up a lucrative tourist economy. The Sandinistas remained a powerful force in Nicaraguan life.

QUESTIONS FOR REVIEW

1. Why did most Nicaraguans fear the Somoza regime?
2. Why was Violeta Chamorro disturbed by the Sandinista government?
3. How did Chamorro show her opposition to the Sandinista government?
4. Why did the Sandinista government fall from power?
5. What problems did the Chamorro government face?

UNDERSTANDING THE STORY

A. Write T for each statement that is true and F for each statement that is false.

1. Nicaragua has had a stable, democratic government for over 50 years.
2. Under the Sandinistas, the people and the press were never allowed to criticize the government.
3. The Sandinistas declared themselves to be the enemies of all foreign Communist governments.
4. Violeta Chamorro always opposed the Sandinistas.
5. The Sandinista government was accused of violating the rights of ethnic minorities.
6. Daniel Ortega believed that he could win a free election.
7. Violeta Chamorro was elected president of Nicaragua by a wide margin over Daniel Ortega.
8. All political groups in Nicaragua supported the Chamorro regime.

B. Imagine that the United States government has sent you to Nicaragua to advise President Violeta Chamorro. What suggestions would you make? How would you try to convince President Chamorro to accept your suggestions?

ACTIVITIES AND INQUIRIES

1. President Chamorro's husband, a newspaper editor, was assassinated by the Somoza regime for what he wrote. Imagine that you are writing for his newspaper. Write an editorial that might put your life in danger.
2. The Somoza regime was replaced by the Sandinista government. Write a news story that could cause the Sandinista government to shut down your newspaper.
3. Write a letter to a friend in the United States describing conditions in Nicaragua under the Sandinista government.
4. Now imagine that a government censor has intercepted your critical letter about the Sandinistas. Draw a line through everything in the letter that the censor does not want the person in the United States to read.
5. Your friend answers your letter and describes life in the United States. Write that letter, and then draw a line through everything that the Sandinista government does not want you to read.

5. The Middle East: Five Minutes to Midnight

In 1917, during World War I, Britain issued the Balfour Declaration, which stated that it favored the establishment in Palestine of a national home for the Jewish people. This angered the Arab people, who believed that Palestine belonged to them.

After World War II, the United Nations voted to divide Palestine into two states: one Arab and one Jewish. The Jewish state of Israel was created in 1948, and a war between Arabs and Jews followed immediately.

The armies of six Arab nations attacked Israel, but the Israeli forces were able to withstand the attack and drive the Arabs from lands they had previously occupied. Hundreds of thousands of Palestinian Arabs fled to neighboring Arab states to escape from the fighting. A truce ended the war, but the Arab states refused to recognize the right of the state of Israel to exist in their midst.

In 1967 the Arab states prepared to attack Israel once again. But Israel struck first, and within six days it had forced the Arab armies to surrender. Israel gained more territory, including the West Bank of the Jordan River and the eastern sector of the city of Jerusalem. Israel vowed that it would not return this territory to the Arabs until they recognized Israel's right to exist and declared that the wars between Arabs and Israelis were at an end.

In 1978 Israel and Egypt signed a peace treaty, and Israel returned the Egyptian land that it had won in battle. But the other Arab nations refused to negotiate with Israel, and they condemned Egypt for signing the peace treaty. Later, President Anwar Sadat of Egypt was assassinated by an Egyptian group that opposed peace with Israel.

And what of the Palestinian Arabs? Many who had been made homeless by the wars were forced to live in refugee camps. Others continued to live in the West Bank and in east Jerusalem and resented being forced to live under Israeli rule. In the 1980s, they showed this resentment by launching an *intifada* (uprising). This was an ongoing battle between the Palestinians and the Israeli army and police. It included bottle-and-rock-throwing, and it led to killings on both sides.

The Palestinians claimed that they were represented by the Palestine Liberation Organization (PLO), a group whose goal was to establish a homeland for the Palestinian Arabs. The PLO resorted to acts of terrorism

561

against Israelis, such as hijacking airplanes, bombing buildings, and killing civilians. The PLO refused to recognize Israel's right to exist, and Israel refused to negotiate with an organization that used terrorist methods.

In our story, two foreign students who are attending a college in the United States discuss the Middle East. One is a Palestinian, and the other is an Israeli. Here is what they have to say to each other.

New York City   1992

Avram had ten minutes in which to eat his lunch and get to his science class. He looked around the crowded college cafeteria and saw one empty seat. A young woman sat alone at the table. She was in his science class, and he knew that her name was Leila.

"Hello. May I sit here?" asked Avram.

Leila nodded her head. Avram put his tray on the table and placed his books next to his chair.

Both Avram and Leila were foreign exchange students. Avram was an Israeli, Leila a Palestinian. They attended several classes together but had never spoken. After a minute of silence, Avram spoke.

"Thank you for letting me sit here," said Avram. "We Israelis don't often get such invitations from Arabs."

Leila looked up sharply. "Perhaps it's because your people behave as rudely as you are behaving now."

"I apologize for my rudeness," said Avram. "Israelis have been pushed so many times that I suppose we're always ready for a fight."

"Please don't make such innocents of the people of Israel," said Leila. "After all, it was you who pushed your way into the Arab world. And you have taken lands that belonged to the Arab people. You Israelis deserve to be pushed. And we Arabs won't stop pushing until we have pushed you into the sea."

"Every time you push us," said Avram, "you leave behind more of your lands. Perhaps it is time for the Arabs to stop this foolishness. We want to talk with you at the peace table."

"Wonderful words," answered Leila, "and Israel repeats these same words before the United Nations and the world. Yet while Israel speaks of peace, it builds settlements on the Arab lands it has stolen. And generations of homeless Arabs waste away in the desert."

"We have stolen nothing. It is you who try to steal our land by making wars. This land has belonged to us for centuries. Even your holy book, the Qur'an, proves it. And you know that many Arabs live in Israel. They are granted citizenship and even hold seats in our government. Most of them live better in Israel than anywhere else in the Middle East."

Leila interrupted. "What about the Arabs you have made homeless?"

"If the Arab countries are truly concerned about the homeless Arabs, why don't they invite them into their own countries? After all, we Israelis invite Jews from all over the world to live in our country."

Leila said, "Arab countries don't take the homeless into their lands because they never want them to forget that Israel has stolen their homeland! You invite Jews to settle in your country because you need soldiers to fight your wars to keep Arab lands."

Avram answered, "Arab countries don't take in the homeless Arabs because they want to use them as terrorists against Israel. And while it is true that the Arabs greatly outnumber us, we invite Jews to Israel for reasons other than building up our armies."

"I know. You're going to tell me all about the concentration camps."

"Yes, my people crawled out of the world's ghettos to go to Israel. They went from countries that had tortured and chased them. They have risen from the ashes of the concentration camps. After two thousand years of persecution, they have the right to live as free people in a land of their own!"

Leila spoke through clenched teeth. "My homeland is not a homeland for Jews!"

"You may be a brilliant student, but you don't know your history," said Avram. "You refuse to understand that Jews have 'lived' in Israel for thousands of years. Many have actually resided and worked there. Others have lived and worked in Israel in their hearts and minds. In recent times we bought useless lands from their Arab owners. We paid dearly for this land—not only with money, but with sweat and blood. We worked hard and made this once-barren land a showplace for the world. The Bible, the Qur'an, our history, and now the United Nations all give us the right to claim this land. And we will not be moved. Never!"

"But we are becoming more powerful," said Leila. "Our Arab countries are rich in oil, and we can buy anything we want. Our armies are getting stronger. Can you really stop us from pushing you into the sea one day?"

Avram answered. "We are not without resources. It has taken too many centuries to reclaim our homeland for us to give it up without a fight."

"And so Arab and Israeli will go on locked together in a death struggle," said Leila.

"Unless we learn to speak with each other."

"What do we have in common to speak about?" asked Leila.

"A great deal," answered Avram. "We are both concerned with homeless people. You are concerned with homeless Arabs, and I am concerned with homeless Jews. Perhaps if we help each other, we can make a good home for all."

Avram and Leila looked quietly at each other. The class bell rang. They gathered their books and coats and walked off silently to class together.

Postscript

In 1992 a new Israeli government, led by Yitzhak Rabin, called for peace with Israel's Arab neighbors. Far too many people on both sides had been killed in a war that seemed to have no end. Rabin believed that only the Palestine Liberation Organization, led by Yasir Arafat, had the power to negotiate an agreement on behalf of the Palestinians and make that agreement work.

In 1993 the two sides began to meet secretly in Norway. In September Israel and the PLO agreed officially to recognize each other. The PLO

Washington, D.C., 1993: A handshake between Israeli prime minister Rabin and PLO chief Arafat seals the peace agreement between the two sides. President Bill Clinton acts as mediator.

renounced terrorism and violence. Israel granted important concessions to the Palestinian people: They would govern themselves in the Gaza Strip and the West Bank town of Jericho. After much debate, the agreement was accepted by both sides, and went into effect in 1994. Israel also established full diplomatic relations with Jordan and continued peace talks with Syria. Most Israelis and Palestinians condemned terrorist acts by extermists on both sides and vowed that they would not allow them to sabotage the peace process. Many believed that by working together the two former enemies had taken a giant step toward peace in the Middle East.

QUESTIONS FOR REVIEW

1. Why were the Arabs in Palestine upset with the Jews?
2. What were the results of the Arab–Israeli war in 1948?
3. What were the terms of the Israeli–Egyptian peace treaty?
4. How did Israel and the PLO view each other? Why?
5. Why did Israel and the PLO agree in 1993 to recognize each other and work toward peace?

ISRAEL AND NEIGHBORING ARAB STATES

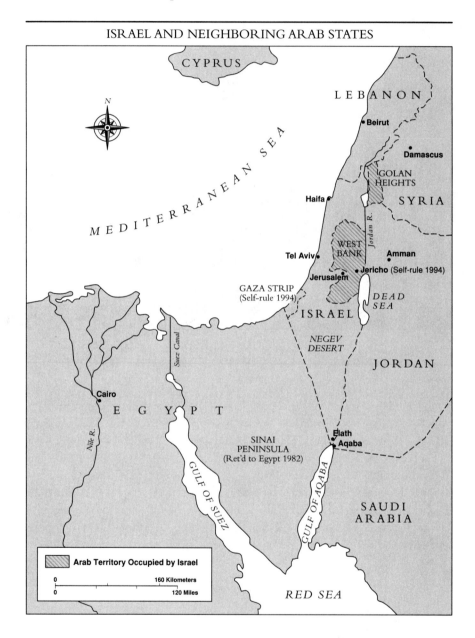

UNDERSTANDING THE STORY

A. Write A for each statement that Avram made or might have made
and L for each statement that Leila made or might have made.

1. We want to talk with you at the peace table.

2. Generations of homeless Arabs waste away in the desert.
3. My people have risen from the ashes of the concentration camps.
4. My homeland is not a homeland for Jews.
5. Can you stop us from pushing you into the sea?
6. My people have the right to live as a free people in a land of their own.
7. You are concerned with homeless Arabs. I am concerned with homeless Jews.

B. Suppose that Avram and Leila come to you for advice. They would like to know how their countries can live in peace. What advice would you give them?

ACTIVITIES AND INQUIRIES

1. Use each of the following key terms in a sentence: Israeli   Arab   terrorism   homeland.
2. The caption of a cartoon is: "Our people have risen from the ashes of the concentration camps!" Who do you think said this? Explain. What does Israel mean to the survivors of the concentration camps? Draw the cartoon.
3. Study the map on page 566. Tell which item makes each statement correct.
    a. The Suez Canal connects (1) Israel and Egypt (2) the Mediterranean and the Nile River (3) the Mediterranean and the Gulf of Suez.
    b. An Arab country to the southwest of Israel is (1) Egypt (2) Jordan (3) Syria.
    c. An Arab country east of Israel is (1) Egypt (2) Jordan (3) Lebanon.
    d. Which of these Arab countries does not actually touch Israeli land? (1) Jordan (2) Saudi Arabia (3) Lebanon.
    e. The city of Jericho is in (1) the Negev (2) the West Bank (3) the Golan Heights.
    f. The Gaza Strip is on (1) the Red Sea (2) the Dead Sea (3) the Mediterranean Sea.

4. You interview Yitzhak Rabin and ask him why he is ready to recognize the PLO. Write his reply.
5. You interview Yasir Arafat and ask him why he is ready to recognize the state of Israel. Write his reply.

6. Last Chance?

In recent years, many people have been taking a long, hard look at Planet Earth. They do not like what they see. They talk about the coming shortages of important natural resources, such as oil and coal. They also talk about dangerous changes that are taking place in the environment.

In our story, a scientist is holding a press conference. The purpose is to awaken the people of the world to the dangers we all face if we continue to abuse the environment. Let us listen in on the press conference so that we can learn more about the scientist's message.

Washington, D.C.   1994

"Doctor," called out a reporter from *The New York Times*. "Would you please repeat those figures?"

"Gladly," said the scientist. "Soon we are not going to be able to grow enough food to feed all the people who live on the planet. Just 100 years ago, there were only 1 billion people on the planet. Forty years ago, there were $1\frac{1}{2}$ billion. Today there are over $5\frac{1}{2}$ billion people living on the earth. The world's population used to double every 1,500 years. Today, it will double in less than 60 years! Soon, we will not be able to feed so many people!"

"What do you suggest?" asked the reporter from the *Chicago Tribune*.

The scientist answered immediately. "We must limit every family in the world to no more than two children."

"But," sputtered the editor of the *National Review*, "that's unthinkable! People have the right to bear as many children as they wish."

The other reporters listened with interest. Most agreed with the editor of the *National Review*. They found it hard to take the scientist's statements seriously.

"Ladies and gentlemen," said the scientist, "I see that most of you do not believe what I am saying."

568

"Oh, we believe you," said the reporter from the *New York Daily News*. "It's just that we don't think the world has anything to worry about for a few hundred years. By that time, scientists like yourself will have invented new ways of feeding the world."

"Ladies and gentlemen," said the scientist, "we don't have a few hundred years left! The crisis is now. The world's natural resources are limited, and they are dwindling rapidly. Oil, lead, zinc, tin, and fresh water are already in short supply. As for food, right this minute, all over the world, countless millions are going to sleep hungry or facing starvation! By the year 2025, in less than a generation, the world's population will have grown from 5 1/2 billion to 8 1/2 billion people. How will we feed so many people?"

"But doctor," protested the reporter from the *Washington Post*, "don't we have enough food to feed the world's people right now? Isn't it just that some countries have too much food and others have too little?

The scientist shook her head. "If all of the world's food supply were evenly divided, there would still not be enough to go around. And, of course, air pollution and water pollution make our problems even more serious. Plants depend upon sunlight, oxygen, and water to live and grow. If plants do not grow, or polluted air and water kill them, the animals that eat these plants will have no food. Soon, animal life will perish. If the plants and animals die off, what will remain for human beings?"

At last the reporters began to understand what the scientist was trying to tell them. They paid rapt attention as she continued to speak. "Our food production around the world has already been seriously affected. Global warming, deforestation, soil erosion, and air pollution have reduced the world's crop yields by about one percent a year since 1984."

"Is there anything we can do?" asked the reporter from the *Los Angeles Times*.

"That's why I called this news conference," said the scientist. "We must stop waste and pollution, and governments must pass tough laws to make sure we stop. Then perhaps there may still be time."

"And if this isn't done?" shouted several reporters.

"Then," said the scientist, "we will learn a bitter lesson from our ancient past."

The reporters looked puzzled. The scientist went on.

"North Africa once supplied the mighty Roman Empire with much of its food. Now, because of the factors I've just discussed, the land is largely desert. This same thing will happen to much of the land that is fertile today if we don't take the necessary steps to stop the damage. If this should happen, we will have nothing to look forward to but pollution, starvation, and war. Advanced civilization and then all human life will disappear. Almost all animal and plant life will die out. A lowly and despised creature will inherit the earth."

"What creature?" cried the reporter from the *New York Post*.

"The one creature that life on earth will be fit for," replied the scientist. "The cockroach!"

Postscript

From the beginnings of recorded history, societies throughout the world have traded goods and ideas with one another. Now, on the brink of the twenty-first century, undoing some of the environmental damage that we have wreaked upon our world will take nothing less than a global effort. But we have made a beginning. Many nations have pledged to reduce their carbon and fluorocarbon emissions by 25 percent. The United States has reduced the soil erosion of its croplands by a third. Denmark has banned the throwing away of beverage containers. Saving the world's environment is perhaps our greatest challenge. We can only hope that the people of the world will join together and meet that challenge peacefully and with a sense of global unity and cooperation.

QUESTIONS FOR REVIEW

1. Why are many people concerned that dangerous changes are taking place in the global environment?
2. Why do some scientists maintain that it will soon be difficult and then impossible to grow enough food to feed all the people who share our planet?

3. What natural resources are already in short supply worldwide?
4. What lessons about the environment can we learn from our ancient past?
5. How are some nations trying to undo environmental damage?

UNDERSTANDING THE STORY

A. Complete each of the sentences below.

1. We are not going to be able to grow enough food to feed all the _____ who live on this _____.
2. The world's _____ _____ are limited, and they are _____ rapidly.
3. The population of the world will double in less than _____.
4. The crisis is _____.
5. All over the world, millions of people are _____ or facing _____.
6. Even if all the world's food were evenly divided, there would still not be _____.
7. We must stop _____ and _____.

B. Assume that you are a member of a presidential commission of natural resources. You have been asked to make a report on the resources of the United States today and in the future. What would you tell the president about our country's resources? How will the careless use of these resources affect the rest of the world?

ACTIVITIES AND INQUIRIES

1. Use each of the following key terms in a sentence: planet   population   environment   natural resources   pollution.
2. Draw a poster that will encourage people to stop waste and pollution.
3. Write an outline telling what the students in your class can do to prevent the waste of resources.
4. If you had been at the press conference in the story, what questions would you have asked the scientist? How would the scientist have answered your questions?
5. Suppose that people continue to abuse the global environment as they do today, and the scientist is correct about the outcome. Write some newspaper headlines that will be printed 50 years from now.

GLOSSARY

abdicate to give up the throne

absolute monarchy form of government in which a king or queen has complete control the nation's affairs

A.D. anno Domini—all the years since the birth of Christ

ancient world societies that flourished thousands of years ago

annexation making an area belonging to one country part of another

apartheid former South African racial policy that kept blacks and whites apart

archeology study of the remains of human groups or societies that existed in the distant past

armistice agreement to stop fighting a war

assassination killing of a head of state

astrolabe device used by sailors to tell how far north or south they were from the earth's equator

balance of power political situation in which two equally strong nations or alliances oppose each other

barbarian outsider, foreigner; one not as civilized as others

B.C. before Christ—all the years before the birth of Christ

Bible holy book of Jews and Christians

bloc groups of countries in the same geographic region or with the same political system

Brahman member of the highest-ranking Hindu caste

Buddhism religion founded in India by Siddhartha Gautama in 500 B.C.

bureaucracy system of government organization and administration

cabinet group of ministers who advise the head of a government

capitalism economic system of free markets and the private ownership of the means of production

caste system social system involving rules and roles for members of each caste

cathedral large church that is the official center of a high church official (bishop)

Christianity religion based on the teachings of Jesus

Church, Roman Catholic dominant religious organization in Western Europe from the fall of Rome (476) to the early 16th century

city-state a city that governed itself and a surrounding area

civilization way of life of a nation or part of the world; refinement of ideas, manners, and taste

civil service system of recruiting and promoting workers in government based on competitive examinations

clan group of people descended from a common ancestor

coalition government in which two or more countries or groups of countries form an alliance for political purposes

cold war ongoing conflict between two countries or alliances that stops short of actual warfare

colony area controlled by a larger, more powerful nation for the purpose of exploiting its resources

commonwealth a group of people or nations organized under a system of laws; English government during the reign of Oliver Cromwell (1649–1660)

communism economic and political system in which all the means of production are the property of the government and are managed by the government

Confucianism philosophy based on the ideas of the Chinese sage Confucius

Congress of Vienna council of European leaders that drew up the peace treaty following the Napoleonic Wars (1815)

constitution a nation's laws, which set down the duties and powers of the government and the rights of the people

crop rotation growing of different crops in succession in one field

Crusades Christian military expeditions to regain control of the Holy Land (Palestine) from the Muslims during the Middle Ages

culture the sum total of a people's history, values, and beliefs; also, their artistic and literary achievements

cuneiform Sumerian wedge-shaped characters that represented ideas or objects

democracy form of government that provides for the expression and realization of the wishes of the majority of the people

developed nation country that is highly industrialized and has a high standard of living

developing nation country that has little of no industry, is primarily agricultural, and has a low standard of living

dictatorship government ruled by one person; the wishes of the majority are not considered or recognized

direct democracy form of government in which all citizens vote on pending laws

divine right belief that a monarch rules because of God's wishes or plans

domestication raising and cultivating plants and animals for food, clothing, and other purposes

domestic system method of manufacturing under which goods were made by hand in the home

dynasty series of national rulers who are related as a family

East, the term used to describe the lands of Asia and India

empire extensive lands or territories controlled by one nation

Estates General legislative assembly of France before the revolution; made up of three estates

factory system production of goods in a factory instead of in workers' homes

fascism form of 20th-century government in which a dictator controls all political life; its economic system is a form of capitalism

feudalism economic and social system; the nobility owned the land, which the peasants or serfs lived and worked on and fought wars to defend

Glorious Revolution replacement of the Stuart kings of England by William and Mary of Orange in 1689; supremacy of Parliament over the king established

global warming scientific theory that world temperatures will gradually increase in the 21st century

golden age period of high artistic and scientific achievement by a society

heresy belief that is counter to official religious doctrine

Holocaust systematic killing of millions of European Jews and others by the Nazi government of Germany during World War II

humanism revival of Greek and Latin classics during the Renaissance; placed emphasis on secular (worldly) matters and activities

imperialism process in which a powerful nation takes control of a weaker one; empire-building

Industrial Revolution shift in technology from handcrafts made at home to machine-made goods produced in factories

Inquisition 16th and 17th century Roman Catholic Church court that punished heretics

Intifada uprising by Palestinians against Israeli rule

Islam religion based on the teachings of Muhammad

Judaism religion of the Jewish people that teaches the belief in one God and keeping God's moral commandments

khan   Mongol ruler
kibbutz   Israeli collective community, often agricultural

land reform   breaking up of large landholdings to give small plots to landless peasants
League of Nations   organization formed after World War I to keep the world at peace

Magna Carta   charter signed by King John of England in 1215, which granted certain basic rights to English barons
mandate   a country under the protection of another, more powerful nation
monotheism   belief in a single god
movable type   method of printing in which the type for each letter is a separate piece of wood or metal
Muslim   person who follows the Islamic religion

nationalism   feeling held by a group of people that they belong together as a separate nation
nation–state   large area in which people share a common culture and language and are governed by a central government
nirvana   state of spiritual bliss and release from worldly cares

oasis   area in a desert that has a water source
Old Regime   system of privileges and absolutism in France before the revolution
oligarchy   dictatorial rule of a government by a small group
oral tradition   knowledge of the past that is handed down by word of mouth

parliament   lawmaking body whose members discuss national problems and enact laws
pass laws   South African laws that required every black person to carry a passbook telling where the person lived and worked
passive resistance   nonviolent opposition to a government's policies
patrician   member of the ruling class in the Roman Republic
peasant   farmer who has little or no land of his or her own
Petition of Right   statement of rights written by the English Parliament and signed by King Charles I in 1628
pharaoh   king or queen of ancient Egypt
philosophes   writers and thinkers in 18th-century France
plebeian   citizen of the Roman Republic who was a farmer or craftsperson

prehistory period of human existence before the invention of written records

prophet person who claims to have access to divine spiritual revelation

Qur'an Muslim holy book

racism belief in the superiority of one race over others

Reformation upheaval in the Church during the 16th century that resulted in the formation of new Protestant Christian churches

Reign of Terror period during the French Revolution marked by violence and death

reincarnation belief that one's soul reappears after death in another living form

Renaissance revival or rebirth of learning and interest in earthly life in Europe during the 15th and 16th centuries

republic democratic form of government that has no monarch and whose officials are elected by voters

revolution great change; overthrow of a government; change in manner of thinking or production

samurai Japanese warrior in feudal times

satellite country that is politically and economically controlled by another, more powerful nation

serfdom system whereby people were bound to the soil as farmers and controlled by the nobility

Shintoism traditional religion of Japan

socialism economic system in which the means of production are publicly owned

soviet Russian council or assembly of workers, soldiers, or farmers

society an organized social group; a community of nation having the same traditions, activities, and interests

state politically organized group of people who inhabit a specific territory

subcontinent major subdivision of a continent

Torah Jewish book of the law

totalitarianism political system in which the government has total control over all areas of society

tradition way of acting or thinking that is handed down from parents to children over a long period of time

treaty written agreement between two or more governments, approved by the lawmaking bodies of these governments

Triple Alliance   agreement of mutual protection by Germany, Austria-Hungary, and Italy; the Central Powers during World War I

Triple Entente   agreement of mutual protection by England, France, and Russia; the Allied Powers during World War I

United Nations   world organization formed after World War II to prevent war and promote freedom

Untouchable   member of the lowest-ranking Hindu caste

warlord   military leader who uses his army to rule over part of a country

ziggurat   Sumerian religious building

INDEX

Acknowledgments

Illustration Credits

Alinari/Art Resource, NY: 57

American Museum of Natural History, Neg. No. 334110, Department of Library Services: 80

AP/Wide World Photos: 513

Art Resource, NY: 4, 89 (Werner Forman)

The Beinecke Rare Book and Manuscript Library, Yale University: 349

The Bettmann Archive: 8, 20, 37, 103, 119, 135, 169, 222, 226, 316, 345 (right), 356, 365, 379, 395, 408, 412, 465

Foto Marburg/Art Resource, NY: 19

The Granger Collection: 14, 25, 44, 50, 63, 87, 124, 147, 156, 160, 173, 191, 195, 218, 227, 247, 258, 266, 278, 288, 322, 336, 345 (left), 403, 416, 429, 461, 472

Giraudon/Art Resource, NY: 113, 327

The Library of Congress: 73, 97, 142, 179, 202, 206, 252, 297, 304 (left & right), 309, 326, 439, 451, 488, 502, 508

Museum of Fine Arts, Boston: 66

The National Archives: 480 (Rudy Vetter), 484, 497 (Rudy Vetter)

Reuters/Bettmann: 540, 549 (Howard Burditt), 553, 558

Royal Ontario Museum, Canada: 31

UPI/Bettmann: 493, 517, 524

The White House: 565

Cover by Ted Bernstein
Map, The Bettmann Archive; wall painting, Egyptian Expedition of the Metropolitan Museum of Art, Rogers Fund, 1930.